CW01653900

City gorged with dreams

MANCHESTER
UNIVERSITY PRESS

The Critical Image

This series explores the historical and contemporary uses of photography. It aims to develop photographic history and criticism and investigates practice. The publications draw on methods and theories widely used in art history, literature, film and cultural studies.

Series editor John Taylor
Department of History of Art and Design
Manchester Metropolitan University

Already published

Jane Brettle and Sally Rice (eds) *Public bodies – private states: new views on photography, representation and gender*

David Brittain (ed.) *Creative Camera – thirty years of writing*

Sarah Kember *Virtual anxiety: photography, new technologies and subjectivity*

Peter Kennard *Domesday book: photopoem*

Roberta McGrath *Seeing her sex: the female body in medical archives*

John Roberts *The art of interruption: realism, photography and the everyday*

Lindsay Smith *The politics of focus: women, children and nineteenth-century photography*

John Taylor *A dream of England: landscape, photography and the tourist's imagination*

John Taylor *Body horror: photojournalism, catastrophe and war*

City gorged with dreams

Surrealism and documentary photography in interwar Paris

Ian Walker

MANCHESTER UNIVERSITY PRESS
Manchester and New York

distributed exclusively in the USA by Palgrave

Published by Manchester University Press
Oxford Road, Manchester M13 9NR, UK
and Room 400, 175 Fifth Avenue, New York, NY 10010, USA
www.manchesteruniversitypress.co.uk

Distributed exclusively in the USA by
Palgrave, 175 Fifth Avenue, New York,
NY 10010, USA

Distributed exclusively in Canada by
UBC Press, University of British Columbia, 2029 West Mall,
Vancouver, BC, Canada V6T 1Z2

British Library Cataloguing-in-Publication Data
A catalogue record for this book is available from the British Library

Library of Congress Cataloging-in-Publication Data applied for

ISBN 0 7190 6214 4 *hardback*
0 7190 6215 2 *paperback*

First published 2002

10 09 08 07 06 05 04 03 02 10 9 8 7 6 5 4 3 2 1

Designed and typeset by Lionart, Birmingham
Printed in Great Britain by Alden Press, Oxford

Contents

List of figures

Acknowledgements

When a project has been developed over such a long time, there are inevitably many people to thank for their help. I regret that I'm unable to acknowledge individually everyone who has contributed to this project.

I began my research on this subject through the Courtauld Institute of Art, where John Golding and Christopher Green made many useful suggestions. Financial assistance from the University of London enabled me to spend extended periods of study in Brussels, Paris and the USA. I will always be grateful for the personal support of Laurie McFadden during this period. More recently, my research has been supported by the University of Wales College, Newport, and I'd particularly like to thank my former colleagues: David Hurn, Keith Arnatt, Carolyn Wilde, Erika Millman, Ialeen Gibson-Cowan, Valerie Swales, Martin Lister and Andrew Dewdney. More recently, Paul Seawright asked me to write a catalogue essay on the *Terrain vague* that followed a complementary trajectory to the chapter in this book.

Other individuals who have helped with particular information or comments are legion. In Britain, they include Eileen Agar, Conroy Maddox, Angus McBean, Humphrey Spender, Elizabeth Cowling, David Sylvester, John Lyle, Bill Brandt, Sir Roland Penrose, George Melly, Adrian Rifkin, Paul Hammond, Mark Haworth-Booth, Anthony Penrose, Krzysztof Fijalkowski and Peter Metelerkamp. In 1986, I was curator of the exhibition *Contrariwise: Surrealism and Britain* for the Glynn Vivian Art Gallery, Swansea. Even though I have been unable to discuss British Surrealist photography at any length in this book, that exercise focused my understanding of Surrealism and I thank the gallery (particularly the former exhibitions officer, Jennifer Hallam) and all the artists who exhibited in the show for their support of the project.

On several occasions in Paris, I've met with artists, writers and photographers, including Philippe Soupault, Henri Cartier-Bresson, Man Ray, Juliet Man Ray, Radovan Ivsic, Annie LeBrun, Alain Brieux, Edouard Jaguer, Patrick Waldberg and Michel Leiris. On an early visit to Brussels, several participants in Belgian Surrealism – Georgette Magritte, Marcel Mariën, Jean Scutenaire and Irène Hamoir – were generous with their time and memories; talking with them was one of the most delightful parts of my research. In

Amsterdam, I talked with Emiel van Moerkerken and Hans Renders about the little known area of Dutch Surrealism. In the USA, individuals I met included Duane Michals, David Hare, André Kertész, John Szarkowski, David Travis and Timothy Baum. In particular, J.H. Matthews kindly made his library and his extensive knowledge of Surrealism available to me.

I regret that a full discussion of Czech Surrealist photography has had to be left to another occasion, but nevertheless that work has affected my thinking in many ways, which I'd like to acknowledge here. My interest in Czech Surrealism was first aroused by Petr Král in Paris in 1979. A decade later, Herta Wolf sent me the catalogue of *Das Innere der Sicht* from Vienna. Subsequent periods of study in the Czech Republic itself were made possible by grants from the Welsh Arts Council and the British Council. In Prague, I was able to talk with Anna Fárová, Petr Kosák and Eva Kosáková, Vladimír Birgus, Jan Švankmajer, Eva Effenbergerová, Michel Resl, Alois Nožička and Zdeněk Kirschner. In Brno, I must thank Antonín Dufek of the Moravian Gallery for his help.

The chapter on *Phantom Africa* has had a specific history. Susan Hiller first pointed me towards the fascinating relationship between Surrealism and ethnography; in entering this different field of enquiry, I have also been grateful for the advice of Jean Jamin and Michael Richardson. An earlier version of this chapter was published in *Cahiers d'études africaines* and my thanks go to the journal's editors for granting permission for the material to be reused here.

There have been two stages in the production of this text. Between 1989 and 1995, I developed it as a D.Phil. dissertation at the University of Sussex. I must above all thank David Mellor for his support as supervisor of that work; his many comments were always valuable and provocative. Likewise, the two readers of the dissertation, Dawn Ades and Thomas Crow, were encouraging of my desire to see this research published.

The text in this book is different, certainly more concise and (I hope) better written. At Manchester University Press, I want to thank John Taylor, the series editor, and Matthew Frost, the commissioning editor, for taking on this project. The title *City Gorged with Dreams* is Richard Howard's rendering of Baudelaire's phrase 'cité pleine de rêves' from the poem 'Les Sept Vieillards'; I am grateful to David R. Godine of Boston, the original publisher of Howard's translation of *Flowers of Evil*, for agreeing to my use of the phrase. As I was finishing my work on the book, I attended a talk by Mike Tooby where he read a few lines from the Sherlock Holmes story 'A Case of Identity'. They seemed so apposite that I've used them as an epigram, and my thanks go to him for that serendipity.

I am particularly grateful to the Kraszna-Krausz Foundation and the University of Wales College, Newport, for their generous funding which has enabled me to illustrate the book so fully. My thanks also go to everyone who has provided images and, for their particular help, Bruno van Moerkerken, Stephen Hauser, Jean-Pierre Marchand, Suzy Lewis at Magnum, Anne Sproat and Barbara Thompson at the Courtauld Institute. Also my thanks to Simon Meddings at Lionart for his patient work with the reproductions.

A word about the translations. Whether or not I have translated titles has depended in large part on the comprehensibility of the original and the felicity of its English counterpart; I have for example preferred *L'Amour fou* to *Mad Love*. For the longer quotations, I have whenever possible used an already existing translation. Where none is available, the translation is my own, though, for their advice, I must thank Susan Butler and Yves Abrioux (French), Jane Boyd (Dutch), Ilona Hamplová and David Short (Czech).

And finally my greatest debt of gratitude is to Susan Butler, whose running commentary and detailed reading of the text has been provoking and enriching in equal measure. Without her encouragement, this book would not be what it is.

Introduction

> My dear fellow ... life is infinitely stranger than anything which the mind of man could invent. We would not dare to conceive the things which are really mere commonplaces of existence ... Depend upon it there is nothing so unnatural as the commonplace. (Sherlock Holmes)[1]

Looking back to the beginnings of this research in the late 1970s, it's now almost impossible to conceive how little literature there was at the time on the relationship between Surrealism and photography. Initially, I intended this project to be a general survey of what seemed to be a finite and marginal area. In the intervening years, however, the literature has increased enormously, but so have the possible areas of enquiry, offering now, not one focus of attention, but many.

As my own project came to centre on the convergence of Surrealism and 'documentary' or 'straight' photography, this meant that some important aspects of the larger subject moved beyond the scope of this text. The manipulated and staged photography produced within Surrealism has by now been extensively examined; here it hovers offstage, a complement rather than a challenge to the work I discuss. Even within the area of 'Surrealist documentary' photography, I have had to choose between making a broad survey or a particular in-depth study. I have chosen the latter, focusing on work made in Paris in the years between the two wars. But this means that other culturally specific forms of Surrealist photography developed in Belgium, Czechoslovakia, Britain and the New World appear only when they are connected with themes also found in Paris.

I want at least to briefly acknowledge here the importance of that Surrealist diaspora, which included several developments of the Surrealist aesthetic of 'straight' photography. In Brussels, René Magritte and Paul Nougé exploited the processes of vernacular photography with a cool irony. In Britain, artists as different as Paul Nash, Eileen Agar, Humphrey Jennings, Lee Miller and Bill Brandt worked between Surrealism and indigenous traditions of landscape or social documentary. The photography of Manuel Alvarez Bravo developed out of his own Mexican culture, but at one point in the late 1930s, it also became connected with Surrealism. During the war in the early 1940s, images by the independent American photographers Frederick Sommer and Clarence John Laughlin, made in the very different environments of Arizona and Louisiana, likewise found a place in the magazine *VVV*, produced in New York by the Surrealist group-in-exile. Finally, and most extensively, the photography of the Czech Surrealists Jindřich Štyrský, Vilém Reichmann, Emila Medková and Jiří Sever was born out of a Surrealist activity of unparalleled longevity and continuity.[2]

In the past twenty years there has been a number of studies of the relationship of Surrealism and photography. The first general work I know of was a slim catalogue by Nancy Hall-Duncan from 1979 entitled *Photographic Surrealism*.[3] The 1982 book by Edouard Jaguer, *Les Mystères de la Chambre Noire*, was much more ambitious, indeed perhaps overly inclusive.[4] Criticised for a lack of objectivity, its strengths lay precisely in the fact that it was written from inside the subject by a long-standing 'fellow traveller' of Surrealism. The catalogue of the 1989 Vienna exhibition organised by Monika Faber, *Das Innere der Sicht*, gave many further insights, and particularly into the work made by the Czech Surrealists.[5] Petr Král's *Fotografie v surrealismu* (1994) viewed the subject from a particular Czech perspective.[6] At the time of writing, I have not had the opportunity to read David Bate's forthcoming study *Photography and Surrealism*, but it seems that it will focus on very different issues from the ones discussed here.[7]

Ironically, the project that really propelled my own research in the direction it took in the late 1980s was that which it least resembles: the major English language study to date, *L'Amour fou*, the 1985 exhibition and book by Rosalind Krauss and Jane Livingston.[8] Many justified criticisms were made of *L'Amour fou* at the time.[9] It passed too easily over the deeply problematic presence of all the many cut-up bits of (mainly female) bodies that it presented as 'Surrealist photography'. In favouring Bataille over Breton, it played havoc with a historical and political understanding of Surrealism. Nevertheless, the exhibition forcefully took up a position on behalf of a body of work which had at that time been neglected and which deserved recognition. And, certainly, its combination of a contradictory revisionism packaged within the authority of museumisation raised the temperature of the debate. However, though the polemical thrust of the project was in one sense altogether evident, there were ways in which it rested upon a set of unspoken assumptions.

Rosalind Krauss (whose two essays were central to the project of *L'Amour fou*) wrote from a post-structuralist position of deep distrust of 'straight' photography, with its hegemonic claims of authenticity and masterliness, and she wished to use the manipulations and excesses of what she called Surrealist photography in order to throw it into disrepute. This is surely a very American position, reacting against, yet still in thrall to a definition of 'straight' photography dominated by the examples of certain American 'masters' promoted by the Museum of Modern Art under its erstwhile Director of Photography, John Szarkowski.[10] From Europe, the arguments look rather different – less polarised – than they might seem in New York. Here, the concept of 'straight' photography is centred on a documentary tradition which often intersects with other areas of practice, be they artistic movements such as Neue Sachlichkeit and Surrealism or modes of enquiry such as anthropology. It's more interesting to examine how these different ways of working converge in specific cultural contexts than to set up reductive oppositions.

However, the most problematic aspect of *L'Amour fou* lay in its after-effect, as the work selected for the exhibition came to represent Surrealist photography generally. This claim, implicit in *L'Amour fou* itself, was taken over explicitly and unquestioningly by most later commentators, even those antagonistic to the position of the exhibition's curators.[11] But, in fact, *L'Amour fou* failed to represent a whole other way of working with the medium: a Surrealist photography which, on the contrary, exploits its very 'straightness', its apparent realism, to Surrealist ends. This text has come out of a belief that this 'Surrealist documentary' photography is in fact more disruptive of conventional norms than the contrivances of darkroom manipulation, and that it deserves a more complex reading than it has had previously.

This is a photography that largely takes place in and around the city, where the banal and the marvellous coexist on a daily basis. Underpinning this study is an investigation of the 'siting' of photographs – how the image moves from the place where it has been taken to the place where it is published and viewed, its meaning shifting as it goes. The very site where the image is made will have its own resonance. Across Paris, the Surrealists identified an array of 'privileged places', especially resonant for personal or cultural reasons, and I examine this re-structuring of city space in Chapter 2.[12] This has always been a crucial element within Surrealism, and it seems important to return to it after all the recent work that has been centred around the Surrealist body. Partly, then, my subject is that city – Paris itself.

But neither the actual places nor the photographs made there can be looked at with an innocent eye. They are always to be viewed through a Surrealist perspective, and a second layer of siting is where these photographs have themselves been placed within Surrealism. Primarily, this means examining the publication of the pictures in Surrealist books and magazines. Less tangibly, it has involved a study of how the photographs were regarded by the Surrealists – and, when there is no hard evidence in that respect, an exploration of how they *might* have been seen from a Surrealist perspective. This last has been particularly important where the work does not come from within Surrealism itself, but can be placed next to, in juxtaposition with, Surrealism.

So the concept of 'site' is complex and involves one other layer: where this study is itself sited. Surrealism looks different now from two decades ago, and what has intervened may be indicated by that universally distrusted but inevitably useful term 'postmodernism'. Though one cannot and should not claim Surrealism as postmodern or even 'proto-postmodern', it is true to say that its awkwardness within the canon of modernism does make more sense through the screen of postmodernity. As Dawn Ades wrote in 1986, 'It could be suggested ... that it was precisely Surrealism's efficacity to have maintained a series of contradictions *without* resolution. But this is uncomfortable for a discipline [Art History] which tends to works towards a unified view of individuals and movements, and to bestow value on them according to the measure of their unity'.[13] It is precisely this resistance to closure that enables us to keep returning to Surrealism.

This study has been undertaken not only in relation to a shift in the perception of Surrealism but also in relation to important developments in documentary photography. Much of my time in the last few years has been taken up in thinking about the implications of postmodernism for documentary – the questions that it raises about authorship, ethical responsibility and the processes of narrative. For many years, the humanist mainstream of documentary was hardly subject to questioning. Then, through the late 1970s and early 1980s, it was problematised almost to the point of paralysis.[14] In the last fifteen years, however, the genre has been reinvigorated by self-reflexivity, a refusal of mastery, an acceptance of ambiguity and a critical awareness of its own history.[15] Documentary is now a complex and multivalent genre that seeks to comment on issues of social and cultural importance without losing sight of the position from which that commentary is made.

It would of course be dangerously ahistorical to claim the same degree of reflexivity for the 'Surrealist documentary' examined here. But it is both intriguing and instructive to look back and view that period through the screen of recent concerns in documentary practice and theory. As scrupulous as one aims to be with primary sources and their placement in an historical context, one must, at the same time, acknowledge that the work studied here looks different from how it would have looked before postmodernism changed the way we think about both Surrealism and documentary.

At an early point in my research, I went to Brussels to talk with the surviving members of the Belgian Surrealist group. I visited Mme Georgette Magritte, who showed me her collection of her husband's photographs, which had just been published.[16] Mme Magritte kept them in a cardboard box – a random, unorganised assortment of tiny faded images. Yet it was impossible to handle these unprepossessing pictures without being affected by the mythologisation of Magritte and his work.

The following day, I visited the Magrittes' old comrades, Louis Scutenaire and Irène Hamoir. And they showed me their own photographs, neatly ordered in yearly albums, for all the world like any other family collection. But many of the pictures were the same as the ones I had seen in Mme Magritte's cardboard box. They explained that only some of the images that were now 'by' Magritte were his alone; many had been made collectively and circulated within the group.

In retrospect, that experience has a significance beyond the anecdotal – as a prefiguration of the experience of studying the other Surrealist photography (or rather photographies) discussed here. In the contrast between the two collections of the same images one can sense how photographs can have significantly different meanings within different contexts. In so far as our apprehension of these anonymous collective pictures is radically affected by our contemporary knowledge of Magritte's position as a twentieth-century 'master', one can also discern some elements of the complex issues of authorship that thread through this text. Photographs originally published anonymously in *La Révolution surréaliste* and *Nadja*, for example, are now significant images in the oeuvre of Eugène Atget and Jacques-André Boiffard respectively. And in examining the ways that, say, Brassaï's work is placed within the context of *Minotaure*, issues are raised around the processes of collaboration involved in any publication.

Most importantly, in questioning the status of these photographs by 'Magritte', one encounters a general issue that underlies the whole of this text. How we understand Surrealist photography now, half a century after it was made, may be quite different from how it was understood by its original audience. I have read the Surrealist use of straight photography as a simultaneous exploitation and subversion of the standard realist frame within which the medium was then primarily situated. It is a conclusion reached through a long process of research, which at the same time I know to be affected by retrospection.

Nevertheless, I believe the result is more than just a reading; I hope it is also – to paraphrase Roland Barthes – a just reading.[17] There are enough internal clues to suggest that even though the questions raised here were not consciously theorised by the Surrealists at the time, they were intuitively embedded in the ways that pictures were made and the ways they were used. And I believe there are many lessons here for contemporary practice: lessons about how documentary can incorporate subjectivity, ambiguity and reflexivity; and about how images can be made which acknowledge both their constructedness *and* their indexicality – images that are both expressions of desire and fragments from the real world.

Notes

1 Arthur Conan Doyle, 'A Case of Identity', in *Sherlock Holmes: The Complete Short Stories* (London: John Murray, 1963), pp. 55–6.

2 It's also worth noting that the photography from Paris I discuss is exclusively male, and it is in these other contexts that one finds work by female photographers such as Miller, Agar and Medková.

3 Nancy Hall-Duncan, *Photographic Surrealism* (Cleveland: New Gallery of Contemporary Art, 1979). Susan Sontag's *On Photography* (New York: Farrar, Straus and Giroux, 1977), with its frequent references to 'surrealism', was surely a major influence in the revaluation of the medium's relationship with Surrealism proper. But in the end, Sontag often uses 'surreal' merely as a synonym for grotesque or disconnected.

4 Edouard Jaguer, *Les mystères de la chambre noire* (Paris: Flammarion, 1982).

5 Monika Faber, *Das Innere der Sicht* (Vienna: Osterreichisches Fotoarchiv im Museum moderner Kunst, 1989).

6 Petr Král, *Fotografie v surrealismu* (Prague: Torst, 1994). In his summary, Král noted that his book had been written twenty years earlier and banned by the censor; otherwise, 'it would have been the first study of its kind in the world'.

7 David Bate, *Photography and Surrealism: Sexuality, Colonialism and Social Dissent* (London: I. B. Tauris, 2002).

8 Rosalind Krauss and Jane Livingston (eds), *L'Amour fou* (Washington: Corcoran Gallery/New York: Abbeville Press, 1985). The catalogue also contained an important essay by Dawn Ades, 'Photography and the Surrealist Text', pp. 153–87. Ades was also the author of a useful small brochure produced when the exhibition came to the Hayward Gallery, London: *An Introduction to Photography and Surrealism* (London: Arts Council of Great Britain, 1986).

9 See Hal Foster, 'L'Amour Faux', *Art in America* (January 1986), 117–28; Nancy Hall-Duncan, 'Out of Context', *Afterimage* (April 1986), 18–9; Ron Horning, 'An Argument with History', *Aperture*, 103 (Summer 1986), 2–6; Steve Edwards, 'Gizmo Surrealism', *Art History*, 10:4 (December 1987), 509–17; Kathleen Campbell, 'Ideology versus History: Deconstructing Surrealist Photography', *Exposure*, 26:1 (Spring 1988), 38–49.

10 On Szarkowski and MOMA, see Christopher Phillips, 'The Judgement Seat of Photography', *October*, 22 (Autumn 1982), 27–63, reprinted in Richard Bolton (ed.), *The Contest of Meaning* (Cambridge, MA: MIT Press, 1989), pp. 14–46, and Andy Grundberg, 'Art and Photography, Photography and Art: Across the Modernist Membrane', in Elizabeth Janus (ed.), *Veronica's Revenge* (Zurich: Scalo, 1998), pp. 43–52.

11 This is true of most of the critics named in n. 9, with the exceptions of Hall-Duncan and Edwards. Steve Edwards' review is a particularly cutting critique of the assumptions of *L'Amour fou*, and his placement of Surrealist photography in the city, and in relationship to Walter Benjamin's writings, were important in reinforcing the direction in which my own research was moving. For a more recent discussion of Surrealist photography in relation to ideas of realism and the everyday, see John Roberts, *The Art of Interruption: Realism, Photography and the Everyday* (Manchester: Manchester University Press, 1998), chapter 5, pp. 98–113.

13 Dawn Ades, 'Reviewing Art History', in A. L. Rees and Frances Borzello (eds),

The New Art History (London: Camden Press, 1986), p. 18.

14 A key concept here was Martha Rosler's characterisation of documentary as 'victim photography', first proposed in 'In, Around and Afterthoughts (on Documentary Photography)', in *Three Works* (Halifax: Nova Scotia College of Art and Design Press, 1981), pp. 59–86, reprinted in Bolton (ed.), *The Contest of Meaning*, pp. 303–33. However, though her critique was often used to discredit documentary, Rosler herself later emphasised that her interest was in repositioning it, rather than destroying it.

15 I have previously examined some of these new forms of documentary in two essays: 'Desert Stories, or Faith in Facts' in Martin Lister (ed.), *The Photographic Image in Digital Culture* (London and New York: Routledge, 1995), pp. 236–52, and 'Documentary Fictions?', *Art and Design*, 10:9/10 (September 1995), 29–33.

16 René Magritte, *La fidelité des images*, text by Louis Scutenaire (Brussels: Service de la Propagande Artistique du Ministère de la Culture française, 1978).

17 Roland Barthes, *Camera Lucida* (New York: Farrar, Straus and Giroux, 1991), p. 70.

1

Between index and construct

To begin this study of Surrealist photography with discussions of a painting and a poem may seem perverse. But this approach can reveal, first, how interlinked photography is – sometimes physically, often conceptually – with the many other media utilised by the Surrealists. Although this book will focus on photography, it cannot be a modernist reading of the medium in isolation. Second and more precisely, these examples may indicate how photography could come to act as a model for a Surrealist conceptualisation of creativity.

But we must be careful. There is very little discussion of photography by the Surrealists themselves, and there is certainly no central body of Surrealist theorisation of photography as developed for painting in Breton's *Le Surréalisme et la peinture* or for collage in Aragon's *La peinture au défi*.[1] Nor would it be possible to put together an anthology of Surrealist texts on photography as has been done for cinema.[2] Any Surrealist theorisation of photography was fragmentary and elusive and our reading of it must be consciously retrospective. Yet it is not mere perversity to concur with Rosalind Krauss in placing photography at the centre of the Surrealist enterprise.[3] Photography does, and I think did, represent certain important Surrealist values, though as we will see, the model that the medium offered the Surrealists was far from unitary. But then the conceptualisation of Surrealism itself was something that was often in flux, varying from group to group and individual to individual.

The painting I want to examine was made by Joan Miró in 1925: *Photo: This is the colour of my dreams* (figure 1). It is one of Miró's most austerely beautiful paintings, featureless but for three elements: the word 'Photo' written large on the upper left, a single patch of blue paint on the right and inscribed below it the phrase: 'This is the colour of my dreams.' Most commentary on the painting concentrates on the patch of blue. As Margit Rowell put it, 'the most important question raised is the meaning of blue';[4] an answer would need to range from Christian symbolism to late Romanticism, from the colour of the Virgin's cloak to Stéphane Mallarmé's poem 'L'Azur'.

That however is to ignore the other, equally significant, element in the painting: the large calligraphic word 'Photo' in the top left corner. With emphatic pedantry but also a certain flamboyance, it states, as Rowell puts it,

Fig 1 Joan Miró, *Photo: This is the colour of my dreams*, 1925. © ADAGP, Paris and DACS, London, 2001.

that 'This is a reproduction of the color of my dreams which is blue'.[5] In this reading, the use of the word 'Photo' asserts this image is a transcription of that blueness, something given in evidence, a kind of documentation. In order to establish the status of his 'blue' as having the force of truth, Miró calls upon a central element in the power of photography: the way that it records, apparently without commentary but precisely and directly, whatever might be before the camera as the image is made.

Barbara Rose is one of the few writers to foreground Miró's use of the word 'Photo' in this painting, but she sees in it a gesture of resistance to the increasingly prevalent role of photography within Dada and Surrealism. Miró, she argues, is asserting, *contra* photography, the continuing potency of his own medium of painting; he 'exposes the imaginative limitations of photography, since dreams, like angels, cannot be photographed'.[6] Yet this is to ignore the way that the transcriptive power of photography can itself seem magical, despite – indeed because of – its chemical directness. Photography's very reliance on chemistry can make it seem alchemical. Does this aspect also lie behind the drama of Miró's use of that word 'Photo', as if that pool of blue had exposed itself on the painting, floating up in his unconscious as the photographic image appears in the darkroom?[7]

Miró's evocation of photography as a metaphor for an apparently contrary form of poetic creativity – a documentation that is also a magic – finds echoes elsewhere in Surrealism. Most pointedly, there is the early remark by André Breton: 'The invention of photography dealt a mortal death blow to old means of expression, as much in painting as in poetry, where automatic writing ... is a veritable photography of thought.'[8] For automatic writing seemed to be the direct, unedited and unmediated workings of the unconscious – or so the early Surrealists hoped. Breton goes on to refer to the camera as 'a blind instrument',[9] an apparently curious characterisation given the very visual nature of the machine. What he surely means is that the camera, unlike the human gaze, looks but it does not know or understand what it is looking at, and it is this very 'blindness' which enables it without prejudice, embellishment and, most important, artistry, to faithfully record all that comes within its frame.

We are now able to theorise the palpability of the link between a thing and its photographic image through the concept of the 'index'. This term derives from the work of the semiotician C.S. Peirce, little known at the time of his death in 1914. The 'index' is a sign where, in Peter Wollen's phrase, there is 'an existential bond between itself and its object'.[10] This may be the smoke created by a fire acting as a sign for the fire, or a weathervane signalling the way the wind is blowing. But if we think in terms of the process of picturing, it means that, in some sense, the object makes its own picture. The photograph, we might say, is made by the thing that is photographed transferring *itself* on to the film. As Peirce wrote, 'photographs, especially instantaneous photographs, are very instructive, because we know they are in certain respects exactly like the objects they represent. But this resemblance is due to the photographs having been produced under such circumstances that they were physically forced to correspond point by point to nature.'[11] That correspondence is in the inherent nature of photography as an optical and chemical process. As one of the inventors of the medium, William Henry Fox Talbot, wrote of his home Lacock Abbey in 1839: 'this building I believe to be the first that was ever known to have drawn its own picture'.[12]

In Peirce's theorisation, the 'index' was one of three types of sign: the other two he called the 'symbol' and the 'icon'. However, these are not as distinctive as the 'index', operating as they do in ways that are very similar to the sign types derived from the work of the other major pioneer of semiology, Ferdinand Saussure. As a linguist, Saussure emphasised the 'arbitrary' relationship between object and sign, where, as with Peirce's 'symbol', there is no causal and necessary connection between the two (the word 'cow' is an arbitrary sign or symbol for the animal who stands in a field munching grass). Later, theorists working in the Saussurean tradition, most notably Roland Barthes, introduced the concept of the 'motivated' sign which resembles (is in some way motivated by) its object. This is in turn very close to Peirce's 'icon' – a sign that connects to its referent through resemblance.[13]

A photograph, then, is a double sign, both an icon – a picture of something – and an index – 'a trace, something directly stencilled off the real'.[14] But it is the index which makes a photograph ontologically distinct from other forms of representation. Peirce's work would not have been known to the Surrealists, nor indeed to most viewers of photography, but he gives voice to a widely held conceptualisation of the medium, which Miró and Breton were expressing as instinctively as we all do when looking through our family album. One of the most eloquent exponents of the argument that the very nature of photography makes it objective is André Bazin, writing in 1945: 'For the first time an image of the world is formed automatically, without the creative intervention of man... Photography affects us like a phenomenon in nature, like a flower or a snowflake... The objective nature of photography confers on it a quality of credibility absent from all other picture-making.'[15] He goes on to evoke the metaphor of the fingerprint (an image of the finger made by the finger), an excellent example of an indexical sign, though it's also unlikely that Bazin knew of Peirce's writings.

For Bazin, this indexicality is essential to photography's realism: reality makes itself through the camera. But he also sees this attribute as integral to the Surrealists' interest in the medium. He argues that for Surrealism, 'the logical distinction between what is imaginary and what is real tends to disappear ... Hence photography ranks high in the order of Surrealist creativity because it produces an image that is a reality of nature, namely, a hallucination that is also a fact'.[16] Indexicality not only underlies our sense of photography's realism; it is also responsible for our sense that we are seeing an uncanny process at work – an image that has 'made itself', the transmutation of a thing directly into its image, an image that in some ways transcends the thing. As Roland Barthes, one of the most controversial proponents of photographic realism, emphasised, 'the realists do not take photography for a "copy" of reality, but for an emanation of *past reality*: a *magic*, not an art'.[17]

In this respect, a photograph is, in Barthes' words, 'superior to everything the human mind can or can have conceived to assure us of reality'.[18] The Surrealists surely valued photography for the same reason, since, much as they prized the imaginative power of the human mind to write poems or paint pictures, there was a worrying flaw in such activity, which could indeed be easily dismissed as 'just' imagination. However, if the power of the camera could be harnessed to record, not only the stolid surface of reality, but also the more obscure relationships that connect within it, the results could be worth more than any number of imagined scenarios. Photography could anchor the surreal in the real, and our common belief in the actuality of the image exploited to convince us that this surreality was also irrefutable.

So we might think of the activity of Surrealist artists not so much as creation but observation, and, whether they are watching the unravelling of their internal unconscious or the intricate patternings of the exterior world, what's important is that these observations achieve the status of objective documentation. This is of course somewhat ironic, for the Surrealists well knew that subjective desire inevitably invades any attempt at objectivity. Indeed it was the unification of the two that was their ultimate aim. But there was reason in the tactic of precise documentary attention, for it was the *reality* of Surrealism that was ultimately at stake. As André Breton wrote in the first Surrealist manifesto: 'What is admirable about the fantastic is that there is no longer anything fantastic: there is only the real.'[19]

When Louis Aragon came in later years to describe his book *Le paysan de Paris*, published in 1926, he coined a term which at first sight looks contradictory: 'Surrealist realism'.[20] But in fact, the phrase goes to the heart of the tactics adopted in the creation of some of the most important Surrealist works. Like Breton's *Nadja* two years later, *Le paysan de Paris* refuses categorisation, as Aragon shifts between cool descriptive exactitude and poetic effusion. The text is interrupted several times by depictions of notices posted in the shops and cafés of the Passage de l'Opéra, a site which Aragon examines with fanatical attention to detail. There are no photographs in *Le paysan de Paris*, but at one point, Aragon does evoke photography as he invites the reader: 'Let us then enter the Baths of the Passage de l'Opéra with a practical mind. And a little Kodak.'[21] For, said Aragon, it was in Surrealism that began 'les royaumes de l'instantané' – 'the realms of the instantaneous, the world of snapshot'.[22]

Despite the irony of Aragon's comments, we see here another Surrealist reworking of the popular conceptualisation of photography. It is the snapshot, the *instantané*, that form of photograph practically synonymous with Kodak,[23] which most centrally represents ideas of photographic immediacy. There are, however, a number of overlapping meanings in the way we use the term 'snapshot'. First, as the word itself implies, these are pictures taken very quickly, so quickly that we assume they could not be contrived. It is instructive that Peirce himself offered the 'instantaneous photograph' as somehow even more indexical than other sorts of photographs. The immediacy of the process offers both extra authenticity and an extra magical charge (think today of the polaroid). Second, to refer to a photograph as a snapshot usually implies one taken by an untrained amateur. However deliberately made, the photograph acquires an aura of innocence, even naivety; it is authentic precisely because its maker does not know *how* to contrive it. (We can see how these parallel concepts of the snapshot might have intrigued the Surrealists if we return to their early espousal of automatic writing, which in order to be unmediated also needed to be done as quickly as possible, the writer hoping to evade any literary skill he or she might have.)

It's evident that the indexicality of photography is a powerful factor in our response to the medium. The Surrealists in turn saw how that power could be exploited for their own ends. But a 'surrealist realism' must consist of more than the reproduction of the surface of reality; it must also try to reveal connections and meanings normally obscured or overlooked. This can be achieved through a range of tactics, some of them interior to the photograph, some exterior. For the Surrealists often exploited the all-too-common passivity of the medium against itself. In some cases, they undermined the intractable stolidity of an image through the use of captioning or accompanying text – a common device in *La Révolution surréaliste*. In a more extended fashion, André Breton's text in *Nadja* draws out the reticence of Jacques-André Boiffard's photographs into a kind of revelation. Photograph could also be set against photograph, as E. L. T. Mesens often did in *Variétés*, or a sequence or block of photographs could be placed together to cumulative effect, as with the spread of Brassaï's *Nuits parisiennes* in *Minotaure*.

Within the single image as well, juxtaposition is often used, locking together within the photographic frame objects from disparate contexts, both defamiliarising the objects themselves and throwing into question the predominating orders of meaning to which they usually belong. The disruption could also come from the photographic process itself. Photographs not only reflect the world but also restructure it, and the flat rectangle of the image is in fact very far from its source material. It is, in effect, 'a new reality: a reality one can no longer touch'.[24] A photographer like Cartier-Bresson will make some of his best early pictures out of that space between the event and its photograph.

In considering how a concept of photograph-as-construct may be placed in relation to the indexicality of the medium, I want to look at a short poem by the main theorist of the Belgian Surrealist group Paul Nougé; it is simply titled 'Instantané'. Obscure in origin, undated and published posthumously,[25] it is nevertheless full of intriguing possibilities:

> The fine straight blade
> too sharp
> ah! truly plunges plunges
> into the too solid too white flesh.
>
> Cold fecundity of the fine blade
> beautiful flesh of certainties here is the fine blade
> a little blood ebbs on the lips
> the needle tears itself away from the dial
> dives toward the North
> a hand dances alone
> the eye explodes from too many images.
>
> Midday – Midnight
> collapses into a vertical sea.[26]

Except for the title 'Instantané', there is nothing in the poem itself that is overtly photographic. But that title – and the evocative quality of Nougé's metaphors – makes it possible to read the poem as referring to the way photography operates on reality.

Thus we might take the cutting of the knife to suggest the snapping of the camera shutter – as the knife might slice through flesh, so the shutter removes a 'slice of reality'. The images produced are cold, the objectivity of the camera rendering the warmth of flesh into something hard and white. The effect is 'beautiful', but the cut made in the 'corpus' of reality is 'too sharp'. The needle breaks from the dial and the hand dances alone. Severed from reality by the photographic frame, things are violently wrenched away from their context and the incisiveness of the cut leads not to clarity but rather a collapse of meaning. The result is a glut of multiplying image-fragments; their variety is overwhelming and 'the eye explodes'. Time is suddenly stopped ('Midday – Midnight'), arrested in the very stillness and flatness – the 'vertical sea' – of the resulting photographic print.

Read in these terms, the poem can point to the way in which photographs do not only record reality, but also reconstruct it. By removing fragments from the flow of experience, photographs create new meanings, which may be powerful in their very isolation but bear little relation to their original context. Photographs cut the world up, they silence it, flatten it and rob it of colour, in a transposition that is both violent and exhilarating. And indeed, so extreme that one must wonder how it is that we can still take photographs to be true documents of the exterior world. Yet, even though we may know better than to trust a photograph altogether, still we cannot escape the pull of its indexical adhesion to the real; in the very physical nature of the medium, there is a tension that is powerful in its ambiguity. The process of recording is inseparable from the process of transformation.

One cannot know Nougé's precise intentions in writing 'Instantané'. But to see the poem as a meditation on the paradoxes of the photographic process is a suggestive reading in the context of some of Nougé's other writings and their relationship with the images of his ally René Magritte. Until their rupture in 1952, the two men worked closely together on a reading of Magritte's work as a dissection of the problematics of representation.[27] One of Magritte's most elegantly direct paintings states that a picture of a pipe is 'not a pipe'. Indeed, the word 'pipe' is not a pipe either. The argument can in retrospect be read in semiological terms, as an insistence on the arbitrariness of both the symbolic sign (the word) and the iconic sign (the painting). Magritte wrenches these signs away from the object with which we too easily identify them, even though it is an identification that is fundamental to our interpersonal and intercultural systems of communication. But what of the index? Would Magritte have extended his scepticism to a photograph of a pipe?[28]

Throughout his work, Magritte played with the central paradox of representational painting – the illusionism of three dimensions represented on two, the way that we treat the realist painting, not as an object hung on a wall, but a window through which we see the world outside. This issue is addressed most famously in the series called *The Human Condition*, where the painted canvas in front of the window fits perfectly over the view seen through the window. We cannot ever know if the two views are indeed identical. However, as the unusually explicit title indicates, this is also a metaphor for human perception itself; Magritte himself explained in 1940, 'we see the world ... as being outside ourselves even though it is only a mental representation of it that we experience inside ourselves'.[29] The 'condition' of photography may be seen as rather ambiguous here. Is it more like a representational painting, standing in for reality – sliding with apparent seamlessness over it – or is it rather an extension of 'natural' vision: the camera seeing as the eye does, the image transferring itself directly on to the film as a kind of 'mental representation' made actual?

In a curious drawing published in 1962, we can see Magritte probing these questions (figure 2).[30] The image has been left in an unfinished state, but it seems to identify three stages in the depiction of reality. At the left is 'the actual image of the object': a vase of flowers on a plinth. To the right are the second and third stages: 'intermediary: vision, more or less accurate' and 'the final interpretation';[31] these are represented by two men, one behind the other. The man in front stands looking at the flowers; over the back of his head and completely covering that of the other man bent over behind him is a black cloth. The man at the front thus seems to be the camera and the man behind him the photographer, a set-up that immediately suggests the ambiguous identification of camera vision and human vision. We are constantly mistaking one form of representation for another, just as we mistake representation for reality. If we start again at the left, we realise that we are not seeing the 'actual' vase, but the 'actual image' of it; already it has become its own image, as it must as soon as we look at it.[32] All we can ever see is a representation; the 'real' vase is presumably somewhere unseen, unseeable, off to the left.

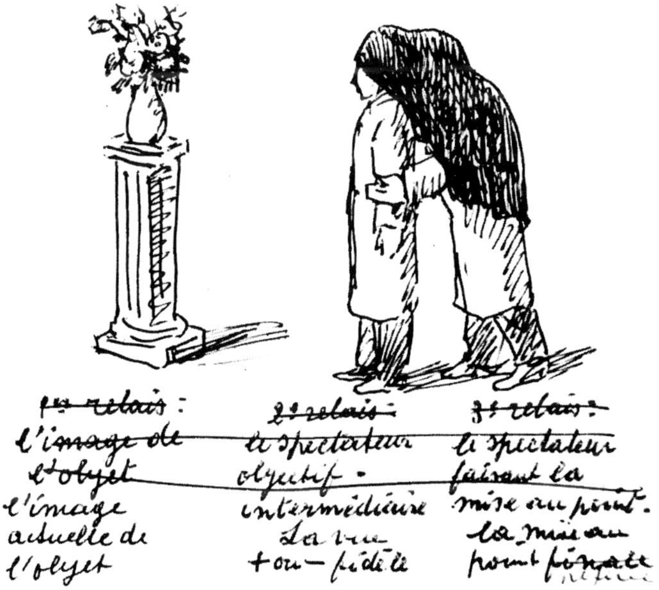

Fig 2 René Magritte, Drawing from *Leçon des choses*, 1962. © ADAGP, Paris and DACS, London, 2001.

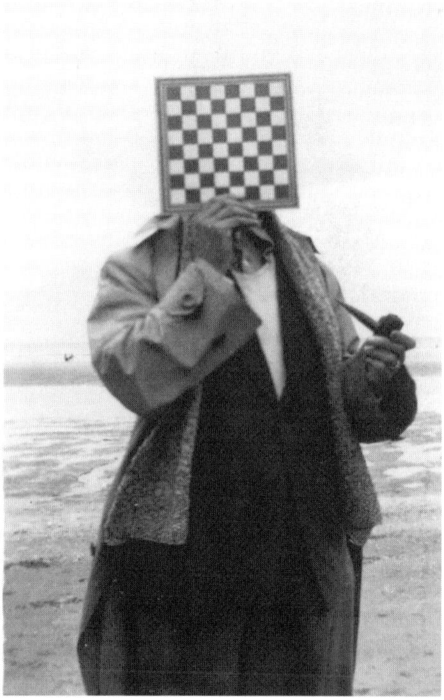

Fig 3 René Magritte, *The Giant (Paul Nougé)*, 1937. The J. Paul Getty Museum, Los Angeles. © ADAGP, Paris and DACS, London, 2001.

One of the most peculiar aspects of the drawing is the way that Magritte has left visible his preliminary captions, crossed out but quite as readable as his final text at the bottom. But should we see this as a simple process of preference – might it not be a staged provisionality, an indecisiveness conspicuously left in the drawing? Certainly, though, the crossed out captions offer other readings to those proposed below them. The central figure of the 'man/camera' is referred to as 'le spectateur objectif', a careful pun which makes him both 'the objective spectator' and the 'spectator-lens', while the far right figure of the photographer is 'le spectateur faisant la mise au point' – the spectator making the final interpretation. But the term 'mise au point' is also a pun; not only does it mean interpretation or restatement, it is also the French term for the focusing of a lens. What is 'brought to the point' is both a physical image – impressed on the film by the action of light – and the mental image – the interpretation made by the viewer.[33] In the aphorism that originally accompanied the drawing, Magritte commented: 'However far one may be from an object, one is never completely separate from it'.[34]

But what we precisely do not see in Magritte's drawing is that 'final interpretation', the new object that has been produced – the photograph. As there is a 'real vase' that we must imagine to the far left, so to the right we must imagine this photograph, and the viewer (another spectator) looking at it. That is our own role in the process and it would probably be a disappointing experience – just a picture of a vase of flowers. But whatever the 'final interpretation', Magritte suggests that the process of producing it is a peculiar

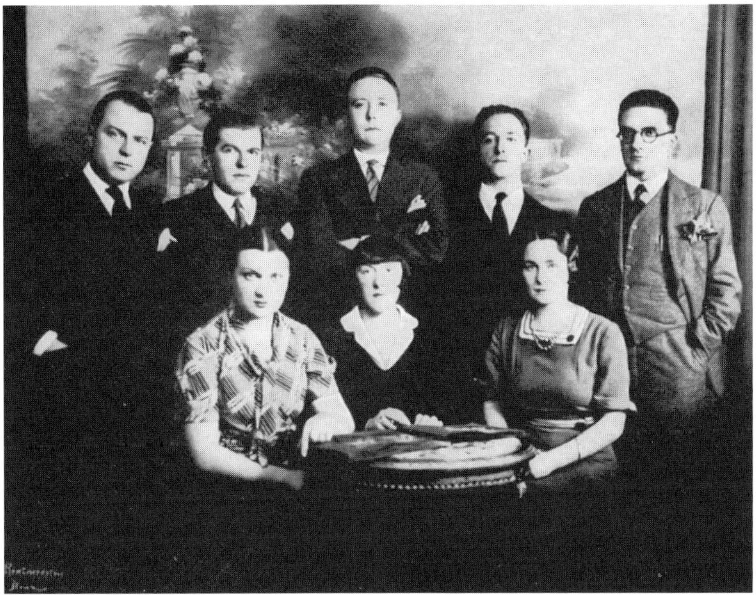

Fig 4 Studio portrait of the Belgian Surrealist group, published as 'Le Rendez-vous de chasse', *Documents 34* (1934).

one. For if we imagine what is happening beneath the cloth, there must be a hole bored through the head of the man at the front so that the man behind him can see the vase. (Or is it the photographer who is the 'blind instrument'?) And also, finally, it is a comic process. The 'photographer' must hold his 'camera' firmly in place so that it doesn't move, and the two figures become as one; indeed, there may only be one – doubled – head under the dark cloth, and both 'photographer' and 'camera' are wearing identical raincoats. It is a small detail, but endearing in its banality.

When Nougé and Magritte came to make their own *instantanés*, one can see something of these ideas in action (figure 3).[35] As the title of Nougé's small volume *Subversion des Images* suggests, one might view these pictures either as active or passive; either exterior reality is being subverted *by* the image or the innocent snapshot is itself being subverted by an overlay of Surrealist ideas.[36] This knowing exploitation of popular photography resonates elsewhere in the Belgians' use of photography. In Paris in 1929, Magritte asked each of the Surrealists to have their photograph taken in one of the newly installed photomaton machines. He did not want merely to confirm their external identity, but rather, to suggest an inner life which photography could not reach; each one kept his eyes shut.[37] In contrast, Nougé in 1934 arranged for the Belgian group to have their photograph formally made in the salon of a professional photographer in order to counter what he perceived as the creeping 'aestheticism' of Parisian Surrealism (figure 4).[38] Nougé and Magritte, then, seem to have been interested in the conventions of photography on two levels;

the physical and material conventions embedded in the medium itself, and the coded social conventions of popular photography. The Belgians' adoption of the forms of popular photography – the snapshot, the identity photo, the studio portrait – were in part humorously parodic, but as with Magritte's elaborate 'Sunday painter' disguise, such postures masked an incisive and highly subversive investigation of the nature of representation.

We might contrast this concern of Magritte and Nougé for the photograph as a double construction – both physical and social – with the earlier examples taken from Miró, Breton and Aragon which evoke a more straightforward model of photograph as 'document'. If the thinking of the Belgians' shows a greater scepticism, we should be careful of making this a simple opposition between Brussels and Paris; as we will see later, there was plenty of sophistication in the way the Parisian Surrealists used actual photographs in their publications. Nevertheless, the tension between the indexicality of photography and its constructedness is also key to a broader theoretical discussion of the medium, and most writing around the nature of photography has tended one way or other: either to see the photograph as a raw piece of reality which can be directly apprehended, or as a mediating language which needs to be decoded.

Some theorists, reacting against the realist view of photography, have indeed gone so far as to suggest that in fact photographs are 'completely arbitrary, conventional and unmotivated'.[39] As Allan Sekula has insisted, we learn to 'read' a photograph 'after learning first that a "reading" is an appropriate outcome of contemplating a piece of glossy paper ... Photographic "literacy" is learned ... The photograph is imagined to have a primitive core of meaning, devoid of all cultural determination ... In the real world no such separation is possible'.[40] In John Tagg's words, 'The photograph is not a magical "emanation" but a material product of a material process ... It requires not an alchemy but a history.'[41] As Mary Price notes, there can apparently be no reconciliation between the arguments of Barthes and Tagg.[42]

It is, however, surely the most compelling quality of photography that it is both actuality and artifice, both 'emanation' and 'material product'. Writing his first full essay on photography in 1961, Roland Barthes referred to the 'photographic paradox' of 'the coexistence of two messages, one without a code (this would be the photographic analogue) and the other with a code (this would be the "art", or the treatment, or the "writing", or the rhetoric of the photograph)'.[43] But it is a paradox central to the medium. This causes perplexity in many theorists of photography: as Geoffrey Batchen points out, even so resolute a conventionalist as Allan Sekula refers to the indexicality of photography as the 'fundamental ground' of the medium. But as Batchen asks: 'what is the status of any ground that is in permanent contradiction with itself, that is apparently both contingent and not contingent?'[44] And, he points out, the search for an 'essence' of photography seems always to result in a listing of dichotomies: 'between activity and passivity, presence and absence, time and

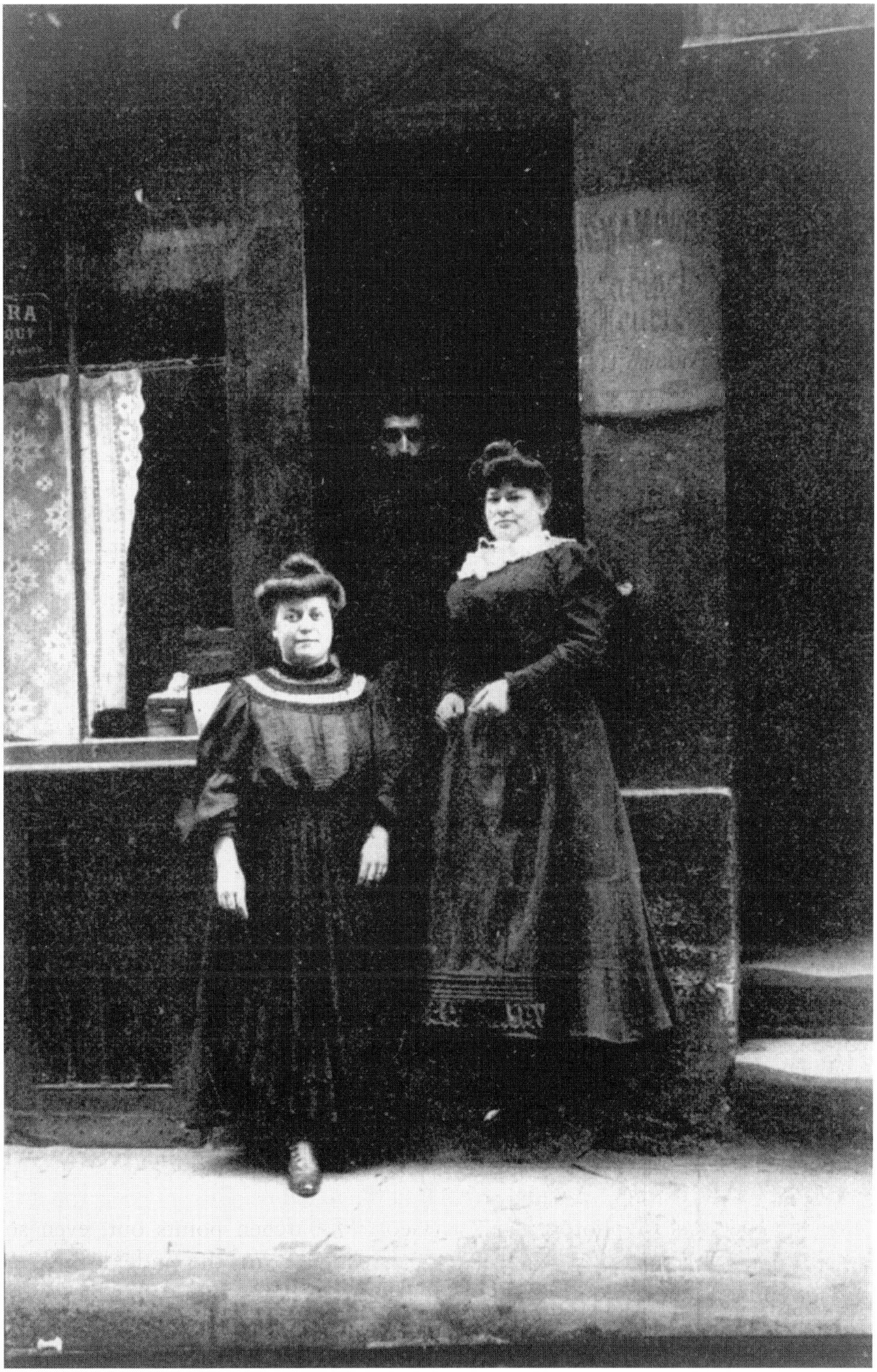

Fig 5 Anonymous photograph reproduced with Salvador Dalí, 'Psychologie non-euclidienne d'une photographie', *Minotaure*, 7 (1935).

space, fixity and transiency, observer and observed, real and representation, original and imitation, identity and difference – and the list could go on'.[45] For those who seek answers, such indeterminacy must be frustrating, but in a Surrealist reading of the medium, it is a provocation.

By the time he came to write *Camera Lucida* at the end of the 1970s, Barthes had not disowned the cultural analysis of photography – it is there in his concept of the *studium* ('a kind of general, enthusiastic commitment ... but without special acuity'). Rather he had lost interest in it. He was now concerned with the *punctum*: 'that accident which pricks me'.[46] The *punctum* is of course located in Barthes' concern for the 'evidential force' of the index, but as Doug Nickel has noted, there is an important difference between Barthes' position and that of other realists: 'Barthes is arguing this essence to be located not in the object itself, but in the process of its cognition by a viewer.'[47] Barthes now offers another photographic paradox: an attachment to external reality that can be only be truly realised through intense subjective investment. So intense, indeed, that at the end of *Camera Lucida*, Barthes declares the photograph 'a new form of hallucination ... a mad image, chafed by reality',[48] a status that is not so far from Bazin's 'hallucination that is also a fact'.

It's suggestive here to juxtapose Barthes' position with an actual Surrealist text.[49] In 1935, Salvador Dalí published an essay in *Minotaure* entitled 'Non-Euclidean Psychology of a Photograph'.[50] The photograph in question was a portrait of three people, two women and a man, perhaps taken towards the end of the nineteenth-century; they are posed in a doorway on to the street, so that the sinister features of the man only half emerge from the shadows (figure 5). These characters are indeed compelling, but Dalí wants us to look elsewhere: 'Do not believe, dear reader, that I draw your attention to this striking photograph because of its obvious pathetic and disconcerting quality, which arises quite naturally from the climate of criminality surrounding the three psychological beings, fixed in a personal, persevering and Euclidean pose.' Rather, in a typically Dalían delirium, he allows his 'paranoiac-critical' methodology to lead him to the bottom left hand corner of the picture, where 'you might observe with amazement – completely naked, completely pale, completely peeled, immensely unconscious, clean, solitary, tiny, cosmic, non-Euclidean – a threadless spool.'[51]

The rest of Dalí's essay swirls around the presence of that spool, which he calls a 'crazy thing' (*chose folle*), a small detail which, once spotted, suddenly undermines any conventional attempt at ordering and understanding the world.[52] To return to Barthes' terminology, we may gaze at and be intrigued by the *studium* of the portrait of the three people posed in the doorway, but it is the *punctum* of the spool which transfixes us, and its very insignificance becomes significant. Now we can't take our eyes off it.[53] There are, of course, important differences between Dalí's *chose folle* and Barthes' *punctum*. Dalí wants to understand the presence of the spool and build a meaning around it where Barthes at this point seems to use the punctum to move beyond established theoretical limits. But nevertheless, there is a commonality in their insistence that such moments of transgression are recognised through the response of individual consciousness. And in both readings, the indexical is far from a mere confirmation of surface; rather it is unsettling, untamable, the element which disrupts the coherence of the photograph (here, that of the 'portrait' convention, with its freight of social meaning). As Barthes put it in the last sentence of *Camera Lucida*: 'Such are the two ways of the Photograph. The choice is mine: to subject its spectacle to the civilised code of perfect illusions, or to confront in it the wakening of intractable reality.'[54]

In the years before the writing of his essay, Dalí had been very concerned with photography. Aside from his description of his own paintings as 'instantaneous colour photography done by hand',[55] he had several times made photographs the subjects of his paranoiac-critical activity (for example, his re-reading of a photograph of an African village hut as a portrait by Picasso).[56] Many of his previous contributions to *Minotaure* had involved photography.[57] And in the late 1920s, Dalí had produced a number of essays on the nature of photography which are among the most perceptive of Surrealist commentaries on the medium.[58] Photography, he wrote, was 'the most agile process for capturing the delicate osmoses which exist between reality and surreality. The mere donnée of photographic transposition already means a total invention: the capture of an UNKNOWN REALITY. Nothing proves the truth of surrealism so much as photography'.[59] Thus, while acknowledging the 'reality' of photographic vision, Dalí also emphasises that at the same time photography constructs a new type of vision for us.[60] Photography here is not only index and construct; it is also at once reality and surreality. But we must be careful not to simply identify the index with the 'real' and the construct with the 'surreal'. As we have seen, the Surrealists' interest shifted between the two, and they valued in different measure both index and construct. Moreover, reality and surreality are not opposing entities. As the Czech film-maker Jan Švankmajer – the most important artist today who still sees his work in explicitly Surrealist terms – affirmed in 1990: 'Surrealism exists *in* reality, not besides it.'[61]

There is one final element to put in place in this discussion – an element that is historical rather than abstractly theoretical. This is the shift that takes place during the period under examination from photograph as 'document' to 'documentary photography'. When, in the mid 1920s, Eugène Atget told Man Ray that his pictures were 'simply documents', he was expressing a common view of his medium.[62] In 1908, Henri Matisse had said: 'The photographer must intervene as little as possible, so as not to cause photography to lose the objective charm which it naturally possesses ... Photography should register and give us documents.'[63] Miró and Breton in the early 1920s were evoking this same concept of the photograph as document, record, evidence. When, in 1929, Georges Bataille named his new magazine *Documents*, the title may have been partly ironic, but it was still the very obviousness, directness (and sometimes brutality) of the photograph that was of interest to him.[64]

By the end of the 1920s, that position was shifting. Eugène Atget modestly termed himself a maker of documents, but as Maria Morris Hambourg has observed, soon after his death he would be transformed into the 'precursor of modern documentary photography'.[65] The apparently slight shift from document to documentary signals an important conceptual change. In English, the first use of the term 'documentary' in relationship to visual media is usually credited to John Grierson, reviewing Robert Flaherty's film *Moana* in 1926.[66] In a popular sense, the word has continued to apply to film (only there is 'documentary' used as a noun as well as an adjective). By the early 1930s, however, it was also applied to a range of other media, including photography, and it has been argued that in Britain and America at least, 'social documentary' was the dominant genre of the period, with significant official investment in organisations such as the General Post Office film unit and the historical section of the Farm Security Administration.[67]

In France, the situation was different. The term *documentaire* had been used as a noun since the start of the century to describe travel and exploration films, and that association had to be superseded before other meanings could take hold. The French concept of documentary remained very distinct; there was no state sponsorship and the term did not carry the overt political connotations it acquired in English. Nevertheless, as early as 1928, a review in *Cahiers d'art* states that 'the first to have given capital importance to documentary photography [*la photographie documentaire*] was E. Atget' and that the forthcoming monograph of his work 'will instruct us in a preemptive fashion of the unsuspecting significance of documentary photography, which already counts among its adherents such well-known names as the Hungarian André Kertész, the American Sheeler, the Belgian E. Gobert, Germaine Krull and Eli Lotar'.[68] E. Gobert may have vanished from sight, but with the work of Parisian photographers such as Krull, Lotar, Kertész, and, a little later, Brassaï and Cartier-Bresson, 'documentary photography' acquired a new self-consciousness. Cutting back and forth between the popular and the avant-garde, they each developed an oeuvre that was at once based in the observation of the reality around them and an expression of their individual artistic convictions.

But therein lies another photographic paradox. The founding definition of 'documentary' was famously offered by Grierson as 'the creative treatment of actuality', a phrase which has caused controversy ever since. As Brian Winston remarks: 'one does not have to be too much of a sceptic to spot the obvious contradiction in this formulation. The supposition that any "actuality" is left after "creative treatment" can now be seen as being at best naive and at worst a mark of duplicity'.[69] But perhaps one might rather take it as an acknowledgement that the direct record of 'actuality' – the pure document – is unattainable, that subjectivity is indeed inherent in the documentary process. From the start, documentarians understood the apparent paradox to be integral to their work. But it also has a particular relevance for Surrealism. Alongside the dialectical tension between index and construct, one might now place the dualities of actuality and creativity, objectivity and subjectivity, document and documentary. As Nick Stanley has written: 'It is when the empirical observation is undertaken with a surreal mistrust of surface that the documentary photograph appears.'[70] If Dalí, and later Barthes, were to speak for the right of the viewer to be suspicious of imposed views, to follow instead his or her own subjectivity, then, from the early 1930s onwards, the conceptualisation of 'documentary' gave a comparable right to the photographer.

Jan Švankmajer's comment on the relationship between Surrealism and reality has already been cited; in 1992, he elaborated on it, saying: 'If my films were perfect, I would like the viewer to think that he had just watched a documentary.'[71] It seems at first a strange comment for Švankmajer's films are manifestly not documentaries – they require much elaborate staging and are tightly controlled. What is important is the aspiration – the desire to persuade us that what we have seen has been actual, to convince us of the reality of (his) Surrealism. It's an aspiration that applies in obvious ways to the Surrealist use of film and photography; equally, though, the spectator must be convinced of the authenticity of an automatic drawing or painted dreamscape. If Pater's dictum that all art aspires to the condition of music may be said to characterise modernist abstraction, then a Surrealist art aspires to the condition of documentary. And, as we noticed at the beginning of this chapter, it is photography that provided – however problematically – an authenticating model, an emblem of this attachment to the real.

It's significant, though, that Švankmajer said 'documentary' rather 'document', because what is being documented is in large part the workings of his own subjectivity. If the Surrealist artist works from the subjective and makes it real, then the documentarian takes the real and filters it through his or her subjectivity. The Surrealist works from the hallucination to the fact, the documentarian from the fact to the hallucination. A Surrealist documentary, we might finally say, would fuse the two together. In different ways, the Surrealists' own use of both photography and the images made by photographers influenced by Surrealism were manifestations of a desire to exploit the camera's ability to simultaneously render the surface of the world palpable and render it marvellous – to reveal it as an hallucination that is also a fact that is also an hallucination.

Notes

1 See André Breton, *Surrealism and Painting* (New York: Icon, 1972), and Louis Aragon, *La peinture au défi* (Paris: Goemans, 1930).

2 Paul Hammond (ed.), *The Shadow and its Shadow* (London: British Film Institute, 1978).

3 See 'Photography in the Service of Surrealism' in Rosalind Krauss and Jane Livingston (eds), *L'Amour fou* (Washington: Corcoran Gallery/New York: Abbeville Press, 1985), pp. 15ff.

4 In Rosalind Krauss and Margit Rowell, *Joan Miró: Magnetic Fields* (New York: Guggenheim Museum, 1972), p. 60.

5 *Ibid.*

6 Barbara Rose, *Miró in America* (Houston: Museum of Fine Arts, 1982), p. 16.

7 For a Surrealist evocation of the darkroom as a site of poetic alchemy, see Chapter 4.

8 From Breton's essay, 'Max Ernst', first published in *Max Ernst* (Paris: Au sans pareil, 1921), and reprinted in *Les Pas perdus* (Paris: Gallimard, 1924). Translated as *The Lost Steps* (Lincoln: University of Nebraska Press, 1996), p. 60.

9 *Ibid.*

10 Peter Wollen, *Signs and Meaning in the Cinema* (London: Secker and Warburg, 1969), p. 122. Wollen was one of the first theorists to point to the appropriateness of the Peircean index in the analysis of film and photography. Rosalind Krauss's essay 'A Note on the Index' (1977) was also important for its analysis of the place of the index in the work of Marcel Duchamp and its connections with photography (reprinted in *The Originality of the Avant-Garde and Other Modernist Myths* (Cambridge, MA: MIT Press, 1985), pp. 196–219).

11 Charles Sanders Peirce, *Collected Papers: Volume II: Elements of Logic* (Cambridge, MA: Harvard University Press, 1960), chapter 3: 'The Icon, Index and Symbol', p. 159.

12 From *Some Account of the Art of Photogenic Drawing*, as quoted by Geoffrey Batchen, *Burning with Desire* (Cambridge, MA: MIT Press, 1999), p. 66. We must be careful, however, not to ascribe too 'primitive' an attitude to the pioneers of photography. As Batchen shows, they were in fact rather ambivalent about the relationship between a photograph and its subject: 'Is nature painted by photography or being induced to paint herself? Is she produced by or a producer of photography?' (p. 63). These are questions that will find an echo later in this chapter.

13 On the arbitrary and the motivated sign, see Roland Barthes, *Elements of Semiology* (London: Jonathan Cape, 1967), pp. 50–4. In the same book (pp. 35–8), Barthes analysed some of the complexities of semiological terminology.

14 Susan Sontag, *On Photography* (New York: Farrar, Straus and Giroux, 1977), p. 154. Peirce himself seems to have wavered between viewing a photograph as an index or an icon; see Michael Leja, 'Peirce, Visuality and Art', *Representations*, 72 (Autumn 2000), 97–122.

15 André Bazin, 'The Ontology of the Photographic Image', in *What is Cinema?: Vol. I* (Berkeley: University of California, 1967), p. 13.

16 *Ibid.*, pp. 15–16. His comment that 'photography ranks high in the order of Surrealist creativity' seems remarkable for 1945, and prescient of more recent views on the significance of the medium within Surrealism.

17 Roland Barthes, *Camera Lucida* (New York: Farrar, Straus and Giroux, 1991), p. 88. There are, by now, many analyses of Barthes' writings on photography; the essays in Jean-Michel

Rabaté (ed.), *Writing the Image after Roland Barthes* (Philadelphia: University of Pennsylvania Press, 1997) are useful: Colin McCabe in 'Bazin and Barthes: The Ontology of the Image' (pp. 71–6) sketches the (unacknowledged) connection between the two writers.

18 Barthes, *Camera Lucida*, p. 87.

19 André Breton, *Manifestoes of Surrealism* (Ann Arbor: University of Michigan, 1969), p. 15. This sentence was quoted by Luis Buñuel in an address on 'Poetry and Cinema' at the University of Mexico in 1953. The text of his talk is given in Joan Mellen (ed.), *The World of Luis Buñuel* (Oxford: Oxford University Press, 1978), p. 109, where the translation is even more to the point: 'the most admirable thing about the fantastic is that the fantastic does not exist; everything is real'.

20 Louis Aragon, *Paris Peasant* (London: Jonathan Cape, 1971), p. 16, quoted from *Je n'ai jamais appris à écrire* (Geneva: Albert Skira, 1969). Aragon was applying the term 'surrealist realism' retrospectively in contradistinction to the 'socialist realism' he went on to espouse.

21 *Ibid.*, p. 69.

22 Translation by Simon Watson Taylor, *ibid.*, p. 78. Walter Benjamin echoed this phrase in the title of his 1929 essay, 'Surrealism, the Last Snapshot of the European Intelligentsia', in *One-Way Street* (London: New Left Books, 1976).

23 For an analysis of the hegemony of Kodak in popular photography, see Don Slater, 'Consuming Kodak', in Jo Spence and Patricia Holland (eds), *Family Snaps* (London: Virago, 1991), pp. 49–59. Within the Parisian avant-garde, this invocation of the Kodak snapshot as a model for a new form of creativity was not limited to Surrealism. In 1924, Blaise Cendrars had published a collection of poems which he called 'photographies verbales' under the very title *Kodak*; he was however prevented from using the title by Eastman Kodak themselves and he retitled it *Documentaires* (see Blaise Cendrars, *Du monde entier: poésies complètes 1912–1924* (Paris: Gallimard, 1975), pp. 133ff.). Cendrars' intentions were however very different from Aragon's and his poems are rather an extension of the exuberant Modernism of the street announced by Apollinaire in his poem *Zone*: 'Handbills catalogues advertisements that sing aloud / Furnish your morning's poetry and for prose there are newspapers' (Guillaume Apollinaire, *Alcools* (Berkeley: University of California, 1965), p. 3).

24 Barthes, *Camera Lucida*, p. 87.

25 Paul Nougé, *L'Experience continue* (Brussels: Les Lèvres nues, 1966), p. 45.

26 'Le fin couteau droit / trop affilé / ah! vraiment plonge plonge / dans la chair trop ferme trop blanche. // Froide fécondité du fin couteau / belle chair des certitudes voici le fin couteau / un peu de sang reflue aux lévres / l'aiguille s'arrache au cadran / s'enfonce vers le Nord / une main danse seule / l'oeil explose de trop d'images. // Midi – Minuit / croule en mer verticale.'

27 Nougé's writings about Magritte's work have been collected in Paul Nougé, *René Magritte (in extenso)* (Brussels: Didier Devillez, 1997).

28 It was presumably in reference to Magritte's conundrum that Roland Barthes wrote that in a photograph, a pipe 'is always and intractably a pipe' (Barthes, *Camera Lucida*, p. 5).

29 'La ligne de la vie', *L'Invention collective*, 2 (1940), translated in Suzi Gablik, *Magritte* (London: Thames and Hudson, 1970), p. 184.

30 The drawing originally accompanied Magritte's text 'Leçon des choses' in *Rhetorique*, 7 (October 1962). This was a sequence of eight aphorisms illustrated with several similar drawings. The full text can be found in René Magritte, *Ecrits complets*, ed. André Blavier (Paris: Flammarion, 1979), pp. 335–7, with an English translation and notes on its complex genesis. Gablik, *Magritte*, reproduces several of the drawings, including this one on p. 103.

31 These are the translations given by Gablik, *Magritte*, p. 103.

32 'Actuelle', in fact, means not so much as 'actual' as 'present'; it usually suggests a temporal rather than spatial placement.

33 It may be significant that the photographic process illustrated by Magritte is not that of the small snapshot camera (the technology he used himself to make his photographs), where the scene is viewed directly through the viewfinder. Rather, he references the old-fashioned process of the plate camera, where the view is already seen as an image by the photographer, focused on the glass screen at the back of the camera.

34 Magritte, *Ecrits complets*, p. 336.

35 See René Magritte, *La fidelité des images* (Brussels: Service de la Propagande Artistique du Ministère de la Culture française, 1978); Marcel Paquet, *Photographies de Magritte* (Paris: Contrejour, 1982) and Paul Nougé, *Subversion des images* (Brussels: Les Lèvres nues, 1968).

36 On Nougé and photography, see Christine de Naeyer, *Paul Nougé et la photographie* (Brussels: Didier Devillez, 1995). *Subversion des images* was published posthumously and, as de Naeyer notes (p. 74), it's possible that the title was in fact coined by the book's editor, Marcel Marïen, himself an expert in incisive subversion. De Naeyer also examines the ambiguous authorship of some of the photographs attributed to Magritte (see the Introduction to the present book), and ascribes several of them jointly to Magritte and Nougé.

37 *La Révolution surréaliste*, 12 (15 December 1929), 72. The first 'photomatons' were opened in Paris in June 1928 (see Robert Delpire (ed.), *Identités* (Paris: Centre Nationale de la Photographie/Editions du Chêne, 1985), p. 117). In Magritte, *La fidelité des images*, p. 8, there is a photograph of Magritte taken on the new machine installed in the Jardin des Plantes in 1928, an experience he undoubtedly remembered a year later for *La Révolution surréaliste*.

38 Taken for the special edition of *Documents 34: Intervention surréaliste* edited by E. L. T. Mesens, where it is titled 'Le Rendez-vous de chasse'. Nougé's 'authorship' and its anti-Paris intention were explained by Louis Scutenaire and Iréne Hamoir in an interview with the author (Brussels: 1978).

39 Umberto Eco, 'Critique of the Image', in Victor Burgin (ed.), *Thinking Photography* (London: Macmillan, 1982), p. 33.

40 Allan Sekula, 'On the Invention of Photographic Meaning', in Burgin, *Thinking Photography*, pp. 86–7.

41 John Tagg, *The Burden of Representation* (London: Macmillan, 1988), pp. 2–3.

42 Mary Price, *The Photograph: A Strange, Confined Space* (Stanford: Stanford University Press, 1994), p. 9. On the conflicting theorisations around the indexicality and constructedness of photography, see also Batchen, *Burning with Desire*, especially pp. 4–21 and pp. 192–202; and Terence Wright, 'Photography: Theories of Realism and Convention',

in Elizabeth Edwards (ed.), *Anthropology and Photography 1860–1920* (New Haven and London: Yale University Press, 1992), pp. 18–31. (I am of course referring here to the traditional chemical photograph; the implications of digital photography are another subject.)

43 Roland Barthes, 'The Photographic Message' in *The Responsibility of Forms* (Berkeley and Los Angeles: University of California Press, 1991), pp. 7–8.

44 Batchen, *Burning with Desire*, p. 195. One way out of this paradox is to propose that the idea of the uncoded photograph is in fact itself a form of coding; as W. J. T. Mitchell puts it, 'one connotation always present in the photograph is that it is a pure denotation' (*Picture Theory* (Chicago: University of Chicago Press, 1994), p. 284). As Batchen points out, there is a parallel suggestion embedded in Peirce's very proposal that an index is a form of sign; following Derrida, he writes that 'Those who follow Peirce for pragmatic evidence of an extra-photographic real ... will, if they look closely enough find "nothing but signs"' (*Burning with Desire*, p. 198). However, what I am rather concerned with here is not the question of whether there is a 'real' in photography, but the persistent and powerful belief that there is.

45 Batchen, *Burning with Desire*, p. 179.

46 Barthes, *Camera Lucida*, pp. 26–7.

47 Doug Nickel, 'Roland Barthes and the Snapshot', *History of Photography*, 24:3 (Autumn 2000), p. 233.

48 Barthes, *Camera Lucida*, p. 115.

49 The connections between *Camera Lucida* and Surrealism are tantalising, but at the time Barthes was writing, Bretonian Surrealism was very much out of favour in French intellectual circles (see Chapter 3 n. 32) and the connections remained unacknowledged. There are however intriguing possibilities; for possible links between *Camera Lucida* and *Nadja*, see Chapter 3 n. 46.

50 'Psychologie non-euclidienne d'une photographie', *Minotaure*, 7 (June 1935), 56–7. This essay comes immediately after André Breton's 'La nuit du tournesol', discussed in Chapter 7. It is translated in Haim Finkelstein (ed.), *The Collected Writings of Salvador Dalí* (Cambridge: Cambridge University Press, 1998), pp. 302–6, where however the photograph has strangely been cropped at the bottom to remove the spool.

51 Dalí's description of the spool as 'immensely unconscious' is reminiscent of Walter Benjamin's evocation of the 'optical unconscious' in photography (see below, Chapter 8). But whereas Benjamin developed such concepts out of his interest in Surrealism, there's no evidence whether the Surrealists in turn knew anything of Benjamin's writings.

52 For a reading of Dalí's text which emphasises his attack on Kantian metaphysics and its insistence on a closure of meaning, see John Roberts, *The Art of Interruption* (Manchester: Manchester University Press, 1998), p. 108.

53 Dalí's emphasis on the threadlessness of the spool might make one recall Sigmund Freud's account of another spool, this one attached to a length of cotton and the plaything of his infant grandson ('Beyond the Pleasure Principle' in *The Pelican Freud Library, Vol. XI: On Metapsychology* (Harmondsworth: Penguin, 1984), p. 284). As the child throws it away from him, he says 'fort' (gone); as he pulls it back, he says 'da' (there). Freud reads the child's act as a coming to terms with the absence of his mother. In this context, I'm

reminded of how the affect of photographs also oscillates between presence and absence. They seem to offer us an actuality, but always they simultaneously deny it: the photography is 'there', but what is in the photograph has 'gone'.

54 Barthes, *Camera Lucida*, p. 119.

55 From 'The Conquest of the Irrational', in Finkelstein, *The Collected Writings of Salvador Dalí*, p. 265. For an analysis of Dalí's early mix of hyper-realist painting and actual collage, see Dawn Ades, *Dalí* (London: Thames and Hudson, 1982), p. 83.

56 'Visage paranoiaque', *Le Surréalisme au service de la révolution*, 3 (December 1931), 40.

57 For example, in issue no. 3–4 (14 December 1933), there are three varied examples of how Dalí worked with photography and photographers. His essay 'De la beauté terrifiante et comestible, de l'architecture Modern style' is a celebration of Art Nouveau, illustrated with images by Man Ray from Barcelona, and by Brassaï from the Paris metro (pp. 69–76). Second, there are the 'Sculptures involuntaires' – a bus ticket, a scrap of soap – which Dalí had anonymously selected with Brassaï (p. 68). Finally, there is the collage 'Le phénoméne de l'extase' (p. 77), which juxtaposes details from Bertillon's analysis of criminal ears alongside elements taken from what look like early pornographic photographs; the central picture of a woman's head thrown back is again by Brassaï.

58 These essays have been usefully translated in Michael Raeburn (ed.), *Salvador Dalí: The Early Years* (London: Thames and Hudson, 1994). See in particular 'Photography, Pure Creation of the Mind', p. 216, and 'The Photographic Donnée', p. 227. On Dalí's early interest in photography, see Dawn Ades, *Dalí*, pp. 47–55, and *Dalí's Optical Illusions* (Hartford, CT: Wadsworth Atheneum/London: Yale University Press, 2000), pp. 10–29.

59 From 'The Photographic Donnée' (1929) in Raeburn, *Salvador Dalí: The Early Years*, p. 227.

60 In her essay in Raeburn, *Salvador Dalí: The Early Years*, p. 142, Dawn Ades proposes that Dalí was here influenced by Moholy-Nagy's *Painting Photography Film* as well as Surrealist publications such as *Nadja*. We will later find another productive conjunction of Surrealism and the 'New Vision' in the work of Eli Lotar.

61 Jan Švankmajer, *Tales from Prague* (BBC Television, 1990).

62 See Chapter 5.

63 Quoted by Molly Nesbit, *Atget's Seven Albums* (New Haven and London: Yale University Press, 1992), p. 15, in the course of a close examination of what 'document' might have meant for a photographer of Atget's generation. French advocates of straight photography continued in the 1930s to promote the importance of the plain 'document' as a counter to the prevalent taste for Pictorialism. Florent Fels in 1928 wrote: 'A good photograph is, above all, a good document', a sentiment echoed three years later by Philippe Soupault: 'a photograph is above all a document'. (Translations from Christopher Phillips (ed.), *Photography in the Modern Era* (New York: Metropolitan Museum of Art/Aperture, 1989), pp. 26 and 51.)

64 For Bataille's interest in non-artistic photography, see Chapter 4.

65 Maria Morris Hambourg, 'Atget, Precursor of Modern Documentary Photography', in David Featherstone (ed.), *Observations: Essays on Documentary Photography* (Carmel: Friends of Photography, 1984), pp. 24–39.

66 This claim has been disputed; there is, for example, the use of the phrase 'documentary

works' by Edward Curtis in 1914. See Brian Winston, *Claiming the Real: The Documentary Film Revisited* (London: British Film Institute, 1995), pp. 8–10, for a useful analysis.

67 This is the argument of William Stott, *Documentary Expression and Thirties America* (Oxford: Oxford University Press, 1973), concerning the United States.

68 This is a review of the 'Exposition de photographie' in Brussels, in *Cahiers d'art*, 3:8 (1928), p. 356; translation from Hambourg, 'Atget, Precursor of Modern Documentary Photography', p. 31. The review is unsigned but Hambourg assigns it to the magazine's editor, Christian Zervos. In another of his early essays, 'Review of Anti-Artistic Tendencies' (1929), Salvador Dalí also talked about 'documentary' in ways that suggest the term was in common use (see Raeburn, *Salvador Dalí: The Early Years*, p. 229).

69 Winston, *Claiming the Real*, p. 11.

70 Nick Stanley, *The Extra Dimension: A Study and Assessment of the Methods Employed by Mass Observation in its First Period, 1937 1940* (Birmingham Polytechnic: unpublished Ph.D. dissertation, 1981), p. 129. On Mass-Observation, see Chapter 9, n. 24.

71 Interview with the author (Cardiff: 1992).

2
Surrealism on the street

On 4 October 1926, 'toward the end of one of those idle, gloomy afternoons', André Breton is drifting aimlessly along the Rue Lafayette, depressed by the crowds in the street: 'No, it was not yet these who would be ready to create the revolution.'[1] Suddenly, he sees a woman, walking toward him. As he looks at her, she looks back, he feels she was already looking at him: 'I have never seen such eyes.' He speaks to her, they walk, they stop in a café. Her name is Nadja. She tells him her story, they agree to meet again.

Thus begins one of the central encounters of Surrealism, potent not only as an event, but also in its setting. For *Nadja*, the book about this relationship that Breton published two years later, is a key representation both of Surrealist *amour fou* and the Surrealist mythology of the street. Photography would be the major visual medium through which Surrealist urbanity was explored, but initially it's important to understand the larger context in which this exploration took place. This chapter, then, will examine the ways that the city is represented within Surrealism, primarily through text and less extensively through paintings and collages.

Though given a particular emphasis by the Surrealists, mythologisation of the city permeated the avant-garde sensibility of the early twentieth-century. Moreover, it was a mythology that by that point in time had a history. Some seventy years before Breton's encounter with Nadja, Charles Baudelaire began his poem 'A une passante' with a more threatening image of the street: 'The traffic roared around me, deafening.'[2] Amid the din, the poet is transfixed by a glance from a woman. The unknown woman looks back, as Nadja will look at Breton. In this case, however, she passes by and Baudelaire is left to regret what might have been: 'You whom I might have loved and who knew that too.' The doubling of gazes, man toward woman and woman toward man, is not of course equal; for a woman to 'walk the streets' implies something quite different than it does for a man. And in both situations, it is the man who recounts the story; as Janet Woolf ironically notes, there is no reciprocal poem written by *la passante* about her encounter with Baudelaire.[3] But at least the look is not solely one way. There is some sense, however problematic, of reciprocity.[4]

The male artist of the street has a designation. He is a *flâneur*, and his activity of strolling and observing is a creative one.[5] Baudelaire, the first great poet of *flânerie*, described the process:

> Thus the lover of universal life enters into the crowd as though it were an immense reservoir of electrical energy. Or one might liken him to a mirror as vast as the crowd itself; or to a kaleidoscope gifted with consciousness, responding to each one of its movements and reproducing the multiplicity of life and the flickering grace of all the elements of life. He is an 'I' with an insatiable appetite for the 'non-I', at every instant rendering and explaining it in pictures more living than life itself, which is always unstable and fugitive.[6]

If the first image of the street presented here is as the scene of a sudden erotic encounter in the midst of urban ennui and the second involves immersion in the unnerving yet exhilarating mass of the crowd, a third view of the city would characterise it as mysterious and unsettling. While Surrealism partook of the erotic (certainly) and the ecstatic (to an extent), its main emphasis was on the 'unstable and fugitive'. As Breton wrote in his first collection of essays *Les Pas perdus* in 1923: 'The street, which I believed could furnish my life with its surprising detours; the street, with its cares and its glances, was my true element: there I could test like nowhere else the winds of possibility.'[7]

Here again, it is Baudelaire who provides a key image with the cry from the poem 'Les Sept Vieillards': 'Swarming city – city gorged with dreams, where ghosts by day accost the passer-by.'[8] This concept of the ghost-ridden street was not only influential for the Surrealists, but was also famously echoed in T. S. Eliot's image of London as the 'Unreal City' of *The Waste Land*.[9] For, though centred in Paris, the dual image of the street as a site of mystery and pleasure, threat and invitation, found expression in the early twentieth-century in all the great cities of Europe: London, Vienna, Berlin and St Petersburg.[10] Later, in the middle of the century, a version of the *flâneur* appeared on the 'mean streets' of the booming new cities of America.[11] The 'street photography' born in New York in the 1950s also had its genesis in the *flânerie* of nineteenth-century Paris.[12]

Undoubtedly, through the first half of the twentieth-century, it was Paris that epitomised the Modernist 'heroism of modern life', first hailed by Baudelaire and subsequently explored by the Impressionists and the Cubists. Guillaume Apollinaire's long poem *Zone*, published in 1913, was an important text in this respect, generally more exuberant in its acceptance of modernity than either Baudelaire or the Surrealists. But, even there, the joyful evocation of 'a fine street whose name slips my mind' is haunted by disturbing visions: 'Today you walk through Paris the women bloodstained.'[13]

Alongside this somewhat self-conscious avant-gardism, there were also more popular dimensions to the romance of the city street which gave expression to the new ways of living in this challenging environment. It is quite possible to

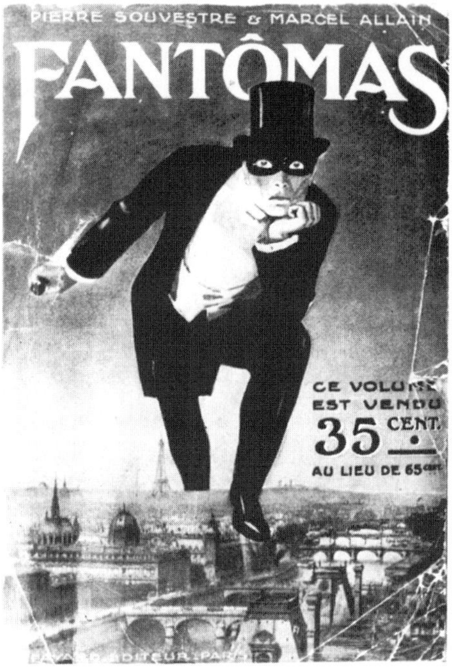

Fig 6 Cover of Marcel Allain and Pierre Souvestre, *Fantômas*, 1912.

write, as Susanna Barrows has, a history of the crowd in nineteenth-century Paris which does not mention Baudelaire.[14] It is important to evoke, as Adrian Rifkin does, a popular life of inter-war Paris where 'modern art movements like Surrealism get a look in from the edges'.[15] But what I want to emphasise is how the avant-garde sense of the street intersected with the popular, with both aspects moving between the political and the fantastic. Pierre MacOrlan, who appears below as a commentator on Atget and Kertész, was a genuinely popular novelist and his 1927 book *Quai des brumes* was turned into an equally popular film by Marcel Carné in 1938. The script was written by the former Surrealist Jacques Prévert who, in his own poetry, sought to express the uncanniness of the everyday in the ballad form of the Parisian *chanson*. His collection *Paroles*, a mix of 'sad love songs and surreal cityscapes',[16] was first published in 1945 with one of Brassaï's photographs of graffiti on the cover and subsequently sold several hundred thousand copies.[17]

Although the Surrealists' sense of the street came quite consciously from the tradition of Baudelaire and Apollinaire, they also responded to the popular life of the city. But they were not interested in the glittering surface of the urban spectacle nor indeed in the working class sociality which concerned MacOrlan and Prévert; rather their concern was with the disruptive forces which lay behind the façade of normality. This is most apparent in their fascination with the master-criminal Fantômas, created in 1911 by 'two inspired hacks' Marcel Allain and Pierre Souvestre, and memorably brought to the cinema screen by Louis Feuillade in 1913.[18] In their admiration, the Surrealists joined a previous

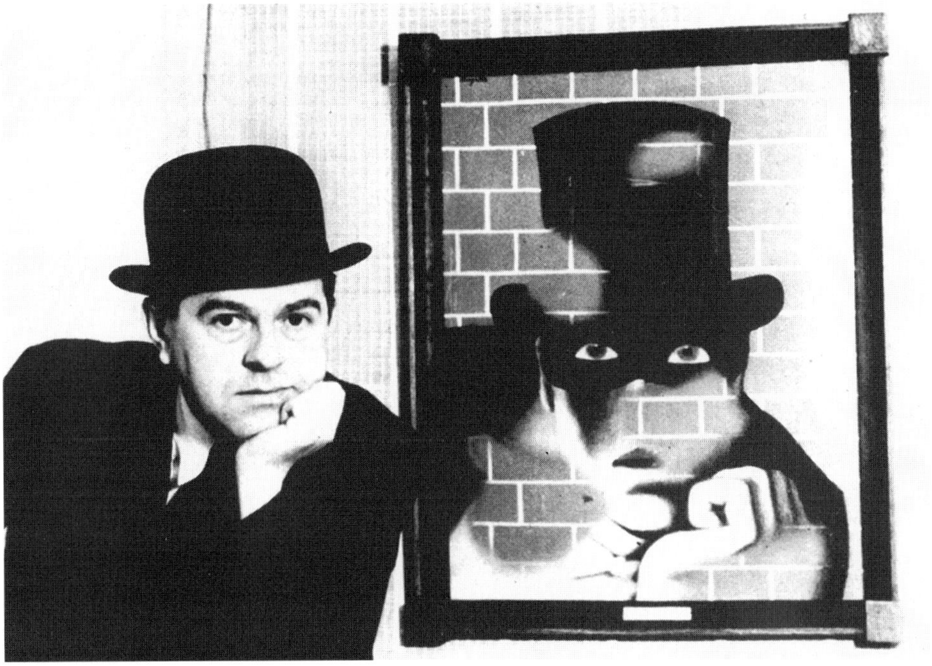

Fig 7 Photograph of René Magritte with *Le barbare*. Painting © ADAGP, Paris and DACS, London, 2001.

generation of avant-garde writers and artists such as Apollinaire, Cendrars and Picasso, but as late as 1933, Robert Desnos could sing the praises of this anti-hero in his poem 'La Complainte de Fantômas':

> Stretching his immense shadow
> Across the world and across Paris
> What is this gray-eyed specter
> Rising out of the silence?
> Fantômas might it be you
> Lurking on the rooftops?[19]

The classic iconic image of Fantômas appears on the cover of the first novel by Allain and Souvestre, showing him as a monstrous but elegant masked figure looming over Paris, dagger in hand (figure 6). Writing in *Documents* in 1930, Desnos observed that the image had 'assumed an enormous importance in Parisian mythology and dreamology'.[20] In his painting *Le retour de flamme* of 1943, Magritte copied the image but substituted a rose for Fantômas' dagger; evidently, the Surrealists had sympathy with the disturbance that Fantômas created in the bourgeois order. Earlier, in 1938, Magritte had already established an ironic identification with the master-criminal, having himself photographed next to another of his paintings of Fantômas, *Le barbare* (figure 7). As Fantômas leans forward, eyes fixed on the spectator, so does Magritte, bowler hat on head.[21]

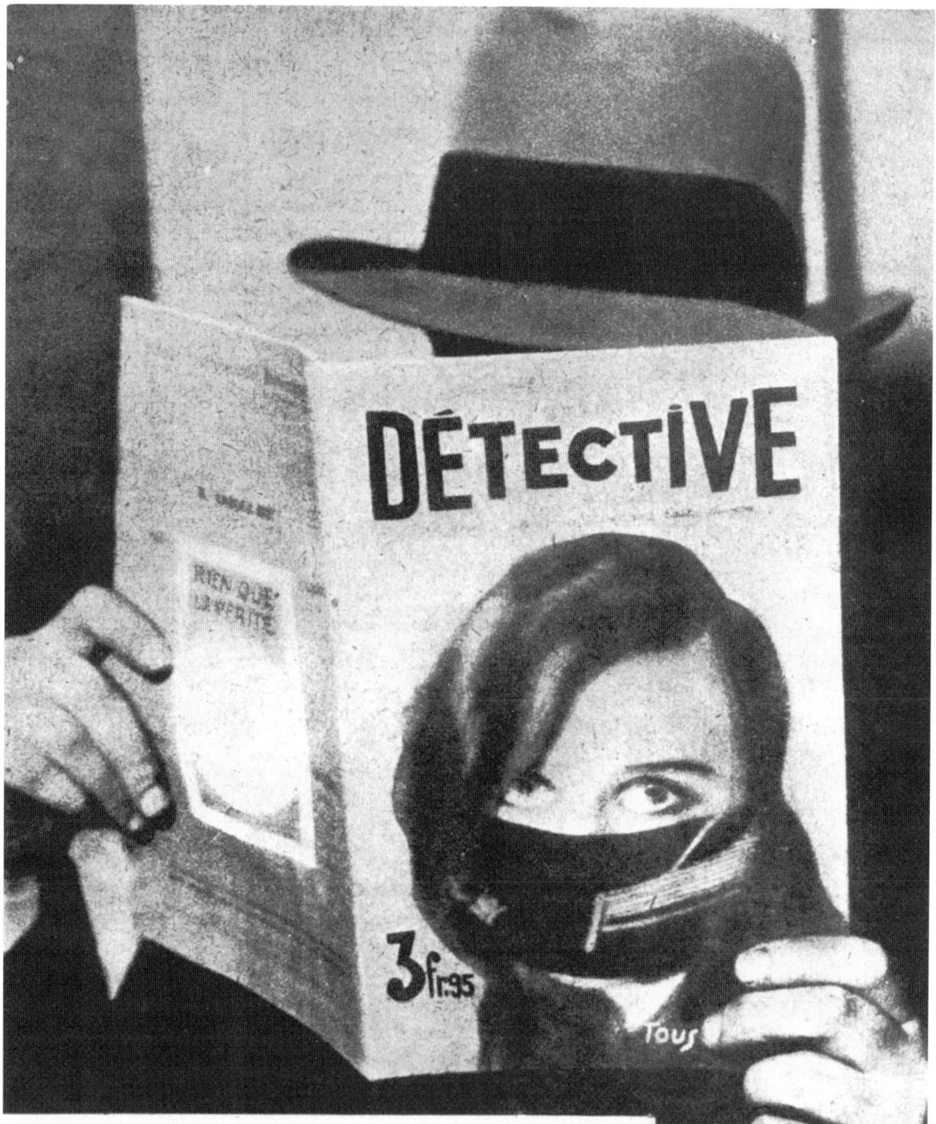

Fig 8 'M. Parain, former editor of *Détective*, is now in charge of the books section of *L'Humanité*', *Le Surréalisme au service de la révolution*, 2 (1930).

Like many avant-gardists of the period, the Surrealists were fascinated by the taste that produced *Détective*, an extremely popular 'true crime' magazine launched in 1928 by Gallimard and used to support their more literary publications (such as André Breton's *Nadja*, published the same year). But the Surrealist desire to 'investigate' the mysteries that lay before them was not that of the police detective aiming at the restoration of public order (just as their espousal of Freudianism was not aimed at any psychic cure). They were indeed deeply critical of *Détective*'s role in 'l'exaltation du flic',[22] and one illustration for *Le Surréalisme au service de la révolution* caustically parodied its lurid style (figure 8).[23] But, as David H. Walker has remarked, that nevertheless shows that the surrealists continued to read the magazine with considerable attention.[24]

If the Surrealists admired and occasionally cultivated a fantasy of criminality that undermined the bourgeois order of the city, they remained somewhat detached observers, critical and analytical. Walter Benjamin's characterisation of the *flâneur* seems apt here: 'turned into an unwilling detective ... [h]e only seems to be indolent, for behind this indolence there is the watchfulness of an observer who does not take his eyes off a miscreant'.[25] Benjamin was certainly aware of the historical parallels here and in his early notes for the *Arcades* project, he wrote: 'Surrealism – *vague de rêves* – the new art of *flânerie*. New past of the nineteenth-century – Paris its classical location.'[26] He conjures a scenario where one can simultaneously imagine Breton's and Aragon's explorations of Paris in the 1920s alongside Baudelaire's in the 1850s.[27]

Benjamin continued his description of the *flâneur* as detective by commenting that 'No matter what trail the *flâneur* may follow, every one of them will lead him to a crime. This is an indication of how the detective story ... participates in fashioning the phantasmagoria of Parisian life.'[28] Again, this evokes the role of the Surrealist observer in the modern city. In Philippe Soupault's 1928 novel *Les dernières nuits de Paris* (written just after his exit from Surrealism proper but still bearing many marks of its influence), the narrator spends his time exploring the city streets by night, searching for meaning and connection in the events he observes.[29] On a more complex level, many critics have noted the elements of a detective story in Breton's *Nadja*; in the rather melodramatic words of Roger Shattuck: 'There is a definite air of mystery surrounding it, with undertones of espionage, cryptography, psychic grand larceny, and possibly worse.'[30] Léo Malet, a member of the Surrealist group in the 1930s, actually turned to writing detective stories in the 1940s; in *120, rue de la Gare* (1943), he introduced the popular *détective de choc* Nestor Burma, a tough guy relative of Philip Marlowe, though with the talent of deciphering clues through his knowledge of the Marquis de Sade![31]

Early in *Nadja*, Breton describes his wanderings on the Boulevard Bonne-Nouvelle, a place where 'I almost invariably go without specific purpose, without anything to induce me but this obscure clue: namely that it (?) will happen here'.[32] However, between beginning his retrospective account of the affair with Nadja and his completion of it, Breton's idea of the Boulevard has been transformed by an intervening event: 'the magnificent days of riot called "Sacco-Vanzetti"', when the proletariat of Paris rose in protest at the condemnation of two Italian immigrants to the electric chair in the USA.[33] This must remind us finally that, alongside the sense of detachment and ennui, the Surrealist engagement with the street often had an important political undertow. When Breton first meets Nadja, their rendezvous takes place on a street named for a revolutionary hero; Breton has just bought a book by Trotsky and is bemoaning the unrevolutionary nature of the crowd. Out of such overt references, Margaret Cohen has developed an argument that for Breton, all the sites in the book were significant because they embodied, albeit usually unspoken, historical, often revolutionary resonances.[34] Paris carried within itself constant reminders of the uprisings of 1789, 1830, 1848, 1871 and for Breton, the political and the poetic were constantly interwoven: 'The magnificent light in Courbet's paintings is for me the same as that of the Place Vendôme, at the time the Column fell.'[35]

The streets of Paris, then, represented a network of potential meanings which were simultaneously erotic, poetic and political, both ecstatic and melancholy. Roger Cardinal, in an important essay on the Surrealist perception of Paris, lists a 'series of complementary models of the city as witnessed by the surrealist ... the city as dream ... as love affair ... as historical palimpsest ... as poetic text ... as psychic labyrinth'.[36] All this suggests complexity, and indeed the Surrealists' city was multi-layered. Yet at the same time, they sought in their exploration of it the directness of lived experience.

The Surrealists were constantly walking the streets. Although their activities there were not innocent – the very tradition of *flânerie* made that impossible – nevertheless they desired to be as open as they could be to whatever they might be presented with. Breton, in describing the central role of Aragon in this activity, conjured up its appeal:

> I can still recall the extraordinary walking companion he was. The areas of Paris I visited with him, even the most nondescript, were enhanced several notches by a magic, romantic fantasising that was never caught short for long, and that burst forth at a bend in the street or before a shop window ... No one was ever a more able detector of the unusual in all its forms; no one was ever more inclined toward such intoxicating reveries on a kind of hidden life of the city.[37]

This experience was paramount and a good Surrealist would not necessarily need to translate it into art. But that of course is exactly what the major writers did, producing the books which represent some of the finest achievements of Surrealism. In the mid-1920s, Aragon's *Le paysan de Paris* (1926) and Breton's *Nadja* (1928) were supplemented by books by other Surrealist writers: Desnos (*La Liberté ou l'amour*, 1927), Soupault (*Les dernières nuits de Paris*, 1928) and Péret (*Il était une boulangère*, 1924).[38] And, in Breton's oeuvre, *Nadja* has often been seen as the first volume in a trilogy, followed in the 1930s by *Les Vases communicants* (1932) and *L'Amour fou* (1937).[39]

However, these books by no means present a monolithic vision of the city, and in this they reflect their different authors. The elements of farce and parody in Desnos' book are very different from Soupault's evocation of the underworld mysteries of the city by night. Aragon's engagement with the detail of his chosen environment, the Passage de l'Opéra, is both obsessive and detached. And Breton's two books *Nadja* and *L'Amour fou* each represent the experience of the city in particular ways, the spare clarity of the former giving way to a rather more lush evocation in the latter. (As we will see, the shift between the two books can also be seen in the photographs chosen to illustrate them: Boiffard's cool images of the city by day in *Nadja* and Brassaï's romantic vision of the night-time city in *L'Amour fou*.)

Writing in 1974, nearly fifty years after *Nadja*, Michel de Certeau wrote about 'a migrational, or metaphorical, city' that 'slips into the clear text of the planned and readable city'.[40] It is surely not an accident that, while the 'readable' city was represented for de Certeau by the view from the top of the World Trade Center in New York, when he wished to elaborate on the idea of the 'metaphorical' city, his examples were Parisian. For the desire to subvert the totalising experience of the modern city through subjective, individual response was by then a century old, with the 'intoxicating reveries' of the Surrealists taking their place midway between the *flânerie* of Baudelaire and the *dérive* of the Situationists.[41] But, as de Certeau argued, the necessity for the exploration of that second city of the imagination and lived experience remains essential, and in that process, the Surrealist model is as significant as ever.

It is curious that there is no central body of Surrealist painting concerned with the city street which one can place besides these texts. To see works that prefigure the Surrealist response to the urban environment, one must go back to the images that Giorgio de Chirico made just before the Great War. A decade later, André Breton, in *Le Surréalisme et la peinture*, made clear the importance of de Chirico's pictures for the Surrealists as an affective cityscape of the imagination: 'How often have we found ourselves in that square where everything seems so close to existence and yet bears so little resemblance to what really exists. It was here, more than anywhere else, that we held our invisible meetings.'[42] De Chirico's city was not only a space to put next to the actual city, but also one to place – palimpsest like – over it, so that the actual city and the imagined city were fused. Reality was infiltrated by the dream, the present infiltrated by the past.

This process, however, had its ironies, since the images by de Chirico most favoured by the Surrealists evoked a tradition – the classicism of de Chirico's native Italy – to which the Surrealists in other circumstances felt a distinct antipathy. (They preferred the medieval, late nineteenth-century art nouveau and the banally modern.) But, while much of the potency of de Chirico's paintings did lie in their nostalgia for a classical otherness, it was nevertheless possible to transplant his vision to Paris, likewise a city of long neo-classical perspectives. Indeed, he himself had done so in 1914, when he titled a painting (otherwise very similar to the rest of his work at this time) *Gare Montparnasse (The Melancholy of Departure)* (figure 9). On the horizon, beyond the ordered grandeur of the abstracted facade, a small black train is belching out smoke as

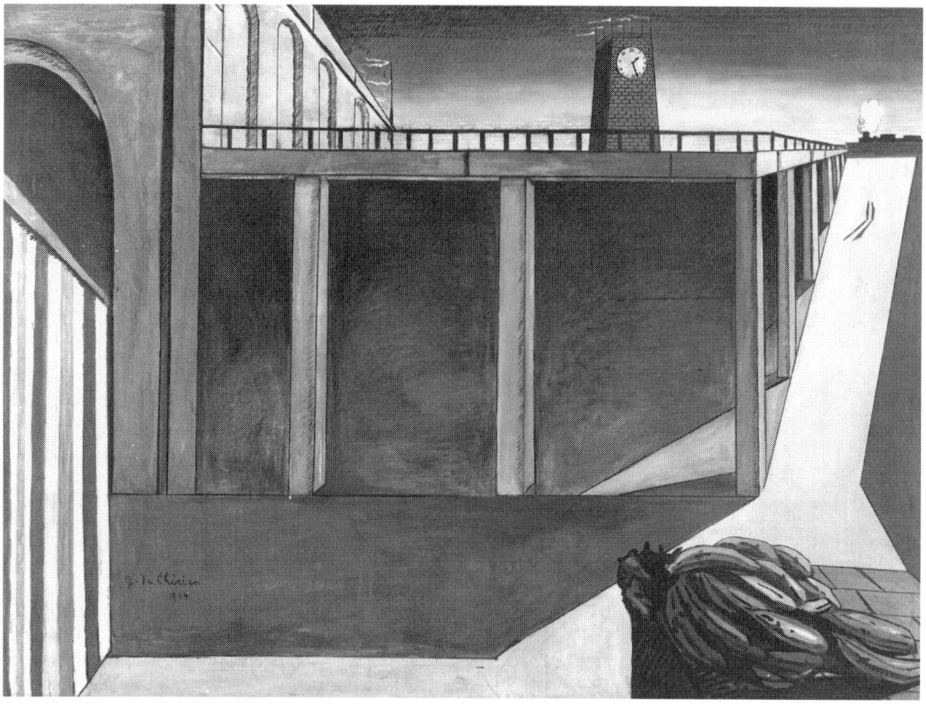

Fig 9 Giorgio de Chirico, *Gare Montparnasse (The Melancholy of Departure)*, 1914. The Museum of Modern Art, New York. © DACS 2001.

it enters the station. Just as, at most actual railway stations built in the nineteenth-century, an elaborate neo-classical frontage served to mask the dirty and noisy process of actually catching a train.

A number of Surrealist artists subsequently made images that envisaged Paris through the screen of de Chirico's work. One of Yves Tanguy's first paintings was of the *Rue de la Santé* (1925), a vigorously crude image of the violently receding perspectives of the Santé prison on one side and a banal row of shops and houses on the other (figure 10). As Tanguy's friend, Marcel Duhamel, later commented: 'The perspective here is unwonted and, under a Breton sky, the prison wall takes on a menacing aspect.'[43] A later work where de Chirico's classicism was brought into direct contact, indeed friction, with contemporary Paris was a photomontage made by Raoul Ubac in 1936: *Hommage à de Chirico*, in which headless classical statues have been placed in an empty street next to a high wall covered with graffiti (figure 11). The result is an image of a 'site' with all the uneasy desolation of the Parisian *banlieue* and the classical statuary seems woefully ill at ease, an effect exacerbated by the overtly montaged character of the image.

The actual statues that inhabited the parks and squares of Paris were the elements in the official classicised cityscape that most obviously affected the Surrealists. Both Aragon, at length in *Le paysan de Paris*, and Philippe Soupault, briefly in *Les dernières nuits de Paris*, conjure up the statues as living beings who

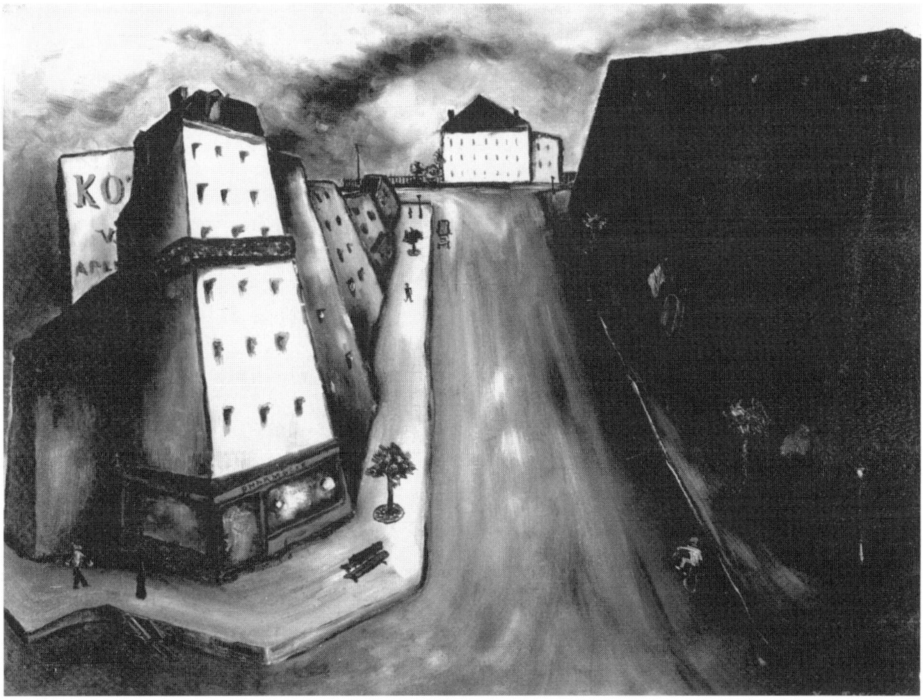

Fig 10 Yves Tanguy, *Rue de la Santé*, 1925. The Museum of Modern Art, New York. © ARS, New York and DACS, London, 2001.

Fig 11 Raoul Ubac, *Hommage à de Chirico*, 1936. © ADAGP, Paris and DACS, London, 2001.

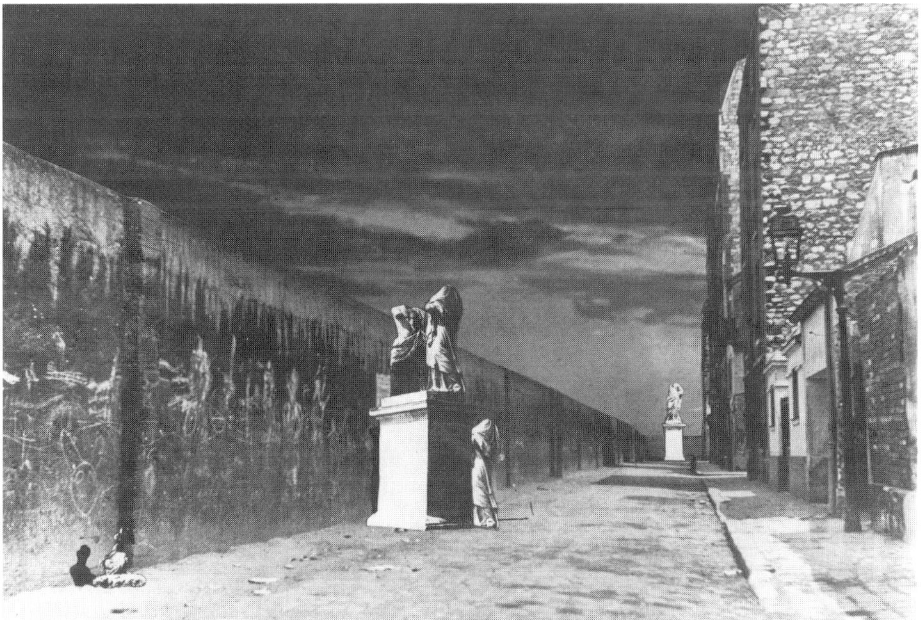

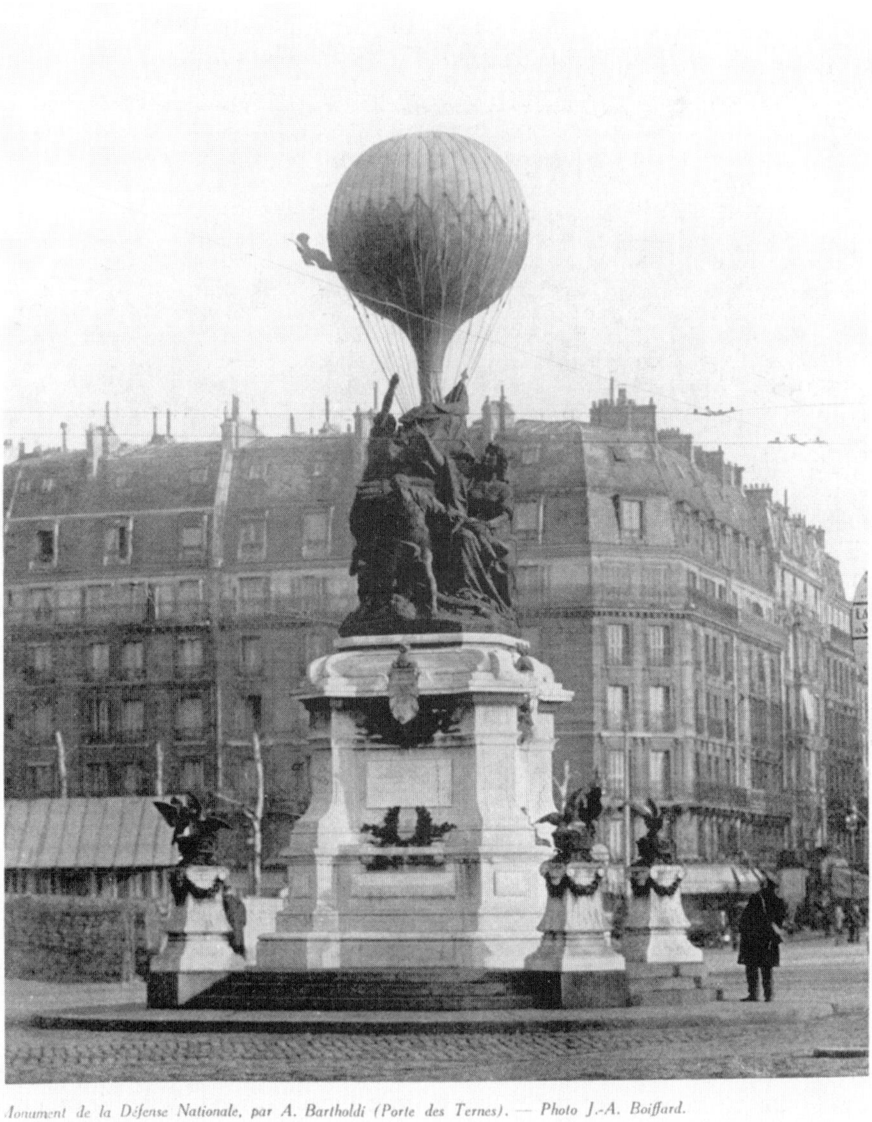

Fig 12 Jacques-André Boiffard, illustration for Robert Desnos, 'Pygmalion et le Sphinx', *Documents*, 2:1 (1930).

reflect ironically on the ordinary mortals passing below them.[44] Breton's reference in *Nadja* to the statue of Etienne Dolet in the Place Maubert which 'has always fascinated me and induced unbearable discomfort'[45] is accompanied by a photograph by Jacques-André Boiffard who later made other images, published in *Documents*, of some of the more absurd statuary of the city: a stone car, a bronze balloon (figure 12).[46]

As Roger Cardinal suggests, these statues 'are examples of objects which punctuate spacious intersections and prompt a sense of dramatic focus. But since

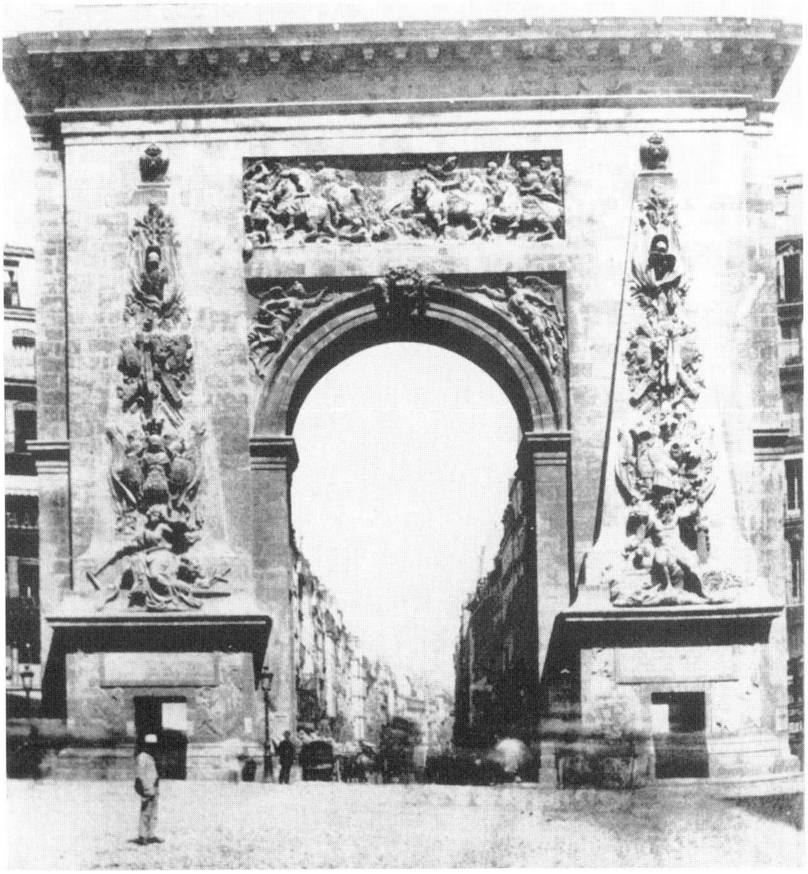

Fig 13 Jacques-André Boiffard, 'No: not even the extremely handsome, extremely useless Porte Saint-Denis', from André Breton, *Nadja*, 1928.

they do not radiate any clear meaning, the response is ambiguous ... Isolation thus gives way to enigma ... the sense of mingled attraction and unease, the intimation of a meaning shrouded in doubt'.[47] In this, the statues of Paris parallel the effect of the classical figures strategically placed by de Chirico in his city squares. Except that the statues that occupy the actual city, as opposed to de Chirico's merely painted ones, have a double-edged ambiguity. They are both physically, palpably present and ambiguously removed from the flow of the everyday, an effect akin to that possessed by another inhabitant of the Surrealist cityscape: the shop window mannequin. (Indeed, this ambiguity is similar to that of the photograph, which offers us the indexical presence of an object while at the same time withholding its actuality from us. Photographs of mannequins and statues serve to double this effect.)

On the whole, the great classical buildings of Parisian triumphalism were ignored by the Surrealists, or, as in the case of the Porte Saint-Denis, condescended to as 'extremely handsome' and 'extremely useless' (indeed 'handsome' because 'useless') (figure 13).[48] However, there were occasions of a

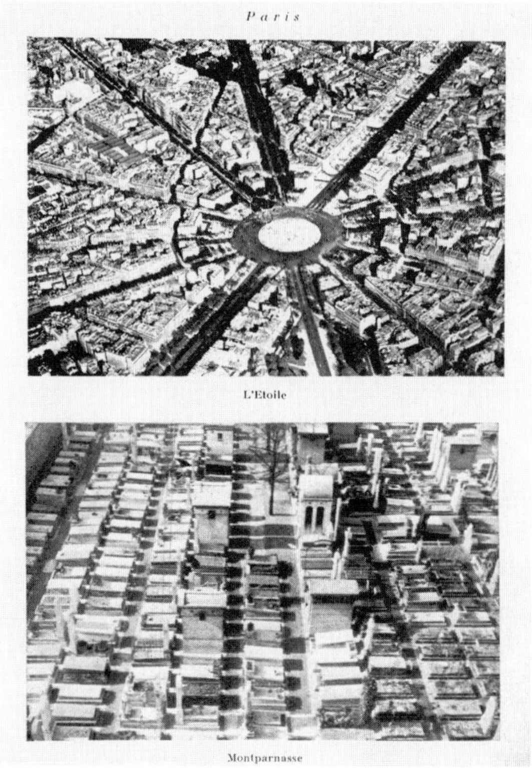

Fig 14 Max Ernst, photomontage in 'Le Surréalisme en 1929', *Variétés* (1929). © ADAGP, Paris and DACS, London, 2001.

more direct sarcasm. In June 1929, the Belgian magazine *Variétés*, edited by the Surrealist E.L.T. Mesens, published a special number: *Le Surréalisme en 1929*, which included a pairing of two aerial photographs of Paris (figure 14).[49] One is of the Place de l'Etoile, but with the Arc de Triomphe 'removed'; the other is titled 'Montparnasse' – it shows a section of the cemetery. One is initially struck by the visual juxtaposition – the wheel of the *rond point* contrasted with the regular rows of tombs – but this formalism is in the service of political satire. Both sites are monuments to the dead, the 'elite' of the nation; beneath the Arc de Triomphe lies the tomb of the Unknown Soldier, while Montparnasse cemetery is the final resting place of many distinguished servants of the state (Baudelaire is there, but only because his father-in-law was a general). However, with the main symbol of this desire 'pro patria mori' – the Arch – quietly obliterated, its associations of glory are reduced back in the picture below to patterns of repetition, the banality of accumulated death.[50]

At the opposite extreme from the deserted vistas of de Chirico is another version of the street, full and bustling with activity, with the constant possibility of confrontation. Yet this street could also be the site of a Surrealist estrangement (as suggested by Breton's reaction to the crowd in *Nadja*). The most vivid painted version of this scenario was by Balthus, in an image simply

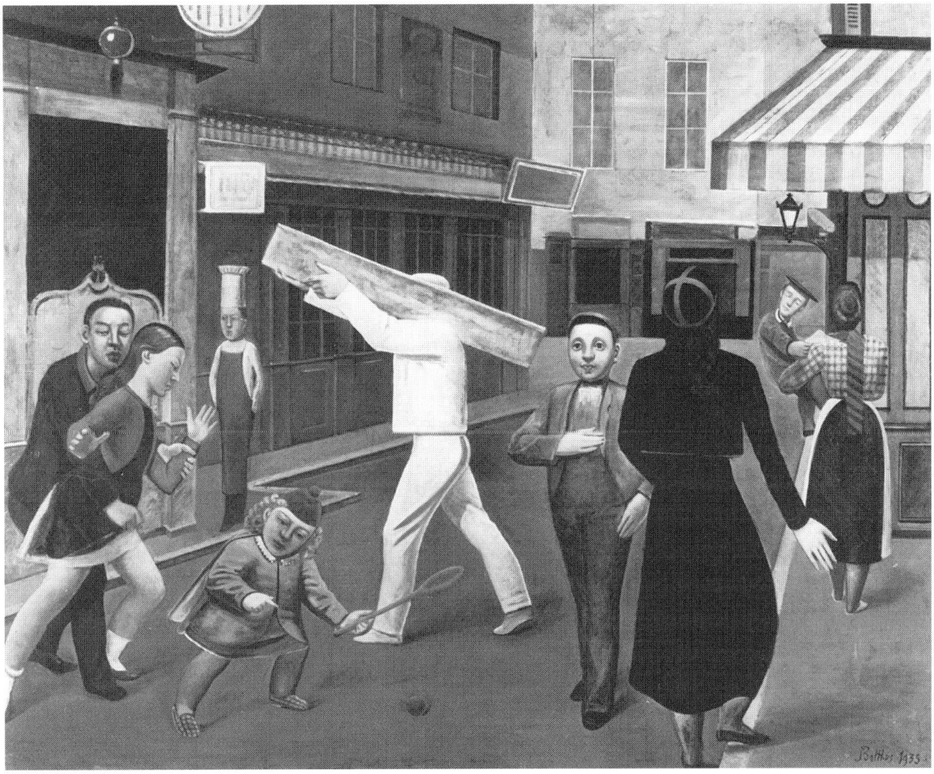

Fig 15 Balthus, *The Street*, 1933. The Museum of Modern Art, New York. © ADAGP, Paris and DACS, London, 2001.

entitled *The Street* (1933) (figure 15). Balthus himself was later to reject all connections between his work and Surrealism, but soon after its completion, this painting was prominently, indeed iconically, displayed in the special number of the Belgian magazine *Documents 34: Intervention Surréaliste*, where it occupied a whole page.[51]

The Street is a painting with sources in Seurat, and further back Masaccio and Piero della Francesca, but it is also a peculiarly modern image, expressive of the disorientation and the alienation that the Surrealists felt on the street. The picture shows an actual Parisian street – the Rue Bourbon-le-Château in the Latin Quarter – but the scene is also dreamlike, removed from that reality. There are elements of violence, eroticism, work and play in the painting, but they are somehow distanced, as if seen through the eyes of the young man in the centre of the picture, who passes through the scene like a sleepwalker.

The paintings of de Chirico and Balthus stand at the poles of the Surrealist dialectic of the street, always in tension between the deserted and the crowded, estrangement and encounter, ennui and the marvellous, passivity and action. As Aragon roamed the Passage de l'Opéra simply absorbing its atmosphere, Benjamin Péret was out in the open insulting a priest.[52] At one point in Buñuel's *L'Age d'or* (set in a Paris pretending to be Rome), a man comes out of a busy cafe covered in white dust and proceeds to clean himself off; no one is concerned. Another man walks along a pavement kicking a violin before him and eventually stamps on it. But these images of humorous provocation take their place in a range of other views of vacant streets, dull facades, a broken window with a letter pasted over it.

These two images of the street – as deserted or crowded – are also to be found throughout the photography being made in proximity to Surrealism itself. The busy but alienated urban environment that Balthus painted in 1933 appears in the work of André Kertész and Henri Cartier-Bresson from the same time. And, as the Surrealists looked back with fascination at the deserted vistas of de Chirico's pictures, so too they would find parallel effects in the photographs of Eugène Atget.[53] But before considering other photographic work related to Surrealism, it is illuminating to look more closely at some of the photographs of the street that appeared in specifically Surrealist contexts. These are dispersed across many kinds of publications, but one must start by returning to André Breton's *Nadja*, the only site where one will find an extended photography of the street at the heart of Surrealist practice.

Notes

1 André Breton, *Nadja* (New York: Grove Press, 1960), p. 63.

2 First published in 1860 and reprinted in *Les Fleurs du mal* (1869). Translated as 'In Passing' by Richard Howard in *The Flowers of Evil* (Brighton: Harvester Press, 1982), p. 97.

3 Janet Woolf, 'The Invisible *Flâneuse*: Women and the Literature of Modernity', *Theory, Culture and Society*, 2–3 (1985), p. 45. On the complex class and gender relationships on the streets of Paris, see also Susan Burck-Morss, 'The Flaneur, the Sandwichman and the Whore: the Politics of Loitering', *New German Critique*, 39 (Autumn 1986), 99–140.

4 Francette Pacteau also suggests a more nuanced reading and makes the connection between Baudelaire and Breton in *The Symptom of Beauty* (London: Reaktion, 1994), chapter 8: 'Love at Last Sight', pp. 161–77.

5 For a range of essays on *flânerie*, see Keith Tester (ed.), *The Flâneur* (London and New York: Routledge, 1994).

6 From 'Le Peintre de la vie moderne' (1863), translated in Charles Baudelaire, *The Painter of Modern Life and Other Essays* (London: Phaidon, 1965), pp. 9–10.

7 From 'The Disdainful Confession', in *The Lost Steps* (Lincoln: University of Nebraska Press, 1996), p. 4.

8 First published in 1859, reprinted in *Les Fleurs du mal* (1869). Translation from Baudelaire, *The Flowers of Evil*, p. 92.

9 From *The Waste Land*, section I, l. 60; in his notes, Eliot makes explicit reference to Baudelaire's 'fourmillante cité' (T. S. Eliot, *Selected Poems* (London: Faber and Faber, 1954), p. 69).

10 For essays on many aspects of this subject, see Edward Timms and David Kelley (eds), *Unreal City: Urban Experience in Modern European Literature and Art* (Manchester: Manchester University Press, 1985).

11 See Marshall Berman, *All That is Solid Melts into Air* (London: Verso, 1983), chapter 5: 'In the Forest of Symbols: Some Notes on Modernism in New York', pp. 287–348.

12 For a general account of street photography, see Colin Westerbeck and Joel Meyerowitz, *Bystander* (London: Thames and Hudson, 1994). Pacteau, *The Symptom of Beauty*, pp. 162–3, draws a parallel between the relationship of Baudelaire and *la passante* and the photographs made by Gary Winogrand for his 1975 book *Women are Beautiful.*

13 Guillaume Apollinaire, *Alcools* (Berkeley: University of California, 1965), pp. 20 and 22.

14 Susanna Barrows, *Distorting Mirrors: Visions of the Crowd in Late Nineteenth Century France* (New Haven: Yale University Press, 1981).

15 Adrian Rifkin, *Street Noises* (Manchester: Manchester University Press, 1993), p. 8.

16 Richard Holmes, *Sidetracks* (London: Harper Collins, 2000), p. 336.

17 This first publication of *Paroles* was in a small limited edition (see Chapter 7), but the book was republished in 1947 in a more available form, with reprints in 1948 and 1949. For a version in English, see *Selections from Paroles* (Harmondsworth: Penguin, 1965). Prévert also wrote the lyrics for one of the most popular songs of the 20th century: 'Feuilles mortes', written in 1946 with Joseph Kosma for the Carné film *Les Portes de la nuit* and subsequently anglicised as 'Autumn Leaves'.

18 The phrase 'two inspired hacks' is from John Ashbery, 'Introduction to Fantômas', in Marcel Allain and Pierre Souvestre, *Fantômas* (London: Picador, 1987), p. 2, a useful summary of Fantômas' avant-garde fame. For a fuller analysis, see Robin Walz, *Pulp Surrealism* (Berkeley and Los Angeles: University of California Press, 2000), chapter 2, pp. 42–75.

19 Originally written for radio transmission (1933), 'La Complainte de Fantômas' was first published in Desnos' book of poems *Fortunes* (Paris: Gallimard, 1942). This translation from Ashbery, 'Introduction to Fantômas', p. 1.

20 Robert Desnos, 'Imagerie Moderne', *Documents*, 1:7 (1929), 377.

21 Reproduced in the *London Bulletin*, 2 (May 1938), 19, with the title 'The Painter and the Barbarian'. David Sylvester, *Magritte* (London: Thames and Hudson, 1992), p. 14, suggests that this was the first time that Magritte adopted the bowler-hat as part of his persona, dismissing this image, however, as a 'photographers' cliché'. But, in the latter half of his career, Magritte's careful construction of his image in fact became inseparable from his art. On Magritte and the bowler hat, see Fred Miller Robinson, *The Man in the Bowler Hat* (Chapel Hill: University of North Carolina Press, 1993), pp. 125–48.

22 Louis Aragon, 'Introduction à 1930', *La Révolution surréaliste*, 12 (15 December 1929), 64. There is another attack on *Détective* in the same issue by Georges Sadoul ('Bonne Année! Bonne Santé', 45–7); see Walz, *Pulp Surrealism*, pp. 148–9.

23 *Le Surréalisme au service de la révolution,* 2 (October 1930). The image is accompanied by the information that 'M. Parain, former editor of *Détective*, is now in charge of the books section of *L'Humanité*', another sarcastic barb in the conflict between Surrealism and the Communist party.

24 David H. Walker, 'Cultivating the *Faits Divers*: *Détective*', *Nottingham French Studies*, 32:2 (Autumn 1992), 71–83; this is an analysis of the relationship between *Détective* and its literary readership which also included Sartre, de Beauvoir and Genet. On *Détective*, see also Rifkin, *Street Noises*, especially pp. 120–7.

25 From 'The Paris of the Second Empire in Baudelaire', in Walter Benjamin, *Charles Baudelaire: A Lyric Poet in the Era of High Capitalism* (London: New Left Books, 1976), pp. 40–1.

26 Quoted in translation by David Frisby: 'The *flâneur* in Social Theory', in Tester, *The Flâneur*, p. 84. Benjamin's notes for the mammoth and incomplete *Arcades* project, containing many other references to Surrealism, have been translated as *The Arcades Project* (Cambridge, MA: Harvard University Press, 1999).

27 On the relationship between Benjamin and Aragon, see Jacques Leenhardt, 'Le Passage comme forme d'expérience: Benjamin face à Aragon', in Heinz Wismann (ed.), *Walter Benjamin et Paris* (Paris: Cerf, 1986), pp. 163–71.

28 Benjamin, *Charles Baudelaire*, p. 41.

29 See Philippe Soupault, *Last Nights of Paris* (Cambridge, MA: Exact Change, 1992). Soupault had been expelled from the Surrealist group in 1926 for his pursuit of a literary career. In so far as *Les dernières nuits de Paris* was part of that pursuit, it was not a Surrealist book. But while there are many *picaresque* elements, the narrator's fascination with a woman he sees wandering the city is so reminiscent of *Nadja* that one must wonder what Breton and Soupault knew of each other's work at this point.

30 Roger Shattuck, 'The Nadja File', *Cahiers Dada Surréalisme*, 1 (1966), 49.

31 Several of Malet's detective novels have been translated into English, including *120, rue de la Gare* (London: Pan, 1991).

32 Breton, *Nadja*, p. 32.

33 Sacco and Vanzetti were executed on 23 August 1927, when Breton was at the Manoir d'Ango in Normandy, at work on the text of *Nadja*.

34 Margaret Cohen, *Profane Illumination: Walter Benjamin and the Paris of Surrealist Revolution* (Berkeley and Los Angeles: University of California Press, 1993), chapter 4: 'The Ghosts of Paris', pp. 77–119.

35 Breton, *Nadja*, pp. 14–5. Gustave Courbet was implicated in the demolition of the Vendôme Column during the Paris Commune of 1871, and after the defeat of the Commune, only avoided having to pay the cost of its restoration by going into exile in Switzerland.

36 Roger Cardinal, 'Soluble City: The Surrealist Perception of Paris', *Architectural Review*, 2–3 (1978), 145.

37 André Breton, *Conversations: The Autobiography of Surrealism* (New York: Paragon House, 1993), p. 27.

38 For an analysis of Surrealist Paris as expressed through these novels, see Marie-Claire Bancquart, *Paris des surréalistes* (Paris: Seghers, 1972).

39 For literary analyses of the connections between the three books, see Victor Crastre, *André Breton: trilogie surréaliste* (Paris: Sedes, 1971), and Anna Balakian, *André Breton: Magus of Surrealism* (New York: Oxford University Press, 1971), chapter 8, pp. 102–24.

40 Michel de Certeau, *The Practice of Everyday Life* (Berkeley and Los Angeles: University of California Press, 1984), p. 93.

41 On the Situationist conceptualisation of the city, including the principle of *dérive* (drift), see Simon Sadler, *The Situationist City* (Cambridge, MA: MIT Press, 1998).

42 André Breton, *Surrealism and Painting* (New York: Icon, 1972), p. 13.

43 Marcel Duhamel, *Raconte pas ta vie* (Paris: Mercure de France, 1972). p. 140. Duhamel is referring here to Tanguy's childhood in Brittany.

44 See Aragon, *Paris Peasant* (London: Jonathan Cape, 1971), pp. 165–8, and Soupault, *Last Nights of Paris*, pp. 160–1.

45 Breton, *Nadja*, p. 24.

46 These accompanied an essay by Robert Desnos, 'Pygmalion et le Sphinx', *Documents*, 2:1 (1930), 33–8. On the Surrealist interest in the statuary of Paris, see also Sergiusz Michalski, *Public Monuments: Art in Political Bondage 1870–1997* (London: Reaktion, 1998), pp. 45–9.

47 Cardinal, 'Soluble City', 145.

48 Breton, *Nadja*, p. 32.

49 Between pp. 6 and 7. On the opposite page are two further images: a photograph of elephants mating above a photomontage of one cathedral 'mounting' another. This spread was reproduced anonymously in *Le Surréalisme en 1929*, but Werner Spies has attributed it to Max Ernst (*Max Ernst – Collagen, Inventar und Widerspruch* (Munich: DuMont Verlag, 1988), plates 199–200). However, such juxtapositions were also typical of the work of Mesens in *Variétés*; in Chapters 5 and 6, I discuss his placement of the works of Atget and Lotar.

50 Another example of the Surrealists' sarcastic attitude toward the monuments of Paris was in the questionnaire: 'Sur Certaines Possiblities d'Embellissement Irrational d'une Ville' in *Le Surréalisme au service de la révolution*, 6 (May 1933), 18–9. There, Breton suggested that the Arc de Triomphe should be blown up 'after burying it in a mountain of manure'.

51 On p. 228. For another placement of Balthus' early work in a Surrealist context, see his illustrations for *Wuthering Heights* in *Minotaure*, 7 (1935), 60–1. For a detailed analysis of *The Street*, see Sabine Rewald, *Balthus* (New York: The Metropolitan Museum of Art/Harry Abrams, 1984), pp. 60–1.

52 See Chapter 4.

53 The comparison with de Chirico has also been a common theme in recent critical writings on Atget. To give one example, Ron Horning, 'Atget's Street Theater', *Aperture*, 101 (Winter 1985), 65, writes that the best of Atget's photographs are 'as evocative and inviolate as de Chirico's early paintings'.

3

Nadja: a 'voluntary banality'?

'When will all the books that are worth anything stop being illustrated with drawings and appear only with photographs?'[1] This demand by André Breton, once so excessive, seems now almost redundant. Yet originally, Breton's question had an urgency, for at the time he posed it in the autumn of 1927, he was himself almost certainly involved in the process of selecting the photographs for his own book *Nadja*, published in May 1928.[2]

The text of *Nadja* is in three parts. The central section recounts the events of nearly two years earlier, starting on 4 October 1926, when, as we have seen, Breton meets Nadja on the Rue Lafayette. He is fascinated by her naivety, her intensity and her clairvoyant abilities. Their time together during the next several days is narrated by Breton in the form of a diary, culminating on 12 October, when he and Nadja spend the night at a hotel in Saint-Germain, a train ride outside the city. After that, they drift apart and Breton later hears she has been committed to an asylum. Before and after this narrative, two other sections explore more general questions about chance and inspiration, beauty and love.

In its original form, *Nadja* contained forty-four images: documents, objects, works of art, a sequence of drawings by Nadja herself and photographs. There are a number of portraits – including three by Man Ray and three by the commercial photographer Henri Manuel – and fourteen images of places which feature in the book – twelve of them in Paris.[3] It is these latter pictures which will be the main focus of attention in this chapter, with a consideration of how they are integrated into the fabric of the text and influence its meaning. I also want to examine what happens to these initially anonymous pictures when their authorship is acknowledged, and they are viewed as images that were made rather merely taken. But first, it's necessary to look at *Nadja* as a whole, at the form of the book and at Breton's text, since a number of other elements radically affect the reading of the photographs.

Nadja has a complicated publishing history. For thirty-five years, there was only the original edition of 1928 in French, translated into English in 1960 by Richard Howard.[4] In 1963, a second French edition 'entirely reviewed by the author' was published, with many small changes to the text and the addition of four illustrations. This version was evidently intended by Breton to be

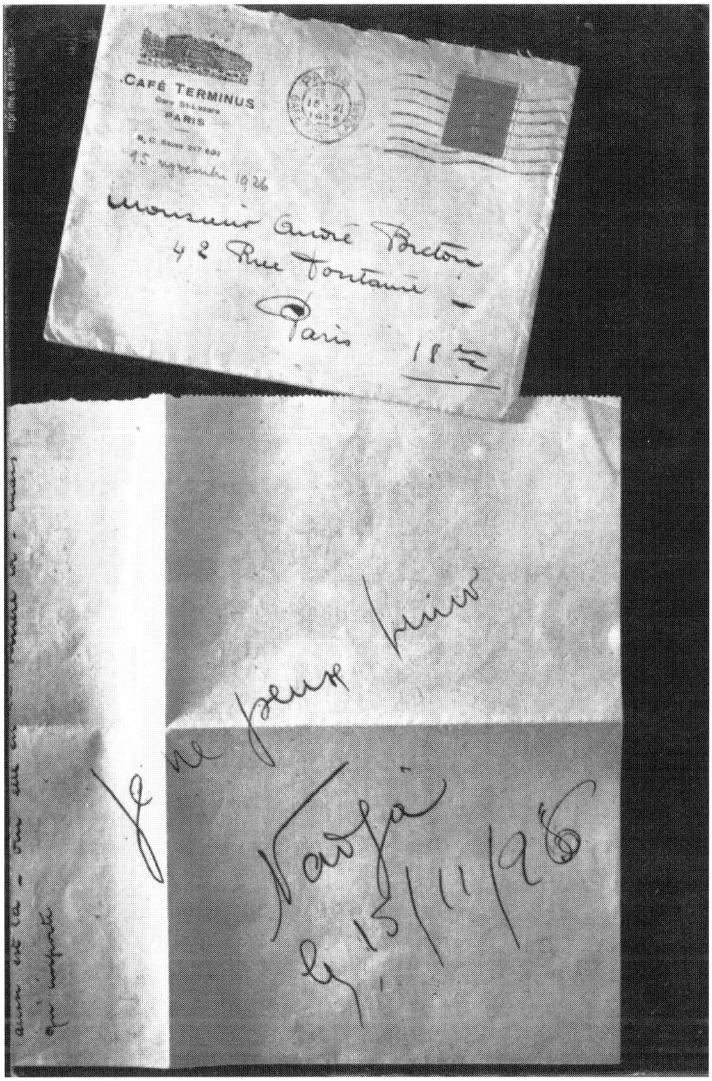

Fig 16 Back cover of André Breton, *Nadja*, first paperback edition, 1964.

authoritative; it is the only one in French available today. But, unlike anything else in Breton's work, the different versions of *Nadja* reflect a process of accretion. As late as the first paperback edition of 1964, one of Nadja's letters to Breton suddenly appeared on the back cover as part of the documentation which Breton's use of photographs in 1928 had initiated – a process which was profoundly equivocal (figure 16). One cannot help but see in such a gesture, and in the coexistence of two *Nadjas*, both and yet neither 'the' *Nadja*, something symptomatic of the nature of Breton's project. For *Nadja* is a slippery work to grasp, full of tactical ruses and devices which inflect even its 'documentary' images.

Walter Benjamin was evidently thinking partly of *Nadja* when he wrote of the Surrealists that 'the writings of this circle are not literature but something else – demonstrations, watchwords, documents, bluffs, forgeries if you will, but at any rate not literature'.[5] That comment is quoted by Dawn Ades who goes on to say of *Nadja*: 'It is a true story'.[6] Franklin Rosemont, latter-day American keeper of the Bretonian flame, is certain on this point. Though *Nadja* is 'often mistaken for a novel', any literary analysis is pointless because '*this book is not fiction!*'[7] Rosemont's protest that the effect of *Nadja* is defused by treating it as fiction is well taken; nevertheless, a leap of faith is required to go further and affirm its absolute veracity.

Certainly, Breton himself wants the reader to believe his story, and he employs several tactics to this end, the use of photographs and other documentary images being one element. As well as Breton's account of his experiences with Nadja, there are many other autobiographical references; real people appear throughout the book and the story is precisely situated in a real city, Paris (indeed one can profitably read *Nadja* side by side with a Paris street-map). Of particular importance is the choice of the diary form, the very genre of personal witness and record, for the central section of the book. As Simone de Beauvoir observed of Nadja (contrasting her with Gérard de Nerval's fictional heroines Sylvie and Aurelie), 'one comes across her, not in a half-dream, but wide awake, on a commonplace day that has its date like all the other days in the calender – 12 April, 4 October, or whatever – in a commonplace setting: a café, some street corner'.[8]

This diaristic effect is compounded by the deliberately flat and unliterary (anti-)style that Breton, in his preface for the 1963 edition, said was 'based on that of medical observation'.[9] Earlier, in writing *L'Amour fou* (1937), Breton had commented on this concept at greater length, eloquently affirming the fundamental principles he had adopted in writing *Nadja*:

> several times, I have recounted a series of facts relating to some intimate circumstances of my life, strange enough to deserve attention. Only a precise and absolutely careful reference to the emotional state of the subject to whom such things happen can furnish any basis for their evaluation. Surrealism has always suggested they be written like a medical report, with no incident omitted, no name altered, lest the arbitrary make its appearance. The revelation of the immediate, bewildering irrationality of certain events requires the most severe authentication of the human document conveying them.[10]

One must be careful, however, not to take Breton's account in *Nadja* simply at face value; it is significant that Benjamin in his comments placed next to 'documents' the apparently opposite concepts of 'bluffs' and 'forgeries'. Indeed, literary critics who have written about *Nadja* have been constantly drawn to the possibilities of fabrication on Breton's part. Anna Balakian, for example, doubted whether Nadja said the things that Breton says she said, observing that a phrase such as 'The blue and the wind' has 'the quality of a surrealist sentence rather than that of a wandering mind'.[11] Her suggestion that Nadja may have been a mouthpiece for Breton's own words opens the door for a series of sceptical questions about just how much of a fiction *Nadja* actually is. For while there can be no doubt that Nadja did exist and that she and Breton had an affair, all we know beyond that is largely the testimony of one – hardly detached – participant.[12]

Evidently, no unilateral subjective account can ever tell the whole truth and nothing but the truth. And indeed Breton himself is at pains to emphasise that the 'truth' of his account is by its very nature ambiguous and equivocal. Early in the book he writes, 'Actually it is of little importance if an occasional error or omission, a genuine anomaly or lacuna casts a shadow across my narrative, across what, taken as a whole, cannot be substantiated.'[13] Later, when Nadja asks to read his books, he comments, 'Life is other than what one writes.'[14] Between the experience and its translation into text must come levels of selection and interpretation, and much must be elided or shifted in the process of telling the story. Breton, however, does distinguish between a strict factuality and events and experiences that move beyond this.

There may indeed be facts which remain just facts – which assert that the statue of Etienne Dolet once stood in the Place Maubert and there was really was a Sphinx Hotel on the Boulevard Magenta – but Breton is not very interested in that kind of factuality. Rather he says he is concerned 'with facts which may belong to the order of pure observation, but which on each occasion present all the appearances of a signal, without our being able to say precisely which signal, and of what'.[15] He is engaged, then, by those facts which enter the arena of the subjective to provoke either a 'special, indefinable reaction' or more threateningly 'a complete lack of peace'. These two types of fact he calls 'faits-glissades' and 'faits-précipes' – facts, as it were, down which we may slide, somewhat in control, as opposed to facts over which we fall, uncontrollably and unpredictably.[16] For Breton, a 'fact' of this kind renders the banal oracular, offering the potential for a sequence of undecidable speculations, the fact operating as a 'sign' and the sign being taken for a 'wonder'. Yet surely what gives these speculations their particular, uncanny resonance is still their very basis in actuality, in 'fact'.

It might be argued that the photographs in *Nadja* are hardly central to the book and many literary critics manage not to discuss them at all. But neither can they be considered simply illustrations, additions to an otherwise completed text. For the integral if apparently tangential relationship of image to text is one of the most powerful devices at work in *Nadja*.[17] If at first the photographs seem intended to merely confirm the book's status as a document, it soon becomes apparent that they rather serve as yet another element in making any straightforward reading of that status problematic.

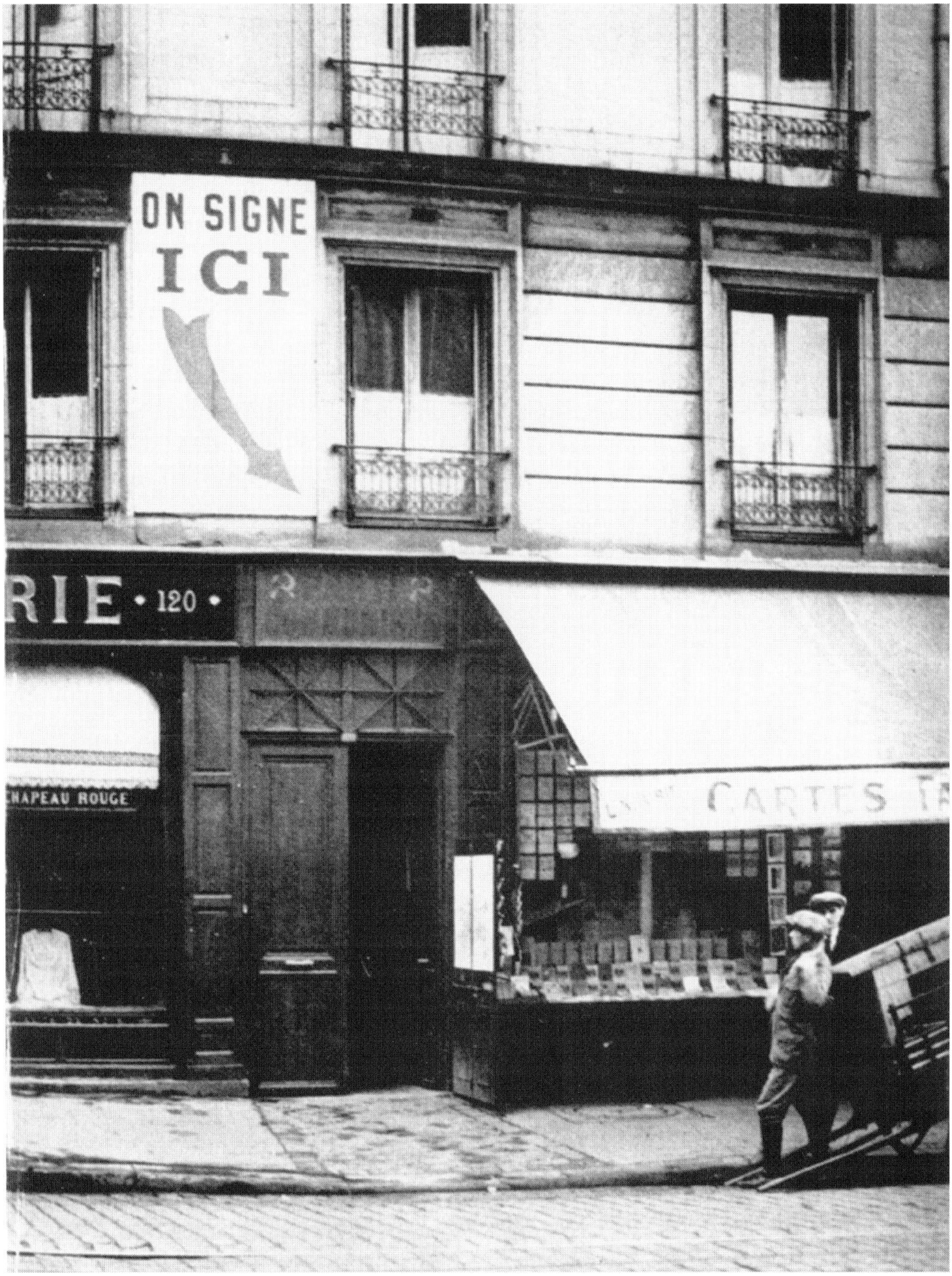

Fig 17 Jacques-André Boiffard, 'The *Humanité* bookstore', from André Breton, *Nadja*, 1928.

The photographs operate on an initial level as direct indices of the sites where the events of the book take place. But our reading of the images themselves is shifted by our knowledge of the text, and the photographs begin to intersect it in unexpected ways. Just before he first meets Nadja, Breton visits the *Humanité* bookshop; the shopfront is subsequently photographed and the photograph reproduced in the book (figure 17). The image is dominated by a large sign, which states 'ON SIGNE ICI' with an arrow pointing towards the shop. At the time, this had an obvious meaning: sign up to the Communist Party here. But, within the context of the book, the sign also becomes a 'sign'. The arrow points into the book, along the Rue Lafayette to where, a few minutes later in his account, Breton will meet Nadja. (Where indeed at the time when the picture was taken, he had already met her.)[18]

Few of the photographs work as dramatically as this, or point so immediately to the mutual implication of text and image in *Nadja*. Rather, the images of Paris have a cumulative effect so that one comes to see in the book not only an account of a love-affair, of the dual trajectories of a disturbed woman and an avant-garde writer, but also an account of the city in which their meeting takes place. Paris, one might say, is itself a character in the book. But it is a curious view of the city we are given, with a few somewhat well-known sites outnumbered by obscure corners, shops, hotels, cafés. This idiosyncratic mapping of Paris becomes clearer if one compares *Nadja* with a typical guidebook to the city. In the wake of Baedeker, many were produced, and by the 1920s, they were beginning to be illustrated with photographs.[19]

There are a couple of sites in *Nadja* which might also have appeared in such a guidebook: the Place du Panthéon and the Tuileries Garden. But, in *Nadja*, the image of the Place du Panthéon perversely does not include the Panthéon itself, while the Tuileries is represented by a solitary fountain watched by a faraway statue in the gloom. (The sun doesn't shine much in this city and, where there are people, they are dressed against the chill; the trees in the Place Dauphine are bare and wintry.) *Nadja* does not include the Arc de Triomphe as would the guidebook, but rather the Porte St Denis, which we have seen Breton describe not only as 'extremely handsome' but also 'extremely useless'.[20] And of course, in *Nadja* there is no Eiffel Tower, no Notre Dame, no Opéra. It is as if the official Paris of spectacle, power and tourism had ceased to exist.

In fact, the images of Paris in *Nadja* might be said to constitute a sort of 'anti-guidebook'. Sites are not chosen because they are the sites 'one must see'; rather they are included because of what happened in these places, either to Breton himself or between Breton and Nadja, or because of the 'uncanny' emotions they create in Breton.[21] A private city has been created within the public city, occupying the same space, but differently, more intensely. The physical geography of Paris is replaced by an affective topography, superimposing a sort of *carte du tendre* over the actual city.[22] Or, to project forward, *Nadja* can be seen as an exemplification of 'psychogeography' – the concept employed by the Situationists in the 1950s to describe a condition

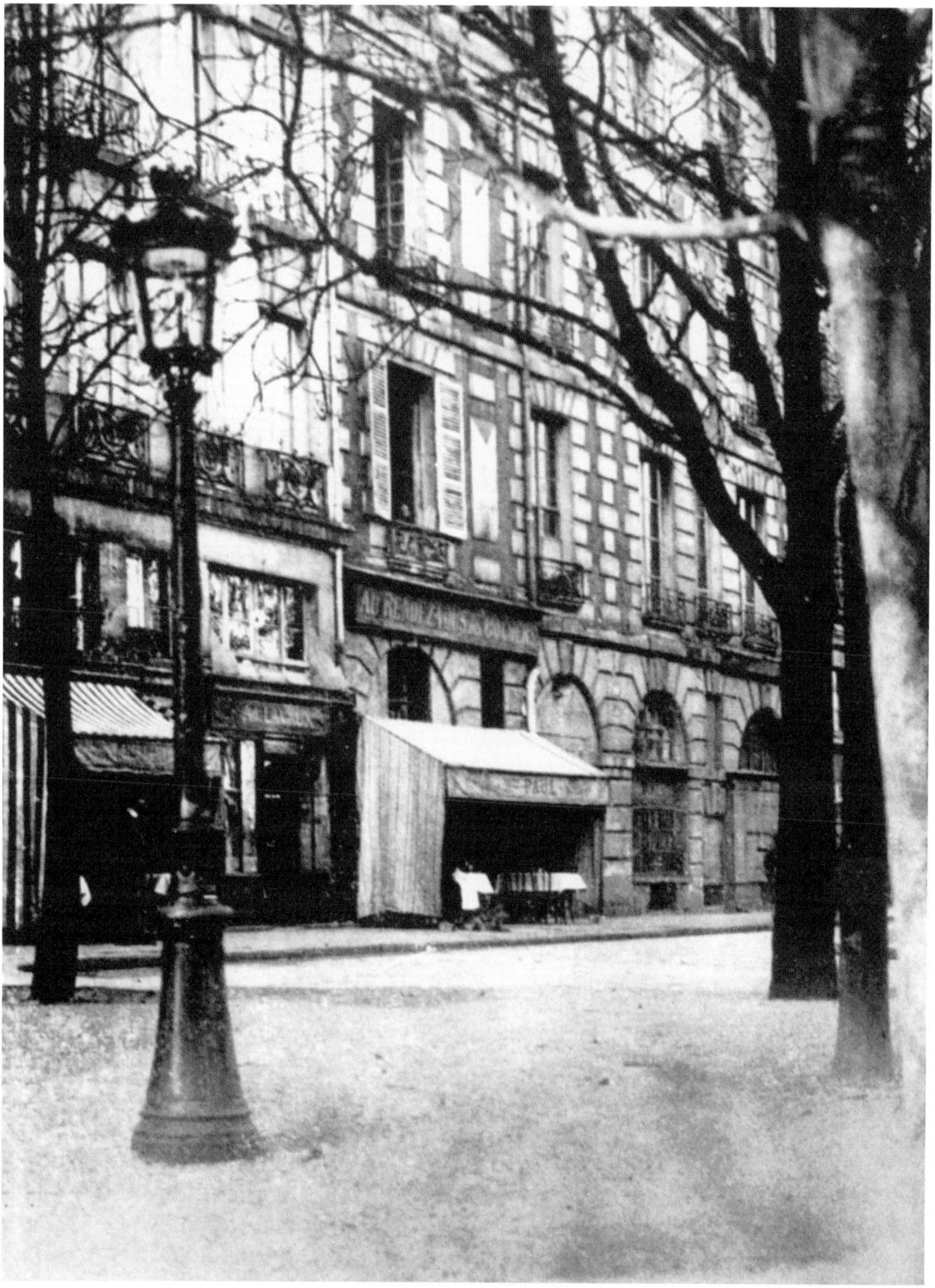

Fig 18 Jacques-André Boiffard, 'We have our dinner served outside by the wine seller', from André Breton, *Nadja*, 1928.

where aspects of the actual city and our subjective response to it have become fused and can no longer be separated.[23]

Nevertheless, the passivity of the photographs continues to disturb. One of the first critics to describe their role in the book, Michel Beaujour, puzzled over their emptiness: 'what we are shown is nothing ... [the places] are perfectly dumb; they suggest nothing in these banal photographs'.[24] But he saw in this a deliberate tactic on Breton's part, which he called a 'voluntary banality'. The phrase suggests that the pictures need to be banal, in order for the events that take place in them to appear truly extraordinary. For Roger Shattuck, their apparent flatness is their strength: 'The quotidian takes on an intensity that makes the wan photographs seem foreboding'.[25] To view the events of the novel as taking place in cold daylight on ordinary streets is to apprehend that the marvellous can and does strike anywhere.

Beaujour continued his comments: 'These photographs, practically void of human presences, return to a degree zero of representation: they are never removed from the amateur cliché or the outdated postcard.'[26] Certainly, these street scenes contrast with the professional portraiture of Man Ray and Henri Manuel. But, as Beaujour recognised, it may have been a deliberate ploy on the part of Breton to make the pictures echo the most popular – and ordinary – of photographs.[27] Produced in quite different ways, the postcard and the snapshot have in common the quality of a talisman. Even when they are pictorially of little interest, they can carry great personal resonance, replete with memories, associations and desires. The 'dumbness' of the photographs in *Nadja* likewise operates in a certain tension with the account of what happens on the streets of the city. That hotel matters because it is where Nadja stayed and that café matters because it is where she and Breton met.

In itself, the photograph of the Place Dauphine confirms only that the Place Dauphine existed (figure 18). It cannot confirm that what Breton says happened there on the evening of 6 October 1926, indeed happened – when, seated at a table outside the restaurant in the photograph, Nadja looked up at a house opposite and predicted that a window would light up red. Which, as Breton tells us, it suddenly did: 'There are, as a matter of fact, red curtains.'[28] Moreover, the photograph cannot begin to suggest why Breton considered the Place Dauphine to be 'one of the worst wastelands (*terrains vagues*) in Paris'.[29] But in its very passivity, the photograph holds open a space where such events can imaginatively reoccur and subjective emotions circulate. Inevitably, as a narrative begins to flow, 'the place' becomes 'the place *where* ...'. But, equally, the image of the place becomes part of the narrative. The two elements – place and narrative, photograph and text – can no longer be pulled apart without damage to both.

In the first edition of *Nadja*, all the Parisian street photographs were uncredited. In contrast with the attribution of the portraiture to Man Ray and Manuel, this emphasised the anonymity of the places photographed, waiting to be filled with significance by Breton's narrative. Moreover, this anonymity served to render the photographs themselves transparent – as if they were merely windows through which we see the actual city.

However, in the 1963 edition, a number of the Paris street scenes – eight of the twelve – were credited to J. A. Boiffard, and, in recent catalogues, nearly all the other Parisian images in *Nadja* have been also attributed to Boiffard.[30] In 1963, the accreditation was still of no great importance; to most of those who looked at the book, the name of Boiffard would have meant very little. However, in the 1980s and 1990s, the status of Jacques-André Boiffard within the body of Surrealist photography changed dramatically, and this, too, necessarily affects our contemporary view of these images in *Nadja*. Within a year of taking the photographs for Breton's book, Boiffard had left the Surrealist group along with several other important dissidents, including Queneau, Desnos, Prévert and Leiris. Like most of the others, he aligned himself with Breton's rival, Georges Bataille, and during 1929–30 made many photographs for the periodical *Documents*, edited by Bataille. It is these images which have transformed Boiffard's reputation, within the larger context of a move to place a 'Surrealism' based on Bataille's principles alongside the more familiar version of Breton.

One can see the beginnings of this realignment in 1978 with the large London exhibition *Dada and Surrealism Reviewed*, which was organised in sections based on periodicals of the period, with *Documents* treated as an equal to *La Révolution surréaliste* and *Le Surréalisme au service de la révolution*.[31] However, the compiler of that catalogue, Dawn Ades, was careful to place *Documents* apart from the main body of Surrealism. No such distinction was made by Rosalind Krauss in her essay 'Corpus Delicti' in *L'Amour fou* (1986), where indeed Bataille's concept of the *informe* was placed at the centre of Surrealist theory.[32] Furthermore, this reorientation took place within a broader context of renewed academic interest in Bataille's writing as a whole.[33]

Undoubtedly, during the period of *Documents*, Boiffard made some extraordinary individual images. And undoubtedly, he played a central role within the pages of the magazine, parallel to Man Ray's role in *La Révolution surréaliste* or Brassaï's in *Minotaure*. Beyond this, however, there is no consistent body of work, like Man Ray's or Brassaï's, to allow for a sustained 'auteurist' reading.[34] But, of course, it is that very fragmentation which makes Boiffard intriguing in a postmodern context, and distinguishes his work from the evidently modernist *oeuvres* of most other significant art photographers of the period.

It becomes even more difficult, however, when one tries to relate Boiffard's work for *Documents* back to his work for *Nadja*. In almost every respect, with one exception, the two sets of pictures are utterly different.[35] Dominique Lecoq, who has written one of the few full accounts of Boiffard's photographic career, criticises Michel Beaujour for his comments on the banality of these images.[36] Certainly Beaujour, in treating the images as if they were made by a visually illiterate snapshooter, was condescending towards Boiffard. But to say that the

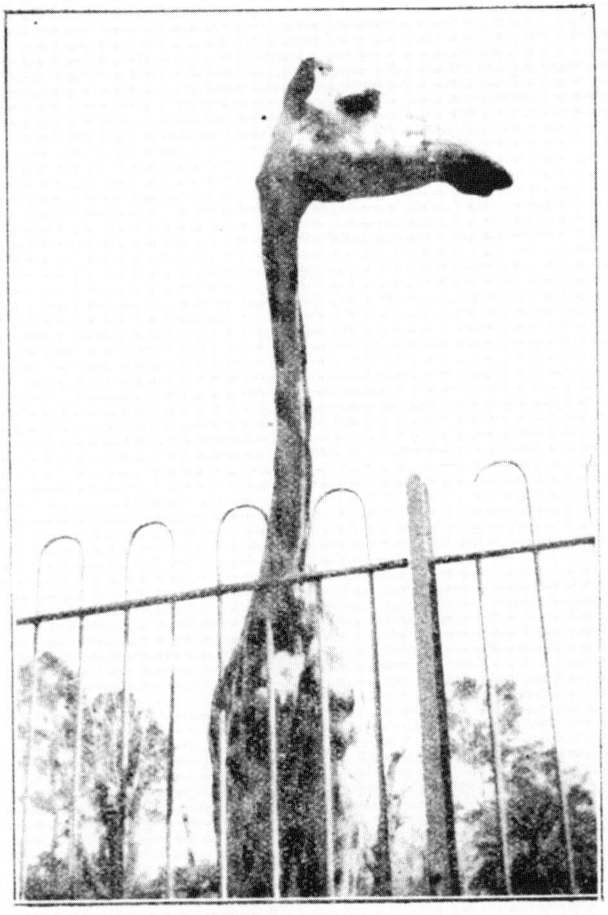

Fig 19 Jacques-André Boiffard (?), untitled photograph, *La Révolution surréaliste*, 8 (1926).

street images in *Nadja* were made with care and deliberation is not the same as saying that the Boiffard of *Nadja* was already the photographer who made the disturbing images of the 'Big Toe' or the 'Mouth' for *Documents*. Still, the remarkable trajectory of Boiffard's work retrospectively affects a reading of the *Nadja* photographs, which come to assume a greater authority than previously. The quotidian wanness now becomes 'masterly'.

What did André Breton himself think of Boiffard's photographs? In a comment towards the end of *Nadja*, Breton says that he wanted 'a photographic image of [the places] taken at the special angle from which I myself had looked at them' (not it should be noted an 'objective' view); however, 'I realised that most of the places more or less resisted my venture, so that, as I see it, the illustrated part of *Nadja* is quite inadequate'.[37] In contrast, Lecoq cites the inscription Breton wrote in Boiffard's own copy of the book: 'To Jacques-André Boiffard, to whom I owe the most beautiful photographs in this book and through whose eyes I have seen the true sites known by mine.'[38] It's impossible seyions un moment. Nous sommes devant un jet d'eau dont elle paraît suivre la courbe. « Ce sont tes pensées et les miennes. Vois d'où elles partent toutes, jusqu'où elles s'élèvent et comme c'est encore plus joli quand elles retombent. Et puis aussitôt elles se fondent, elles sont reprises avec la même force, de nouveau c'est cet élancement brisé, cette chute... et comme cela indéfiniment. » Je m'écrie : « Mais Nadja, comme c'est étrange ! Où prends-tu justement cette image qui se trouve exprimée presque sous la même forme dans un ouvrage que tu ne peux connaître et que je viens de lire ?» (Et je suis amené à lui expliquer qu'elle fait l'objet d'une vignette, en tête du troisième des *Dialogues entre Hylas et Philonous*, de Berkeley, édition de 1750, où elle est accompagnée de la légende : *Urget aquas vis sursum eadem, flectit que deorsum*, qui prend à la fin du livre, au point de vue de la défense de l'attitude idéaliste, une signification capitale). Mais elle ne m'écoute pas, toute attentive qu'elle est au manège d'un homme qui passe à plusieurs reprises devant nous et qu'elle pense connaître car ce n'est pas la première fois qu'elle se trouve à pareille heure dans ce jardin. Cet homme, si c'est lui, s'est offert à l'épouser. Cela la fait penser à sa petite fille, une enfant dont elle m'a appris avec tant de précautions l'existence, et qu'elle adore, surtout parce qu'elle est si peu comme les autres enfants, « avec cette idée de toujours enlever les yeux des poupées pour voir ce *qu'il y a* derrière ces yeux. » Elle sait qu'elle attire toujours les enfants : où qu'elle soit, ils ont tendance à se grouper autour d'elle, à venir lui sourire. Elle parle maintenant comme pour elle seule ; tout ce qu'elle dit ne m'intéresse plus également, elle a la tête tournée du côté opposé au mien, je commence à être fatigué. Mais, sans que j'aie donné aucun signe d'impatience : « Un point, c'est tout. J'ai senti que j'allais te faire de la peine. (*Se retournant vers moi :*) C'est fini. » Nous sortons du jardin et ne tardons pas à nous arrêter encore dans un bar de la rue Saint-Honoré qui s'appelle « Le Dauphin ». Elle observe que nous sommes venus de la place Dauphine au Dauphin. (A ce jeu qui consiste à se chercher des correspondances avec tel ou tel animal, on s'est généralement accordé à faire de moi un dauphin). Nadja ne peut supporter la vue d'une bande de mosaïque qui se prolonge du comptoir sur le sol et nous devons quitter le bar peu après y être entrés. Elle se fait arrêter devant le Théâtre des Arts. Nous convenons de ne nous retrouver à « La Nouvelle France » que le soir du surlendemain.

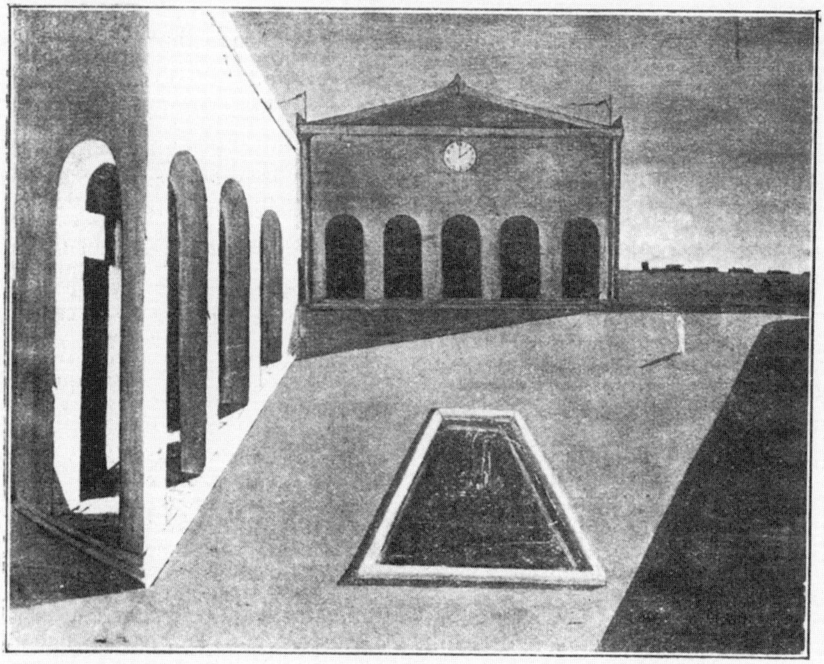

Chirico

André BRETON

to determine now what caused this shift in Breton's view. Was he just writing a flattering dedication for Boiffard? Or was it that, between writing the book and seeing it published, his opinion of the photographs changed? Or perhaps it was in their very nature, within the context of this book, that these photographs could indeed be both 'inadequate' and 'beautiful'? Their inadequacy in conventional aesthetic terms may have been exactly what Breton responded to, which may indeed have made the images beautiful. Not however in the sense of the 'convulsive' beauty that Breton demanded at the end of *Nadja*, but something altogether more elusive, that existed in the space between the plainness of the actual pictures and the meanings that they held for Breton himself.

One cannot now determine the level of independence that Boiffard was given by Breton. Breton's own comment would suggest that he intended to retain tight control of the pictures: 'taken from the special angle from which I myself had looked at them'. Moreover, little in Boiffard's biography up to that point had marked him out as more than a rather minor member of the Surrealist group. He worked between 1924 and 1929 as Man Ray's assistant,[39] contributing at least one photograph to *La Révolution surréaliste* in 1926: a curiously distorted image of a giraffe more like some of his later work than the images in *Nadja* (figure 19).[40] Michel Beaujour commented that if Breton had wanted images of 'les merveilleux des yeux', he would have asked Man Ray, the 'photographer-in-residence' of Surrealism.[41] Perhaps the task of taking the pictures for Breton's book was passed on to Boiffard by Man Ray. Perhaps it was felt (by Breton? by Man Ray?) that a less sophisticated photographic eye than Man Ray's was needed here.

But, minor or not, no member of the Surrealist group in the 1920s could really be considered unsophisticated. Boiffard's training with Man Ray, and his own apparent inclination towards an expressive style, would ensure that no more than Man Ray could he approach the picture-making process with unalloyed naivety. To put it more positively, it is probable (as Dawn Ades has suggested)[42] that Boiffard, an ex-medical student like Breton himself, would have understood the style of passive 'medical observation' Breton wanted, in ways that Man Ray, far more securely placed in modernist experimentation, could not have. It is probably too much to claim for Boiffard, as would some recent proponents, a total authority over his pictures. But, equally, one cannot propel him back into the anonymity from which he emerged in 1963. From a study of both the circumstantial material surrounding these pictures and a careful consideration of the pictures themselves, one can only see this part of the project as the result of a collaboration – however one weighs it – between Breton and Boiffard.

A closer examination of the images may reveal more of what Boiffard brought to the exercise. A persistent comparison is made between this work of

Fig 20 (left) Extract from André Breton, *Nadja*, with untitled painting by Giorgio de Chirico, *La Révolution surréaliste*, 11 (1928). Painting © DACS 2001.

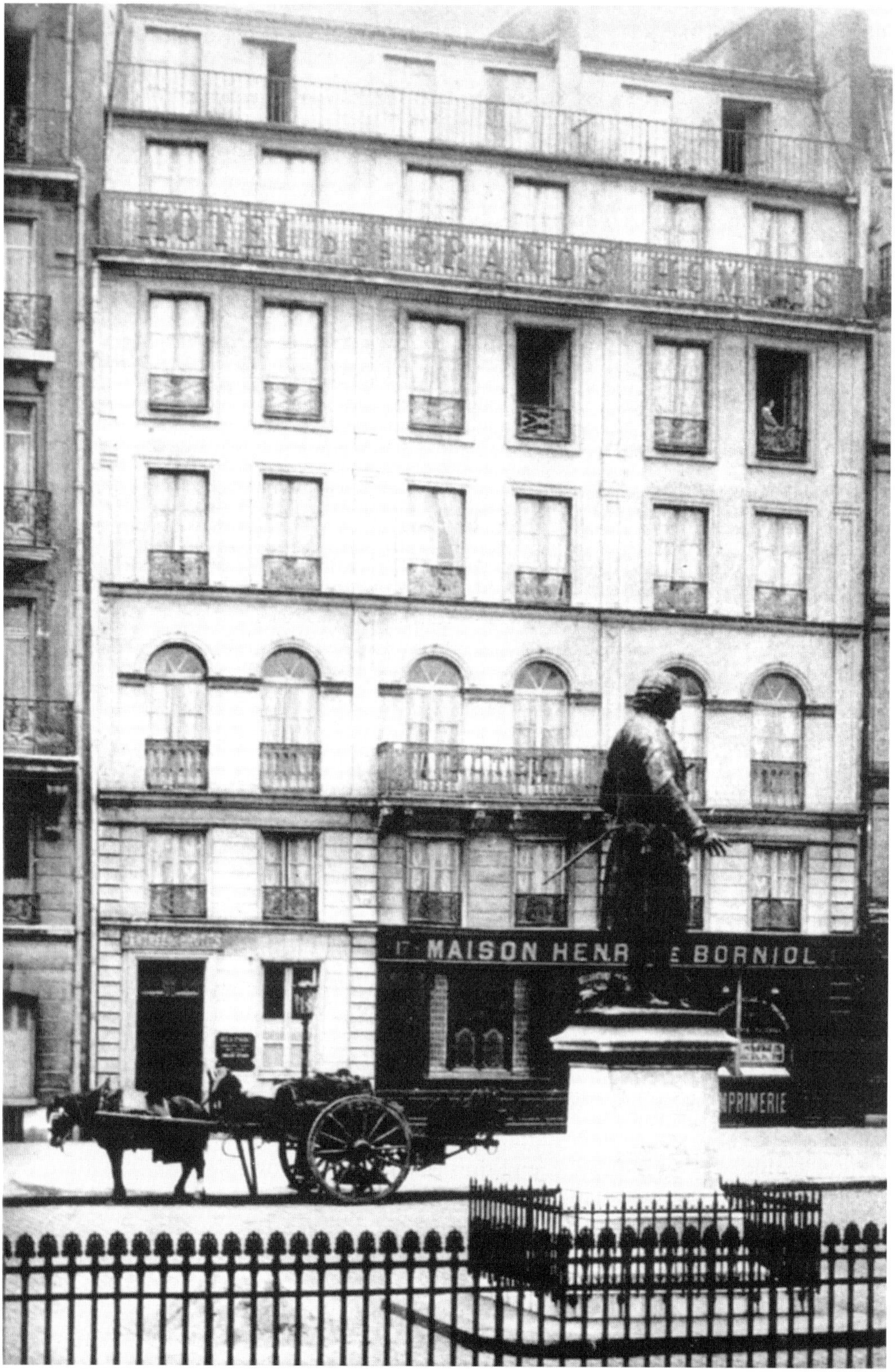
HOTEL
MAISON HENR
BORNIOL

Boiffard and that of Atget, voiced eloquently by Annette Michelson:

> Boiffard's photographs in illustration of the promenades and expeditions of *Nadja* introduce us ... into the theater of the surrealist encounter. This is the space of daily existence from which the stream of life has been evacuated, in which movement is cancelled. The social arena has been transformed into the theater of the private encounter. This is also the space of Atget's Paris. To Walter Benjamin his photographs evoked, in their vacant stillness, the scene of a crime. Let us say, rather, that they project a sense of imminence, of occurrences past or still to come. In them time is suspended: we are between times. These streets, squares, boulevards, arcades are cleared for the emergence of *le merveilleux*; their emptiness is ecstatic.[43]

The influence of Atget on Boiffard seems plausible, given that the images for *Nadja* were being made just a couple of years after Man Ray had discovered Atget's work and had it published in *La Révolution surréaliste*.[44] In many ways, though, Boiffard has learnt the lesson of Atget's pictures better than Man Ray – how to make quite unadorned images haunting and resonant of unspoken meanings. Moreover, just as the work of Atget and Boiffard might be linked in their having this 'sense of imminence, of occurrences past or still to come', so both can be related to the pre-1914 paintings of Giorgio de Chirico. When an extract of *Nadja* was published in *La Révolution surréaliste* – the sequence where Breton and Nadja have dinner in the Place Dauphine – it was accompanied by a de Chirico cityscape rather than a photograph (figure 20).[45]

But photographs operate differently from paintings. 'Every photograph', wrote Roland Barthes, 'is a certificate of presence'.[46] It offers us something that we know was there, that we still see as (having been) there. Yet, as he added, it is 'a reality one can no longer touch'. The presence the photograph offers is also an absence. The events we know must have occurred on the streets in Atget's and Boiffard's photographs have gone and the onlooker must imaginatively refill the space. Except that we can never quite do so, for whatever scenes we may imaginatively stage, these can never be as palpable as what actually happened. The marvellous, as it occurs in the chance encounter in the flux of the crowd, does so in ways which cannot be generally imagined. Rather, the empty street makes us feel that what has happened there, or will happen there, is unpredictable in its particularity, and thus essentially unknowable.

The notion of 'ecstatic emptiness' is very seductive, but in fact, only a few of the *Nadja* photographs are indeed deserted. These are mainly close-ups – the 'Camées Durs' shop front or the 'Nouvelle France' café, for example. However, looking carefully at the other photographs, one can see many peripheral signs of

Fig 21 (left) Jacques-André Boiffard, 'My point of departure will be the Hôtel des Grands Hommes', from André Breton, *Nadja*, 1928.

people, perhaps as many as one might expect to catch in casually photographing such public spaces. They are usually in transit, on their way across and out of the photograph, or they soon will be – they have paused and will then move on. We cannot know them, and their presence seems fleeting and ghost-like. This sense of transitoriness is emphasised by the carts or carriages which wait to be moved in four pictures: outside the Hôtel des Grands Hommes, in front of the *Humanité* bookshop, beside the Château at Saint-Germain and beneath the poster for Mazda lightbulbs. There is evidently a world of work going on in this city which is quite separate from the activities of either writer or photographer.

Most haunting, however, are those moments when someone stops to look back. At the base of the Porte St-Denis, a man stands and stares at the camera; at the flea market, one of the traders returns our gaze. And in an upper window of the Hôtel des Grand Hommes, there is a woman sitting, static, gazing out (figure 21). She is as unmoving as a statue or mannequin – and of course now will never move. Such a palpable evocation of presence is as haunting as any absence, for while she can be glimpsed, she also cannot be known.[47] While one may engage with the photographs as an observer, one cannot enter them as a participant.

Why is it that these multiple presences have not been noted, and the photographs too simply described as empty and void? Perhaps it is the very seductiveness of the myth of emptiness that offers a form of certainty – of absolute exclusion – which the actual pictures don't possess. But it is also true to say that the figures in the photographs are small and, in the published versions, difficult to read. The woman sitting at the hotel window, for example, can hardly be seen at all in later editions of the book, in which the photographic reproduction has become progressively muddier. It's only by turning to the original 1928 edition, the 1963 reprint or a more recent reproduction of an original print that she can be clearly seen.[48] Once noticed, however, she cannot be ignored – indeed the picture now seems to pivot around her rather than the statue of Rousseau (or it oscillates between them). And that raises the question of how different the relationship between text and images would seem if the reproduction was that much better, or if the images had been printed larger.

In an important sense, however, the reason the photographs work in the book is precisely because they are small, grey and indistinct. It was something of this effect that Walter Benjamin responded to when he wrote of *Nadja*: 'In such passages in Breton, photography intervenes in a strange way. It makes the streets, gates, squares of the city into illustrations of a trashy novel, draws off the banal obviousness of this ancient architecture to inject it with the most pristine intensity toward the events described, to which, as in old chambermaids' books, word-for-word quotations with page numbers refer.'[49] Benjamin's account of a shift from banality to 'pristine intensity' is related to the transformation of the everyday through subjective investment. But it is instructive that he aligns that effect with the fascination with the 'outmoded' which he discerns throughout Surrealism.[50] Certainly, as a book about Paris,

Nadja must be set against the modernist imagery of the dynamic metropolis, which was beginning to appear in books of photographs such as Germaine Krull's *100 x Paris*, also published in 1928. In *Nadja*, Breton rejected that modernism in favour of something visually more restrained and in its own way more intense.

Breton had written his book and he knew the pictures he wanted. Boiffard was in sufficient sympathy to provide them for him. Above all, however, the achievement of this 'voluntary banality' needed the anti-modernist context of Surrealism in the late 1920s. To make and utilise photographs as insolently 'dumb' as those in *Nadja* in fact required the highest degree of sophistication – and also a degree of nerve, given the way the medium was at that point in time being positioned on the cutting edge of modernist experimentation. As, all around, images were being tilted, reversed, cut up, collaged and juxtaposed, it required a very particular vision to allow an apparently direct, simple image just to sit there on the page, against the text.

Notes

1 André Breton, *Surrealism and Painting* (New York: Icon, 1972), p. 32.

2 Noted by Dawn Ades, 'Photography and the Surrealist Text', in Rosalind Krauss and Jane Livingston (eds), *L'Amour fou* (Washington: Corcoran Gallery/New York: Abbeville Press, 1985), p. 161.

3 The two exceptions are the pictures of the Manoir d'Ango, near Varengeville on the Normandy coast, where Breton wrote the book, and the château at Saint-Germain. On the use of photographs in *Nadja*, see Jean Arrouye, 'La photographie dans Nadja', *Melusine*, 4 (1981), 123–51.

4 All translations here are from this edition (New York: Grove Press, 1960), with additional reference to the revised French edition (Paris: Gallimard, 1963). Howard's translation was reprinted by Penguin in 2000 with the same pagination and a useful introduction by Mark Polizzotti; there has not however been a translation of Breton's 1963 version.

5 Walter Benjamin, 'Surrealism, the Last Snapshot of the European Intelligentsia', in *One-Way Street* (London: New Left Books, 1979), p. 227.

6 Ades, 'Photography and the Surrealist Text', p. 161.

7 Franklin Rosemont, *André Breton and the First Principles of Surrealism* (London: Pluto Press, 1978), p. 61 (his emphasis).

8 Simone de Beauvoir, *The Second Sex* (Harmondsworth: Penguin, 1983), p. 262. Denis Hollier has developed an argument that the use of indexical tactics, both textual and photographic, is intrinsic to Breton's anti-novelistic stance in *Nadja* ('Surrealist Precipitates (Shadows Don't Cast Shadows)', *October*, 69 (Summer 1994), 124–30).

9 From the 'Avant-Dire (dépeche retardée)' ('Preface (dispatch delayed)') in the 1963 Gallimard edition.

10 André Breton, *Mad Love* (Lincoln: University of Nebraska, 1987), p. 39.

11 Anna Balakian, *André Breton: Magus of Surrealism* (New York: Oxford University Press, 1971), p. 112.

12 What can now be known of the life of the real Nadja – Léona-Camille-Ghislaine D. born

near Lille in 1902 – is recounted by Marguerite Bonnet in her notes in André Breton, *Oeuvres Complètes, Vol. I* (Paris: Gallimard, 1988), p. 1509ff. See also Mark Polizzotti, *Revolution of the Mind: The Life of André Breton* (London: Bloomsbury, 1995), pp. 265–6. An account of meeting Nadja is given by another member of the Surrealist group, Pierre Naville, in *L'Espérance mathématique: Vol. I – Le temps du surréal* (Paris: Galilée, 1977), p. 359. Two handwritten letters from Nadja to Breton were included in the exhibition 'Surrealism: Desire Unbound' at Tate Modern, London, in 2001.

13 Breton, *Nadja*, pp. 23–4.

14 *Ibid.*, p. 71.

15 *Ibid.*, p. 19.

16 Translated by Howard as 'slope-facts' and 'cliff-facts' (*Ibid.*, p. 20).

17 Breton's tactics in *Nadja* had something of a precedent in Louis Aragon's *Le paysan de Paris*, published two years earlier (*Paris Peasant* (London: Jonathan Cape, 1971)). Several times, Aragon interrupted his text with reproductions of signs posted in the shops and cafés of the Passage de l'Opéra. However, these were of necessity typographical reworkings of the actual signs; in *Nadja*, the use of photography offers a more direct indexical link back to an exterior reality.

18 A lot of the photographs in *Nadja* contain phrases or names – Camées Durs, Bois Charbons, Sphinx Hotel, Mazda – and Breton's account constantly demonstrates his fascination with their poetic potential. Their appearance in the photographs as well as his text serves to give the phrases a physical presence that heightens their effect. In one case, there is a strange slippage between text and image. The photograph of BOIS CHARBONS in the first edition (and in the 1960 translation) in fact says BOIS CHABBONS! Breton made no comment on this, but perhaps he deliberately left it as it was – an unacknowledged misregistration. In 1963, however, a stroke of the retoucher's brush removed the bottom of the first B. This silent erasure suggests an unfortunate desire on Breton's part to retrospectively make the image conform to the text, in the process removing one of the little awkward moments that are in fact a significant feature of the original publication.

19 As an example, one might take *Pruvodce Paříží a Okolím* (*A Guide to Paris and its Environs*) (Prague: Odeon, 1927). Hardbound in red cloth, hand-sized, with photographs of the monuments to visit, nothing in this guidebook would indicate anything unconventional. In fact its authors were three young Czech artists: Vincenc Nečas, a writer, and two painters, Toyen and Jindřich Štyrský. All three were then members of the Czech avant-garde group Devetsil, and, in 1934, the latter two would help found the Surrealist group in Prague.

20 Breton, *Nadja*, p. 31.

21 The use of this term must of course evoke Freud's essay 'The Uncanny' (*The Pelican Freud Library, Vol. XIV: Art and Literature* (Harmondsworth: Penguin, 1985), 335–76). Victor Burgin has related *Nadja* to Freud's own memory of 'walking one hot day through the deserted streets of a provincial town in Italy' ('Chance Encounters', in *In/Different Spaces* (Berkeley and Los Angeles: University of California Press, 1996), pp. 93–4).

22 The *carte du (or de) tendre* was 'an allegorical map of the region of the tender sentiments' devised in the seventeenth century salon of Mme de Scudery (*Oxford Companion to French Literature* (Oxford University Press, 1959), p. 105).

23 On 'psychogeography', see Thomas F. McDonough, 'Situationist Space', *October*, 67 (Winter 1994), 59–77, and Simon Sadler, *The Situationist City* (Cambridge, MA: MIT Press, 1998), especially pp. 76–81.

24 Michel Beaujour, 'Qu'est-ce que *Nadja*?', *Nouvelle Revue Française*, 15:172 (April 1967), 797.

25 Roger Shattuck, 'The Nadja File', *Cahiers Dada Surréalisme*, 1 (1966), 55.

26 Beaujour, 'Qu'est-ce que *Nadja*?', 797. There is a pun here in the original French on 'cliché' as photographic negative and as commonplace. Also, in using the term 'degree zero', Beaujour was echoing the title of Roland Barthes' *Le degré zero de l'ecriture* (1965) and perhaps even making an implicit claim for the precedence of Breton with this concept, which was so influential in the 1960s.

27 Indeed, one of the pictures – that of the Château at Saint-Germain – looks as if it is from an actual postcard. In *L'Amour fou*, Breton used a postcard of Tenerife as an illustration (*Mad Love*, p. 72). Perhaps these are examples of Breton ironically doing what, in the Surrealist Manifesto, he had said a realist novelist did: 'slipping [us] his postcards' (*Manifestoes of Surrealism* (Ann Arbor: University of Michigan, 1969), p. 7).

28 Breton, *Nadja*, p. 83.

29 *Ibid.*, p. 80. In his later essay 'Pont-Neuf', Breton explored the resonance of the Place Dauphine, discovering in its siting within the city a very specific sexual meaning (translated in *Free Rein* (Lincoln: University of Nebraska Press, 1995), pp. 221–8).

30 The attribution of the street photographs in *Nadja* to Boiffard has been a haphazard affair. The eight photographs attributed to Boiffard in 1963 were: the Hôtel des Grands Hommes, Bois Charbons, the Porte St Denis, the L'Humanité bookshop, the Place Dauphine, Camées Durs, the Sphinx Hotel and the Mazda sign. However, in the paperback edition of 1964, two of these attributions (the Hôtel des Grands Hommes and the Place Dauphine) were inexplicably dropped. Since then, the image of the statue of Etienne Dolet has been credited to Boiffard in Philippe Sers (ed.), *Atelier Man Ray* (Paris: Centre Georges Pompidou, 1982), p. 39 (it was replaced in the 1963 edition of *Nadja* by another closer view). The images of the Tuileries and the flea market are attributed to Boiffard in Agnès Angliviel de la Beaumelle *et al.*, *André Breton: la beauté convulsive* (Paris: Musée nationale d'art moderne, 1991), p. 500. Of the original Paris photographs, this only leaves the 'Nouvelle France' which has never been formally credited to Boiffard, though it seems unlikely that anyone else took the picture.

31 Dawn Ades, *Dada and Surrealism Reviewed* (London: Arts Council of Great Britain, 1978), pp. 228–9.

32 Krauss and Livingston, *L'Amour fou*, pp. 57–100.

33 Susan Rubin Suleiman, *Subversive Intent: Gender, Politics and the Avant-Garde* (New Haven: Harvard University Press, 1990), pp. 72–83, gives a brief account of the developing interest in Bataille's work, and on p. 222 n. 5, lists some of the English language books on and translations of Bataille produced in the 1980s. For a study of Bataille which emphasises the connections between him and Breton rather than their antagonism, see Michael Richardson, *Georges Bataille* (London: Routledge, 1994); Richardson has also translated a selection of Bataille's post-war texts which amply demonstrate that sympathy (see Bataille, *The Absence of Myth* (London: Verso, 1994)).

34 See, for example, the extraordinarily heterogeneous collection of images by Boiffard reproduced in Sers, *Atelier Man Ray*.

35 The exceptions are the photographs of Paris statues taken to accompany Robert Desnos' article 'Pygmalion et le Sphinx' in *Documents*, referred to in Chapter 2. These are visually so similar to the images made for *Nadja* that in Sers, *Atelier Man Ray*, pp. 38–9, the two sets of pictures are mixed together as 'Illustrations pour *Nadja* d'André Breton, 1928'. However, the presentation of the photographs in *Documents* was quite different from that in *Nadja*; large-scale, one to a full page, they acquire an authority, even though they were probably taken on the same camera that made the images for *Nadja*.

36 Dominique Lecoq, 'Jacques-André Boiffard ou l'histoire d'un oeil' in *Georges Bataille et Raymond Queneau 1930–1940* (Clermont-Ferrand: L'association Billom-Bataille, 1982), p. 40.

37 Breton, *Nadja*, pp. 151–2.

38 Lecoq, 'Jacques-André Boiffard ou l'histoire d'un oeil', p. 40 (trans. Ades, 'Photography and the Surrealist Text', p. 161). Presumably, since Lecoq cites Boiffard's widow Denise as a source, the book was in her possession.

39 He can be seen in this role at the start of Man Ray's film *Le Mystère du Château de Dés* (1929).

40 *La Révolution surréaliste*, 6 (1 December 1926), 10. The picture is uncredited in *La Révolution surréaliste*, but one can confidently assign it to Boiffard, since it closely resembles a distorted photograph of two giraffes by Boiffard from the Julien Levy Collection, now in the Art Institute of Chicago and exhibited in Ades, *Dada and Surrealism Reviewed*, cat. no. 9.5.

41 Ades, 'Photography and the Surrealist Text', p. 189, states that Lucien Treillard, Man Ray's former assistant, informed her that Man Ray *had* photographed some of the sites in the novel. If so, they have never been published, but for some of Man Ray's other cityscapes (more 'avant-garde' in appearance), see Jean-Hubert Martin, *Man Ray Photographs* (London: Thames and Hudson, 1982), pp. 188–200.

42 Ades, 'Photography and the Surrealist Text', p. 163.

43 Annette Michelson, 'Dr. Crause and Mr. Clair', *October*, 11 (Winter 1979), 42. Michelson's main focus in this essay is on Rene Clair's film *Paris qui dort* (1924), and her comments are made in the context of the depiction of a deserted Paris in that film.

44 Ades, 'Photography and the Surrealist Text', p. 163, specifically compares the 'Camées Durs' photograph by Boiffard, made in the Palais Royale, with the photographs of shop windows that Atget made there.

45 *La Révolution surréaliste*, 11 (15 March 1928), 11.

46 Roland Barthes, *Camera Lucida* (New York: Farrar, Straus and Giroux, 1991), p. 87. As suggested in Chapter 1, there are a number of striking parallels between *Nadja* and *Camera Lucida*, albeit unacknowledged by Barthes. The way that Barthes used quotations from his text to accompany and inflect the meaning of the photographs he illustrated is very reminiscent of *Nadja*. Carol Armstrong has noted how the captions in *Camera Lucida* 'help to expose the photograph's inverted logic of illustration, by which the text supplements the image and the image naturalizes the text that colonizes it' (*Scenes in a Library* (Cambridge, MA: MIT Press, 1998), p. 441 n. 29). This points to deeper levels of connection in the ways

that subjective resonances are revealed as potentially embedded within the apparently objective status of the photograph.

47 In his poem 'The Photographs in *Nadja*', Paul Carroll evoked this presence with the line: 'The nimbus of those windows with curtains of thin flesh' (in *The Luke Poems* (Chicago: Big Table Publishing Company, 1971), p. 25).

48 See, for example, Sers, *Atelier Man Ray*, p. 39. However the photograph is cropped very differently from the versions that have appeared in the various editions of *Nadja*.

49 Benjamin, 'Surrealism', p. 231.

50 This connection is explored further in Chapters 4 and 5.

4
La Révolution surréaliste and the urban spectacle

The second half of the 1920s was when Surrealism was at its most uncompromising – the time when Aragon and Breton wrote *Le paysan de Paris* and *Nadja*, when painters as different as Miró and Magritte were producing their most radical works, when Buñuel and Dalí made their film *Un Chien andalou*. But the project that surely defined the ambitions of the Surrealist group as a whole during this period was the magazine *La Révolution surréaliste*. The span between the first issue published on 1 December 1924 and the twelfth and final issue (15 December 1929) was described by Aragon as 'a sort of mental year which lasted five years'.[1]

The format of *La Révolution surréaliste* was very different from that of its Dadaist predecessors, with each page containing two columns of closely set, dense type into which were dropped small grey illustrations. In fact, it was laid out in imitation of the popular scientific magazine *La Nature*. As Dawn Ades has observed, 'the effect visually is to bind the pictures ... very closely to the text, in that they look like documents, like evidence – none of the 'halo' of a beaux arts review – and their really enigmatic, unexpected, dream-like quality is made all the more startling'.[2]

This layout was the idea of Pierre Naville, initially co-editor of *La Révolution surréaliste* with Benjamin Péret. Naville had seen issues of *La Nature* at Breton's apartment: 'I asked that we copy, for the material presentation, this periodical inspired by positivism. That was, to my mind, the guarantee that our enterprise would not turn too quickly to the display of aesthetic production as one always finds a little everywhere.'[3] He saw how, under 'an identical austere cover', Surrealist provocation could produce 'an effect of surprise and rupture'. Moreover, the guise of positivism and evidentiality fitted in with the Surrealists' initial intention to leave Art and Literature behind and move into a sphere of 'scientific' research. Although their espousal of science – like their adoption of certain documentary strategies – always carried an element of scepticism, even irony.

Breton himself later said that 'in the beginning, the stress was placed on pure Surrealism – Surrealism, let's say, in its native state – and that's why the editorship was entrusted to Pierre Naville and Benjamin Péret, who at the time seemed the most completely driven by the new spirit and the most resistant to compromise'.[4] Although Naville and Péret were the editors of *La Révolution surréaliste*, all the members of the group were actively involved in the process of putting it together. Another central participant at this time, Philippe Soupault, has emphasised the collaborative nature of the publication, in which the gathering of material was quite unsystematic and often incorporated chance findings by the various group members.[5]

The moment of 'purity' does not last long. It is most apparent in the first issue; within a year, it has been considerably eroded, being replaced by something less astringent, though arguably richer. There are no poems in the first issue; rather there are 'Surrealist texts'. On the visual side, there are no paintings, but there are drawings – by writers such as Desnos and Naville as well as artists like de Chirico, Masson and Ernst. These drawings are credited, though, unlike the photographs, which are all anonymous and untitled; some were found images, some were made by Man Ray.[6] The lack of titling and attribution lends these photos an air of irresolution and undecidability. With all the images, both drawings and photographs, aesthetic delectation is of little importance, even suspect as being decidedly detrimental to the Surrealist value of the images.

As Ades says, the choice of imagery within *La Révolution surréaliste* was intimately bound up with broader arguments that were going on around the role of the visual within Surrealist practice.[7] This came to a head in issue no. 3, when Naville published a brief polemic with the heavily ironic title 'Beaux Arts'. His main aim was to disparage, *contra* Breton, the idea of a Surrealist art *per se*: 'Everyone knows there is no Surrealist painting.' What he offered instead he called 'spectacles': 'Memory and the pleasure of the eyes; that is the whole aesthetic'. It is worth quoting at length the examples he gave:

> The cinema, not because it is life, but the marvellous,
> the agency of chance elements.
> The street, kiosks, automobiles, screaming doors,
> lamps bursting in the sky.
> Photographs: Eusebius, L'Etoile, Le Matin, Excelsior, La
> Nature – the smallest ampoule in the world, route followed
> by a murderer. The circulation of the blood in the
> thickness of a membrane.
> To get dressed, – to get undressed.[8]

Naville was of course fighting a rearguard action and some of his examples do sound like warmed-over Futurism. Because Naville was so wrong about Surrealist painting, it is tempting to dismiss the rest of his credo. But it's not such an easy target. He is accurate about the Surrealist space of cinema and his list of photographic 'spectacles' remains intriguing. His specific examples are obscure, though 'La Nature' is surely a reference back to the magazine's source and a

'Tournée Excelsior' – a fairground act perhaps – appears in the second issue of *La Révolution surréaliste*.[9] This suggests that the others are also images from popular or non-artistic culture, which would accord with Naville's evident lack of interest in photography as an artistic practice. Finally, a couple of Naville's general images are remarkably prescient. The 'route taken by a murderer' must make one think of the Surrealists' later interest in *Détective* and the 'blood in the thickness of a membrane' presages the scientific images – often enormous enlargements – which are to appear in many Surrealist publications.

Moreover, one can see something similar to Naville's agenda being pursued by editors of the various Surrealist (or Surrealistic) magazines which would appear by the end of the decade. Bataille in *Documents*, Mesens in *Variétés*, Ribemont-Dessaignes in *Bifur* were all to employ a rich mixture of images from journalistic or scientific sources alongside those by 'art' photographers. As Bataille wrote in what seems to be his only direct comment on photography, 'informational photographs or film-stills are much more pleasurable to look at and often more alive than most masterpieces which are submitted to the admiration of the public'.[10]

Since Naville used the word 'spectacle' in 1925, it has acquired other layers of meaning. After the Situationist Guy Debord published *La société du spectacle* in 1967, the term came to stand for the way that, under modern Capitalism, 'everything that was directly lived has moved away into a representation'.[11] In his essay, 'Spectacle, Attention, Counter-Memory', Jonathan Crary attempted a historiography of the term.[12] He discussed the application by T. J. Clark of the concept of the spectacle to the Second Empire in Paris, the era of the grand boulevards of Haussmann and the department stores that lined them, the era, as we have seen, of the *flâneur*.[13] The moment at which Naville was writing, then, is midway between Baudelaire and Debord. Debord himself seemed to date the birth of the spectacle to the 1920s,[14] and Crary points to a number of events that might have led to this position: the advent of television and the sound film, the rise of Fascism, the writings of Walter Benjamin.

Crary concludes his essay with two 'different responses to the new texture of modernity taking shape in the 1920s': the work of Fernand Léger and the example of Surrealism.[15] In the first instance, he cites Léger's 1924 essay 'Le Spectacle':

> Life rolls by at such a speed that everything becomes mobile. The rhythm is so dynamic that a 'slice of life' seen from a café terrace is a spectacle. The most diverse elements collide and jostle one another there. The interplay of contrasts is so violent that there is always exaggeration in the effect you glimpse. On the boulevards two men are carrying some immense gilded letters in a handcart; the effect is so unexpected that everyone stops and looks. There is the origin of the modern spectacle.[16]

On one level, this sounds remarkably like Naville's 'spectacle': the sight caught from the flow of life which arrests the viewer. (One is reminded of two other workmen who, later in this chapter, will look down a manhole on the cover of *La Révolution surréaliste.*) But Crary suggests that in his work Léger then attempts to find his way into the spectacle, to somehow make it work for him, like many later artists 'who believe, or at least claim, they are outwitting the spectacle at its own game'.[17]

For Naville, however, the sights of urban life were to be left simply as that – fleeting incidents glimpsed in passing – perhaps because he implicitly understood that to try to build them into a system was to be co-opted into the spectacle. But one must be careful about making too retrospective a reading of his position. Despite the fact that Naville was one of the most committed Marxists in the Surrealist group, his concept of the 'spectacle' does not have an overt political dimension, and one cannot simply overlay the connotations the term has since acquired. Rather, it seems he meant it, not even in the sense of the spectacularly grand or overwhelming, but rather as something simpler, even deliberately naïve: whatever immediately feeds 'the pleasure of the eyes'. Such images can haunt the memory precisely because they seem to have no other role and no obvious explanation. While there are no explicit politics here, one can see in this espousal of the trivial but compelling a side-stepping of accustomed aesthetic and social norms.

Jonathan Crary concludes his text by citing the Surrealist refusal of the spectacle. However, he does not specifically refer to Naville's use of the term, but more generally evokes the Surrealist strategy of 'turning the spectacle of the city inside out through counter-memory and counter-itineraries. These would reveal the potency of outmoded objects excluded from its slick surfaces, and of derelict spaces off its main routes of circulation. The strategy incarnated a refusal of the imposed present, and in reclaiming fragments of a demolished past it was implicitly figuring an alternative future'.[18] Crary is here echoing Walter Benjamin in emphasising the Surrealist involvement with the 'outmoded' and we can surely see a link between the placement of the photographs in *Nadja* (which Benjamin described as looking as if they came from 'old chambermaids' books'),[19] and the placement of the 'spectacles' in *La Révolution surréaliste* – deliberately fragmented, modest, unexplained. In both cases, many of these 'spectacles' are photographic – transposed through the medium with an apparent capacity both for the direct recording of fact and for the transmutation of that fact into memory. A photograph is in a sense always outmoded, the present having just slipped into the past.

With issue no. 4, Breton assumed the editorship of *La Révolution surréaliste* and began the serialisation of *Le Surréalisme et la peinture*. From now on, many more (and more important) paintings were to be reproduced in the magazine. Yet, long after Naville had lost this particular battle with Breton, photographic 'spectacles' such as he had advocated continued to play an important role in the magazine. Two types of photograph figured: found, appropriated images and

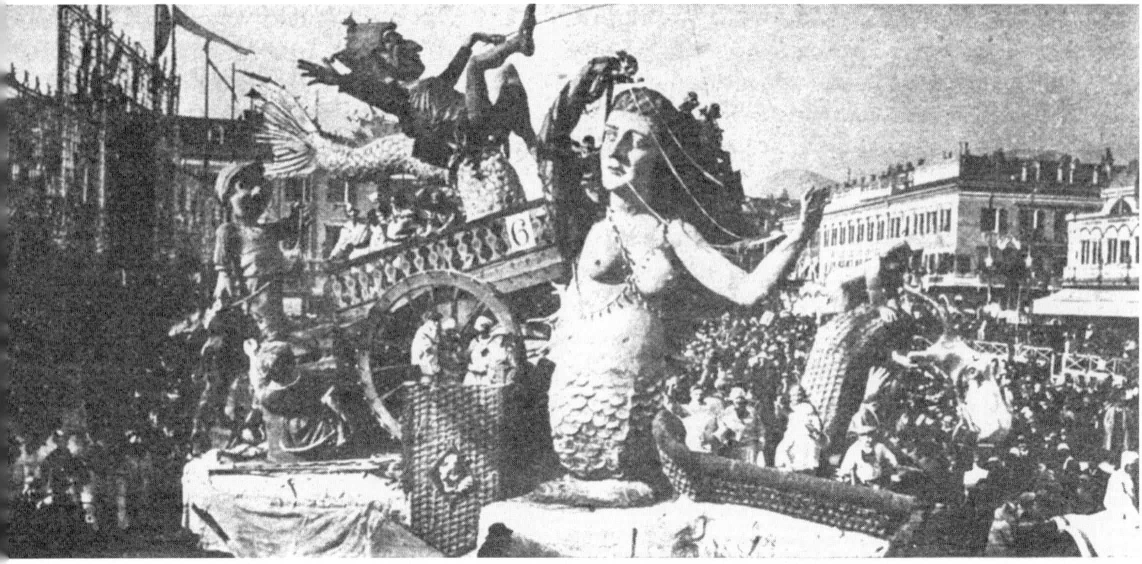

Fig 22 Untitled photograph, *La Révolution surréaliste*, 1 (1924).

photographs made as Surrealist images. In later issues, Man Ray's contribution to the magazine was increasingly acknowledged, though many of the individual pictures remained uncredited and untitled. This continued to blur the distinction between authored and unauthored work, giving the photographs the status of a 'thereness' rather than a 'madeness'.

There was a variety of intended effects in the use of photography in *La Révolution surréaliste*, but it can be broadly categorised as either satirical or celebratory. One should be wary of separating the tactics of attack and affirmation, which for the Surrealists were dialectically complementary rather than opposed. Nevertheless, while the images of satire were part of an assault on the fundamental tenets and assumptions of bourgeois society in a continuation of the Dadaist tradition of provocation, the more positive images show something different: the desire of the Surrealists to construct an edifice of approved, non-respectable icons. In some cases, the Surrealist meaning of the image may be continuous with its original, intended meaning. More often, the image is repositioned within a Surrealist context. This process is two-fold: a turning away, a *détournement* (as the Situationists would call it)[20] of the image from its manifest meaning, followed by an avowal of its latent, oblique, Surrealist meaning.

I want to look here at four specific anonymous images from *La Révolution surréaliste*, selected on a dual basis. As fragmentary, almost arbitrary examples snatched from the larger context of the magazine, they may stand for the way that texts and images, theory and poetry, the subjective and the documentary are collaged together in the publication, through tactics parallel to those of Breton in *Nadja*. Except that here there are many voices, many sights. These four

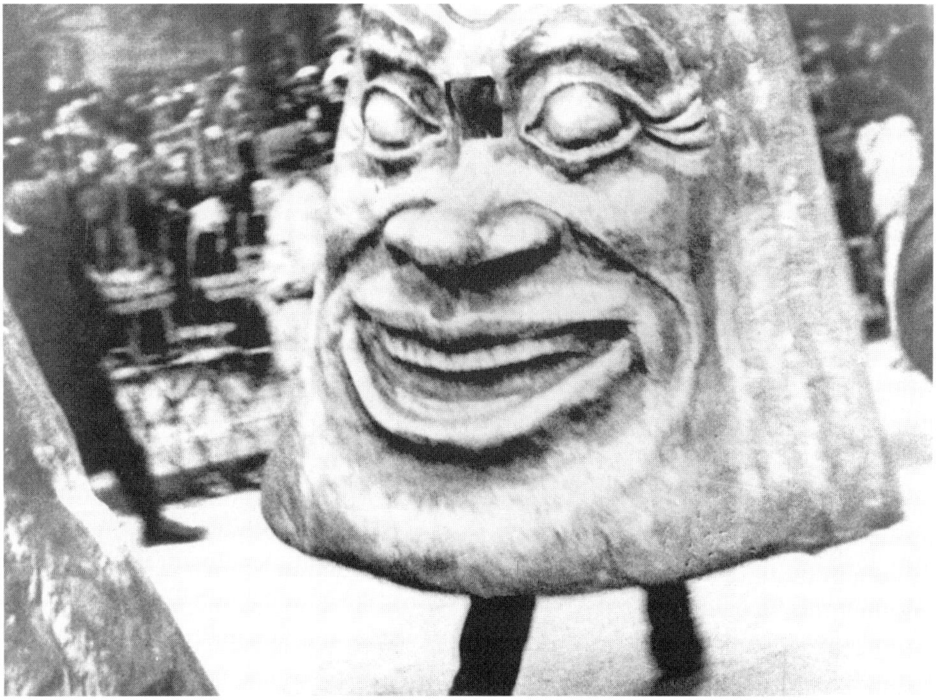

Fig 23 Frame still from Jean Vigo, *A Propos de Nice*, 1929.

images have also been chosen because of their subject matter. They comprise four different representations of the street which will serve to amplify some of the themes already examined – the street as a site of active participation and passive contemplation, of sardonic observation and impassioned intervention.

Seven pages into the first issue of *La Révolution surréaliste* is an image of a very traditional form of popular street culture, the carnival (figure 22). It is placed between the title TEXTES SURREALISTES and the actual texts by Marcel Noll and Robert Desnos. Woven into the very fabric of the magazine, the image itself becomes a 'Surrealist text'; whatever its original source (a postcard perhaps?), it is now thoroughly implicated in the web of Surrealist subversion.

This photograph is of course untitled. But it may well show the carnival at Nice, the best known surviving celebration of its kind in France. The young film-maker Jean Vigo, whose work had many affinities with Surrealism, included shots of the carnival in his short film *A Propos de Nice* (1929), placing them against images of social hypocrisy and bourgeois repression (figure 23).[21] But one cannot be sure whether Vigo saw the carnival as a revolt against that repression or, more negatively, as the appropriation of the popular by the bourgeois hegemony.[22] There is a similar ambiguity in this Surrealist representation of the carnival – is this an event to be celebrated or critiqued? Only its placement in the magazine suggests the former – its co-option as a 'Surrealist text' and the link with other images of the popular in the rest of magazine.[23]

As with the concept of the spectacle, this debate also strikes a more recent theoretical resonance. Since the translation into English of his study of *Rabelais and his World*, Mikhail Bakhtin's discussion of the carnival and more broadly the 'carnivalesque' in popular culture has had great influence.[24] But there has also been disagreement. Bakhtin's broadly positive image of the carnival as a 'potent, populist, critical inversion of all official words and hierarchies'[25] has itself been countered by an alternative critical view of carnival as 'a licensed affair in every sense, a permissible rupture of hegemony, a contained blow-off as disturbing and relatively ineffectual as a revolutionary work of art'.[26] Both these positions resonate with Surrealist views of the popular. Certainly, they saw popular culture as an important antidote to the stifling restrictions of high art; equally, though, the profound pessimism which permeates early Surrealism may well have led them to doubt its efficacy.

At one point in *Rabelais and his World*, Bakhtin himself considered the relationship between carnival and spectacle:

> Because of their obvious sensuous character and their strong element of play, carnival images closely resemble certain artistic forms, namely the spectacle ... But the basic carnival nucleus of this [folk] culture is by no means a purely artistic form nor a spectacle and does not, generally speaking, belong to the sphere of art. It belongs to the borderline between art and life. In reality, it is life itself, but shaped according to a certain sense of play.[27]

By 'spectacle', Bakhtin evidently means a ritualised, public event, and not the simpler, more spontaneous phenomenon suggested by Naville's use of the term. Nevertheless, Bakhtin's comments do strike a chord in this discussion, for the anonymous illustrations appropriated for *La Révolution surréaliste* also occupy a no man's land on 'the borderline between art and life'. They are drawn into the magazine by its insistent layout, woven into its web of 'surprise and rupture', one element in a polemic of interest only in advanced artistic circles. But they cannot be contained there, they keep sticking out, awkwardly reconnecting with their original context in the popular.

If the photograph of the carnival represents the filled, teeming street (excessively so), then its opposite, the empty, haunted street, also appears in the magazine. The image I want to examine appears in the last issue of *La Révolution surréaliste*, dropped into a dense essay by André Thirion, 'Note sur l'argent'.[28] Thirion, one of the most politically committed in the Surrealist group, later described his text as 'a sort of Marxist fantasy ... an apologia for poverty'.[29] In

Fig 24 (right) Extract from André Thirion, 'Notes sur l'argent', with uncredited photograph 'Maison-Attentat', *La Révolution surréaliste*, 12 (1929).

et que de ce fait, la valeur qu'il avait essayé de lier par des chaînes d'acier à la durée de la fatigue des prolétaires, reprenait peu à peu sa liberté, animant une foule d'objets de-ci, de-là, au hasard des désirs, des hasards et des escroqueries.

Voici donc mon heureux imbécile qui fait sonner comme il se doit ses pièces de vingt francs dans sa poche. Comme c'est demain le 25 décembre, jour où l'on souhaite leur fête aux gens qui s'appellent Noel (le seul prénom du calendrier que jamais un saint ne porta) il achètera une oie, volatile qu'il aime entre tous et qu'il va échanger contre le petit poids d'or qu'il a dans la main. Il se ravise, il paiera le 26 au matin, en allant à son bureau. Pour quelle raison, ce matin du 26, quand il donnera sa pièce d'or au rôtisseur, ne lui demandera-t-il pas, à cet homme, une nouvelle oie? J'ai connu des escrocs qui reprenaient leur argent à chaque achat qu'ils faisaient, sous prétexte qu'il était inutile que cet argent servît à d'autres pour le même usage. Aucun tribunal ne peut les condamner à l'aide d'un raisonnement logique. Imbécile mon frère, si tu imitais ces escrocs, tu aurais de l'oie tous les jours à ta table.

Je sais ce qui t'empêche de te livrer à des manœuvres aussi productives. Tu n'as pas d'or dans ta poche (les pièces de la stabilisation étant toujours à la frappe) mais des billets de banque, c'est-à-dire un morceau de papier dont tu te doutes un peu que la valeur n'est pas bien sûre?

On ne te laisse même plus en main, sauf à de rares instants, la substance qui est l'incarnation matérielle de la monnaie. Quoique tout ce qu'il fasse en ce sens s'oppose tous les jours davantage à cette augmentation, c'est une question de vie ou de mort pour le capitaliste que d'augmenter sans cesse la force productive du travail social. La production de l'or et de l'argent constituant une part importante des faux frais de la production capitaliste, on a été amené à développer les moyens accessoires, le crédit, qui représente de la valeur en marchandises, joue le rôle de la monnaie, mais sous quelque forme qu'il aille jusqu'à toi (lettre de change, chèque, billet de banque) ne constitue qu'une habile tromperie, car tu penses bien qu'on n'a jamais eu l'idée saugrenue de faire du papier un équivalent général.

Pauvre marchand d'hostie, tu reçois des mains du prêtre, amateur d'hostie comme le porc l'est de truffes (que le noble animal porte jambon m'excuse de cette comparaison désobligeante) un petit franc de laiton garanti par les Chambres de commerce sur de la camelote dont tu n'auras jamais la vue, qui est à la merci d'un raz-de-marée aux Antilles, ou plus simplement d'une chiure de mouche, pauvre marchand, tandis que dans l'heureux temps de l'avant-guerre tu avais la joie de contempler, dans ta main sale, un peu de la sueur humaine que ton idéalisme transformait en argent. Mais rassure-toi, bien que tu vives à l'époque de la Révolution prolétarienne, tu as encore des chances. C'est avec le crédit, cette fausse monnaie sans laquelle la société capitaliste est impossible, que tes pareils du quartier Saint-Sulpice se sont enrichis.

« Dans la mesure (*) où les moyens acces-

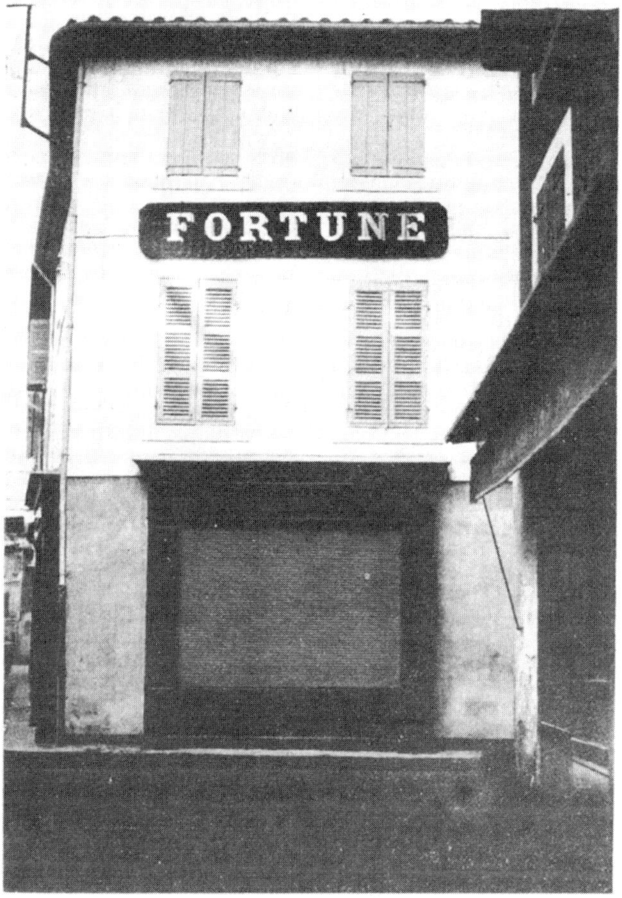

MAISON-ATTENTAT

(*) Marx : *Capital*, Le procès de circulation du capital, 2e Section, Ch. XVII.

the middle of this solid text is placed a photograph of a closed-up shop façade on which a sign is emblazoned with the single large word FORTUNE (figure 24).[30] Below the image is a caption: MAISON-ATTENTAT. It is a curious phrase that can best be rendered as 'murdering-house'. The secretive, blank façade becomes sinister; its placement within Thirion's text suggests the fortune within is being nefariously and possibly violently acquired.

This was not, however, the only site in which this photograph was published. Its other, parallel placement was far less public, in a now obscure volume of poems by René Char entitled *Le tombeau des secrets*. Char was, after the Second World War, to become one of the best known of contemporary French poets. But in the early 1930s, his adherence to Surrealism, though short-lived – he was formally a member from 1930 to 1934 – was a crucial phase in the development of his work.

In 1929, Char was living at the family home in L'Isle-sur-Sorgues near Avignon. His introduction to the Surrealist group was made via Eluard, to whom he had sent a copy of his book of poems *Arsenal* (published earlier that year). He joined the Surrealist group and his next volumes were all published by Editions Surréalistes, culminating in the 1934 anthology, *Le Marteau sans maître*. Since this latter volume was republished in 1945, it has come to represent Char's Surrealist period.[31] But *Le tombeau des secrets*, privately published in 1930 in a small edition (103 copies), presumably at Char's own expense, has been forgotten. The book has been discussed by few writers on Char, and Virginia A. La Charité has attributed this critical neglect to the fact that several poems from *Le tombeau des secrets* were reprinted (and slightly rewritten) in *Le Marteau sans maître* as if they had been part of *Arsenal*.[32]

Whether intentionally or not, Char himself in effect removed *Le tombeau des secrets* from his *oeuvre*. But it is a book of great interest in the present context, for in the slim, large format volume, Char juxtaposed a series of ten short poems with a selection of found and often antiquated photographs. Only one literary critic of Char's work, Jean Claude Mathieu, seems to have discussed the photographs in the book;[33] no critic of Surrealist photography has done so. It deserves more extended attention that can be given here as an important example of the Surrealist juxtaposition of poems and found photographs.

The photographs are plain yet hauntingly distanced; they seem to be mainly family or personal images, yet no clues are given within the book as to their provenance. The poems are brief and epigrammatic, their language also plain enough but the meaning elusive. As the photographs are poeticised by the text, the poems are rooted in an everyday reality by the pictures. The personal connotations of the pictures are abstracted in the elusive language of the poems, but the language is in turn humanised and individualised by the presence of the photographs. Yet this does not lead to comprehension or elucidation; any precise meanings slip away from both poem and picture, slip down the space between the two, in some senses, irreconcilable forms of expression.

The photograph of the closed shop which a year before had been published in *La Révolution surréaliste* appears in *Le tombeau des secrets*, opposite one of Char's more epigrammatic poems:

> La respiration
>
> L'apparition de l'arme à feu
> La reconnaissance du ventre.

The poem is, like most of those in *Le tombeau des secrets*, gnomic in its brevity: a title and two juxtaposed lines asking the reader to make connections. Char's poetry is difficult to translate, since the deceptively simple phrases can carry a range of nuanced meaning. 'La respiration' can be read as 'breathing' or 'a (single) breath', but it may also indicate a pause for breath at the end of a musical phrase – or between the two lines of the poem. 'L'apparition de l'arme à feu' may be directly rendered as 'The apparition of the fire-arm', though 'l'apparition' can carry a range of meanings between physical appearance and ghostly manifestation. 'La reconnaissance du ventre' is a colloquial term indicating gratitude toward a person who has looked after one (rather like the English 'cupboard love' though without the pejorative connotations). But its component parts carry additional meanings. 'Ventre' can be stomach, bowels, womb – perhaps 'belly' is the best English equivalent – while 'reconnaissance', as well as gratitude, can mean recognition or discovery. It is also, as in English, a military term – reconnoitring – which would connect with the firearm.[34]

One proposal as to the poem's meaning has been made by Mathieu, who sees it as bringing together 'the formula of the historian ("L'apparition de l'arme à feu") and the proverbial saying ("La reconnaissance du ventre") to unite the death instinct and sexual desire, to "recognise" the belly only through the wound inflicted on it'.[35] Certainly, one might see the two lines as working both with and against each other, to suggest simultaneous processes of violence and protection, the potential for death and for procreation. And in that, it works similarly to the phrase 'Maison-Attentat', which also yokes together ideas of the home and violent death; indeed, that phrase could have been Char's starting point for the poem.

Later, when the poem was reprinted without the photograph in *Le Marteau sans maître*, Char changed 'La respiration' to 'Les poumons' ('The lungs'),[36] emphasising the bodily organ itself rather than the action it performs. Perhaps this compensates for the absence of the photograph, for in *Le tombeau des secrets*, the picture suggests a parallel effect, the building becoming a body that ambiguously holds both the organs that breathe and those that procreate. Compared with the blunt irony of the use of the image in *La Révolution surréaliste*, such ambiguity suggests the other meaning of fortune – chance occurrence, random luck – also comes into play here. Still, in both *La Révolution surréaliste* and in *Le tombeau des secrets*, the façade acts as a mask for something we cannot see, be it violent or ineffable, social or sexual, and that

N° 11 — Quatrième année 15 Mars 1928

LA RÉVOLUTION SURRÉALISTE

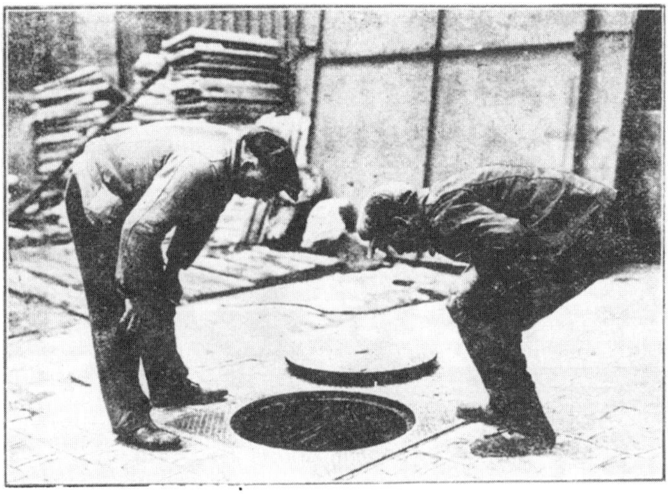

LA PROCHAINE CHAMBRE

SOMMAIRE

ADMINISTRATION : 16, Rue Jacques-Callot, PARIS (VIe)

ABONNEMENT,
les 12 Numéros :
France : 55 francs
Etranger : 100 francs

Dépositaire général : Librairie GALLIMARD
15, Boulevard Raspail, 15
PARIS (VIIe)

LE NUMERO :
France : 5 francs
Etranger : 7 francs

single word FORTUNE seems to offer a suggestive but indefinite comment on whatever activity is going on back there – behind just one of the many frontages which line the street. As with Atget's photographs of brothels or Magritte's paintings of bourgeois houses, the façade represents the barrier between the interior and the exterior, the open and the hidden.[37]

In *Le tombeau des secrets*, the photograph does not have the overtly sinister quality it has in *La Révolution surréaliste*, and this is of course mainly because that title 'Maison-attentat' is missing. One might therefore assume that it was added to point up the meanings the image was to carry in the magazine. But this was not so. When Char himself gave a copy of the book to Valentine Hugo, he annotated it, indicating that most of the photographs indeed had a personal source, as talismans of family or friends. Beneath this picture he noted 'Maison de mon ami Jean Fortune à l'Isle. Maison dite Maison-attentat'.[38] So, after all, FORTUNE was the name of the man who owned the building. But still there is no explanation as to why the house should have acquired its sinister designation. Perhaps its source was similar to that of the 'House of the Hanged Man' that Cézanne painted – except that here there's an implication that it is the house itself that is murderous.[39]

So this plain photograph, depending on its context, can hold meanings that are political and satirical (in *La Révolution surréaliste*), poetically suggestive (in *Le tombeau des secrets*) or finally personal and irretrievable. Its very flatness and impenetrability enables it to operate in all these contexts. There is no need to choose between these meanings; there is no 'correct' reading.

The photograph used on the cover of issue no. 11 of *La Révolution surréaliste* (15 March 1928) is an image of two workmen looking down an open manhole (figure 25). The original context of the photograph has been removed and we can never know why the two men were actually there. The picture is also accompanied by a caption which inflects its meaning decisively, a tactic commonly used on the cover of the magazine. In several early issues, these captions had been bluntly satirical: a scarecrow representing 'French Art at the Start of the Twentieth Century', for example.[40] Later, the device was used to throw open more ambiguous possibilities, such as when a blank-eyed schoolgirl who probably originally featured in a titillating piece of nymphettéism became the 'muse' of 'Automatic Writing' on the cover of issue nos 9–10.[41]

The phrase that accompanies the two workmen is vigorously polemic and subtly suggestive at the same time. It reads LA PROCHAINE CHAMBRE ('the next room'). Immediately, one's concentration is centred on the oval of the black hole, no longer a void but an active presence in the picture, holding untold mysteries which lie down below the flat surface of the pavement. As Paul Eluard wrote in an assertion of Surrealist materialism: 'There exists another world. But

Fig 25 (left) Cover of *La Révolution surréaliste*, 11 (1928).

it is assuredly in this one.'[42]

Several readings come simultaneously into play as one considers what that room might contain. 'Chambre' is often used in French specifically to refer to the Chambre des Députés – the Parliament – and read thus, the text becomes another example of the directly satirical image–text combinations already mentioned. In addition, it is possible that the photograph was intended as a satirical jibe at the workers themselves. This image was, after all, appearing in the middle of the troubled relationship between the Surrealists and the Communist Party. Just a year before, several of the Surrealist group had joined the Party and André Breton had been assigned to a cell of gas-workers. Asked however to write a report on the Italian situation and 'to stick strictly to the statistical facts (steel production, etc.) and above all not get involved with ideology', he said, 'I couldn't do it'.[43] The dumbfounded, uncomprehending stares of the two workmen may well recall the reaction Breton had received from the comrades. For what the Surrealists could not accept was the conventional leftist piety in the face of manual work; 'And War on Work' was one of their slogans.[44] They insisted that the 'black hole' of imagination had to be acknowledged as a crucial force in any revolutionary politics.

But perhaps there were other resonances that could be read obliquely between this image on the magazine's cover and the contents inside, as if the black hole led into the interior of the magazine. Issue no. 11 contained, for example, the 'Recherches sur la Sexualité', a group discussion about sexual practices and desires.[45] Consequently, one might envisage the 'next room' into which the men gaze so avidly as thc *chambre à coucher*, the *chambre d'amour*. Suddenly the photograph becomes an image of voyeurism. However, another major feature of this issue was a celebration of 'Le Cinquantenaire de L'Hysterie', which could suggest that the mysterious blackness represented a 'descent' into mental disturbance. (In fact, given that the Surrealists' celebration of hysteria had a decidedly erotic edge to it, these two elements in the magazine – *amour fou* and madness itself – might well begin to merge.)

Finally, and more tentatively, one might allow the literal blackness of the hole to combine with its metaphorical status as a 'chambre' to produce the image of a *chambre noire*, the photographic darkroom where the image came into existence in the first place. The transformative power of photography was often evoked by Surrealist writers; in his prose poem 'Nuits partagées', Eluard wrote: 'But the light has given me beautiful pictures of the negative of our encounters.'[46] Such poetic evocations of the magical processes of the darkroom are usually associated with manipulative processes such as solarisation, 'bas-relief' or the Rayograph.[47] But even photographs as plain and apparently straightforward as this image of the two workmen must be 'reborn' in the darkroom, passing through the alchemy of the photographic process to emerge as something still linked to but abstracted from its origins.

Of course, none of these readings is any more correct than any other, nor are they mutually exclusive. Rather, the range of meanings – marvellous, satirical, sexual, psychiatric and self-referential – interpenetrate to create a complex web of possibilities. The quotidian reality of the original event has been transmuted into a photographic image, and that in turn has been repositioned by the addition of the caption.

Edouard Jaguer has written of the encounter of the Yugoslav poets Djordje Kostic and Oskar Davico with this image and, through it, with Surrealism.[48] Walking in Paris together, the two men suddenly found themselves on the edge of an open manhole. Looking up, they saw the cover of *La Révolution surréaliste* outside a nearby bookshop, with the two workers poised in exactly the same situation. They bought the magazine and, upon their return to Yugoslavia, became leading members of a Surrealist group there. If today we can only examine *La Révolution surréaliste* in the museum or the library, in 1928 it could be found fluttering on the street – where an image such as this of the two workmen could re-enter real life and transform it.

There are many photographs of the Surrealists themselves threaded through their publications – enough to suggest these pictures were part of a highly conscious formation of group identity. This effect is most obvious in the first and last issues of *La Révolution surréaliste*, where whole pages are taken up by photographs of the (male) Surrealists grouped around a picture of a woman. In the first issue, this picture is a photograph of the anarchist Germaine Berton, who had recently assassinated Plateau, the leader of the extreme right-wing 'Camelots du roy';[49] in the last issue, a painting by Magritte of a female nude is surrounded by photomat images of the Surrealists with their eyes closed.[50] In addition, there were many photographs of individual Surrealists that served to dramatise their personae. Man Ray's formal portraits of group members, such as his photographs of Eluard, Péret and Desnos in *Nadja*, served this function as much as his group portraiture.[51]

Not all these individual pictures were so formal, however, and on other occasions, the connotations of the crudely-made snapshot were deliberately exploited. Perhaps the most extreme example was the photograph that appeared in issue no. 8 of *La Révolution surréaliste*, with the caption: 'Our Colleague Benjamin Péret Insulting a Priest' (figure 26).[52] This is a very famous image within the canon of Surrealism, highly expressive of the antagonistic aspect of the movement which revelled in pure insult. But it's hard to know what sort of photograph we are looking at. Is this a completely spontaneous picture, hastily snapped as the action unfolds? The photographer would have had to move very fast. Is it, on the other hand, a completely staged image, with Péret and the priest (a friend dressed up?) both acting out their roles for the camera? Again unlikely – and somewhat pointless. Perhaps the best estimate is to see this photo as a partly staged set-up, worked out between Péret and photographer, grabbed from behind a parked car and perhaps already intended for the pages of the magazine.[53]

Whatever its provenance, the image in itself is undistinguished. But in the

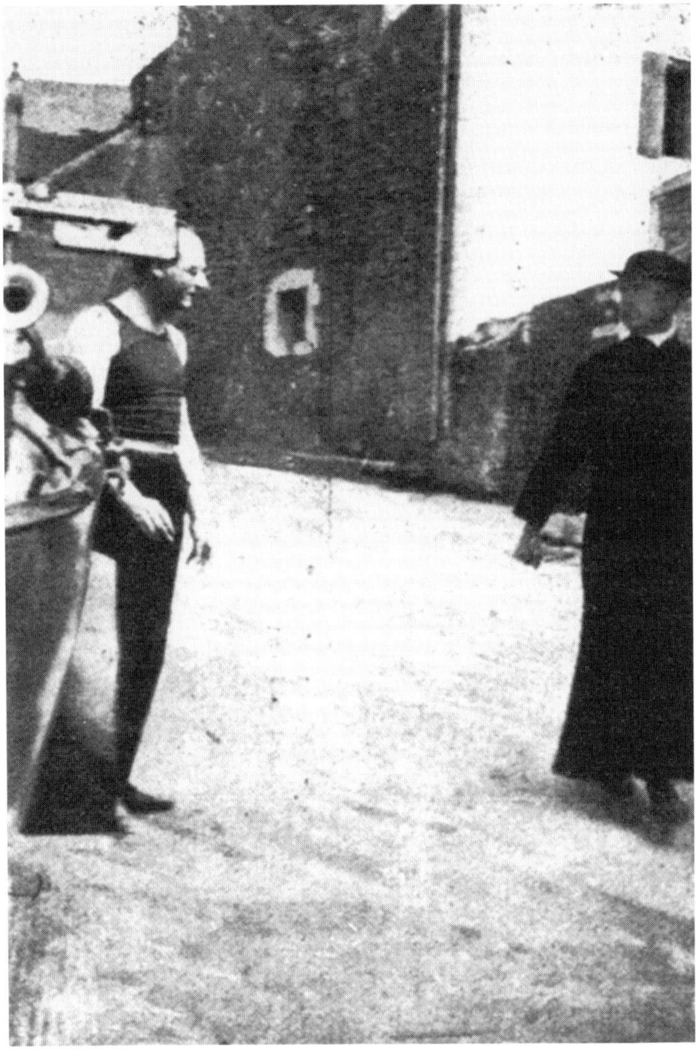

Fig 26 'Our Colleague Benjamin Péret Insulting a Priest', *La Révolution surréaliste*, 8 (1926).

context of what has already been said here about the images in *Nadja* and *La Révolution surréaliste*, one might see in the crudeness of the photograph another example of a willed and wilful insufficiency, an insistent dumbness.[54] We can't really tell what Péret is doing; perhaps the irony of recording a verbal attack through the silence of a still photograph was intentional. The empty space of a road, a wall and a window holds the centre of the image, squeezing both Péret and the anonymous priest out to the edge. That space is where the presumed insult hangs.

Inevitably, the power of this 'insult' has faded. Two recent popular critics – Robert Hughes and Greil Marcus – have both been rather disparaging about its potency and its relevance. Both acknowledge, however, how very different it must have seemed in 1926, Marcus commenting that it was the image that first attracted Buñuel to Surrealism, 'which only proves that at the right time and place the most marginal poetics – here, an ambiguous photo titled by fiat – can lead somewhere; in this case to *L'Age d'or*, which still changes lives'.[55] Given this historical placement, it is somewhat unjust of Robert Hughes to grant the image a status only as the 'forerunner of a thousand equally trivial actions that would be recorded on Polaroid or videotape by American artists in the seventies'.[56] The photograph must be seen in its context. To use the camera in this way had not occurred to Jacques Vaché when he waved a revolver in a crowded theatre or Arthur Cravan when he gave a lecture to the smartest New York society while taking his clothes off. Their actions remain undocumented, and all the more mythic for that. This gesture of Péret's, then, can be seen as a forerunner of those later performances which were enacted so as to be photographed – an example, perhaps, of the Surrealists' innovative use of the camera both to record and to construct events.[57]

But this is to consider the photograph as just a 'performance', merely art, which it was not. For Péret, it seems, insulting priests was a way of life. Nine years later, the Czech Surrealist Vítězslav Nezval met him on the Pont du Carrousel. Suddenly Péret started shouting 'Vache! vache!' and Nezval turned to see a(nother) priest crossing the bridge. Péret explained that 'he so detested religion that he was not able to hold himself back from making it known in a loud voice every time he met a priest or a nun'.[58] This repeated action is now represented by a single snapshot, a 'permanent revolution' within a small grey image.

These four individual photographs – a carnival, a blank façade, an open manhole and an insulted priest – did not stand alone in *La Révolution surréaliste*. They were not isolated, as they must be here, but rather were surrounded by other images and texts, by a complex web of poetics and politics. Only occasionally do the images in the magazine 'illustrate' the text in any conventional sense; equally, though, they are rarely quite disconnected from the texts surrounding them. The relationship is usually more ambiguous, with a less tangible 'third meaning' being produced by the juxtaposition of image and text.

Many of the anonymous photographs that appeared in *La Révolution surréaliste* have an ambiguous status; we cannot now know where they came from or what violence has been done to their original meaning. As with the photograph of the two workmen, this can have a liberating effect, the image released to be read anew. (One might prefer *not* to know the source.) But four other photographs that appeared in *La Révolution surréaliste* have a different value. When these were published in 1926, they too were uncredited, retitled, *detournées* by the text around them. Now their status has shifted, for they had been made by a photographer who was very soon after to become famous, and whose fame was to increase steadily for the rest of the twentieth-century – Eugène Atget.

Notes

1 Louis Aragon, 'Introduction à 1930', *La Révolution surréaliste*, 12 (15 December 1929), 62.

2 Dawn Ades, *Dada and Surrealism Reviewed* (London: Arts Council of Great Britain, 1978), p. 189.

3 Pierre Naville, *L'Espérance mathématique: Vol. I: Le temps du surréal* (Paris: Galilée, 1977), p. 104.

4 André Breton, *Conversations: The Autobiography of Surrealism* (New York: Paragon House, 1993), p. 83.

5 Interview with the author (Paris: 1979).

6 Most of the images by Man Ray have since appeared under his name in other publications. The credits on the cover of the magazine include a general attribution: 'Photos: Man Ray'.

7 Dawn Ades, 'Photography and the Surrealist Text', in Rosalind Krauss and Jane Livingston (eds), *L'Amour fou* (Washington: Corcoran Gallery/New York: Abbeville Press, 1985), p. 159; she specifically refers to an essay by Max Morise: 'Les yeux enchantés', *La Révolution surréaliste*, 1 (1 December 1924), 26–7.

8 Pierre Naville, 'Beaux Arts', *La Révolution surréaliste*, 3 (15 May 1925), 27. This translation is based on that in Ades, 'Photography and the Surrealist Text', p. 160.

9 *La Révolution surréaliste*, 2 (15 January 1925), 30.

10 In the same text, though, Bataille does express his admiration for the work of Man Ray, Atget and Boiffard. This brief essay was probably written as a review of an exhibition of photography at the Galerie d'art contemporain, but was unpublished at the time. It was finally printed in Georges Bataille, *Oeuvres complètes, Vol. II: Ecrits posthumes, 1922–1940* (Paris: Gallimard, 1970), p. 122.

11 Guy Debord, *Society of the Spectacle* (London: Rebel Press, 1987), chapter 1, paragraph 1.

12 Jonathan Crary, 'Spectacle, Attention, Counter-Memory', *October*, 50 (Autumn 1989), 97–107.

13 T. J. Clark, *The Painting of Modern Life: Paris in the Art of Manet and his Followers* (Princeton: Princeton University Press, 1984).

14 In his *Comments on the Society of the Spectacle* (London: Verso, 1990), p. 13, Debord writes 'the society of the spectacle has continued to advance. It moves quickly for in 1967 it had barely forty years behind it, though it had used them to the full'.

15 Crary, 'Spectacle, Attention, Counter-Memory', 106.

16 Fernand Léger, 'The Spectacle: Light, Color, Moving Image, Object-Spectacle', in Edward Fry (ed.), *Functions of Painting* (London: Thames and Hudson, 1965), p. 35.

17 Crary, 'Spectacle, Attention, Counter-Memory', 106.

18 *Ibid.*, 107.

19 Walter Benjamin, 'Surrealism, the Last Snapshot of the European Intelligentsia', in *One-Way Street* (London: New Left Books, 1979), p. 231. For the full quotation, see Chapter 3. Following Benjamin, the concept of the 'outmoded' has become important for theorisations of Surrealism; see, for example, Hal Foster, *Compulsive Beauty* (Cambridge, MA: MIT Press, 1993), chapter 6: 'Outmoded Spaces', pp. 157–92. The term is an anglicisation of the French *démodé*, but that carries the slightly different connotation of 'old-fashioned'; as Foster notes (p. 159), the German word used by Benjamin – *veraltet* – is closer to 'obsolete'.

I return to the outmoded in discussing the work of Atget in Chapter 5.

20 As Simon Sadler notes, '*Détournement* can be translated most simply as "diversion", though at the loss of the nuances encoded in the original French – "rerouting", "hijacking", "embezzlement", "misappropriation", "corruption", all acts implicit in the situationist use of society's "preexisting aesthetic elements"' (*The Situationist City* (Cambridge, MA: MIT Press, 1998), p. 17).

21 On *A Propos de Nice*, see P. E. Salles Gomes, *Jean Vigo* (London: Secker and Warburg, 1972), pp. 55–68, and John M. Smith, *Jean Vigo* (London: November Books, 1972), pp. 21–63. Vigo's relationship with Surrealism was ambivalent; friends with Buñuel and Painlevé, he does not seem to have had any direct connection with the Surrealist group more generally. For a reading of the connections between Surrealism and a later Vigo film, see Marina Warner, *L'Atalante* (London: British Film Institute, 1993), pp. 41–6.

22 Peter Stallybrass and Allon White, in *The Politics and Poetics of Transgression* (London: Methuen, 1986), p. 177, note that 'in 1873 the famous Nice carnival was taken over by a "comité des fêtes", brought under bureaucratic bourgeois control and reorganised quite self-consciously as a tourist attraction'.

23 The central figure in the carnival photograph is a giant mermaid. Fifteen pages later, there is a film still in which a young woman, wrapped only in a shower curtain, greets a perplexed Buster Keaton. She is a more popular, even parodic, version of the siren, a Surrealist icon of woman that will find its fullest expression in the image of Jacqueline Lamba as 'L'Ondine', photographed by Rogi André for *L'Amour fou* (*Mad Love* (Lincoln: University of Nebraska, 1987), p. 62). (Though the film still is untitled, it is from *One Week* (1920) and Keaton's co-star is Sybil Seely.) Buster Keaton was a Surrealist favourite; see the review by Luis Buñuel of *College* in Paul Hammond (ed.), *The Shadow and its Shadow* (London: British Film Institute, 1978), pp. 34–5, and more recently and at greater length, Robert Benayoun, *The Look of Buster Keaton* (New York: St. Martin's Press, 1983).

24 Mikhail Bakhtin, *Rabelais and his World* (Cambridge, MA: MIT Press, 1968); the text was in fact written in the 1940s and first published in the USSR in 1965. For a discussion of Bakhtin's influence, see Stallybrass and White, *The Politics and Poetics of Transgression*, especially pp. 6–26. For a connection between the 'carnivalesque' and Surrealism, see Susan Rubin Suleiman, *Subversive Intent: Gender, Politics and the Avant-Garde* (New Haven: Harvard University Press, 1990), pp. 142ff.

25 Stallybrass and White, *The Politics and Poetics of Transgression*, p. 7.

26 Terry Eagleton, *Walter Benjamin: Towards a Revolutionary Criticism* (London: Verso, 1981), p. 148.

27 Bakhtin, *Rabelais and his World*, p. 7.

28 *La Révolution surréaliste*, 12 (15 December 1929), 25.

29 André Thirion, *Revolutionaries without Revolution* (London: Cassell, 1975), p. 189.

30 The centrality of this word within the photograph is reminiscent of the way that words or phrases appear in Boiffard's photographs in *Nadja* (see Chapter 3, n. 18).

31 René Char, *Le Marteau sans maître* (Paris: José Corti, 1945); the book has had several subsequent editions and is still in print.

32 Virginia A. La Charité, *The Poetics and the Poetry of René Char* (Chapel Hill: University of North Carolina Press, 1968), p. 45. Char was a constant reviser of his work and many of

his Surrealist poems were changed for the 1934 and 1945 editions of *Le Marteau sans maître*. La Charité lists the variations in an appendix.

33 Jean Claude Mathieu, *La Poèsie de René Char: Vol. I – Traversée du surréalisme* (Paris: José Corti, 1984), pp. 83–90.

34 My thanks to Yves Abrioux for his elucidation of the complexities of this poem and also the connotations of 'Maison-attentat'.

35 Mathieu, *La Poèsie de René Char*, p. 89.

36 In *Le Marteau sans maître*, it is 'Arsenal': XVIII, p. 36.

37 'Maison' (as in 'maison close') is, in French, a brothel. It can also be a firm or business, where it would usually be followed by the family name of the firm's owner (here, 'La Maison Fortune').

38 This copy was later acquired by Yvonne Zervos and is now in the Bibliothèque Jacques Doucet, Paris. Mathieu, *La Poèsie de René Char*, pp. 83–90, notes some of the other annotations in the book. Two other copies of the book are in the Bibliothèque Nationale, Paris, and in the Library of the Museum of Modern Art, New York (from the collection of Paul Eluard). The copies vary in the addition of a collage that was individually pasted over the last photograph in the book by Breton and Eluard.

39 The biography of Char by Philippe Castellin (*René Char* (Paris: Editeur les Evidents, 1989)), reproduces several of the photographs from *Le tombeau des secrets*, but without citing them in its text; the 'Maison-attentat' is on p. 82.

40 *La Révolution surréaliste*, 2 (15 January 1925).

41 *La Révolution surréaliste*, 9–10 (1 October 1927). The term 'muse' is from Roger Cardinal and Robert Stuart Short, *Surrealism: Permanent Revelation* (London: Studio Vista, 1970), p. 22.

42 Cited by J. H. Matthews, *An Introduction to Surrealism* (University Park: Pennsylvania State University Press, 1965), p. 67.

43 André Breton, *Manifestoes of Surrealism* (Ann Arbor: University of Michigan, 1969), p. 143.

44 On the cover of *La Révolution surréaliste*, 4 (15 July 1925), the phrase 'Et Guerre au travail' acts as the caption for a photograph of a fashion mannequin by Man Ray.

45 Collected in book form in José Pierre (ed.), *Investigating Sex* (London: Verso, 1992).

46 This translation is from Mary Ann Caws, *The Poetry of Dada and Surrealism* (Princeton: Princeton University Press, 1970), p. 165, where the passage it comes from is analysed in detail (p. 166). The poem was originally published in Paul Eluard, *La vie immédiate* (Paris: Gallimard, 1932).

47 Solarisation is a process where a flash of light is applied to the image during development to create sharp edges and a grey fogginess. It was used by Man Ray mainly on nudes and portraits. Raoul Ubac exploited solarisation in the late 1930s, when he also developed the technique of 'bas-relief', the creation of a three-dimensional effect by slightly offsetting a positive and a negative image. The 'Rayograph' was Man Ray's version of the cameraless image or 'photogram', made directly by placing objects on the photographic paper.

48 Edouard Jaguer, *Les mystères de la chambre noire* (Paris: Flammarion, 1982), p. 20.

49 *La Révolution surréaliste*, 1 (1 December 1924), 17.

50 *La Révolution surréaliste*, 12 (15 December 1929), 72. For more information on this image,

see Chapter 1, n. 38.

51 An example of another use of portraiture was in *La Révolution surréaliste*, 3 (15 April 1925), 8–9, where a text by Robert Desnos, 'Pamphlet contre Jerusalem', was accompanied by a photograph of a young boy at his communion; though the image was uncaptioned, this was Desnos himself (see Marie-Claire Dumas, *Robert Desnos ou l'exploration des limites* (Paris: Librarie Klincksieck, 1980), p. 20). The text is an attack on Zionism, which gives the use of this particular photograph an edge of sarcasm.

52 *La Révolution surréaliste*, 8 (1 December 1926), 13.

53 The opposition between a documentary photograph and a staged photograph, once so common, has now become blurred and in some ways untenable. Snapshots have always been ambiguous in this respect; many of them are in fact highly directed, but this does not affect their personal value as 'documents'.

54 See also Chapter 3 on *Nadja*.

55 Greil Marcus, *Lipstick Traces* (London: Secker and Warburg, 1989), pp. 311–12.

56 Robert Hughes, *Shock of the New* (London: BBC Books, 1980), p. 249.

57 For an analysis of how performance artists such as Yves Klein and Joseph Beuys have used photography in their work, see David Briers, 'Some Notes on the Relation of Photography/Performance', *Creative Camera*, 238 (December 1984), 1627–9.

58 Vítězslav Nezval, *Rue Gît-le-Coeur* (Paris: Editions de l'Aube, 1988), pp. 31–2.

5
A Surrealist Atget

In 1926, Man Ray introduced into *La Révolution surréaliste* four images by another, very different photographer – Eugène Atget. Seventy-five years later, Atget is one of the most famous of photographers, whose work seems to form a bridge between nineteenth-century topographical photography and twentieth-century modernism. That fame, though, only began to accumulate after Atget's death in 1927, when a number of different factions within modernist photography each came to claim him for their own cause. The construction of a 'Surrcalist Atget' was a significant part of that shift in reputation, but it was the later phase of a Surrealist interest in Atget's work first evident prior to his death with the publication of those four pictures.

This initial appearance of Atget's pictures in a Surrealist context was however anonymous and unremarked upon at the time: three photographs unobtrusively slid into issue no. 7 of *La Révolution surréaliste* in June 1926 and one more in no. 8 the following December. Only in retrospect do these disparate images stand out as being by 'Atget', their presence inflected by his posthumous status as a master photographer. In 1926, they would have looked very different – decontextualised single images, 'spectacles' (in Naville's modest sense) with no authorial connotations.

Although only four photographs by Atget were actually reproduced in the magazine, it also published several other images similar to his. In some cases, indeed, the resemblance has led to misattribution.[1] Partly this has to do with the repertory of images – deserted streets, *terrains vagues* and shop window displays – which Atget and the Surrealists shared. But it is also an effect of how this urban iconography is represented. What we might now call an 'Atgetian' aesthetic – the everyday recorded with such understated directness that it comes to seem haunting, somehow inexplicable – can be found throughout early Surrealist practice, and was allied to the impulse that gave *La Révolution surréaliste* its air of ascetic formality.[2]

Eugène Atget lived on the same street as Man Ray (the Rue Campagne-

Fig 27 (right) Cover of *La Révolution surréaliste*, 7 (1926), with uncredited photograph by Eugène Atget.

Nº 7 — Deuxième année 15 Juin 1926

LA RÉVOLUTION SURRÉALISTE

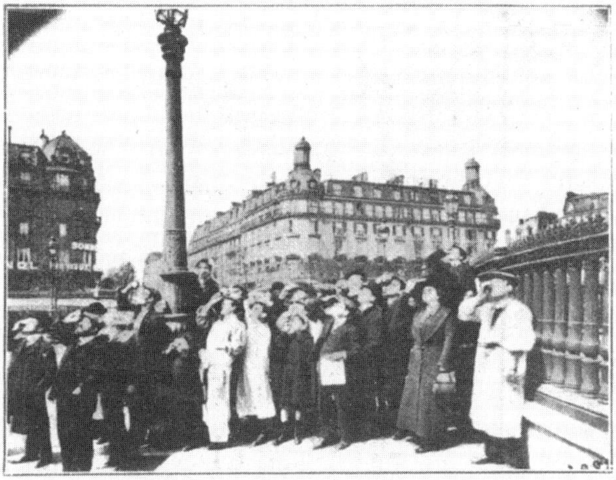

LES DERNIÈRES CONVERSIONS

SOMMAIRE

ADMINISTRATION : 42, Rue Fontaine, PARIS (IXe)

ABONNEMENT, les 12 Numéros :
France : 55 francs
Étranger : 75 francs

Dépositaire général : Librairie GALLIMARD
15, Boulevard Raspail, 15
PARIS (VIIe)

LE NUMÉRO :
France : 5 francs
Étranger : 7 francs

Première in Montparnasse) and had been photographing Paris and its environs for over twenty-five years before Man Ray 'discovered' him in the early 1920s.[3] Man Ray bought a number of prints from Atget,[4] and arranged for the appearance of his pictures in *La Révolution surréaliste*. Man Ray later stated that it was Atget who asked that the pictures should be used anonymously: 'he said: "Don't put my name on it. These are simply documents that I make." You see, he didn't want any publicity.'[5] This suggests that Atget was at least unconcerned about, and possibly dismissive of, this use of his pictures. However, given the standard practice of *La Révolution surréaliste*, it's doubtful whether the magazine's editors would have wished to credit them anyway.

The first of the three photographs by Atget in issue no. 7 of *La Révolution surréaliste* appears on the cover and shows a crowd of people standing looking up towards the left corner of the image (figure 27).[6] In fact, they are gazing at the eclipse of the sun, an untypically newsworthy event for Atget to photograph.[7] The title added by the Surrealists gives a different explanation for what the crowd is looking at: 'The Last Conversions'. The image thus takes its place in a range of Surrealist jibes at Catholicism, with the additional edge that here it is a crowd of ordinary Parisians in a recognisably ordinary Paris who seem to be engaged in some form of mass hysteria. Moreover, in the top corner towards which the crowd are looking, the tipped-up lens of Atget's camera has created a penumbra of black which acts as an ironic metaphor for the eclipsed sun – or the coming miracle.[8]

Inside the magazine, there are two more Atget photographs. On page 6, an image of a corset shop is inserted into an account of a dream by Marcel Noll (figure 28). In the dream, Noll is a courtier during the Revolution; he is in love with the King's daughter Augustina, who in turn is in love with the Marquis de Sade! At one point in the story, he rescues her from a mob that have attacked her; she is 'almost nude, her back covered in the traces of blows from a riding-whip'. Atget's image of the corsetted dummies interacts with this surrounding dream-recitation to become dreamlike itself; one reads across from text to image and the photograph also becomes charged with connotations of sexuality and violence (including, because of the Revolutionary setting, decapitation), connotations indeed of 'Sadism'.

The third image by Atget in this issue (p. 18) also carried an oblique association with the Ancien Regime. This is one of his photographs of prostitutes; the woman is small in the centre of the frame, standing in front of a large doorway (figure 29). Again, there is a connection between the image and the surrounding text by René Crevel, which is set in a seaside port peopled by, among others, prostitutes. However, the multicultural environment that Crevel evokes is very different from that depicted in the photograph, which is simply entitled 'Versailles'. Atget's bluntly factual caption had caused Man Ray some

Fig 28 (right) Page from *La Révolution surréaliste*, 7 (1926), with uncredited photograph by Eugène Atget.

de la liberté, nous garderons intacte l'étrange espérance que nous ont donné ses premières œuvres. Nous les interrogerons tant que nous vivrons, sans que l'embarrassante personne de leur auteur parvienne à nous en détourner. C'est là-même, nous en sommes toujours aussi sûrs, à l'heure prévue pour l'arrivée de ce train, à cette heure qui ne peut tarder, c'est parmi ces arcades et quand se sera calmé le vent qui monte abominable de la terre à lancer verticalement le rouge des oriflammes, que le livre dont nous avons si longtemps contemplé la reliure muette s'ouvrira au feuillet marqué. C'est seulement alors qu'en signes fulgurants se précisera pour tous le sens, je crois extrêmement particulier, de notre intervention. Car *nous ne sommes pas*, dans la littérature et dans l'art. Toute notre impatience vient de ce que nous savons qu'un jour, en ayant bien fini avec tous ceux qu'on nous compare encore, nous aurons seuls à *intervenir.*

André Breton.

RÊVES

Marcel Noll :

I

C'est la révolution. Le matin de ce jour Sade a été conduit en prison par un détachement de chevaux-légers. Le roi (dont je suis un des conseillers), sa suite et la majeure partie du peuple qui lui est restée fidèle, habitent un ensemble de vieilles maisons (apparemment l'Hôpital Civil de Strasbourg) qui, entourées d'un haut mur et protégées de tourelles composent la résidence royale.

Sans l'avoir vue encore, je sais que je dois aimer la fille du roi, Augustina, qui admire et estime hautement le marquis de Sade qu'elle a vainement protégé contre les poursuites de son père.

Je suis avec le roi et deux de ses conseillers dans une pièce carrée dont l'unique fenêtre domine la route nationale. Accoudé à cette fenêtre, j'assiste à cette scène : quelques cavaliers accourent au trot, se dirigeant vers la résidence, sans doute pour y rendre compte d'une mission remplie. Une jeune fille que je reconnais aussitôt pour être Augustina, s'élance vers eux et tente d'arrêter les chevaux. Mais elle est bientôt traînée à terre et maltraitée par les cavaliers. Me rendant compte du danger couru par la jeune fille, je veux m'élancer au dehors pour la secourir. Mais le roi, devinant mon projet, ordonne à ce moment à toutes les personnes présentes de s'agenouiller à l'effet de prier. Fou de colère, je sors mon revolver et le décharge à plusieurs reprises sur le roi. Celui-ci part d'un énorme éclat de rire et me fait savoir que la meilleure façon qu'il avait de me punir était de me laisser tranquille. Il me tient une sorte de discours où revient constamment le sens de cette phrase : « La prison ou la mort ne sont pas pour les amoureux. »

Pendant ce temps, la jeune fille a eu la force de se traîner jusqu'à notre porte. Elle est poursuivie par toute la populace de la résidenc qui l'injurie et la menace de mort. J'ai grande peine à laisser entrer Augustina et à empêchee les manifestants d'envahir la pièce. J'y réussis pourtant, et bientôt, devant moi, se tient la jeune fille, presque nue, le dos couvert des traces de coups de cravache. Je remarque quelques ecchymoses sur son sein droit. Elle m'enlace sans mot dire.

Des servantes s'empressent bientôt autour d'Augustina pour lui laver les blessures qui disparaissent aussitôt sans laisser de traces. Durant tout le temps que durent ces opérations, je suis muet, en admiration devant la

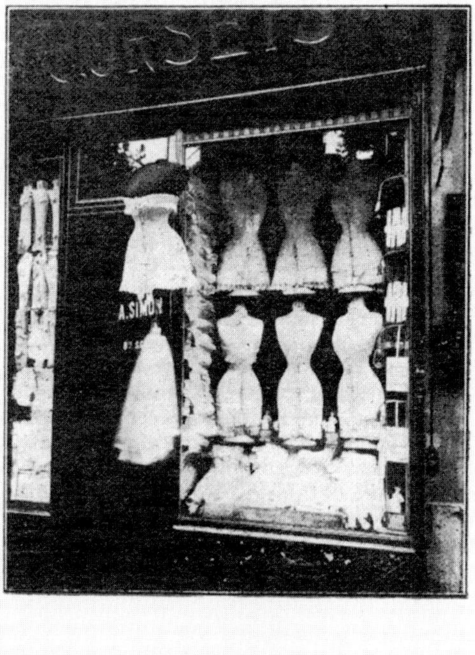

28 LE PONT DE LA MORT

ne sont pas de couleur noire. Et elle, inspirée, tandis qu'elle nettoyait ce qu'elle-même avait gâté, trouvait de quoi séduire. Elle s'emparait de l'étranger, se pavanait à son bras et avec lui, revenue jusqu'à son taudis, montrait des dents si blanches, que dames putains, ses collègues, frissonnaient dans leurs chiffons roses.

Les marins qui avaient assisté à tout ce manège riaient à grands coups. Ils étaient connaisseurs en bons tours et, par exemple, savaient comment pour quelques centaines de francs, sous prétexte d'une traversée à prix réduit, on persuade aux Africains qui apprendrait la peur de la chaleur aux fils du soleil ? — de se laisser rôtir près d'une chaufferie. Le bateau rendu au port, il suffisait de déboulonner les plaques de tôle qui tenaient prisonniers ces passagers spéciaux. Simple histoire, des hommes bruns sont devenus des hommes bleus. Grâce à des pierres qui remplacent dans leurs pauvres poches l'arc-en ciel plat des portefeuilles marocains, leur corps prend avec du poids une discrétion suffisante pour qu'on les laisse doucement, doucement glisser jusqu'au centre même de cette obscurité clapotante, qui dans quelques heures, à l'aube, pour les poissons et les navigateurs redeviendra la mer, la vie.

Or, quel soir ? Enfin, les prostituées ont compris que les pieds n'étaient pas faits pour des tortures de velours noir mais pour une nudité de peau à même une nudité de sable. Alors les talons, sur lesquels, depuis des siècles, elles chaviraient, tous les talons se sont brisés, et des fleurs sans semence ont jailli du macadam. Parce que nul mensonge ne pouvait plus être toléré, fût-il celui si mince des semelles de ficelle, les voyous ont jeté plus loin que l'horizon leurs espadrilles. Eclatez couleurs. Les criminels ont les mains bleues. Et vous, filles, si vous voulez des bouches rouges, passez sur vos lèvres le doigt taché de vos dernières amours. Au font des océans, tous les Africains crédules qui voulurent faire des voyages à bon compte et moururent près des chaufferies, ressuscitent. Sans doute bientôt seront-ils poissons, puisque déjà leurs jambes deviennent transparentes. Ecoutez leurs chansons sans mot, à la lumière des monstres électriques Les hyppocampes appuient sur leur nombril, comme sur le bouton d'une sonnette électrique. Est-ce pour le thé? Mais non, Des forêts d'eau, ils montent, points d'interrogation à tête de cheval, jusqu'aux yeux des savants européens, qui éclatent dans leur peau terrestre. Le vaisseau fantôme écrit sa danse en plein ciel. Les murs s'écartent entre lesquels on voulut enchaîner les vents de l'esprit. Derrière les plis d'un velours trop lourdement paisible s'allume un soleil de soufre et d'amour. Les hommes du monde entier se comprennent par le nez. Un geyser imprévu envoie au diable des pierres dont on a tenté d'habiller le sol. Il y a un pont de la planète minuscule à la liberté.

Du pont de la mort, venez voir, venez tous voir la fête qui s'allume. René Crevel.

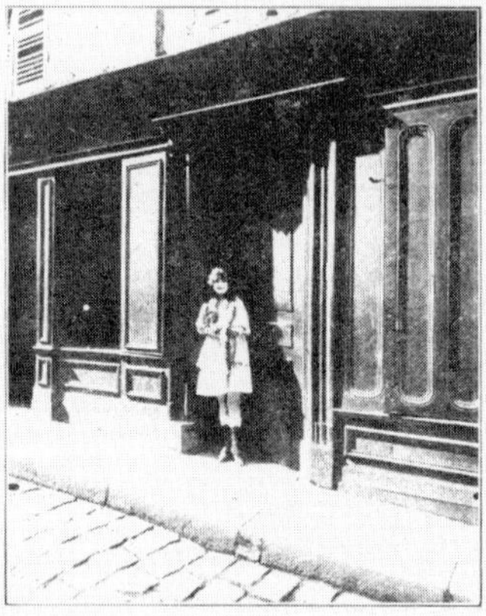

VERSAILLES

Fig 29 Extract from René Crevel, 'Le Pont de la mort', *La Révolution surréaliste*, 7 (1926), with uncredited photograph by Eugène Atget.

amusement at what he considered Atget's naivety.[9] It was taken over in *La Révolution surréaliste* and converted to an ironic iconoclasm, for that single word must conjure up the contrasting grandeur of the Sun King's palace, somewhere not far away outside the picture.

A fourth image by Atget appeared in the next issue of *La Révolution surréaliste*: a photograph of an elaborate balustrade descending a curving staircase (figure 30).[10] How Atget himself thought of such a structure can be surmised from the text accompanying a similar image in his own album *L'Art dans le vieux Paris*: 'Rue Charlot, 83 (3rd Arrt) – Hotel de Marquis de Mascarini (disappeared). Splendid extension, wrought iron, of the Hotel staircase'.[11] The caption is tersely factual, with hints of delight ('splendid') and regret ('disappeared'). In *La Révolution surréaliste*, Atget's photograph of the balustrade was once more surrounded by a Surrealist text, this time by Paul

LES DESSOUS D'UNE VIE OU LA PYRAMIDE HUMAINE

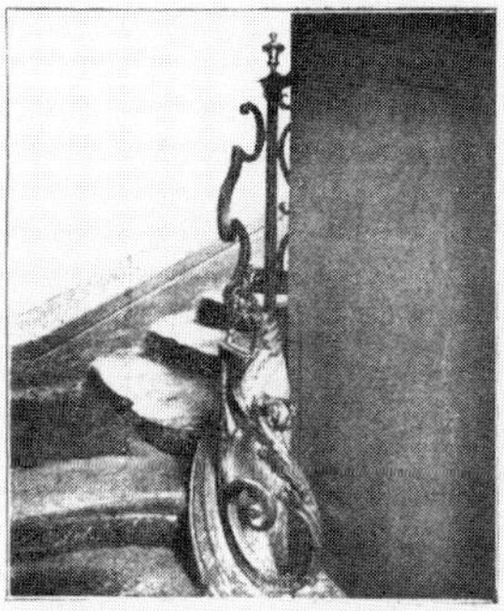

à Marcel Noll.

D'abord, un grand désir m'était venu de solennité et d'apparat. J'avais froid. Tout mon être vivant et corrompu aspirait à la rigidité et à la majesté des morts. Je fus tenté ensuite par un mystère où les formes ne jouent aucun rôle. Curieux d'un ciel décoloré d'où les oiseaux et les nuages sont bannis. Je devins esclave de la faculté pure de voir, esclave de mes yeux irréels et vierges, ignorants du monde et d'eux-mêmes. Puissance tranquille. Je supprimai le visible et l'invisible, je me perdis dans un miroir sans tain. Indestructible, je n'étais pas aveugle.

LES CENDRES VIVANTES

Plus j'avance, plus l'ombre s'accroît. Je serai bientôt cerné par ses monuments détruits et ses statues abattues. Je n'arriverai jamais. Mes pensées orgueilleuses ont trop longtemps été liées au luxe de la lumière. Je déroule depuis trop longtemps la soie chatoyante de ma tête, tout ce turban avide de reflets et de compliments. Il n'y a qu'une façon maintenant de sortir de cette obscurité : lier mon ambition à la misère simple, vivre toute ma vie sur le premier échelon nocturne, à peine au-dessus de moi, à peine celui des oiseaux de nuit. Détaché de cette terre, de cette ombre qui m'ensevelit. Le ciel a la couleur de la poussière.

•

Trois heures du matin. Un cortège, des cris, des chants, des armes, des torches, des brutes. Je suis, je suis obligé de suivre je ne sais quel pacha, quel padishah sonore. J'ai trop sommeil et je me révolte. Je mérite la mort. Mange ton pain sur la voiture qui te mène à l'échafaud, mange ton pain tranquillement. J'ai déjà dit que je n'attendais plus l'aube. Comme moi, la nuit est immortelle.

Dans un bouge ma mère m'apporte un livre, un si beau livre. Je l'ouvre et je crache dedans. Ma fille est assise en face de moi, aussi calme que la bougie.

•

La nuit des chiffonniers. Je tiendrai ma promesse de rendre visite aux chiffonniers. Leur maison brûle. Ces gens sont vraiment aimables. Je ne méritais pas tant d'honneur : leurs chevaux brûlent. On cherche dans les fossés les trésors que l'on doit m'offrir. Que le feuillage invisible est beau. J'ai fait un geste incompréhensible, j'ai mis ma main en visière sur mes yeux.

L'AUBE IMPOSSIBLE

« Le grand enchanteur est mort !
et ce pays d'illusion s'est effacé. »
YOUNG

C'est par une nuit comme celle-ci que je me sais privé du langage pour prouver mon amour et que j'ai eu affaire à une sourde.

C'est par une nuit comme celle-ci que j'ai cueilli sur la verdure perpendiculaire des framboises blanches comme du lait, du dessert pour cette amoureuse de mauvaise volonté.

C'est par une nuit comme celle-ci que j'ai régné sur des rois et des reines alignés dans un couloir de craie. Ils ne devaient leur taille qu'à la perspective et si les premiers étaient gigantesques, les derniers, au loin, étaient si petits que d'avoir un corps visible, ils semblaient taillés à facettes.

C'est par une nuit comme celle-ci que je les ai laissé mourir, ne pouvant leur donner

Fig 30 Extract from Paul Eluard, 'Les Dessous d'une vie ou la pyramide humaine', *La Révolution surréaliste*, 8 (1926), with uncredited photograph by Eugène Atget.

Eluard. Entitled 'The Underside of a Life or The Human Pyramid', it is a sequence of poetic fragments: 'All my living and corrupted being aspires to the rigidity and the majesty of the dead. I was tempted then by a mystery where forms played no role ... I suppressed the visible and the invisible, I lost myself in an unsilvered mirror.' These phrases do not relate directly to the image, but the staircase now potentially descends towards 'the Underside' through an atmosphere where its 'rigidity' strikes a line through an unformed space both 'visible' and 'invisible'.

Once resited within a Surrealist context, it was possible for oblique connections to be discerned with other Surrealist works. When Julien Levy, a young American newly arrived in Paris, saw the photograph of the balustrade in *La Révolution surréaliste*, it reminded him of a Surrealist painting by Pierre Roy of a snake slithering down a staircase: *Danger on the stairs* (figure 31).[12] So the

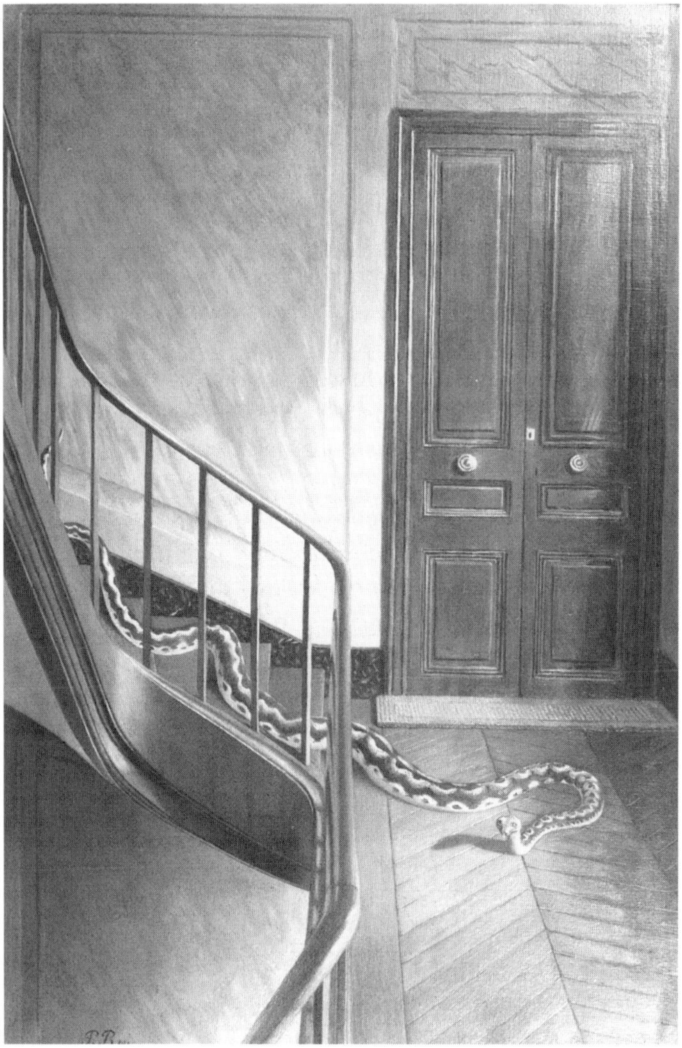

Fig 31 Pierre Roy, *Danger on the stairs*, 1927 or 1928. The Museum of Modern Art, New York. © ADAGP, Paris and DACS, London, 2001.

metal balustrade becomes yet more animate, 'serpentine', and the space around it filled with a silent threat.[13] Some fifty-five years later, in his book on Surrealist photography, Edouard Jaguer read across from Atget's image of hanging corsets to André Breton's poem 'Le Corset Mystère',[14] a connection which Jaguer admitted may be quite arbitrary, but which was made plausible within the context of several generations of males who had still been 'born in the time of corsets'.[15] One cannot know if either of the connections made by Levy or Jaguer had already been considered by the Surrealists themselves but, even though these are 'second order' readings, one can surmise that such elusive, sidelong meanings are indeed what they also found in Atget's images in 1926.

The selection of Atget's photographs and the way they are positioned within

La Révolution surréaliste suggests that what the early Surrealists particularly valued in these pictures was the appearance of the outmoded: the nineteenth-century ironwork, the display of corsets, the evocation of Versailles, perhaps even the scene in the Place de la Bastille. (To us, there may be little difference between such a scene in 1912, when the picture was shot, and 1926, when it was reproduced; in the fourteen-year gap, though, it may also have acquired the patina of a slight out-of-dateness, in the clothes worn by the crowd as well as in the photographic technology that Atget persisted in using.)

It was Walter Benjamin who best defined this taste of the Surrealists for the outmoded, writing of Breton: 'He was the first to perceive the revolutionary energies that appear in the "outmoded", in the first iron constructions, the first factory buildings, the earliest photos, the objects that have begun to be extinct, grand pianos, the dresses of five years ago, fashionable restaurants when the vogue has begun to ebb from them.'[16] Jonathan Crary's suggestion that this was part of the Surrealist resistance to the encroachment of the 'spectacle' is important here,[17] and may indeed be applied to Benjamin's own revolutionary project. As Dan Graham has commented, 'Benjamin wished to demonstrate that for his generation slightly out-of-date – just-past – objects of mass culture possessed a latent revolutionary power, a notion he developed from surrealism ... For Benjamin, this was one way in which "the commodity dream" might be broken'. This process would reveal 'an actual though hidden past, mostly eradicated from consciousness but briefly available in moments of dreams, hallucinations, stoppages etc'.[18]

And, one might add, in photographs such as these by Atget, though in fact Benjamin himself does not specify that connection. Indeed, he claimed that the value of Atget's work lay above all in the removal of what he famously called 'aura': 'He [Atget] was the first to disinfect the stifling atmosphere generated by conventional portrait photography in the age of decline. He cleanses this atmosphere, indeed he dispels it altogether.'[19] In Benjamin's terms, it would seem that 'aura' is a stifling nostalgia, whereas the outmoded represents a more productive, critical use of the past. Yet it is now rather difficult to unpick the two elements – the 'aura' of a long gone Paris is in part created for us now by all those elements which Benjamin in 1929 read as outmoded. It is impossible today to know how Atget's pictures would have looked in the mid-1920s, for the passage of the century has pushed Atget even further into the past, and refilled his work with 'aura'. Partly this is to do with the look of the images – the soft glow of the warm sepia – and partly to do with our growing distance from the scenes that Atget photographed. But it is also an effect of the later cumulative readings of Atget's work (including, as we will see, Benjamin's own) which make it impossible to unpick the photographs themselves from the connotations they now carry.[20]

The appearance of four images in two issues of the same magazine would, in another career (that of Man Ray, for example), be a minor event. But, given the lack of any other publication or exhibition of Atget's work during his lifetime, the reproduction of these pictures in *La Révolution surréaliste* assumes an importance it might not otherwise have.[21] In this respect, also, it is impossible to put ourselves back in time to 1926. For the modern spectator, these pictures are authored, touched by genius, they are 'Atgets'. For most readers of the magazine at that point in time, these were just four more images that took their place among many similar found photographs used in the magazine.

What happened soon after Atget died – on 4 August 1927 – radically shifted the perception of his work. Atget left his archive to his close friend André Calmette, who placed two thousand negatives with the *Monuments Historiques*, where they presumably continued to be catalogued as neutral records of old Paris. However, the bulk of the images was bought by Man Ray's assistant, the young American photographer Berenice Abbott, who had come to know Atget in the last two years of his life. Abbott's response to the work was very different from that of Man Ray; in 1964, she remembered her first impression as 'the shock of realism unadorned'.[22]

In 1928, the year after Atget's death, pictures from Abbott's collection were shown in exhibitions in Paris and Brussels alongside work by the Parisian avant-garde – Man Ray, Krull, Kertész – and most reviews of the exhibitions referred to him as a forerunner of contemporary photography.[23] Two years later, in 1930, the first monograph of Atget's photographs was published simultaneously in Paris, Leipzig and New York, a selection of ninety-six images with an introduction written by Pierre MacOrlan.[24] Rather than a few isolated images, it was now Atget's larger *oeuvre* that was revealed and that revelation provided the ground for the construction of Atget as author.[25] When Walker Evans reviewed the 1930 book, he wrote that the poetry of these photographs was 'not "the poetry of the street" or "the poetry of Paris" but the projection of Atget's person'.[26]

In the process whereby Atget's images were transformed from anonymous documents to modernist masterpieces, the Surrealist interpretation was but one among many. Some other early writers on Atget concurred with Abbott's view of him as a realist – 'a Balzac of the camera'[27] – or perhaps a romantic like Gérard de Nerval 'who also loved the mysterious beauties of Paris'.[28] Other sitings of the work emphasised its objectivity and formal precision. In 1929, the photograph of the corset shop that had been reproduced in *La Révolution surréaliste* was the first image in the volume *photo-eye*, published to accompany the exhibition *film and foto* in Stuttgart.[29] Here, it was positioned as a preface to an anthology of the most radical photographic work of the age, from Russia, France and the United States as well as Germany itself, by photographers such as El Lissitsky, Man Ray, Edward Weston and Laszlo Moholy-Nagy. Thus Atget's work was placed firmly at the heart of the 'New Photography'.

The Surrealist response to Atget was less focused and must be excavated from a number of sites, both literary and visual. Two Surrealists wrote about Atget shortly after his death: Robert Desnos and Albert Valentin. Desnos had of course been a central member of the Parisian group through the 1920s, though at the time he wrote about Atget he was beginning to drift away.[30] By his own statement, he visited Atget once (arranged through Man Ray) and bought some prints; his protegé Alain Brieux remembered that in the 1930s one of these hung in Desnos's apartment.[31] Through the 1920s, Desnos also operated as a journalist,[32] publishing two magazine articles on Atget. In September 1928, he wrote a brief memoir for *Le Soir*, with the resonant title: 'Les Spectacles de la rue'; this was followed in May 1929 by a longer text in *Merle* which looked forward to the posthumous publication of Atget's work in book form.[33]

Albert Valentin was a Belgian novelist, associated with Surrealism between 1928 and 1931, when he was expelled for working on René Clair's film *A nous la liberté*. He was connected with both the French and Belgian groups and his photomontages were published in *La Révolution surréaliste* and *Variétés*.[34] It was in the latter journal that Valentin's essay on Atget was published in December 1928, along with a portfolio of Atget photographs discussed below.[35] Valentin's essay is longer than those by Desnos, more discursive and perhaps consciously emulating the fragmented and ironically philosophic tone of Breton or Aragon. There is no reference to Atget himself until nearly halfway through the text.

Yet if these texts by Desnos and Valentin are different in form, the stance of the two writers towards Atget is remarkably similar and might be indicative of a Surrealist position towards his work at the end of the 1920s, albeit with certain provisos. First, that attitude may not have extended very far into the group – we have no comments from Breton, Aragon or Eluard. Moreover, these posthumous statements by Desnos and Valentin in 1928–29 cannot be conflated with any particular attitude towards Atget prior to his death in 1927. Desnos indeed remarks that Atget needed to die before he was appreciated, even by the Surrealists, 'for whom, no doubt haunted by his ghost, the fabulous country reconstituted on the sensitive gelatin of the glass plates appears to its visitors in all its splendour'.[36] Only with Atget's death could the pictures float free, to be appropriated by the various camps then forming in modernist photography.

One persistent image of Atget, within and without Surrealism, was that of the *naif*. The Surrealists would not have intended any condescension here. They wished to erase the distinction between the self-conscious artist (such as themselves) and the artisan such as Atget whom the Surrealists viewed as an unwitting avant-gardist. Both Desnos and Valentin compared Atget to the obvious model of the Douanier Rousseau. This comparison was already common in the late 1920s; outside Surrealism, other writers on Atget such as Pierre MacOrlan and Waldemar George made the link.[37] But Desnos and Valentin placed this comparison next to more sophisticated references. Desnos wrote that Atget had 'the innocence of soul of a Douanier Rousseau, and the attention to detail of a Parisian *flâneur*',[38] while Valentin made reference to Rousseau alongside the 'poètes maudits', Rimbaud, Lautréamont and Nerval as rebels whether 'conscious or unconscious' against established order.[39]

In both his texts, Desnos listed a selection of Atget's images: 'He worked in the midst of a fabulous quantity of documents ... But what documents!'[40] (It is as if Desnos was responding to the comment that Man Ray was later to attribute to Atget himself – 'These are simply documents that I make' – but with an echo of Cézanne describing Monet as 'only an eye – but what an eye'.) He continued, 'Atget has photographed all of Paris with the marvellous objective of creating a dream and a surprise'.[41] Valentin's initial statement ran parallel to this sense of how Atget's photographs could be both factual and dreamlike, 'opening the way to that extraordinary cerebral landscape which has compelled our attention and which maintains an equilibrium between fact and dream'.[42] For both writers, the paradox was that Atget had been able to present not only exterior reality but also his own interior reality: 'his viewpoint of the world, determined by an apparently mechanical medium, is also the vision of his soul'.[43]

Although these evocations of the city as dreamscape strike many chords with the Surrealist sense of the urban, neither Desnos nor Valentin made this connection explicit. This was left to a writer from outside Surrealism, the art critic Waldemar George, who wrote about Atget on two occasions – in a short review of the Salon de l'Escalier exhibition in 1928 and as part of a longer text in the special number of *Arts et métiers graphiques* devoted to photography in 1930.[44] In these texts, George linked the work of de Chirico and Atget – the only major early writer to do so – and in his later essay, he also wrote: 'Before the Surrealist painters, Adget [*sic*] understood the potential and meaning of facts juxtaposed, confronting each other without any logical line to justify their juxtaposition. A quarter of a century before Louis Aragon, he wrote the *paysan de Paris*, while probing, while clearing away the waste rock, while stripping naked this immanent mystery that has for a name: banality.'[45] It's a reference that is elegant and trenchant, placing Atget's work in a very precise relation with fundamental Surrealist attitudes.

Both Desnos and Valentin were concerned with the image of Paris in Atget's work. For Desnos, the pictures bring out the marvellous inherent in everyday reality: 'His albums ... comprise the most fantastic dossier of marvels that our eyes can see each day but to which too often they do not pay attention.'[46] Both of Desnos's texts end on a note of flux and dissolution. In 1928, he concluded with a very grand image: 'The city dies. Its ashes are scattered. But the dream capital, created by Atget, raises its unconquerable ramparts under a gelatin sky.'[47] A year later he wrote more simply: 'Matter remains and form is lost'.[48] Desnos's reveries powerfully convey the sense in which Atget's images could take their place in the Surrealist notion of the urban, what Roger Cardinal has called the 'soluble city'.[49]

Valentin also referred to Atget's vision of the city, but not in such apocalyptic terms. He concentrated his attention on Atget's photographs of the edges of Paris – 'Those dead-end streets in the outlying neighbourhoods, those peripheral districts' (figure 32) – reading them as images of discomfort and threat: 'We experience a certain malaise in contemplating the world we discover in the ten

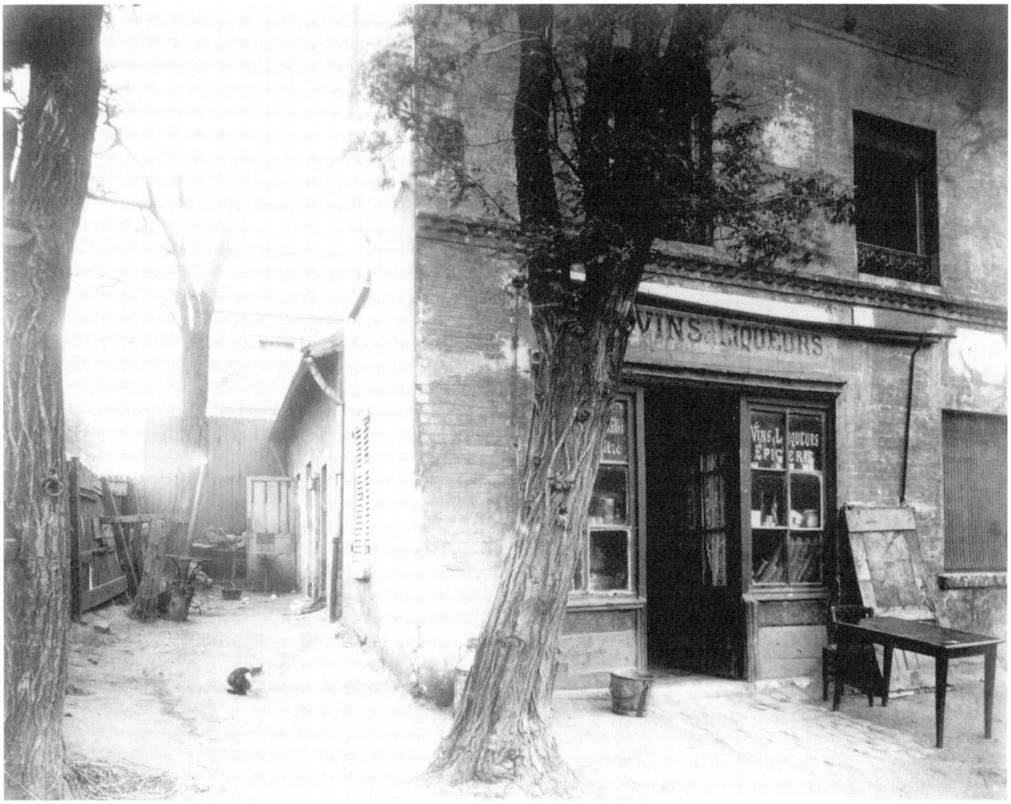

Fig 32 Eugène Atget, *Porte d'Ivry, impasse Masséna, 18 and 20 Boulevard Masséna*, *c.* 1907–8. © Photothèque des Musées de la Ville de Paris.

thousand plates Atget printed, although it is every inch our own.'[50] For Valentin, this quality resided in the sense that 'Everything has an air of taking place somewhere else, somewhere beyond'.

Valentin continued with a comparison with the work of another artist much admired by the Surrealists – the film-maker Louis Feuillade, who shot his exterior scenes in those same 'peripheral districts' which 'constituted the natural theatre for violent death, for melodrama'.[51] Valentin did not cite any specific films by Feuillade, but the most obvious reference for a Surrealist would of course be the crime serial *Fantômas*.[52] What made the connection significant was not only the way that Atget's pictures 'project a sense of imminence',[53] but also a feeling in both Atget and Feuillade for the disturbing poetry of the banal. Francis Lacassin's description of Feuillade's films suggests this very well: 'He had understood that nothing is more beautiful than a certain suburban poetry that emanates from disjointed paving stones, from working class districts, from a dismal suburb, silent and deserted, from vacant lots beyond which, at a distance, the blurred profiles of buildings under construction are silhouetted against the sky.'[54]

Desnos also referred to *Fantômas* in such a way as to suggest that the connection with Atget was being commonly made in Surrealist circles. In his second essay, he recalled Apollinaire's comment that *Fantômas* provided 'the exact description of the Paris of 1910', and proposed that Atget's photographs would provide 'the face of Paris during the same period'.[55] Indeed, in his earlier text, Desnos had suggested that Atget's photographs be used as illustrations for a re-publication of the original *Fantômas* books by Allain and Souvestre.[56] Another early critic, reviewing the Brussels exhibition for *Variétés* in 1928 and only signing his text as F. L., made a parallel comment when he wrote that Atget had 'unconsciously illustrated the modern police novel'.[57]

These connections woven around Atget's images later found a potent resolution in the most famous single statement on Atget's work – Walter Benjamin's much-quoted comment that Atget had photographed the streets as if they were the scene of a crime. In fact, Benjamin made this observation in two different essays. In 'A Small History of Photography' (1931), he wrote: 'Not for nothing have Atget's photographs been likened to those of the scene of the crime. But is not every square inch of our cities the scene of a crime? Every passer-by a culprit? Is it not the task of the photographer ... to reveal guilt and to point out the guilty in his pictures?'[58] In the later 'The Work of Art in the Age of Mechanical Reproduction' (1936), he said of Atget and his images of deserted city streets: 'It has been quite justly said of him that he photographed them like scenes of crimes. The scene of a crime, too, is deserted; it is photographed for the purposes of establishing evidence.'[59]

Benjamin's emphases were slightly different in each case – the first text emphasises a sense of collective social guilt missing from the second, while the detective-like role of the photographer slips from that of an accuser 'point[ing] out the guilty' to a more passive and functional provider of evidence. Nevertheless, the analogy was an extravagant one, and its melodrama has haunted Atget studies ever since. Writers now find themselves (as we saw previously with Annette Michelson)[60] backing away from it; indeed, there is an ambiguity in Benjamin's own choice of words, for the term he uses – 'tatort' – can mean 'scene of action' as well as 'scene of a crime'.[61] This ambiguity opens out the possible readings of Atget's images. Benjamin emphasises the sense that something *has* happened on this site, while Annette Michelson, for example, sees it also as the stage where something will or could happen. The photograph itself presents only a moment of time, from which the spectator can in imagination move forward or backward.

A close reading of Benjamin's texts, though, reinforces the sense that the idea of 'crime' was in his mind.[62] For his observations are couched in terms which seem to repeat or inflect a previously held opinion: 'It has been said ...', 'Atget's photographs have been likened to ...'. No such exact previous analogy can be found, but Benjamin was surely putting into different terms the link that Desnos, Valentin and F. L. had already made between Atget's photographs and contemporary crime fiction. Benjamin's phrasing suggests that, by the early 1930s, to make a comment of this kind about Atget's work was fairly commonplace.

Moreover, there is one other identifiable source lying behind Benjamin's remarks. An author who did write about both Atget and 'scene of the crime' photography, though not in the same place, was Pierre MacOrlan. MacOrlan's 1929 essay, 'Elements de fantastique social', was illustrated by an anonymous police photograph of a blood soaked bedroom;[63] the following year, he wrote the preface for the first book of Atget's work: *Atget: Photographe de Paris*. For MacOrlan, both the police photo and the work of Atget were manifestations of what he called the 'social fantastic' – a concept that has on occasion been conflated with a Surrealist viewpoint, though, as we will see, it has rather different connotations.[64] In addition, MacOrlan often wrote for the popular magazine *Détective*, and this is a connection that may also have been behind Benjamin's comment. Like its modern counterparts, *Détective* often featured photographs of deserted streets where the *frisson* lay in the knowledge of the awful crime that had been committed there. (Now such images carry a reverse effect; as Adrian Rifkin neatly puts it, 'a crime begins to look like the scene of an Atget'.[65])

It is not only in critical texts that one must look for this 'Surrealist Atget', but also in the influence his work exerted on the next generation of photographers. In 'A Small History of Photography', Benjamin wrote of Atget's photographs as 'the forerunners of surrealist photography', in the 'emancipation of object from aura'. He continued: 'When avant-garde periodicals like *Bifur* or *Variété* [*sic*] publish pictures captioned Westminster, Lille, Antwerp or Breslau but showing only details, here a balustrade, there a tree-top whose bare branches criss-cross a gas lamp, or a gable wall, or a lamp-post with a life-buoy bearing the name of the town – this is nothing but a literary refinement of themes that Atget discovered.'[66]

Benjamin's reference here is mainly to a couple of picture spreads in *Variétés* with the titles 'Paysages méconnus' and 'Mélancholie des villes'.[67] The photograph of the lifebuoy next to the Thames at Westminster is anonymous and the gable wall is most probably the frontage of an Amsterdam warehouse photographed by Germaine Krull (figure 33). (There is, though, also a picture of a half-demolished wall by Eli Lotar and a wall next to the sea by Michel Seuphor (figure 34).) The balustrade is at Versailles and was photographed by Herbert Bayer and the bare tree and gas-lamp are in a picture by Maurice Tabard entitled 'Paysage' in the rival magazine *Bifur*.[68]

These were indeed the photographers who learned from Atget, though Benjamin was unjust in suggesting that their projects were the same as Atget's had been. The formalism and sense of estrangement in their work was wilful and deliberate. Some of these photographers are important figures in the narrative of Surrealist documentary, but what Benjamin noticed, and what remains striking today, was not the individual images but their grouping together in *Variétés*, where photographs from cities across Europe and America are brought together to create a complex multilayered sense of urban *ennui*. These two

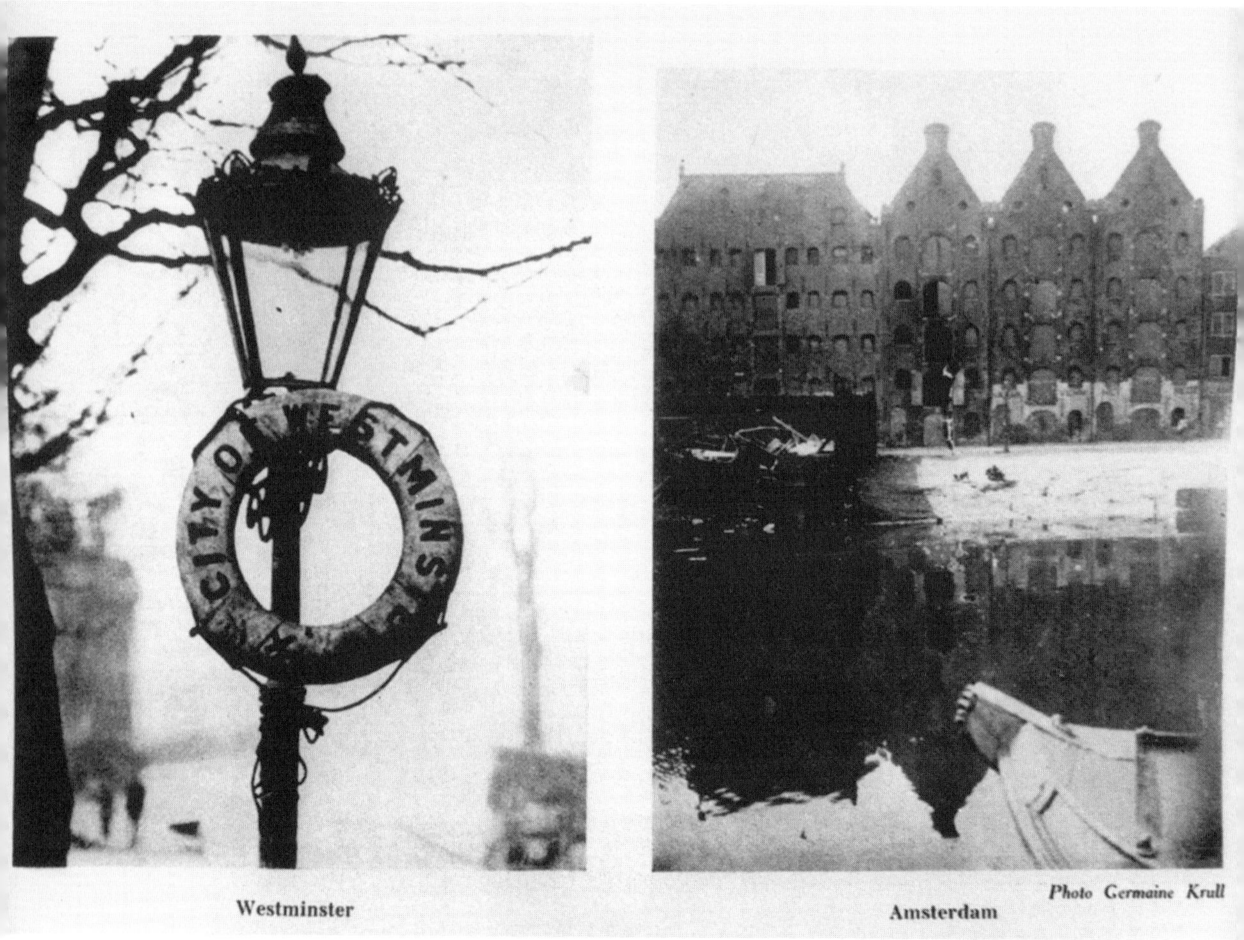

Fig 33 'Paysages méconnus', photographs by Germaine Krull and anonymous photographer, *Variétés*, 2:8 (1929).

picture spreads were the work of E. L. T. Mesens, picture editor of *Variétés* and member of the Belgian Surrealist group. As Jacques Brunius later suggested, Mesens brought a Surrealist aesthetic to the job of picture layout: 'Each page [of the magazine] became an unacknowledged collage by the sole game of confrontation.'[69] Mesens also used the work of Atget himself on several occasions and it is in the creative montage that he made with those photographs in *Variétés* where one will find yet another Surrealist reading of Atget to place alongside other constructions of his work: Man Ray's personal selection of his pictures, the reproductions in *La Révolution surréaliste* and the texts of Desnos and Valentin.

Mesens employed several tactics in his picture layouts. The simplest was one-to-one juxtaposition, such as the placement next to each other of Atget's image of a *zonier*'s cabin with a photograph of the Eiffel Tower by Germaine Krull, brought together under the title: 'Paysages de Paris' (figure 35).[70] The

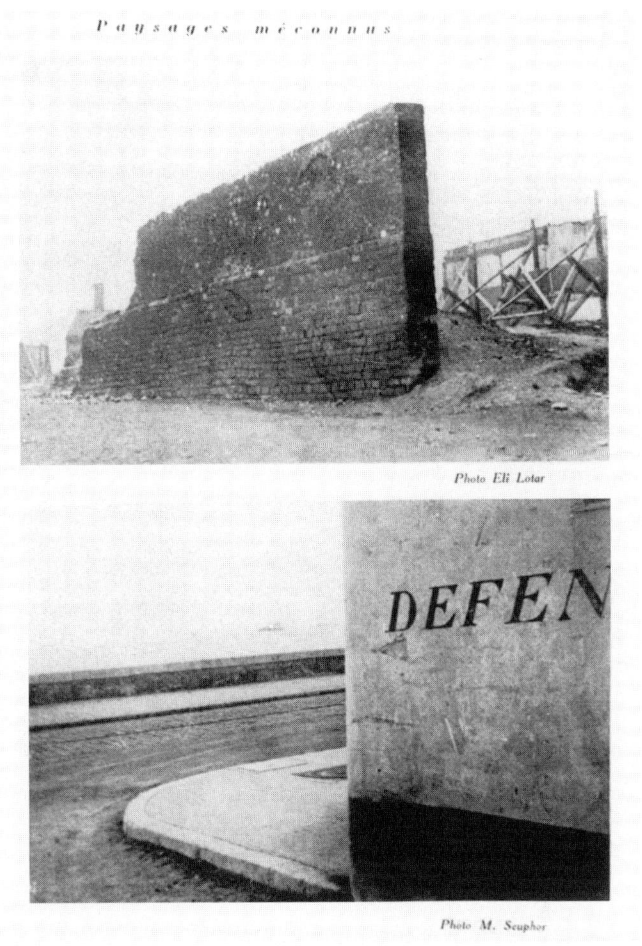

Fig 34 'Paysages méconnus', photographs by Eli Lotar and Michel Seuphor, *Variétés*, 2:8 (1929).

juxtaposition sets up a series of contrasts: the homemade versus the industrial, the antiquated versus the modern, the periphery versus the centre, and – for the knowledgeable reader – the conservative old man versus the young woman whose work represented the latest in photographic innovation. Another tactic employed by Mesens was to place together an overwhelming proliferation of images across a page, within which one photograph might suddenly stand out in its very stillness. This he did with the sequence called 'Galerie des phénomènes', where a welter of photographs of dwarfs, bearded ladies and man-dogs surround one of Atget's most quietly eloquent photographs: 'Hommage au géant Armand' (figure 36).[71]

But the most complex example of Mesens using the tactics of juxtaposition to create his own reading of 'Atget' occurred when he reproduced eight of Atget's own photographs in a spread which accompanied Albert Valentin's text in December 1928 (figure 37).[72] Mesens arranged the photographs in pairs and

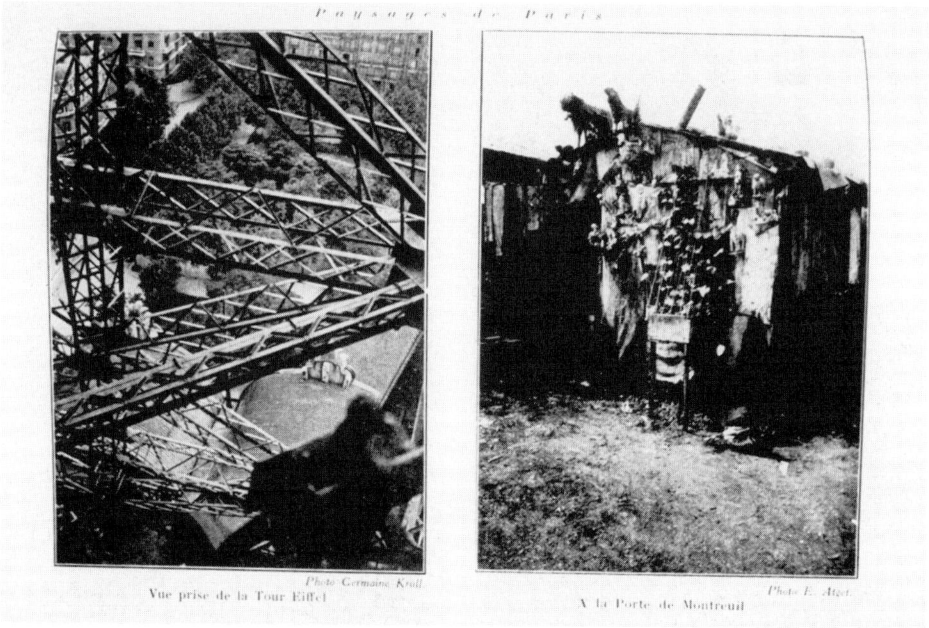

Fig 35 'Paysages de Paris', photographs by Germaine Krull and Eugène Atget, *Variétés*, 1:5 (1928).

their combination was not accidental. The first pair juxtaposed the image of the eclipse in the Place de la Bastille with a row of male headless dummies (two crowds, one 'all eyes', the other sightless). The second pair was the gorilla skeleton in the window of a naturalist's shop and a young female 'porteuse de pain' (a sort of everyday King Kong scenario, animal and human, male and female, even bestiality and innocence). The third pair was a group of female mannequins in a coiffeur's window in the Palais Royale and an image of a robust prostitute on a street corner (two images of women, both suggesting their commodification under capitalism). The fourth pair was of the decorations on the front of the Manfretta circus and the brothel with the repeated figure five on it (two façades of pleasure).

The 'Atget' that Mesens found – indeed created – here is far from the maker of poetic, somewhat nostalgic images with which we have grown so comfortable. The work of this 'Atget' is resonant with unspoken ironies, cutting perceptions about the social placement of the individual. (It is a reading that in some respects prefigures the view of Atget as a political artist developed most recently by Molly Nesbit.)[73] The crowd is a thoughtless mass, the city a façade behind which unknowable events take place, and, most uncomfortably of all, the role of women in particular is constrained and under threat. This last component may suggest those elements of misogyny which have been examined in feminist studies of Surrealism, but it is in the nature of Mesens's deliberately

Fig 36 (right) 'Galerie des phénomènes', *Variétés*, 2:1 (1929).

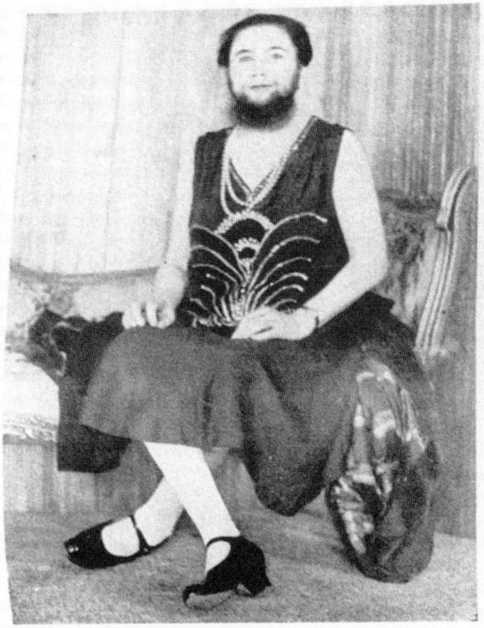

Madame Adriana, la femme à barbe

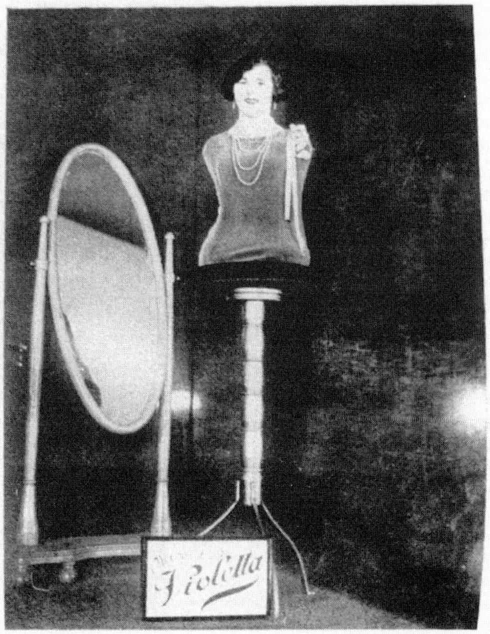

Miss Violetta, la femme-tronc

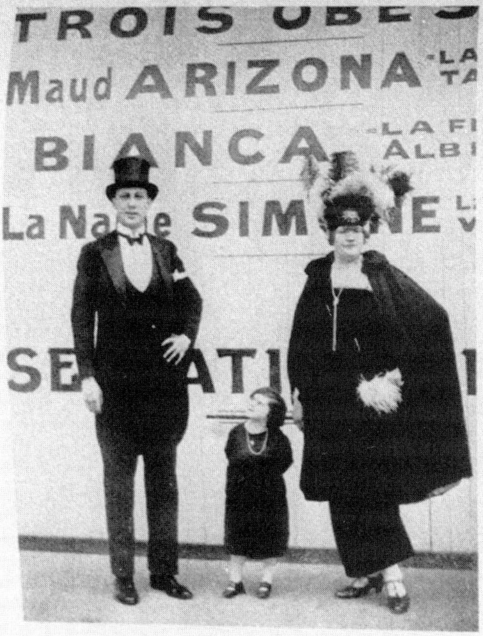

Le géant Uranus, la naine Simone et la géante Londy

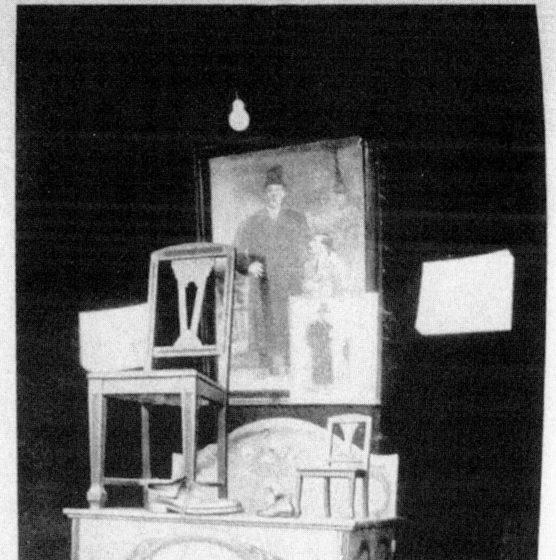

Hommage au géant Armand

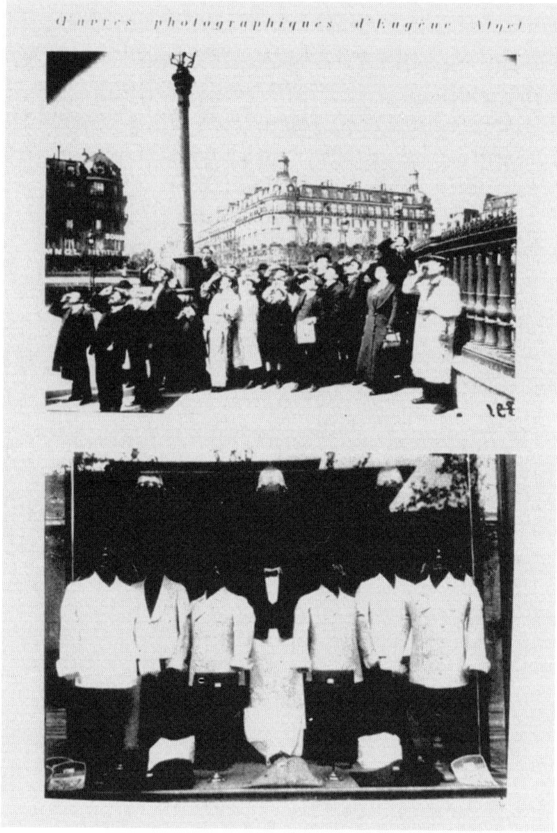
Œuvres photographiques d'Eugène Atget

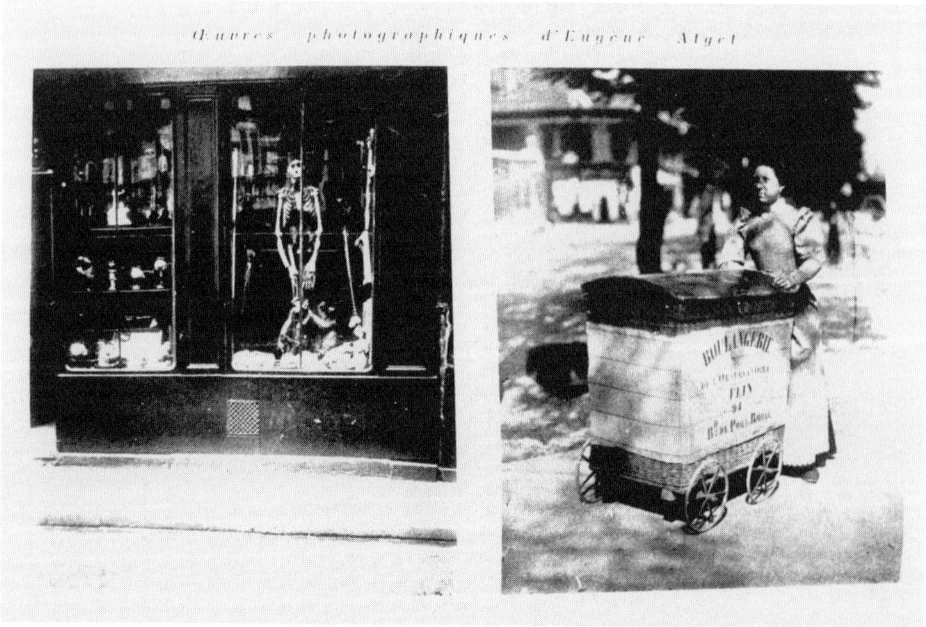
Œuvres photographiques d'Eugène Atget
BOULANGERIE

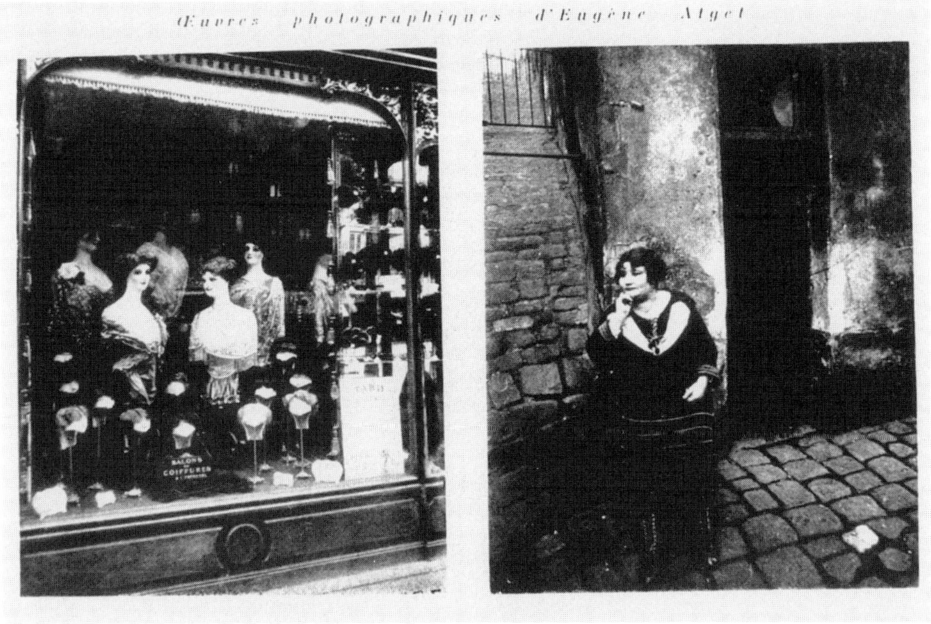

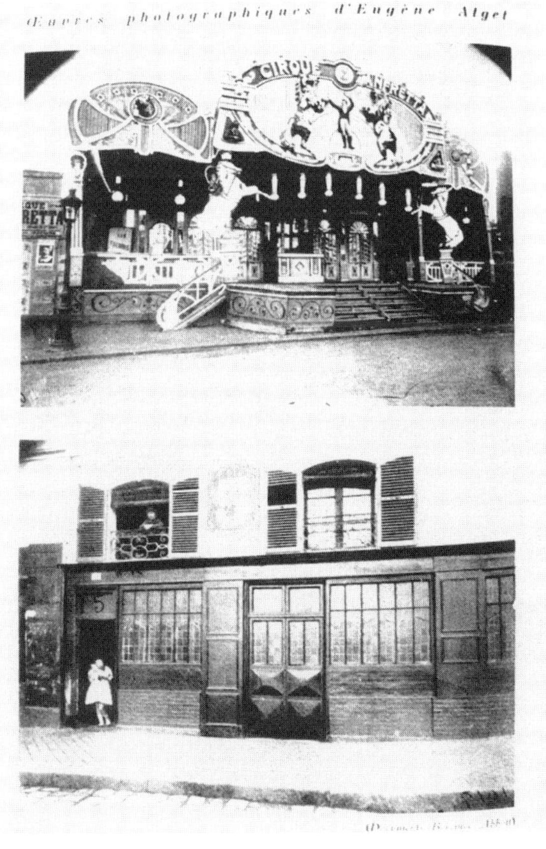

Fig 37 'Oeuvres photographiques d'Eugène Atget', *Variétés*, 1:8 (1928).

'dumb' use of juxtaposition that one cannot tell if his own attitude was one of acquiescence or critique. Nevertheless, as an ambiguous and problematical reading of Atget – a reading made through the photographs themselves – it remains pungent and disturbing, restoring something of the disturbance which Atget's earliest Surrealist viewers found in his work.

Many later writers on Atget's work have been very sceptical of a Surrealist reading, even at times ridiculing it: 'As regards Atget and surrealism, this is simply the outcome of a joke by Man Ray'.[74] Of course, the Atget presented here isn't the 'real' Atget, the photographer who made however many thousand pictures over a career of thirty years. Nor can one simply turn him into a Surrealist. Rather, the views of Atget's work presented in this chapter trace the development of a Surrealist construction of 'Atget'. Any reading of Atget must involve a lesser or greater degree of construction, for there is a lack of closure in his work that allows for a multiplicity of readings. Our view of Atget is now more comprehensive, but it still cannot achieve resolution. Certainly, the Surrealism of Atget's images has been often overplayed, and we must now see the Surrealists' response to his work in its historical context. But it will not go away. It remains part of the myth that Atget has become, for no longer can his photographs be thought of as 'simply documents'.

Notes

1 John Fuller, 'Atget and Man Ray in the Context of Surrealism', *Art Journal*, 36:2 (1976/77), 130, assigns the photograph of a man wrestling with a crocodile in a tank of water (issue no. 2, 20) to Atget, while Edouard Jaguer, *Les mystères de la chambre noire* (Paris: Flammarion, 1982), p. 20, attributes the cover image of no. 11 (the two workmen gazing down the manhole) to 'Atget(?)'.

2 See Chapter 4.

3 'Discovered' is Man Ray's own term (Paul Hill and Thomas Cooper, *Dialogue with Photography* (New York: Farrar, Straus and Giroux, 1979), p. 17).

4 The prints bought by Man Ray from Atget are now in the George Eastman House collection, Rochester, New York. They have been reproduced by Thomas Michael Gunther, 'Man Ray and Co.: la fabrication d'un buste', in Pierre Barbin (ed.), *Colloques Atget*, special number of *Photographies* (March 1986), 66–73.

5 Hill and Cooper, *Dialogue with Photography*, p. 17.

6 However, this may not have been the first photograph by Atget reproduced in a (proto)Surrealist context. In 1922, the magazine *Littérature*, published by the Paris Dadaists, printed an uncredited photograph of a butcher's shop decorated with Chinese-style lanterns (2:5 (1 October 1922)). Dawn Ades has queried whether this image was 'either by Atget himself or someone who knew his work well' ('Photography and the Surrealist Text', in Rosalind Krauss and Jane Livingston (eds), *L'Amour fou* (Washington: Corcoran Gallery/New York: Abbeville Press, 1985), p. 189 n. 5). There is also a comment by Robert Desnos, who, in 1929, wrote of Atget, 'It is after the war, around 1922, that the revue *Littérature* first published his photographs' ('Emile Adget [*sic*]' in *Nouvelles-Hebrides et autre textes 1922–1930* (Paris: Gallimard, 1978), p. 436). Yet the photograph does not really resemble any known image by Atget, and the question must be left open.

7 The photograph was in fact taken in the Place de la Bastille on 17 April 1912.

8 Fuller, 'Atget and Man Ray in the Context of Surrealism', p. 132.

9 Man Ray's comments are cited by Jean Leroy, 'Who was Eugène Atget?', *Camera* (March 1978), 41. A fuller caption: 'Versailles: maison close, Petite Place, March 1921' is given in John Szarkowski and Maria Morris Hambourg, *The Work of Atget: Vol. IV: Modern Times* (New York: Museum of Modern Art, 1985), plate 67.

10 *La Révolution surréaliste*, 8 (1 December 1926), 20.

11 Molly Nesbit, *Atget's Seven Albums* (New Haven and London: Yale University Press, 1992), p. 326.

12 Cited by John Szarkowski and Maria Morris Hambourg, *The Work of Atget: Vol. II: The Art of Old Paris* (New York: Museum of Modern Art, 1982), p. 176.

13 This encounter led Levy to visit Atget, buy some prints for the gallery he was opening in New York and subsequently fund the purchase by Berenice Abbott of Atget's posthumous legacy. See Julien Levy, *Memoirs of an Art Gallery* (New York: Putnam, 1977), pp. 90–5.

14 Jaguer, *Les mystères de la chambre noire*, p. 19. For a translation of the poem, see André Breton, *Earthlight* (Los Angeles: Sun and Moon Press/Toronto: Coach House Press, 1993), p. 31.

15 Quoted by Jaguer from René Crevel: *Le Claveclin de Diderot*. Breton's own title had in fact been inspired by a shop sign 'on a second floor balcony on the Rue de la Paix' – see

Marguerite Bonnet, *André Breton et la naissance de l'aventure surréaliste* (Paris: José Corti, 1975), p. 186.

16 Walter Benjamin, 'Surrealism, the Last Snapshot of the European Intelligentsia', in *One-Way Street* (London: New Left Books, 1979), p. 229.

17 See Chapter 4.

18 Dan Graham, 'Legacies of Critical Practices in the 1980s', in Hal Foster (ed.), *Discussions in Contemporary Culture, no. 1* (New York: Dia Art Foundation/Seattle: Bay Press, 1987), p. 89.

19 Walter Benjamin, 'A Small History of Photography', in *One-Way Street*, pp. 249–50.

20 A complete historiography of Atget's reputation remains to be written, but the best brief guide to the early period is Maria Morris Hambourg, 'Atget, Precursor of Modern Documentary Photography', in David Featherstone (ed.), *Observations: Essays on Documentary Photography* (Carmel: Friends of Photography, 1984), pp. 24–39. On more recent debates, Abigail Solomon-Godeau, 'Canon Fodder: Authoring Eugène Atget' in *Photography at the Dock* (Minneapolis: University of Minnesota Press, 1991), pp. 28–51, and Gerry Badger, 'Garden of Critical Delights: The Meaning of Atget', in Peter Turner and Gerry Badger, *Photo-Texts* (London: Travelling Light, 1988), pp. 108–18, lay out the arguments and offer strikingly different interpretations.

21 During his lifetime, Atget sold his photographs to institutional archives and to individuals, either connoisseurs of 'old Paris' or artists seeking source material. Full details of his clients are given by Maria Morris Hambourg: 'A Biography of Eugène Atget' in Szarkowski and Hambourg, *The Work of Atget: Vol. II*, pp. 9–31.

22 Berenice Abbott, *The World of Atget* (New York: Horizon Press, 1964), p. xxxi.

23 The two exhibitions were the 'Premier Salon Indépendent de la Photographie' held in the Salon de l'Escalier, Comédie des Champs-Elysées, Paris in May 1928, and an exhibition at the Galerie L'Epoque in Brussels in October. Details of the participating photographers and press coverage are given by John Szarkowski, 'Understandings of Atget' in Szarkowski and Hambourg, *The Work of Atget: Vol. IV*, pp. 9–10.

24 *Atget: photographe de Paris* (Paris: Henri Jonquières/New York: E. Weyhe Gallery, 1930). German edition: *Eugène Atget: Lichtbilder* (Leipzig: Jonquières, 1930). MacOrlan's text was in fact only used in the French and American editions; in the German edition, it was replaced by an introduction by Camille Recht. For a translation of MacOrlan's essay, see Christopher Phillips (ed.), *Photography in the Modern Era* (New York: Metropolitan Museum of Art/Aperture, 1989), pp. 41–9.

25 However, it was more than fifty years before the full scope of Atget's work was revealed, with the publication of the Abbott/Levy collection in Szarkowski and Hambourg, *The Work of Atget*, and Atget's own arrangement of his images in Nesbit, *Atget's Seven Albums*. The various collections holding his work in France were annotated in Barbin (ed.), *Colloques Atget*, and the images in those collections reproduced in Laure Beaumont-Maillet, *Atget's Paris* (London: Thames and Hudson, 1993), where, far from Szarkowski's construction of Atget as a great photographic artist, the work is presented primarily as a portrait of Paris, arranged by arrondissement.

26 Walker Evans, 'The Reappearance of Photography', *Hound and Horn* (October–December, 1931), p. 126.

27 Abbott, *The World of Atget*, p. xxxi.

28 Florent Fels in his review of the Paris exhibition (*L'art vivant*, 1 June 1928, p. 445). Quoted in translation by Szarkowski, 'Understandings of Atget', p. 9.

29 Franz Roh, *photo-eye* (Stuttgart: Akademischer Verlag, 1929).

30 After his appearance in *Nadja*, published in May 1928, Desnos became detached from the group around Breton and by the time of the publication of the *Second Surrealist Manifesto* in *La Révolution surréaliste*, 12 (15 December 1929), he was firmly identified with the dissident *Documents* group.

31 Interview with the author (Paris: 1979). This was a now famous image of a street singer, interestingly not one of the more evidently 'Surrealist' images, which suggests how broad Desnos's – and perhaps the Surrealist – taste for Atget was.

32 His film reviews in particular form a key part of the Surrealist writings in that area. See Robert Desnos, *Cinéma* (Paris: Gallimard, 1966).

33 The text in *Le Soir* has been translated as 'Spectacles of the Street – Eugène Atget', in Phillips (ed.), *Photography in the Modern Era*, pp. 16–17. The text in *Merle* has not been translated, but was reprinted in Desnos, *Nouvelles-Hebrides,* pp. 435–6. In this second text, Desnos gives Atget's name as 'Emile Adget'. This was a common mistake at the time, but it's strange that Desnos should have got both names wrong nine months after he had got them right in his first article.

34 See *La Révolution surréaliste*, 12 (15 December 1929), 47, and *Variétés* (15 August 1929), between 248–9. Valentin also participated in the 'recherches sur la sexualité' of the Paris group (see Sessions nos. 8 and 9 (November 1930) in José Pierre (ed.), *Investigating Sex* (London: Verso, 1992)).

35 *Variétés* (15 December 1928), 403–7. Valentin's essay was translated as 'Eugène Atget', in Phillips (ed.), *Photography in the Modern Era*, pp. 18–22.

36 Desnos, 'Emile Adget', p. 436.

37 See MacOrlan's text for the 1930 monograph (Phillips (ed.), *Photography in the Modern Era*, p. 49) and George's text 'Photographie: Vision du monde', in *Photographies*, special issue of *Arts et métiers graphiques*, 16 (1 March 1930), 134.

38 Desnos, 'Emile Adget', p. 435.

39 Valentin, 'Eugène Atget', p. 20.

40 Desnos, 'Spectacles of the Street', p. 16.

41 This is another pun on the different meanings of 'objectif' in French – as objective and as camera lens.

42 Valentin, 'Eugène Atget', p. 20.

43 Desnos, 'Spectacles of the Street', p. 17.

44 See Waldemar George, 'Le Salon de la photographie au Salon de l'Escalier', *Presse et Patrie* (11 June 1928) and 'Photographie: Vision du monde'.

45 This translation is by John Szarkowski, who praises its prescience in the description of Atget's project ('Understandings of Atget', pp. 14–15).

46 Desnos, 'Emile Adget', p. 435.

47 Desnos, 'Spectacles of the Street', p. 17.

48 Desnos, 'Emile Adget', p. 436.

49 The phrase 'soluble city' was, I think, coined by Cardinal in the title of his essay: 'Soluble

City: the Surrealist perception of Paris', *Architectural Review*, 2–3 (1978), 143–9. It plays off the title of André Breton's automatic text 'Soluble Fish' (in *Manifestoes of Surrealism* (Ann Arbor: University of Michigan, 1969), pp. 51–109).

50 Valentin, 'Eugène Atget', pp. 20–1.

51 *Ibid.*

52 Christopher Phillips, *Photography in the Modern Era*, p. 22 n. 4, suggests that Valentin may have been referring here to the real-life films that Feuillade also made on location around Paris, but Valentin's comments about violent death and melodrama surely suggest he was indeed thinking of *Fantômas*.

53 Annette Michelson, 'Dr. Crause and Mr. Clair', *October*, 11 (Winter 1979), p. 42. For the context of this phrase, see Chapter 3.

54 Translated from Francis Lacassin, *Louis Feuillade* (Paris: Seghers, 1964), by John Ashbery, 'Introduction to Fantômas', in Marcel Allain and Pierre Souvestre, *Fantômas* (London: Picador, 1987), p. 8.

55 Desnos, 'Emile Adget', p. 436.

56 Desnos, 'Spectacles of the Street', p. 17.

57 *Variétés*, 7 (15 November 1928), 400–1. F. L.'s review also describes the setting of Atget's pictures in terms that echo Valentin, referring to 'desolate suburban landscapes' and 'tragic Parisian facades'. It's interesting to speculate on the identity of F. L. – perhaps a pseudonym for E. L. T. Mesens, one of the organisers of the Brussels exhibition?

58 Benjamin, 'A Small History of Photography', p. 256.

59 Benjamin, 'The Work of Art in the Age of Mechanical Reproduction', in *Illuminations* (London: Fontana, 1973), p. 228.

60 See Chapter 3.

61 Indeed one translator of Benjamin has rendered the phrase this way, with 'täter' translated as actor rather than culprit; see 'A Short History of Photography', translated by Stanley Mitchell, *Screen* (Spring 1972), p. 25.

62 Molly Nesbit concluded that 'given Benjamin's interest in detective stories and social injustice, 'crime' is probably not too strong' (Nesbit, *Atget's Seven Albums*, p. 219 n. 54).

63 MacOrlan's text is translated but without illustrations as 'Elements of a Social Fantastic', in Phillips (ed.), *Photography in the Modern Era*, pp. 31–3. The photograph of the bloodstained bedroom is reproduced in Szarkowski and Hambourg, *The Work of Atget: Vol. IV*, p. 12. The original article was also illustrated with Daumier's lithograph *Rue Transnonain*.

64 The 'social fantastic' is discussed further in Chapter 7.

65 Adrian Rifkin, *Street Noises: Parisian pleasure, 1900–40* (Manchester: Manchester University Press, 1993), p. 124.

66 Benjamin, 'A Small History of Photography', p. 250.

67 *Variétés,* 2:8 (15 December 1929). 'Paysages méconnus' is between pp. 558–9 and 'Mélancholie des villes' between pp. 582–3.

68 *Bifur*, 5 (30 April 1930), after p. 105. *Bifur*, edited by the former Dadaist Georges Ribemont-Dessaignes, ran for eight issues between May 1929 and June 1931. Its use of pictures was generally more limited and cruder than that in *Variétés* and *Documents*, but it did publish images by photographers such as Krull, Lotar and Kertész, as well as Tabard.

69 Jacques Brunius, *E. L. T. Mesens* (Knokke Le Zoute Albert Plage: Salle 'La Reserve', 1963), unpaginated.

70 *Variétés*, 1: 5 (15 September 1928). The picture by Krull was plate 54 from her book *Métal* (see Kim Sichel, *Germaine Krull: Photographer of Modernity* (Cambridge, MA: MIT Press, 1999), p. 183). For a further discussion of Atget's photographs of the Zone, see Chapter 6.

71 *Variétés*, 2: 1 (15 July 1929), between 152–3. The image has been severely cropped on either side; the full photograph is reproduced in Szarkowski and Hambourg, *The Work of Atget: Vol. IV*, plate 116.

72 *Variétés*, 8 (15 December 1928), between 406–7.

73 Nesbit, *Atget's Seven Albums*.

74 Jean Leroy, 'The Truth about Atget', *Camera* (November 1979), 42.

6
Terrain vague

The Surrealists' celebration of Paris was always ambiguous, for their immersion in urban modernity – walking the boulevards, meeting in the cafés – was often interrupted and even undercut by other values: the natural, the primitive, the raw. For the Surrealists, nature was not to be separated from culture. Rather the intrusion of the 'natural' into the city disrupted the veneer of urbanity and, in turn, undermined the coherence of the bourgeois, capitalist system. In this process, the city was revealed not as the monolithic and coherent structure of the modernist dream, but something more like a complex organism, fraught with contradictions, unstable, even sometimes on the edge of collapse.[1]

In the very title of that key Surrealist text *Le paysan de Paris*, Louis Aragon pointed to an intersection of the rural and the urban, the primitive and the sophisticated, as a nodal point within Surrealism.[2] In the first half of the book, Aragon describes his intensely detailed investigation of the Passage de l'Opéra in the heart of the city. Strolling through the glass-roofed arcades, he conjures up a sense of 'the modern light radiating from the unusual' that he finds in 'these human aquariums'.[3] They are, he says, 'the secret repositories of several modern myths', as potent as any conjured up by ancient cultures.

In the second half of the book, however, he moves out of the city centre to search for 'A Feeling for Nature at the Buttes-Chaumont'. But, as George Melly points out, the Buttes-Chaumont, 'a nineteenth-century park in a vaguely sinister inner suburb of Paris, is almost absurdly artificial'.[4] Aragon asks what can the venerable Romantic notion of 'a feeling for nature' mean in the context of the urbanised 'mythology of the modern' which he had discovered in the Passage de l'Opéra.[5] He centres his answer around the concept of the Garden, rhapsodising on the subject and conjuring up images of childhood, eccentricity, leisure, paradise, the feminine, love, the Orient. Aragon's panegyric, genuinely lyrical, is at the same time deeply ironic; the garden (in particular the classical French garden) is after all the quintessential site of a cultivated and culturalised nature.[6] Nevertheless, for Aragon, a garden is a place 'where the city dwellers' wild dreams stir', where is found 'every lingering remnant in adults' memory of the atmosphere of enchanted forests'.[7]

Yet he acknowledges no actual garden can adequately embody such dreams,

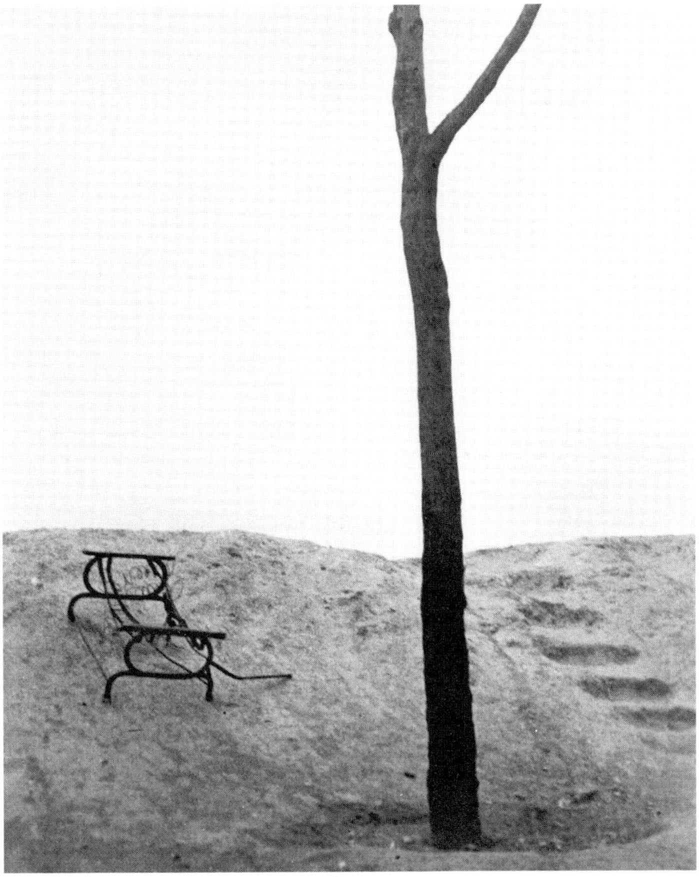

Fig 38 Man Ray, *Terrain vague*, 1932. The Museum of Modern Art, New York.
© Man Ray Trust/ADAGP, Paris and DACS, London, 2001.

and, evincing a characteristic Surrealist refusal of the infantile happiness of nostalgia, Aragon calls the ideal of the garden 'this cretinous symbol of happiness'.[8] Still it is important that Aragon, much as he ironised the 'natural', did not reject it. He asks whether there might exist 'some specific mythical feeling restricted to what was once thought of as nature, but still effective today. Are there modern natural myths?'[9] For the Surrealist, the point was not to choose the natural over the urban or vice versa, but rather to explore the discomfiting hybridisation resulting from the interpenetration of the two. This chapter will examine a number of hybrid sites around the city where this interpenetration is evident – the Zone, the flea market, the abattoir – through a number of images made in each setting by different photographers, including Eugène Atget, Emiel van Moerkerken and Eli Lotar.

An appropriate starting point is with one extraordinary and unsettling photograph by Man Ray, entitled *Terrain vague*: waste ground, unused land (figure 38). The image is visually very coarse. A bank of earth or grass fills the bottom third of the frame. Steps roughly cut into the bank indicate this is a place

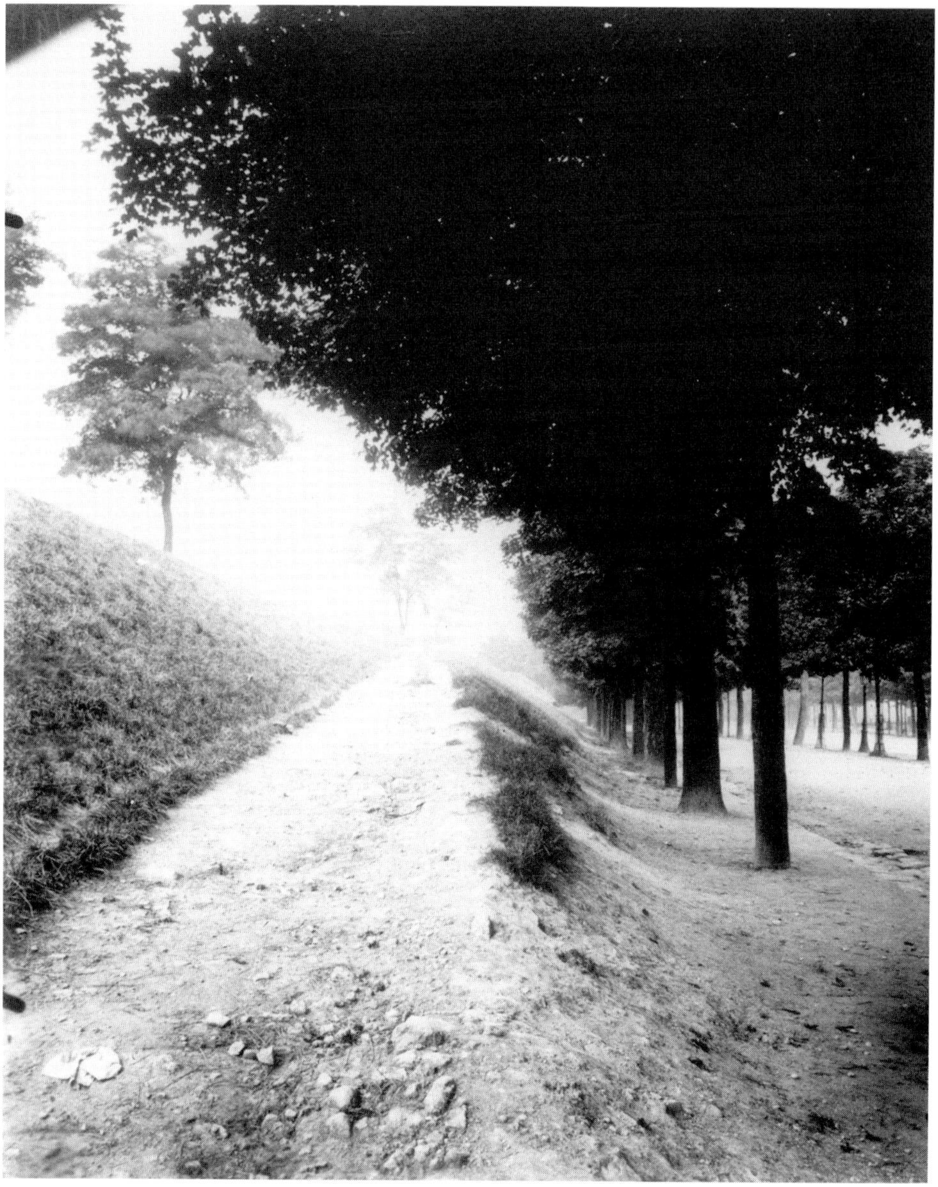

Fig 39 Eugène Atget, *Porte de Gentilly, Paris 13*, 1910–13. © Photothèque des Musées de la Ville de Paris.

through which many people have passed, but now it is uncannily empty. We cannot know what this site is. Is it part of a larger natural landscape entered, corrupted, by the human, or is it a corner of an urban space – a park perhaps – in which the natural is trying to survive?

Halfway up the bank, almost sliding down, is a misshapen, half-recognisable piece of ironwork; given the context, it might be the remains of a park bench, but it seems to have coiled springs attached to it. It might, in truth, have been anything – industrial, recreational or domestic. The ambiguity of this object is an essential element in the overall indecisiveness of the scene. It figures as the central character in a desolate existential drama – like one of the tramps that Samuel Beckett was to place beneath a similar tree in a similarly desolate landscape in *Waiting for Godot*. But such pessimistic desolation was never far from Surrealism itself, especially in its first years. Throughout *Le paysan de Paris*, what Aragon called 'the sense of the useless'[10] alternated with flashes of visionary insight; his discourse on gardens was interrupted by a 'meditation' on boredom.

Man Ray probably made *Terrain vague* in 1932, but it is completely unrelated to any of his other work, usually so controlled and staged.[11] However, a better connection might be made to the work of his neighbour, Eugène Atget. Looking through Atget's pictures, Man Ray would surely have come across the photographs that Atget had made back in 1910–13 of somewhat similar earth embankments, likewise covered in meandering paths and stunted trees – the fortifications surrounding Paris (figure 39). Molly Nesbit has evoked the lack of definition in this marginal landscape and likewise in Atget's depiction of it: 'We have come to a land where even the surfaces suffer from ellipse, where culture would never be seen as more than a trace ... Form was rendered obtuse, thick, blank.'[12]

With the spread of industrialisation across Europe in the mid-nineteenth-century, the distinction between city and country became increasingly blurred.[13] The situation in nineteenth-century Paris was however very particular, for in the 1840s the limits of the city were precisely defined by a new ring of fortifications, with entrance in and out of the city restricted to a number of 'portes'. Although on several occasions, the fortifications proved quite ineffective as a defence for the city, it was more than 120 years before they were finally disposed of. As Atget's photographs show, during that time they fell into a quiet neglect, used mainly for weekend outings.[14]

Beyond the fortifications lay the *banlieue* – the suburbs – and by the late nineteenth-century, that space had a particular poetic resonance. T. J. Clark has discussed this meaning, citing a passage from the 1861 edition of Victor Hugo's *Les Miserables*:

> To wander in a kind of reverie, to take a stroll as they call it, is a good way for a philosopher to spend his time; particularly in that kind of bastard countryside, somewhat ugly but bizarre, made up of two different natures, which surrounds certain great cities, notably Paris. To observe the banlieue is to observe an amphibian. End of trees, beginning of roofs, end of grass, beginning of paving stones, end of ploughed fields, beginning of shops, the end of the beaten track, the beginning of the passions, the end of the murmur of things divine, the beginning of the noise of humankind – all of this holds an extraordinary interest. And thus, in these unattractive places, forever marked by the passer-by with the epithet sad, the promenades, apparently aimless, of the dreamer.[15]

The fascination of Hugo's text lies in its attempt to evoke a new kind of landscape, simultaneously entrancing and disturbing in its lack of definition, or rather its confusion of possible definitions. His figure of the melancholy passer-by is also ambiguous. In one sense, it continues a tradition of Romanticism, as if Rousseau's eighteenth-century *promeneur solitaire* had wandered in from the natural landscape he had previously inhabited.[16] But we might also be reminded of that new sort of wanderer of the mid-nineteenth-century, the *flâneur* of the city streets. Tired of the spectacle of the boulevards, he has perhaps here strolled out into this 'amphibian' landscape and found in it a different, more contemplative aspect of the rampant urban growth of the period.

For in Paris, the nineteenth-century experience of boulevard and *banlieue* as alienating yet compelling had a common source in the process of Haussmannisation – the radical rebuilding of the city by Baron Haussmann, Prefect of the Seine in the regime of Napoleon III.[17] Other key Surrealist sites around Paris – the park made from the quarries of Buttes-Chaumont and the abattoir relocated to La Villette – had also resulted from Haussmann's effort to rationalise the city. But this imposition of order was for the Surrealists ironically undermined by the raw passions that continued to flow beneath this cultured surface. The Surrealist desire to be a 'Paris peasant' was not a simplistic attempt to live a pre-Haussmann life in a post-Haussmann environment. Rather, this desire was another element in the Surrealists' 'refusal of the imposed present' of the urban spectacle, as they explored rather 'the potency of ... derelict spaces off its main routes of circulation'.[18] For the determined metrophile or metrophobe, the indeterminate territory that lay between the city and the country was tainted, impure. But in a Surrealist reading, that sense of unease was a stimulation.

The most extensive of these derelict spaces lay between the Parisian fortifications and the *banlieue*: the Zone. This was a strip of land about 250 metres wide immediately in front of the fortifications where building had been forbidden for defensive purposes. But the Zone outlived such practicalities, and by the late nineteenth-century, it was inhabited by gypsies, ragpickers, itinerants – known collectively as the *zoniers* – whose presence had become integral to the myth of the city itself.[19] When Guillaume Apollinaire took *Zone* as the title of his seminal poem of 1912, he was echoing the way the bohemian writers of the mid-nineteenth-century had often identified themselves with these outcasts of society.[20] As Walter Benjamin described it, 'the poets find the refuse of society on their street and derive their heroic subject from this very refuse'.[21]

In 1910–12, as well as the overgrown fortifications, Eugène Atget had also photographed the *zoniers* and their environment.[22] In photographing the 'villas' of the *zoniers*, his characteristic directness brought out the unsettling bricolage with which such dwellings might be decorated. One of these photographs was, as noted earlier, reproduced by E. L. T. Mesens in *Variétés* next to Germaine Krull's photograph of the Eiffel Tower.[23] Beyond a stretch of flat earth, on which sit the ragpicker's discarded boots, is a shack seen from an oblique angle (figure 40). The shack is covered with a multitude of dolls and toys, like so many

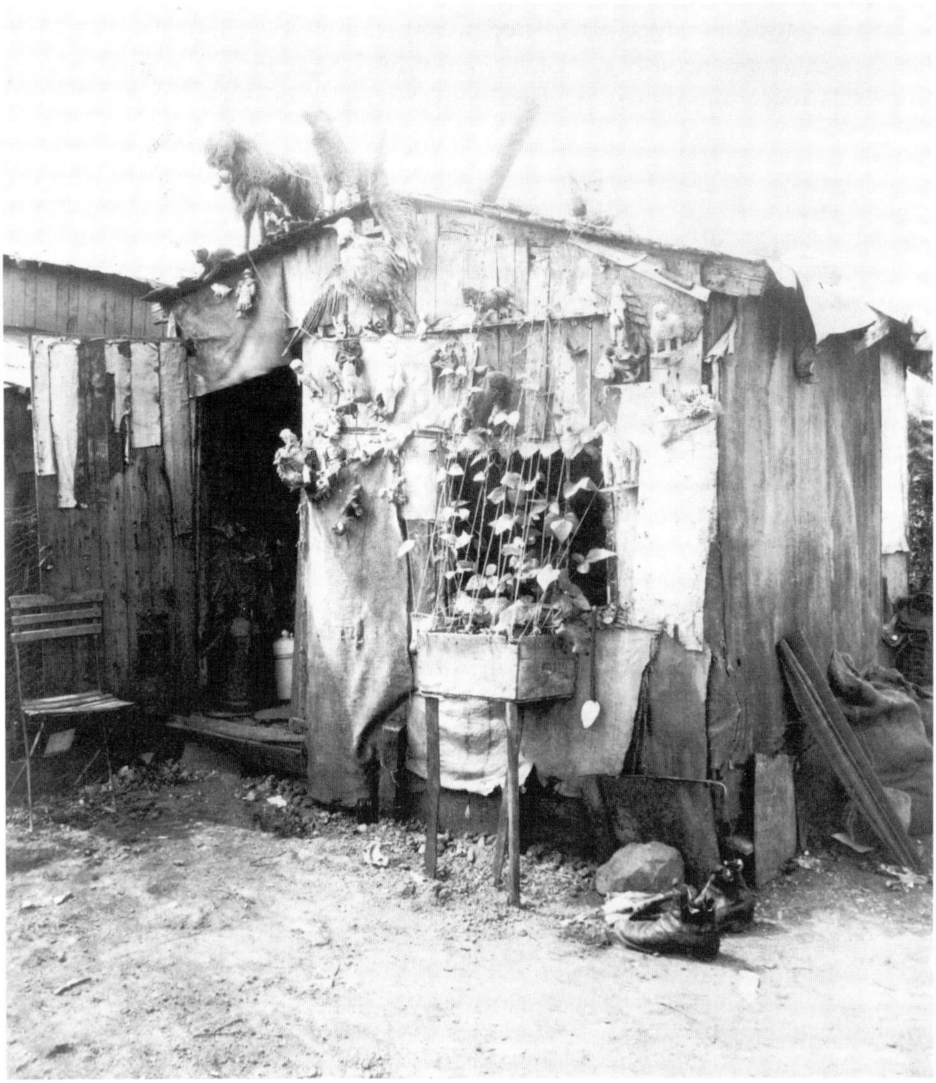

Fig 40 Eugène Atget, *Villa d'un chiffonnier*, 1912. The Museum of Modern Art, New York.

magical fetishes and talismans. On the roof are several animals: a dog, a sheep and a cat. They might be dummies or stuffed. Or, just possibly, alive.

We now think of Atget primarily as a photographer of the city streets, but for a number of early critics, his central subject was the *terrain vague*. Waldemar George, for example, writing in 1930, referred to him as a photographer of a 'Paris terre en friches [waste ground], no man's land'.[24] For some recent writers who have been concerned to construct Atget primarily as a maker of pictures full of balance and grace, this aspect of his work can be unsatisfactory: 'Atget made a considerable number of pictures in the Zone that could be characterised as extraordinarily chaotic, and it is only occasionally that these pictures manage

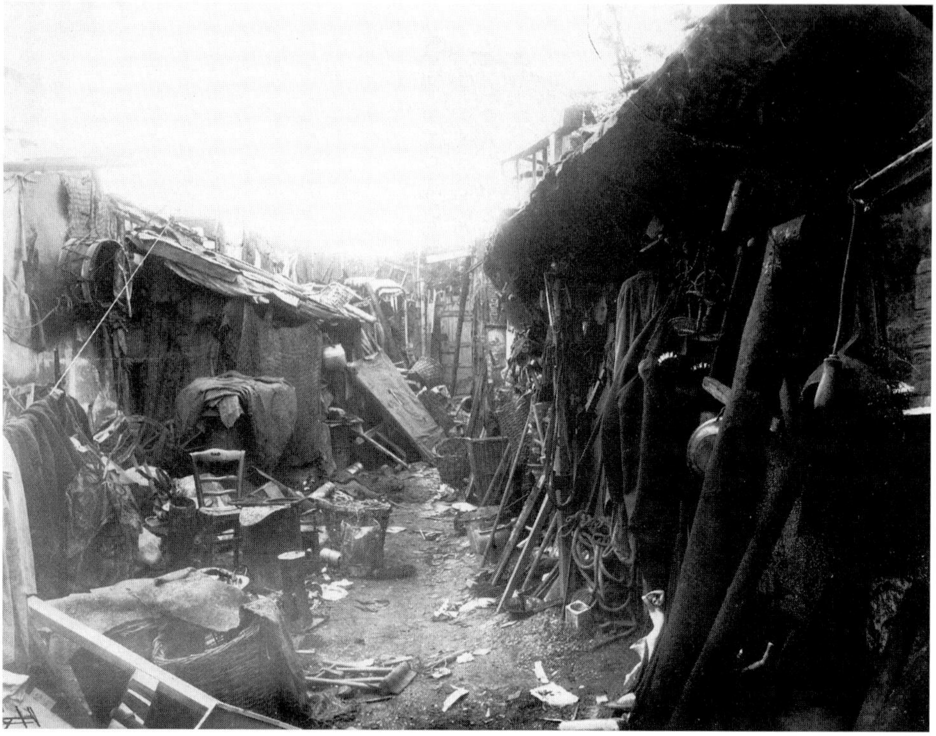

Fig 41 Eugène Atget, *Boulevard Masséna*, 1910. The Museum of Modern Art, New York.

to achieve ... a clarified essence of chaos.'[25] Maybe, though, this lack of clarity is the point of these images.

When Man Ray bought some of Atget's photographs for himself, he chose seven pictures of the Zone.[26] Some show the shacks of the *zoniers* and others the great piles of junk and rags through which they made their precarious living (figure 41). Perhaps he was interested in these pictures as images of an environment where composition can no longer cohere, where order struggles hopelessly against an impending chaos which seems to flow out beyond the edge of the frame. Images, in other words, of a real life Dadaism. In 1920, Man Ray himself had attempted to depict this state of entropy through contrivance, tipping out his ashtray in order to photograph it; he called the resulting picture *New York* – a microcosm of the city as debris.[27] In Atget's photographs of the Zone, this disorder was revealed as actual and on a scale at which no mere artwork could compete.

When, in 1929, Georges Bataille started quite unsystematically to compile entries for a 'Dictionnaire' in his new magazine *Documents*, one of his first entries was on 'Dust': 'dismal sheets of dust constantly invade earthly habitations and uniformly defile them ... One day or another, it is true, dust, supposing it persists, will probably begin to gain the upper hand over domestics, invading the immense ruins of abandoned buildings, deserted dockyards'.[28]

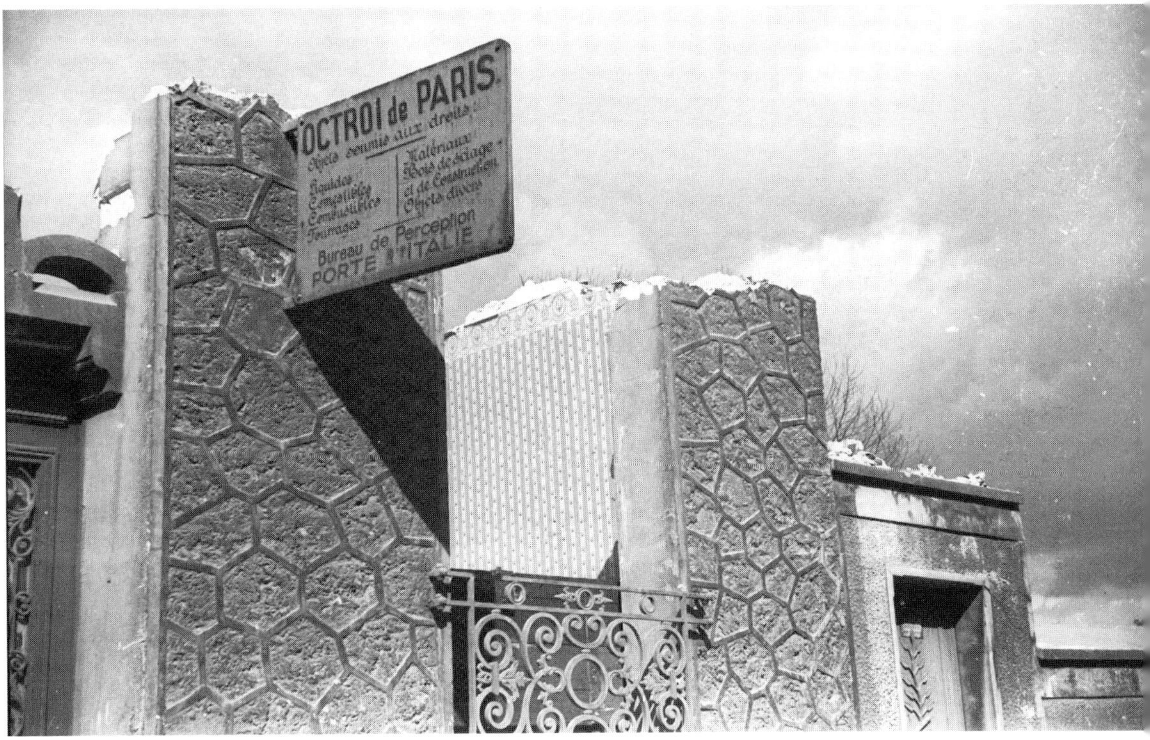

Fig 42 Emiel van Moerkerken, *Octroi de Paris*, 1935. © Emiel van Moerkerken.

What Bataille imagines then is an accumulation of domestic dust such that it takes over the now empty city, turning it all into the Zone. As Yves-Alain Bois comments, 'On an urban scale, the zone is what dust is on the scale of the single dwelling: it is the waste that inevitably accompanies production (which is necessarily, according to Bataille, overproduction).'[29] The project of urbanism is a constant attempt to keep this waste at bay, clear it away, keep it out in the Zone, but of course it returns – in an endless cycle of ruination, renewal, ruination.

One winter's day in 1935, the Dutch photographer Emiel van Moerkerken was wandering on the edge of the Zone.[30] Van Moerkerken was then nineteen; he had discovered Surrealism the year before, through his father's copy of *Documents 34: 'Intervention surréaliste'*, and this was the first of several visits to Paris during which he met Breton, Dalí, Bellmer and became particularly close friends with Brassaï. On this day, van Moerkerken was near the Porte d'Italie, photographing impoverished housing conditions (like many well-off young men of the time, van Moerkerken was fervently leftist) when he saw and photographed a ruined tollhouse building – *Octroi de Paris* (figure 42). Later, as Edouard Jaguer reports, van Moerkerken showed the image to Salvador Dalí who declared it to be 'one of the most surrealist photos he had ever seen'.[31] (In fact, van Moerkerken's own account played down the encounter; he said that Dalí's comment was made very quickly – a brief 'très surréaliste' – before passing on.[32])

The photograph is in fact quite plain, not at all 'paranoiac-critical', working by insinuation rather than confrontation through a number of very precisely placed elements. The eye is first drawn to the sign of the 'Bureau de Perception' (the collector's office), a phrase that suggests the way the building would have operated as an centre for official surveillance, but now only the tight rectangle and precise lettering of the sign support that process of bureaucratic regulation. The attempts at bourgeoisification, suggested by the intricate railing and the regular wallpaper seen through the window, now seem merely pathetic amid the destruction of the building, its insistence on order rendered hopeless. The best laid plans of tax collection fall apart.[33]

Though the building is in ruins, it looks relatively new – demolished rather than naturally decayed. Its now irregular form is ironically paralleled by the 'crazy paving' (another bourgeois attempt to achieve a stabilised naturalness) on the wall. The far door seems to be decorated with plant forms that are echoed in the winter tree beyond. (To extend that reading, one might see the cloud above the tree as foliage). Within the precise framing of the picture, the tip of that bare tree is all that suggests the larger landscape that lies around the tollhouse, which, even though we cannot see it, we know to be the *terrain vague* between city and country. The 'amphibian' connotations of that landscape as Victor Hugo had defined it underpins the amorphous character of this ruined building.[34]

The Surrealist interest in the Zone was related to the broader role it played in Parisian culture, a role that it occupied until after the Second World War. When Robert Doisneau published his first book of photographs *La banlieue de Paris* in 1949, Blaise Cendrars in his introduction dubbed him 'un photographe zonier'.[35] (Doisneau had been born in the *banlieue* at Gentilly.) In its fascination with the tarnished and often grubby surfaces of this landscape, Doisneau's work exemplified the romantic attachment that many Parisians felt for the edges of the city. Already though that romance was threaded through with nostalgia, for the Zone would soon disappear. When the city planners of post-war Paris decided they needed a new dual-carriageway ring road to facilitate movement around the city, they already had its route laid out for them. In 1973, the *boulevard périphérique*, occupying precisely the land that had been the Zone, was finally completed. Paris was – is – now surrounded by a very different *terrain vague*.[36]

If the Zone in general offered a spectacle of dissolution and entropy, then the flea market was a concentrated instance of that experience, both physically and imaginatively. In this, its siting was crucial, poised at the point where the city and the Zone met on the north of the city near the Porte de Saint-Ouen. (It is still there, next to the *périphérique*.) The flea market was a favourite Surrealist haunt, particularly for André Breton, who wrote about his visits in both *Nadja* and *L'Amour fou*. Breton continued to come here regularly every Saturday

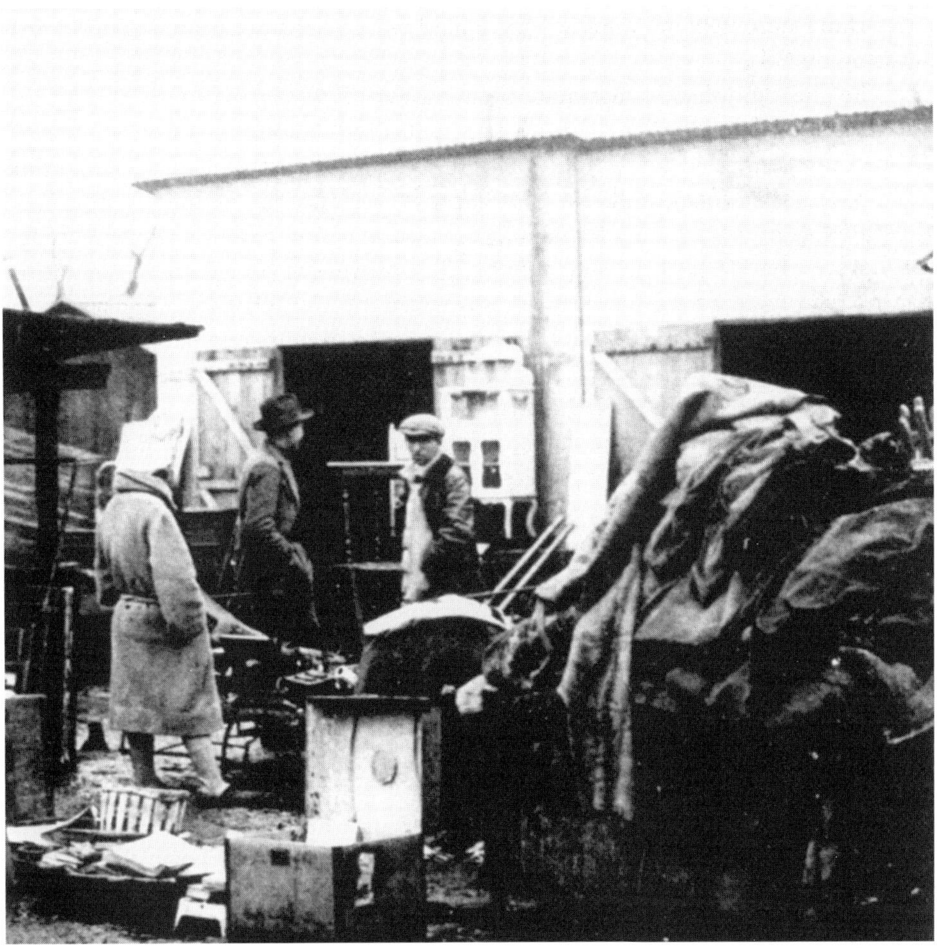

Fig 43 Jacques-André Boiffard, 'When I went one Sunday to the Saint-Ouen flea-market', from André Breton, *Nadja*, 1928.

throughout his life, accompanied by Surrealist comrades and favoured friends such as Jean Dubuffet and Claude Lévi-Strauss.[37] Late in life, he was photographed in the market by Gisèle Freund.[38]

In *Nadja*, the flea market was represented by one of Boiffard's photographs, characteristically distanced and removed, with three anonymous occupants of the market viewed beyond a pile of bric-à-brac (figure 43). The anonymity of these figures was quite deliberate, for the woman with her back turned is Fanny Beznos, a stallholder who talks with Breton about Shelley, Nietzsche, Rimbaud and Surrealism.[39] Her role in the book as an active, female presence would hardly have been evident from this photograph. Shot on a heavy grey winter's day, the image may suggest something of the desolation of the market, but it does not convey the sense of magical encounter which Breton experienced there with 'objects that can be found nowhere else: old-fashioned, broken, useless, almost incomprehensible, even perverse':[40] objects such as the white half-cylinder

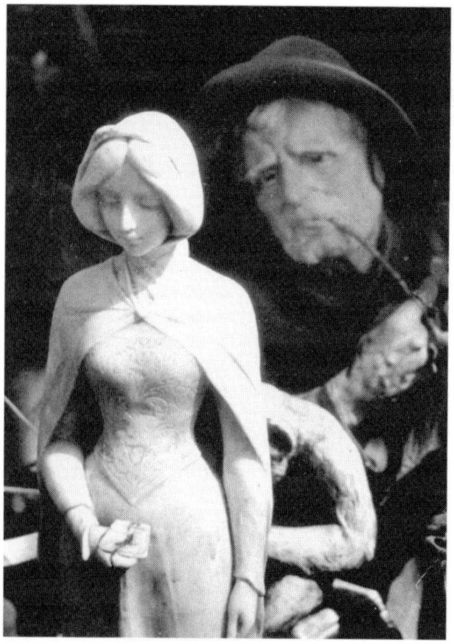

Fig 44 Emiel van Moerkerken, *Marché aux puces*, 1936-37. © Emiel van Moerkerken.

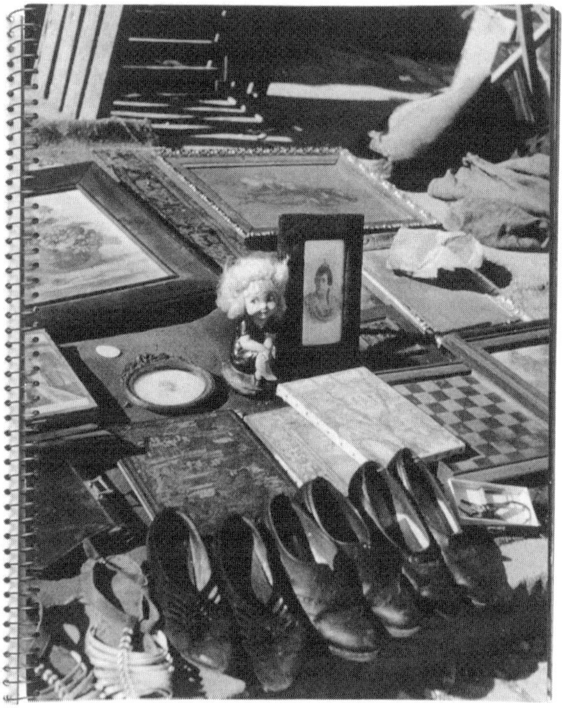

Fig 45 Jiří Sever, image from *Bez Protijedu*, 1946. Uměleckoprůmyslové museum, Prague.

pictured in *Nadja* or the mask in *L'Amour fou*.

The flea market evidently held a particular frisson for Breton, but none of the other central participants in the Surrealist group seems to have written or made images about it; perhaps it was in a sense felt to be 'his' place. To find more obviously 'surreal' representations of the flea market, one must turn to the photography that was going on around Surrealism – made by artists influenced by but not strictly affiliated with the movement itself. André Kertész, for example, photographed there in the 1930s; in *Day of Paris*, published in New York in 1946, there is a brief sequence on the flea market.[41] An image of two naked female mannequins in apparently fervent conversation, seen past a painting of the crucifixion, is a good example of a certain sort of flea market photography, which exploits the inherent bricolage of the place to comment on the vicissitudes of human communication.

In 1936, the year after he had made his *Octroi de Paris* photograph, Emiel van Moerkerken visited the market. Among the images he made was a photograph of two statues, a scowling peasant seeming to eye a pious young girl (figure 44).[42] This gives a very particular twist to this commentary on failed communication, ironically emphasising the hopelessness of male desire. It was a theme that was developed by the Czech photographer Jiří Sever, who photographed in the flea market on his visit to Paris in 1946. He made a book of the pictures called *Without Antidote* in which a graffitied scrawl on a

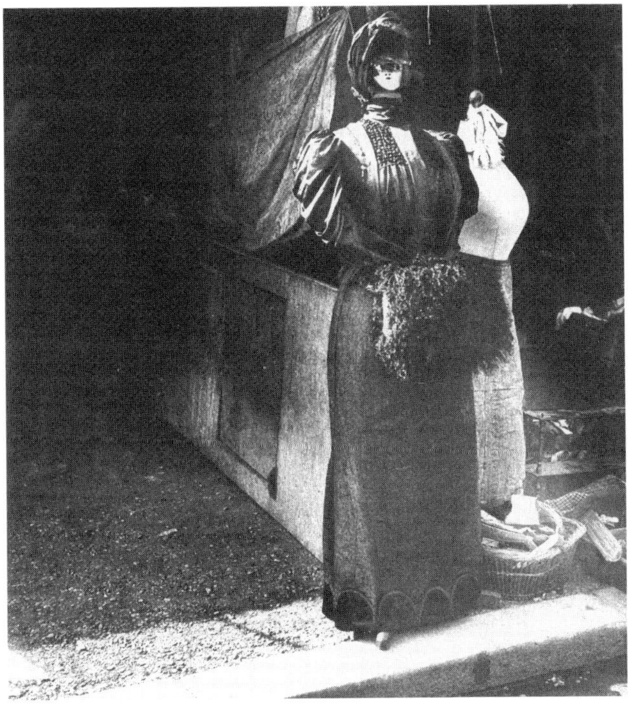

Fig 46 Bill Brandt, *Flea market, Paris*, 1930. © Bill Brandt/Bill Brandt Archive.

tarpaulin – 'On demande une jeune fille pour tenir' – is followed by fantasies of femininity in two images of 'jeunes filles': a sentimental painting and a small frizzy haired doll (figure 45).[43] A very different image of the feminine appears in Bill Brandt's forbidding figure of the 'Grand Mannequin', made at the flea market in 1930, when he was working as Man Ray's assistant (figure 46).[44] Brandt's photographic tactics are also quite distinct, for he isolated the figure against the surrounding darkness, eliminating all the other bric-à-brac that would have surrounded it.

At the same time, many foreign photographers inspired by Surrealism explored their own flea markets. Jindřich Štyrský in Prague in the 1930s and Vilém Reichmann in Brno after the war made pictures that echoed those taken at the Paris flea market, while inflecting them with resonances particular to their own cultural milieu.[45] Upon his return to Amsterdam in 1938, van Moerkerken made the three-part sequence *Great Expectations*. The first image centres on a grinning dummy in a bathtub surrounded by other flea market objects (figure 47); van Moerkerken later wrote of the picture: 'Taken on a walk with Chris van Geel in a market in Amsterdam, I do not remember whether we found the lady in the bath-tub or put her there.'[46] On one level, of course, his remark raises the issue of whether it matters if this scenario was staged or found. More to the point here, however, is that van Moerkerken's comment suggests how predictable and easily replicable certain Surrealist scenarios had become,

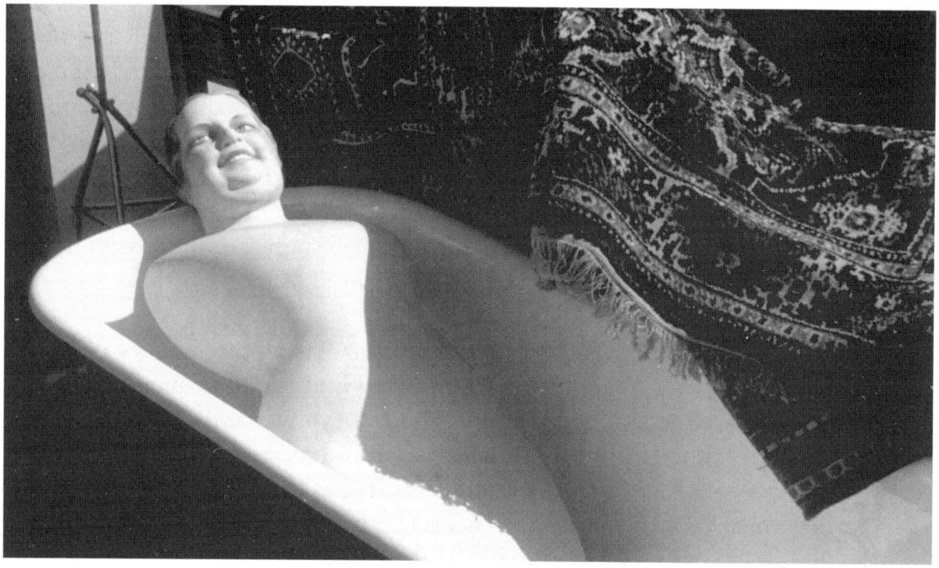

Fig 47 Emiel van Moerkerken, *Great Expectations: 1*, 1938. © Emiel van Moerkerken.

especially in the flea market where encounters like that between an umbrella and a sewing machine would in fact be commonplace.

Perhaps by the late 1930s, the photography of the flea market offered only a plethora of superficial juxtapositions; perhaps the mythology of the Zone also too often resulted in a facile vision of dissolution. The taste for the strange and outmoded was also part of fashionable society; Adrian Rifkin acidly remarks that Breton in the flea market probably encountered 'no more than the couturier Balmain in search of a rare colour of silk'.[47] (This was not a new danger. T. J. Clark notes that already in the 1880s, the *zoniers* were being sentimentalised by fashionable painters.[48]) Nevertheless, the Zone and the flea market were important Surrealist sites of estrangement and entropy. Perhaps finally, one must return to Atget's pictures of dissolution in the Zone, Boiffard's image of the flattened banality of the flea market and the hybrid landscape of Man Ray's *Terrain vague* to find photographs which eschew the predictable pleasure of juxtaposition in favour of a more nuanced indeterminacy – images that continue to trouble because they refuse to offer the easy formula of readymade collage.

Of all the encounters between nature and culture that fascinated the Surrealists, the most brutal and raw was to be found in the abattoir. Haussmann had sited the largest of the Paris abattoirs on the north-eastern edge of the city at La Villette, and most Parisians would have known of the place without ever having ventured near it. In 1929, though, two artists came here to experience it for themselves – the painter André Masson and the photographer Eli Lotar. The result of Masson's visit was a series of drawings and paintings on the theme of massacre and sacrifice. Although pictorially rooted in the 'convulsive' automatism Masson had developed as a member of the Surrealist group, these images were thematically allied to the ideas of his close friend Georges Bataille.[49]

The photographs that Lotar made at La Villette are very different in mood. Three of them were shortly afterwards published in *Documents*, juxtaposed with a short 'Dictionnaire' text by Bataille: 'Abattoir' (figure 48).[50] It was a subject ideally suited to the pages of *Documents*, typical of Bataille's assault on the higher aspirations of mankind and his belief in the impossibility of extricating the violent from the sacred (indeed from life itself):

> The slaughterhouse is linked to religion insofar as the temples of by-gone eras (not to mention those of the Hindus in our own day) served two purposes: they were used both for prayer and for killing ... In our time, nevertheless, the slaughterhouse is cursed and quarantined like a plague-ridden ship. Now the victims of this curse are neither butchers nor beasts, but those same good folk who countenance, by now, only their own unseemliness ... The curse ... leads them to vegetate as far as possible from the slaughterhouse, to exile themselves, out of propriety, to a flabby world in which nothing fearful remains and in which ... they are reduced to eating cheese.[51]

On the whole, the photographs in *Documents* were selected to illustrate an already written text. But, according to Bataille's colleague, Michel Leiris, the use of Lotar's pictures of the abattoir was one occasion in the magazine when the text was written in response to the images.[52] Evidently, Bataille was impressed with the pictures, yet the passion and sarcasm of his comments is at odds with the dispassionate mood of Lotar's photographs, which offer no such judgements.

In *Documents*, it is the first photograph in Lotar's 'Abattoir' sequence that is most striking (and by now best known). It depicts a row of cows' hooves propped up against a wall in the middle distance, surrounded by solid masonry and sightless windows. The wall above them is pocked and scratched, with the name PICHARD repeated twice, presumably that of the trader whose property they now are. It is as if these animals had been executed in the heart of an impenetrable prison; the only way through the space would seem to be on a twisting path where one would have to pass close by these remains. This powerful yet impassive image is reproduced full-page in *Documents*, a sober counterweight to Bataille's florid evocation of massacre and religion opposite.

That contrast between Lotar's image and Bataille's text was surely deliberate, for as Yves-Alain Bois observes, if Bataille wanted simply to reinforce the horror of the slaughter, there were plenty of other more blatant images to use, or on a more mediated level, he might have reproduced one of Masson's paintings. 'Violence', Bois suggests, 'is not a theme here, rather the question of its repression ... the photographs exhibit nothing that is not extremely orderly, and

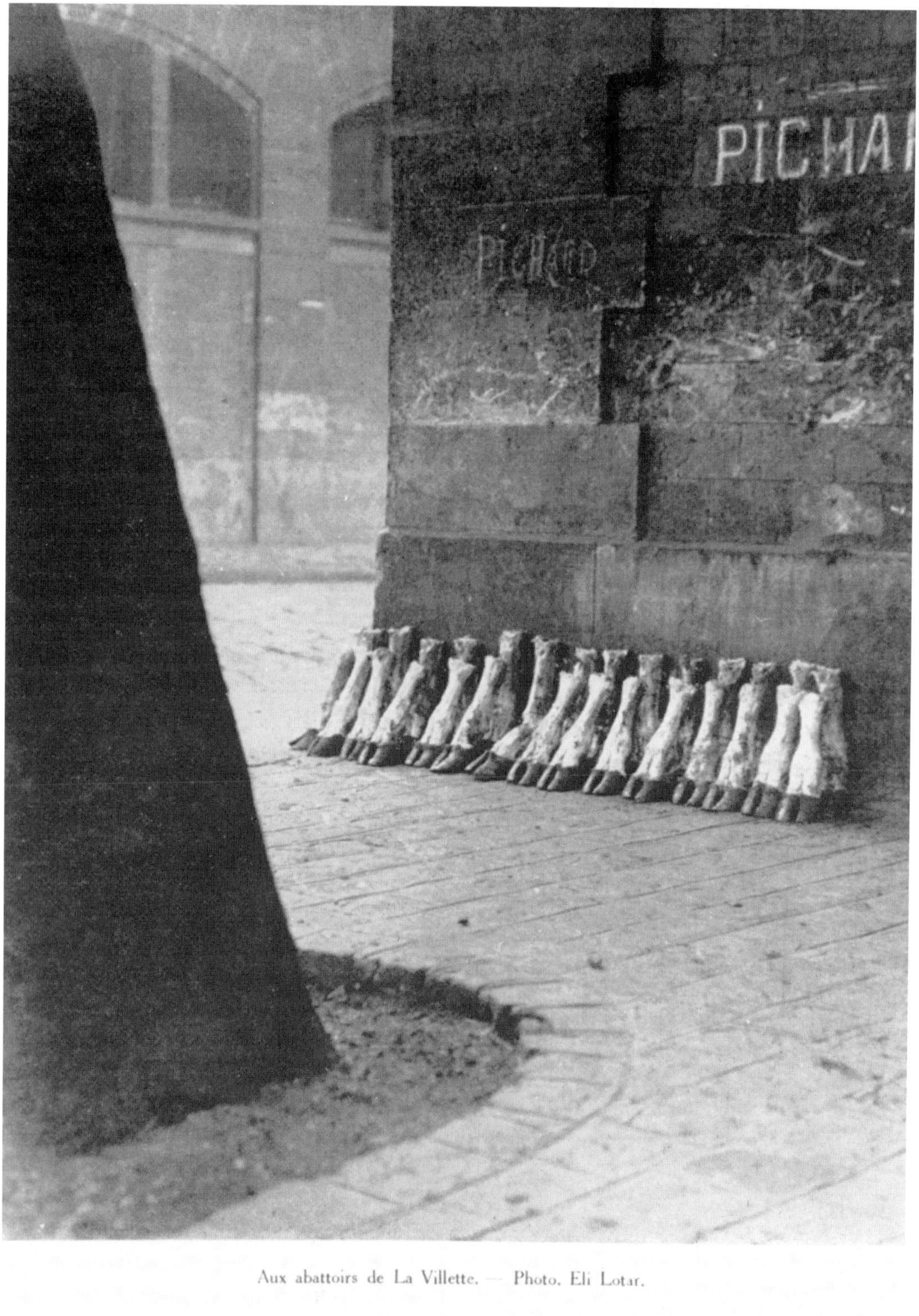

Aux abattoirs de La Villette. — Photo. Eli Lotar.

CHRONIQUE

DICTIONNAIRE

ABATTOIR. — L'abattoir relève de la religion en ce sens que des temples des époques reculées, (sans parler de nos jours de ceux des hindous) étaient à double usage, servant en même temps aux implorations et aux tueries. Il en résultait sans aucun doute (on peut en juger d'après l'aspect de chaos des abattoirs actuels) une coïncidence bouleversante entre les mystères mythologiques et la grandeur lugubre caractéristique des lieux où le sang coule. Il est curieux de voir s'exprimer en Amérique un regret lancinant : W. B. Seabrook (1) constatant que la vie orgiaque a subsisté, mais que le sang de sacrifices n'est pas mêlé aux cocktails, trouve insipide les mœurs actuelles. Cependant de nos jours l'abattoir est maudit et mis en quarantaine comme un bateau portant le choléra. Or les victimes de cette malédiction ne sont pas les bouchers ou les animaux, mais les braves gens eux-mêmes qui en sont arrivés à ne pouvoir supporter que leur propre laideur, laideur répondant en effet à un besoin maladif de propreté, de petitesse bilieuse et d'ennui: la malédiction (qui ne terrifie que ceux qui la profèrent) les amène à végéter aussi loin que possible des abattoirs, à s'exiler par correction dans un monde amorphe, où il n'y a plus rien d'horrible et où, subissant l'obsession indélébile de l'ignominie, ils sont réduits à manger du fromage. — G. BATAILLE.

(1) *L'Ile magique*, Firmin-Didot, 1929 (cf. plus loin, p. 334).

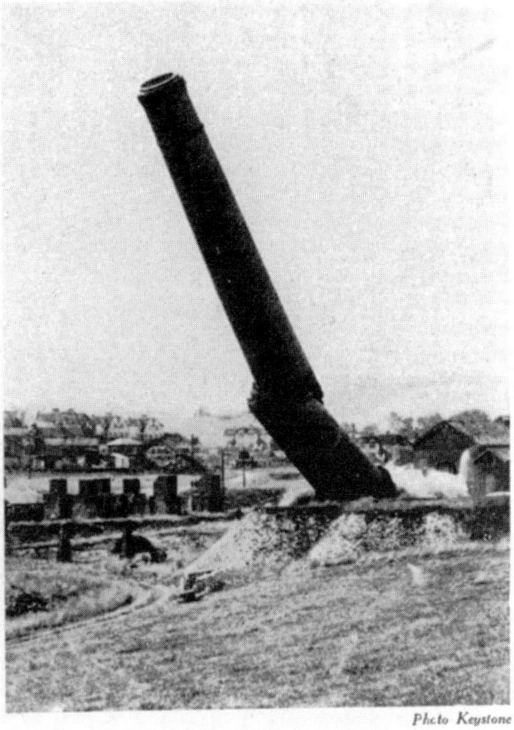

Photo Keystone

Chute d'une cheminée haute de 60 mètres
Banlieue de Londres.

CHEMINÉE D'USINE. — Si je tiens compte de mes souvenirs personnels, il semble que, dès l'apparition des diverses choses du monde, au cours de la première enfance, pour notre génération, les formes d'architecture terrifiantes étaient beaucoup moins les églises, même les plus monstrueuses, que certaines grandes cheminées d'usine, véritables tuyaux de communication entre le ciel sinistrement sale et la terre boueuse empuantie des quartiers de filatures et de teintureries.

Aujourd'hui, alors que de très misérables esthètes, en quête de placer leur chlorotique admiration, inventent platement la *beauté* des usines, la lugubre saleté de ces énormes tentacules m'apparaît d'autant plus écœurante, les flaques d'eau sous la pluie, à leur pied, dans les terrains vagues, la fumée noire à moitié rabattue par le vent, les monceaux de scories et de mâchefer sont bien les seuls attributs possibles de ces dieux d'un Olympe d'égout et je n'étais pas halluciné lorsque j'étais enfant et que ma terreur me faisait discerner dans mes épouvantails géants, qui m'attiraient jusqu'à l'angoisse et aussi parfois me faisaient fuir en courant à toutes jambes, la présence d'une effrayante colère, colère qui, pouvais-je m'en douter, allait devenir plus tard ma propre colère, donner un sens à tout ce qui se salissait dans ma tête, et en même temps à tout ce qui, dans des états civilisés, surgit comme la charogne dans un cauchemar. Sans doute je n'ignore pas que la plupart des gens, quand

32?

Fig 48 Spread from *Documents*, 1:6 (1929), with photograph by Eli Lotar.

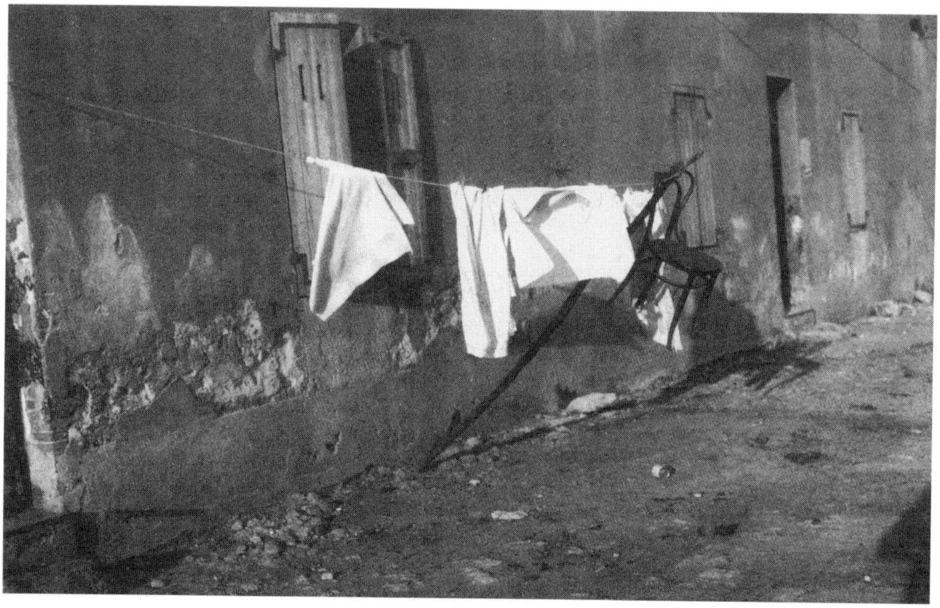

Fig 49 Eli Lotar, *Somewhere in Paris*, 1929.

it is the banality of this very order that is sinister.'[53] The deaths of these animals is a bureaucratic process – they are placed in a row as if on an assembly line. But Lotar's abattoir photographs are not themselves banal. Denis Hollier has called them 'crude', adding that '*Documents* specialised in this sort of illustrations [*sic*], ones resolutely turning their back on surrealism's erotic aestheticising'.[54] There is an aesthetic here, though. The distance of these photographs is surely highly measured and formal, but it is not a formality that serves a merely aesthetic end; rather, it serves to re-emphasise the very orderliness of the abattoir, the efficient administration of animal death.

To understand these pictures, we need in addition to turn to Eli Lotar's other work.[55] Lotar learnt his photography from Germaine Krull, whom he had met in 1926; they quickly became partners, both personally and professionally. By 1928 he was publishing and exhibiting his own work, and in 1929 his photographs, along with those of Atget, Man Ray, Kertész and Krull, was chosen by *L'Art vivant* to help answer the question: 'La Photographie est-elle un art?'[56] The spread of pictures chosen emphasised radical, formalist composition, industrial subject-matter and large intense close-ups, which all suggest a strong affinity with the style of Krull, the leading exponent in Paris of the 'new objectivity' then dominant in Germany.[57]

One photograph in the spread, entitled (in English) 'Somewhere in Paris', is very different (figure 49). It depicts a curious little genre scene: the side of a house from which the plaster is peeling, washing hung out to dry and, at the far end, a chair also hanging in mid-air. As the title suggests, the scene is both ordinary and resonant in its indeterminacy, a sort of domestic *terrain vague*. It

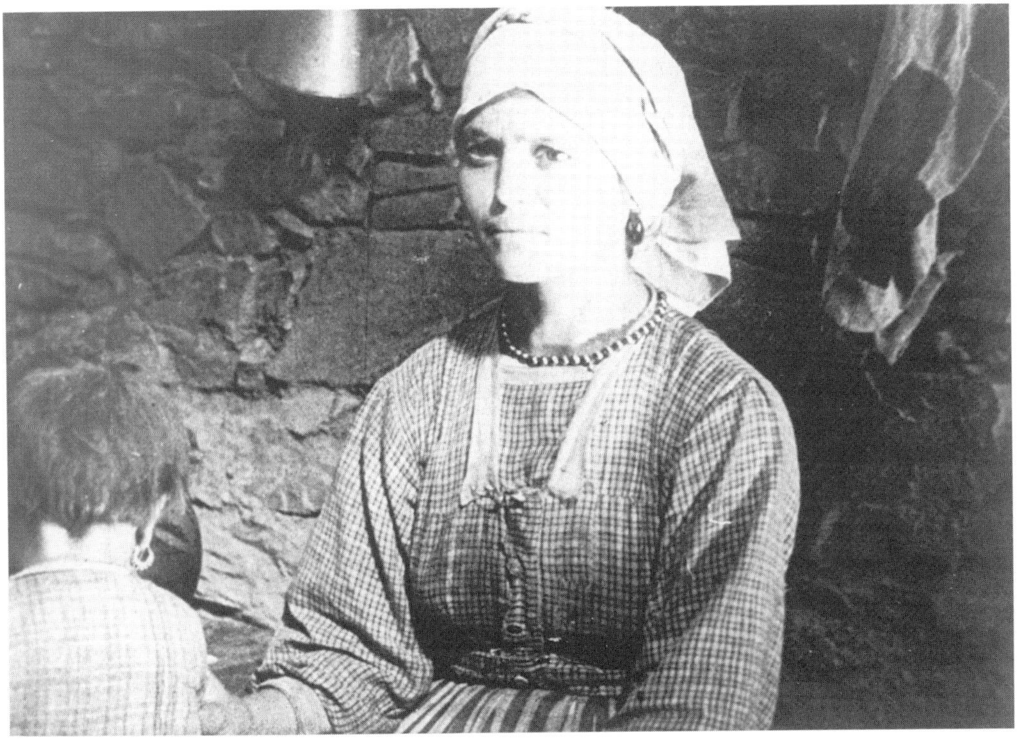

Fig 50 Frame still from Luis Buñuel, *Las Hurdes (Land without Bread)*, 1933.

seems that Lotar had an affinity with Surrealism that Krull did not and this was borne out when, in 1929, he set up a studio in partnership with his friend Jacques-André Boiffard. Lotar's work, then, can be seen as a point of conjunction between a 'new objectivity' approach to photography and a 'surrealist' one.

The studio did not last long, and in the early 1930s Lotar turned increasingly to documentary film, working as cameraman for Joris Ivens (Krull's husband at the time), the natural history film-maker Jean Painlevé and for Luis Buñuel on *Las Hurdes* (*Land without Bread*), his 1933 film about the impoverished peasants of Las Hurdes in Spain (figure 50). There, in Buñuel's excursion into documentary, one can see an attitude very similar to that which Lotar brought to his abattoir photographs: a clinical gaze at a reality that is so far beyond the bounds of accustomed normality that it becomes surreal. It is in the very strictness of its documentary approach that its Surrealism lies.[58]

The same mood predominates in a later documentary film that may well have taken as its starting point Lotar's photographs of the abattoir: Georges Franju's *Le sang des bêtes* of 1949 (figure 51). With an equally unflinching gaze, Franju also recorded the slaughter of La Villette and its 'sister' abattoir at Vaugirard, showing the two slaughterhouses firmly set in the landscape of the Zone, 'at the gates of Paris, on the wastelands, gardens of poor children' where

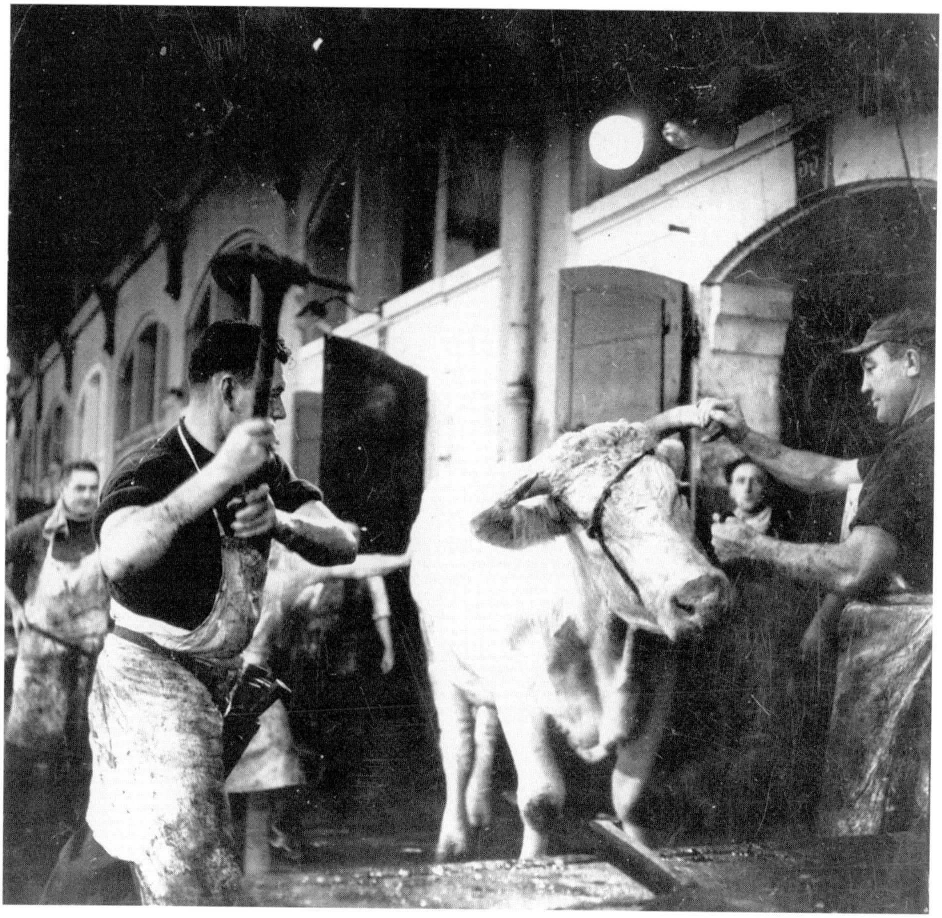

Fig 51 Frame still from Georges Franju, *Le sang des bêtes*, 1949.

'is scattered the peculiar debris of uncertain wealth'.[59] The film opens by revealing surreal arrangements of second hand goods laid out on the waste ground: a print of a Renoir painting and an umbrella, a chandelier hanging from a tree, a nude mannequin and the horn of a record player. Then the camera moves away to enter the brutal interior world of the abattoir; as it does so, it passes a young couple in an embrace.[60]

The commentary for *Le sang des bêtes* was written by Jean Painlevé, who brought to it the clinical edge of his own natural history films. Painlevé was another important link in the chain of connections here, and he was working particularly closely with Lotar at the time he made his photographs at La Villette. Painlevé had been friendly with the Surrealists since the mid-1920s. Because his father, Paul Painlevé, was a Minister of State, he was able to obtain the blotting pads from a ministers' meeting which were published to scandalous effect in *La Révolution surréaliste*.[61] By the end of the decade, he was closer to the dissident group, particularly to Lotar and Boiffard.[62] Lotar worked as

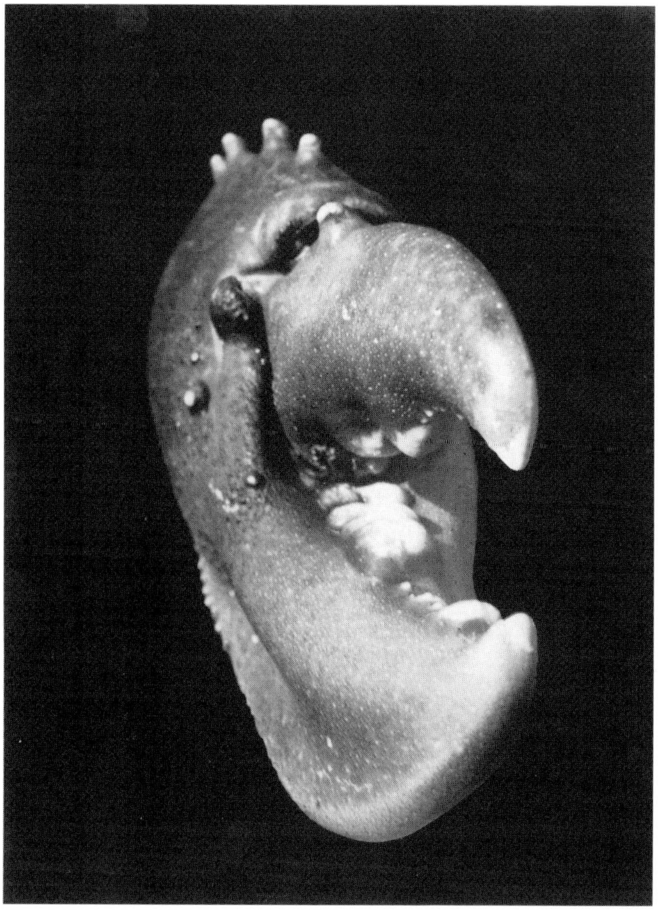

Fig 52 Jean Painlevé, *Lobster claw*, 1929. © Les Documents Cinématographiques.

Painlevé's cameraman on *Caprelles et Pantopodes* (1929) and *Crabes* (1930). They also collaborated on still photographs of the same subjects; one set of images – some by Lotar, some by Painlevé – was published in *Art et Decoration* in 1931, though as the siting would suggest, the emphasis there was on the formal rather than the surreal qualities of the undersea creatures.[63] Elsewhere, Lotar and Painlevé have also individually been credited with still images which relate to Painlevé's films, though one may suspect throughout an element of collaboration.[64]

Though he worked in a scientific genre, Painlevé's films were often studded with ironic humour and a strong sense of the bizarre (figure 52). His approach to the creatures he filmed (most famously, the seahorse in his 1934 film: *L'Hippocampe*) represents another sort of hybridisation between nature and culture. For though Painlevé filmed natural forms very distant from our own, the creatures within the film were anthropomorphised through the voice-over commentary, resulting, as it were, in a sort of *un*natural history.[65] (The same

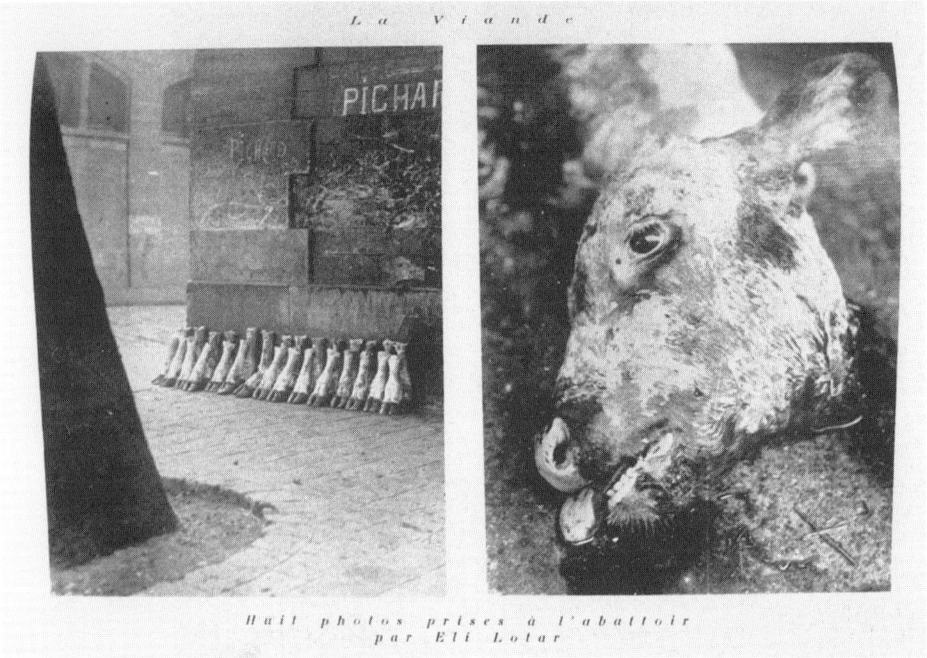

Fig 53 Eli Lotar, 'La Viande', *Variétés*, 2:12 (1930).

quality is to be found in the introductory sequence to Buñuel's *L'Age d'or*, where the images of scorpions fighting could have come from a Painlevé film.[66] Perhaps this was a reciprocation of Painlevé's admiration for the coldly clinical opening sequence of *Un Chien andalou*.)

The 'Dictionnaire' section of *Documents* which began with 'Abattoir' also contained an entry on 'Crustacea', and a double-page spread juxtaposed two of Lotar's abattoir photographs with two stills from Painlevé's films. These images of a 'tête de crevette' and a 'tête de crabe' are as discomfiting in their viscerality as the abattoir scenes opposite; in both cases, the order – of man and of nature – seems tenuously balanced against a threat of chaos. This placement of Painlevé's work was part of an intricate set of juxtapositions around Lotar's photographs. The entry in the 'Dictionnaire' immediately after 'Abattoir' was 'Factory Chimney', and Bataille reproduced a small photograph of a chimney being demolished (again in an industrial wasteland: the 'Banlieue de Londres') (figure 48). The chimney falls as we imagine the cattle fell.

Documents was not the only site of publication for Lotar's abattoir photographs. The following year, in *Variétés*, E.L.T. Mesens reproduced a larger selection of eight images in a section of four pages.[67] As elsewhere, it was through the layout that Mesens made his own mute comment. On the left of the first page was reproduced the same powerful image of the row of hooves that had appeared full page in *Documents*. Here its distanced sobriety is placed next to and disrupted by a large and bloody close-up of a staring calf's head (figure

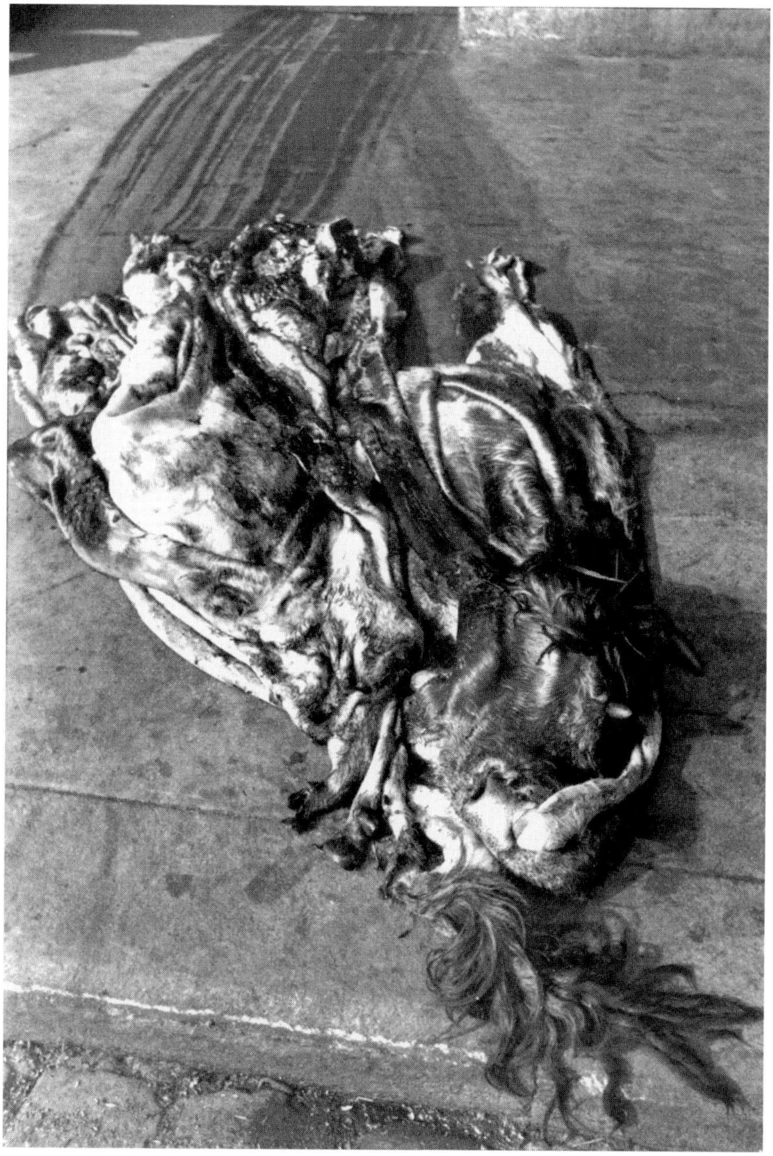

Fig 54 Henri Cartier-Bresson, *La Villette, Paris, 1932*. © Henri Cartier-Bresson/Magnum Photos.

53). On the following pages, the messy process of slaughter is juxtaposed with the ordered, carefully arranged aftermath, the dismembered animal forms placed in a context of work and industry. The other major difference between the appearance of these pictures in *Documents* and *Variétés* is the absence of all text in the latter. Or nearly all, for there is a title: LA VIANDE. Succinctly, Mesens pinpoints the process that is going on here: nature becoming culture, the raw in the first stage of its transformation into the cooked. Mesens' cool, almost imperceptible irony is surely closer to the tone of Lotar's photographs than

Bataille's melodrama. Nevertheless, all three would have agreed with the need to challenge the silence of bourgeois culture, this 'flabby world in which nothing fearful remains', a culture that would prefer not to know anything about the brutal processes that underpin its comfort.[68]

In 1932, another young photographer, Henri Cartier-Bresson, visited La Villette, 'evidently ... inspired' by Lotar's photographs.[69] Only one image survives from Cartier-Bresson's visit there, unprinted until 1986 (figure 54). But it is an extraordinary picture, remarkable even in the disorientating context of Cartier-Bresson's work of the time. A large animal skin has been dragged across the pavement to the edge of the kerb, and the photographer has gone in low and close so that it recedes sharply away from us. The effect is sensuous; one could reach out and fondle the fur. Whereas Lotar (and Franju after him) came to La Villette in overcast, grey weather, Cartier-Bresson photographed in bright sunlight. Yet the skin is also intensely disturbing, because the hank of hair in the immediate foreground is unnervingly human-like, almost as if a (female) human body had evaporated from beneath a fur coat. The result is both fascinating and repulsive, immediately physical yet suggestive, even metaphorical, in a way that Lotar refused to be. Where Lotar stands back, Cartier-Bresson moves to within touching distance, where Lotar is 'objective', Cartier-Bresson's image is 'convulsive'. For as we will see, in his work of the early 1930s Cartier-Bresson offered an approach to Surrealist documentary photography radically different from the studied neutrality established by Boiffard and Lotar under the influence of Atget.

The selection of photographs examined in this chapter has been fragmentary in nature, and it is appropriate that the *terrain vague* should be pictured in images whose status remains shifting and uneasy. But there is one final image that offers, if not resolution, then at least a compilation of the varied elements discussed here. This is a collage by an artist on the fringes of Surrealism, Kurt Seligmann, entitled *Les animaux surréalistes* and first reproduced in the *Dictionnaire abrégé de surréalisme* published in 1938 (figure 55).[70] Constructed in the manner of Max Ernst's *Loplop presenting the Surrealists*, the most obvious feature of the collage is a collection of pictures of 'surrealist' animals: a praying mantis, a giraffe, a rhinoceros, a pelican, a platypus and a little group of seahorses placed as if hooked on at the top.

But it is the background of the image that is the main point of interest here. It is a rough-hewn stone wall, isolated and left standing in a state of ruination: a sort of nameless monument to which the animal pictures are attached. To the bottom right is a glimpse of the sea, while in the top left opposite corner is a factory chimney. Across the image – across the wall – is drawn then the dialectical opposition between unbounded nature and industrialised culture which we have examined in this chapter. The animals, natural creatures transformed through photographic reproduction, straddle this divide. In the middle of the image is another element, for apparently drawn directly on the

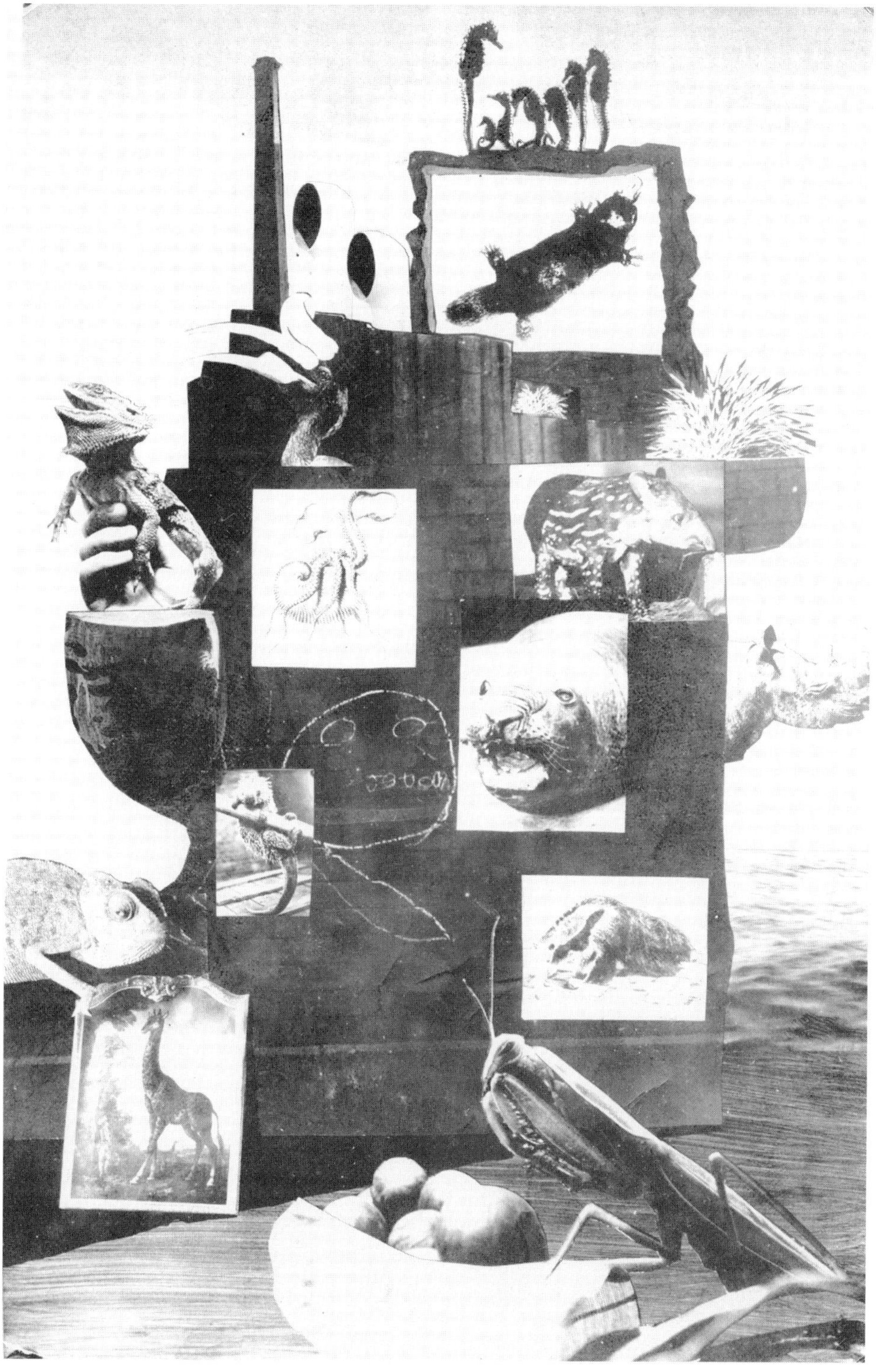

Fig 55 Kurt Seligmann, *Les animaux surréalistes*, 1938. © Orange County Citizens Foundation.

wall is a childish graffito of a face, both fearsome and laughable. It also partakes of the various elements of this discourse, simultaneously 'cultural' and 'natural', a paradigm of the primitive within modern culture. Such graffiti appeared throughout Surrealism, but there is one body of work in which it was extensively explored. These were the set of photographs of *Graffiti parisiens* which Brassaï first published in 1933. Along with his images of Paris by night, it is this work which best represents the development of a Surrealist realism into the mid-1930s.

Notes

1 The literature on the modern city is of course enormous, but useful introductions can be found in Elizabeth Wilson, *The Sphinx in the City* (London: Virago, 1991) and James Donald, 'Metropolis; the city as text', in Robert Bocock and Kenneth Thompson (eds), *Social and Cultural Forms of Modernity* (Cambridge: Polity Press, 1992), pp. 417–70. Specifically on Paris, see Michael Sheringham (ed.), *Parisian Fields* (London: Reaktion, 1996).

2 For an elaboration of Aragon's choice of title, see Robin Walz, *Pulp Surrealism: Insolent Popular Culture in Early Twentieth Century Paris* (Berkeley and Los Angeles: University of California Press, 2000), p. 26.

3 Louis Aragon, *Paris Peasant* (London: Jonathan Cape, 1971), p. 28.

4 George Melly and Michael Woods, *Paris and the Surrealists* (London: Thames and Hudson, 1991), p. 97.

5 Aragon, *Paris Peasant*, p. 130.

6 The garden as site of the nature/culture debate has also been been the subject of critical exploration in recent times. For a pithy introduction, see Dan Graham, 'Garden as Theater as Museum', in *Rock My Religion* (Cambridge, MA: MIT Press, 1993), pp. 286–307; a more extensive analysis can be found in Mark Francis and Randolph T. Hester (eds), *The Meaning of Gardens* (Cambridge, MA: MIT Press, 1990).

7 Aragon, *Paris Peasant*, p. 134.

8 *Ibid.*, p. 135.

9 *Ibid.*, p. 141.

10 *Ibid.*, p. 62.

11 The picture is dated 1932 on a typed list from Man Ray himself in the George Eastman House Museum, Rochester. *Terrain vague* seems to have been first reproduced, untitled, in Man Ray's anthology, *Photographs 1920–34* (Paris/Hartford, Connecticut: James Thrall Soby, 1934). There, *Terrain vague* is placed between two images that are more definite in their sense of place. Before it is one of Man Ray's rare photographs of a purely natural landscape, a view between two rows of shadowy trees, and after it a photograph taken by night of the Place de la Concorde. The indeterminacy of *Terrain vague* serves to undercut the easy contrast between a feminine Nature on the one hand and a masculine Culture on the other.

12 Molly Nesbit, *Atget's Seven Albums* (New Haven and London: Yale University Press, 1992), pp. 193–4. Atget's album 'Fortifications de Paris' is reproduced in full, pp. 414–28.

13 As Charles Dickens wrote of suburban London: 'It is neither of the town nor country. The former, like a giant in his travelling boots, has made a stride and passed it, and has set his brick-and-mortar heel a long way in advance; but the intermediate space between the giant's feet, as yet, is only blighted country, and not town.' (from *Dombey and Son*, chapter 33, quoted by Phillip Collins, 'Dickens and the City', in William Sharpe and Leonard Wallock (eds), *Visions of the Modern City* (Baltimore: Johns Hopkins University Press, 1987), p. 117).

14 A few fragments of the fortifications still remain. In Didier Daeninckx's contemporary crime novel *Murder in Memoriam*, two of the characters visit some remains near the Porte d'Italie and discuss the historical status of the Zone (London: Serpent's Tail, 1991, pp. 107–9).

15 T. J. Clark, *The Painting of Modern Life: Paris in the Art of Manet and his Followers* (Princeton: Princeton University Press, 1984), pp. 25–30. Clark notes that this passage was added to the 1861 edition of *Les Miserables*. He also discusses a small painting of the *banlieue* by van Gogh: *The Outskirts of Paris*, 1886.

16 Jean-Jacques Rousseau's *Rêveries du promeneur solitaire* was his final work, written before his death in 1778 (translated as *Reveries of the Solitary Walker* (Harmondsworth: Penguin, 1979)).

17 For a historical account of the process of Haussmannisation, see David H. Pinkney, *Napoleon III and the Rebuilding of Paris* (Princeton: Princeton University Press, 1972). The cultural implications are discussed by Clark, *The Painting of Modern Life*, chapter 1: 'The View from Notre Dame'. Marshall Berman, *All That is Solid Melts into Air* (London: Verso, 1983), p. 150, discusses this process as it is reflected in the writings of Baudelaire and his notes give further references (p. 359).

18 Jonathan Crary, 'Spectacle, Attention, Counter-Memory', *October*, 50 (Autumn 1989), p. 107. For the full quotation, see Chapter 4.

19 For the importance of the Zone in Parisian popular culture, and further primary sources, see Adrian Rifkin, *Street Noises: Parisian pleasure, 1900–40* (Manchester: Manchester University Press, 1993).

20 Warren Ramsey, in his foreword in Guillaume Apollinaire, *Alcools* (Berkeley: University of California, 1965), p. xxvi, suggests the identification with the 'outer margin of society'.

21 Walter Benjamin, *Charles Baudelaire: A Lyric Poet in the Era of High Capitalism* (London: New Left Books, 1976), p. 79. Benjamin is here specifically referring to Baudelaire's poem, 'Le vin des chiffonniers' ('The ragpickers' wine') in *Les Fleurs du mal* (1857).

22 Atget's album *Zoniers* is reproduced with further discussion of the myth of the Zone in Nesbit, *Atget's Seven Albums*, pp. 398–412.

23 See Chapter 5. Krull also worked in the Zone; in 1928, at the Porte de Bagnolet, she photographed 'La refuge', a house made from many pieces of scrap metal, collaged together to form a sort of parody of the structures she had photographed for *Métal*. See Kim Sichel, *Germaine Krull: Photographer of Modernity* (Cambridge, MA: MIT Press, 1999), p. 187.

24 'Photographie: Vision du monde', in *Photographies*, special issue of *Arts et métiers graphiques*, 16 (1 March 1930), p. 134. 'No man's land' is in English in the original.

25 John Szarkowski and Maria Morris Hambourg, *The Work of Atget: Vol. IV: Modern Times* (New York: Museum of Modern Art, 1985), p. 167.

26 On Man Ray's collection of Atget prints, see Chapter 5 n. 4.

27 In the following year, 1921, Man Ray travelled by ocean liner from New York to Paris, where he made a collage incorporating the *New York* photograph and a fragment of a map of Paris; he called it *Transatlantique*. For illustrations and more details, see Merry Foresta (ed.), *Perpetual Motif: The Art of Man Ray* (Washington: National Museum of American Art/New York: Abbeville Press, 1989), pp. 136–7.

28 Translated in Georges Bataille *et al.*, *Encyclopaedia Acephalica* (London: Atlas Press, 1995), pp. 42–3. Originally published in *Documents*, 1:5 (October 1929), p. 278, accompanied by a photograph of a group of mannequins in a dusty storeroom.

29 Yves-Alain Bois and Rosalind Krauss, *Formless: A User's Guide* (New York: Zone, 1997), p. 226.

30 Edouard Jaguer, *Les mystères de la chambre noire* (Paris: Flammarion, 1982), p. 84, gives the date as 1937, but in van Moerkerken's *Reportages in licht en schadeuw* (Amsterdam: Geert van Oorschot, 1947), it is dated 1935 and this was confirmed in an interview with the author (Amsterdam: 1993).

31 Jaguer, *Les mystères de la chambre noire*, p. 84.

32 Interview with the author (Amsterdam: 1993).

33 One might be reminded here of Walter Benjamin's comment: 'Balzac was the first to speak of the ruins of the bourgeoisie. But it was Surrealism which first allowed its gaze to roam freely over it.' (Benjamin, *Charles Baudelaire,* p. 176).

34 In the late 1930s, several Surrealists responded to the political events of the period with images of the ruin as sterility – notably Max Ernst with his *Entire City* paintings. But others continued to see the ruin as a site of liberation. In the last issue of *Minotaure*, there is an article by Benjamin Péret: 'Ruines: ruine des ruines' (12–13 (1939), 57–61). What ruins, he asks, will Paris leave to be discovered by another era? 'Not the churches ... not the banks; but perhaps someone will one day find ... the gigantic fossil of a unique animal, the Eiffel Tower.' The text was accompanied by three images in which Raoul Ubac utilised the 'bas relief' technique to show Paris monuments – the Bourse, the Eiffel Tower and the Opéra – as 'fossils'. They are among the most culturally resonant of Surrealist manipulated photographs – the Eiffel Tower transformed into the fossilised animal evoked by Péret.

35 Robert Doisneau, *La Banlieue de Paris* (Paris: Seghers/Lausanne: La Guide du Livre, 1949).

36 For contemporary photographs of this *terrain vague* under and around the *périphérique*, see *Paul Seawright* (Salamanca: Ediciones Universidad de Salamanca, 2000), pp. 135–61. This publication also contains a text by the present author discussing the varied connotations of the *terrain vague* in twentieth-century art and culture.

37 Dubuffet's presence is referred to in Agnès Angliviel de la Beaumelle *et al.*, *André Breton: la beauté convulsive* (Paris: Musée nationale d'art moderne, 1991), pp. 402–3. Lévi-Strauss described his own participation with the comment: 'it was a great honour to be allowed to accompany Breton on this occasion' (Didier Eribon, *Conversations with Claude Lévi-Strauss* (Chicago: University of Chicago Press, 1991), p. 33).

38 See de la Beaumelle *et al.*, *André Breton*, p. 425. Freund's photograph was taken in 1960.

39 Noted by Marguerite Bonnet in André Breton, *Oeuvres Complètes, Vol. I* (Paris: Gallimard, 1988), p. 1539 n. 2.

40 André Breton, *Nadja* (New York: Grove Press, 1960), p. 52.

41 André Kertész, *Day of Paris* (New York: J. J. Augustin, 1946), pp. 42–3.

42 Van Moerkerken included several images from the flea market in two anthologies of his work: *Reportages in licht en schadeuw*, nos 36 and 83, and *Foto's* (Amsterdam, De Bezige Bij, 1989), no. 14.

43 *Without Antidote* (*Bez Protijedu*) is one of a number of hand-made books by Sever now in the collection of the Museum of Decorative Arts in Prague. Some of the images are included the anthology of his work: *Jiří Sever* (Prague: Odeon, 1968). In 1966, another Czech Surrealist Emila Medková also visited Paris and photographed in the flea market.

44 This 'title' derives from the text that René Crevel wrote to accompany the publication of Brandt's image in *Minotaure*: 'La Grande Mannequin cherche et trouve sa peau', 5 (May 1934), 18–19.

45 This was an aspect of the fascination with decay and entropy that runs through Czech Surrealist photography. For an image made by Štyrský at a flea market, see Anna Fárová, 'Un Tcheque: Jindřich Štyrský', in Pierre Barbin (ed.), *Colloques Atget*, special number of *Photographies* (March 1986), p. 80. After the war, Vilém Reichmann made many images in Brno of the flotsam left by a culture torn apart. When he came to later title a sequence of flea-market photographs made in 1947, he gave them the caustic title *Co zanechali Sudetáci*: 'What Was Left by the Sudeten Germans.' (See Antonín Dufek, *Vilém Reichmann* (Ceské Budéjovice: Foto Mida, 1994), plates 41–2.) However, when Reichmann showed his work in Germany, he gave these images less provocative titles: 'Reading the Dream Book' and 'Good Forsaken' (*Fotografien*, Berlin: Ex pose, 1989, p. 52).

46 Van Moerkerken, *Foto's*, p. 170. The other two photographs in the *Great Expectations* sequence were also of female mannequins (*ibid.*, nos 21 and 30). Van Moerkerken had met Chris van Geel at the International Surrealist exhibition in Amsterdam in 1938 and they subsequently made a number of 'performance photographs' together (see Jaguer, *Les mystères de la chambre noire*, p. 115) and formed the nucleus of the Dutch Surrealist group (see Hans Renders, *Verijdelde Dromen* (Haarlem: Joh. Enschede en Zonen, 1989)).

47 Rifkin, *Street Noises*, p. 125.

48 Clark, *The Painting of Modern Life*, pp. 26–7.

49 On Masson's relationship with Bataille, see Dawn Ades: 'Movement and Metamorphosis', in David Sylvester *et al.*, *André Masson: Line Unleashed* (London: South Bank Centre, 1987), pp. 38–9. A spread of the 'Massacre' drawings were reproduced in the first issue of *Minotaure* and in an interview with Jeanine Warnod in 1983 (Charles Georg (ed.), *Focus on Minotaure* (Geneva: Musée d'Art et d'Histoire, 1987), pp. 246–7), Masson said that André Breton had also been very interested in the images.

50 Georges Bataille, 'Abattoir', *Documents*, 6 (November 1929), 328–30.

51 Translation from Bataille *et al.*, *Encyclopaedia Acephalica*, pp. 72–3.

52 Interview with the author (Paris: 1979).

53 Bois and Krauss, *Formless*, p. 43.

54 Denis Hollier, *Against Architecture: The Writings of George Bataille* (Cambridge, MA: MIT Press, 1989), p. xii.

55 For a long time, it seemed that Lotar's work was lost except for those few images published at the time. However, his negatives were rediscovered in 1991 and prints made from them exhibited at the Pompidou Centre in 1993, with a very informative catalogue (Annick Lionel-Marie, *Eli Lotar* (Paris: Musée national d'art moderne, 1993)).

56 All the portfolios were accompanied by short texts by Jean Gallotti. Lotar's spread was in the issue for 1 August, following p. 605. It is reproduced in Horacio Fernández, *Fotografía Pública (Photography in Print 1919–1939)* (Madrid: Museo Nacional de Arte Reina Sofia, 1999), p. 165. On the same page is also reproduced the complete spread of his abattoir photographs from *Variétiés* (see below, n. 67).

57 On Krull, see Sichel, *Germaine Krull*. Her relationship with Lotar is detailed on pp. 85–6. Sichel also makes some connections between Krull and Surrealism (pp. 116–17); noteworthy in this context are her photographs showing the debris left by Parisian street markets (pp. 196–8).

58 For further references to *Land without Bread*, see Chapter 9.

59 Georges Franju and Jean Painlevé, 'Le sang des bêtes', *L'Avant-scène du cinéma*, 41 (1 October 1964), 46.

60 On the surrealism of Franju's early documentaries, see Gérard Leblanc, *Georges Franju: une esthétique de la déstabilisation* (Paris: Maison de la Villette, 1991). See also Franju's own essay 'Réalisme et surréalisme', in Georges Vialle, *Georges Franju* (Paris: Seghers, 1968), pp. 84–7, where he cites as an example of a film which is simultaneously realist and surrealist a medical study of *Trépanation pour crise d'épilepsie*.

61 *La Révolution surréaliste*, 6 (1 March 1926), 16–7.

62 Boiffard photographed him at work; see Philippe Sers (ed.), *Atelier Man Ray* (Paris: Centre Georges Pompidou, 1982), p. 35.

63 See Jean Cassou, 'L'Art sous-marin', *Art et Décoration*, 59 (January–June 1931), 143–50.

64 There is, for example, a photograph of a shrimp's tail which, in the Julien Levy collection (Art Institute of Chicago), is attributed to Lotar (see also Lionel-Marie, *Eli Lotar*, p. 19), but which has also been attributed to Painlevé (see Andy Masaki Bellows and Marina McDougall, *Science is Fiction: The Films of Jean Painlevé* (Cambridge, MA: MIT Press, 2000), p. 110).

65 On Painlevé, see also Brigitte Berg (ed.), *Jean Painlevé* (Paris: Les Cahiers cinématographiques, 1991). A compilation of Painlevé's films was issued on video in Britain in 1995: *Surrealism and Science: The Weird World of Jean Painlevé* (Connoisseur Academy Video: CAV 036).

66 In fact, the sequence was 'appropriated' from a popular science documentary *Le scorpion languedocian* (see Paul Hammond, *L'Age d'or* (London: British Film Institute, 1997), p. 8).

67 *Variétés*, 2:12 (15 April 1930), between 320–1.

68 In light of Aragon's comments on gardens in *Le paysan de Paris*, it's ironic that the former abattoir at La Villette has now been converted into a post-modern version of a classical French garden (see Graham, 'Garden as Theater as Museum', pp. 301–7).

69 The phrase is Peter Galassi's (*Henri Cartier-Bresson: The Early Work* (New York: Museum of Modern Art, 1987), p. 35). He does not indicate however whether this is based on information from Cartier-Bresson himself.

70 André Breton and Paul Eluard (eds), *Dictionnaire abrégé de surréalisme* (Paris: Galerie des Beaux-Arts, 1938).

7
Brassaï: Paris night and day

When Man Ray bought his selection of prints from Atget in the mid-1920s, he was possibly planning to use them in a book of photographs of Paris.[1] The photographs he himself made of the city at the same time may well have been for the same project.[2] The book, however, remained unpublished. If it had appeared, it would have been one of the first of a new type of photographic book about Paris which began to be produced in the late 1920s, providing an alternative to the traditional guidebook (if not the radical antidote that *Nadja* represents).

These books generally featured the work of a single photographer, supported by a text from a well-known writer associated with the city.[3] The 1930 volume of Atget's pictures with an essay by Pierre MacOrlan was a fairly conservative example of this format; the photographs are laid out very formally – one per page – printed with a sepia tint that emphasises the sense of retrospection. Though earlier, Germaine Krull's *100 x Paris* of 1928 was more innovative, with both pictures and layout reflecting the modernist dynamism of the city.[4] MacOrlan also provided the text for *Paris vu par André Kertész* (1934), which presented a gentle, wistful image of the city.[5] It was this romanticism which came to dominate the genre after the war, with Robert Doisneau's *La Banlieue de Paris* (1949, text by Blaise Cendrars), Willy Ronis' *Belleville-Menilmontant* (1954, MacOrlan again) and Izis' *Paris de rêves* (1950) where the photographs were accompanied by short texts from a range of Parisian writers, including André Breton.[6]

But of all the books in this genre, the one that made the greatest impact was *Paris de nuit* by Brassaï, published in 1932 with an introduction by Paul Morand.[7] This was Brassaï's first book and quickly became a nodal point both of his own career and of Parisian photography at the time. In the phrase coined by his friend Henry Miller, Brassaï was perceived as the 'eye of Paris', and his images have come to represent a central aspect of the mythology of the city.[8]

Brassaï was thirty-three when *Paris de nuit* appeared. Born Gyula Halász in Brasso, Transylvania (the pseudonym he adopted means 'from Brasso'), he came to Paris in 1924 to pursue a career as a journalist. Gradually, through a friendship with his fellow Hungarian André Kertész and a meeting with Eugène

Atget,[9] he became more interested in photography, and in about 1930, started to make his nocturnal pictures of Paris. These photographs have been much discussed, and I will concentrate here only on their relationship to Surrealism, and the actual placement of a number of them within a Surrealist context.[10] In the second half of this chapter, I want to consider another body of work which Brassaï also began to develop in the early 1930s – his photographs of Parisian graffiti. I will argue that, even though these were less centrally sited within Surrealism, there is a stronger connection between that work and Surrealist values.

In discussing Brassaï's photography of Paris by night, one needs to be specific as to which pictures are in question, for there are in effect three different strands of this work and they hardly intersect. First, there is the selection of pictures published in *Paris de nuit* in 1932. The book meshes together two different cities: the world of ordinary workers labouring through the night to keep the city going and alongside that, a Paris of culture and pleasure; evidently, there was a need to strike a balance between the social value of the book and its touristic appeal. What hardly appears at all in *Paris de nuit* – and in fact formed a somewhat different project – is the most celebrated of Brassaï's different versions of Paris by night – the underlife of the city, its bars, brothels and nightclubs. Only in 1976 was this aspect of his *oeuvre* fully revealed with the publication of *The Secret Paris of the 30s*.[11]

None of this would seem to have held much interest for the Surrealists. However, there is a third siting of Brassaï's night-time photographs which is quite distinct: their reproduction in Surrealist publications, most notably the (Surrealist-influenced if not controlled) magazine *Minotaure* and later in André Breton's book *L'Amour fou*. The photographs used in those publications did not overlap with the pictures published either in *Paris de nuit* or in *The Secret Paris of the 30s*, and it is this selection of images we must consider more closely to understand properly the relationship that Brassaï had with Surrealism. In fact, Brassaï's work was featured predominantly in six of the first seven issues of *Minotaure*, and his night photography was central to issue no. 7 (June 1935): 'The Nocturnal Side of Nature'. This issue contained articles on Uccello and Georges de la Tour, extracts from Young's *Night Thoughts*, Balthus' illustrations for *Wuthering Heights* as well as André Breton's text 'La Nuit du tournesol'. But Brassaï has a dominating presence in this issue of the magazine with seventeen photographs in all.[12]

The appeal of Brassaï's night pictures for the Surrealists seems on one level quite obvious. As he himself said: 'They considered my photographs "surrealist", because they revealed a ghostly, unreal Paris, drowned in the night and the fog.'[13] Manuel Borja-Villel has developed this connection: 'Night was the natural setting for Surrealist actions; the place where dreams are dreamed and passions awake, crimes are committed and evil lurks.'[14] This is the city of Fantômas. Yet Brassaï's night photographs are not on the whole so melodramatic as this, and there may have been more specific and subtle reasons

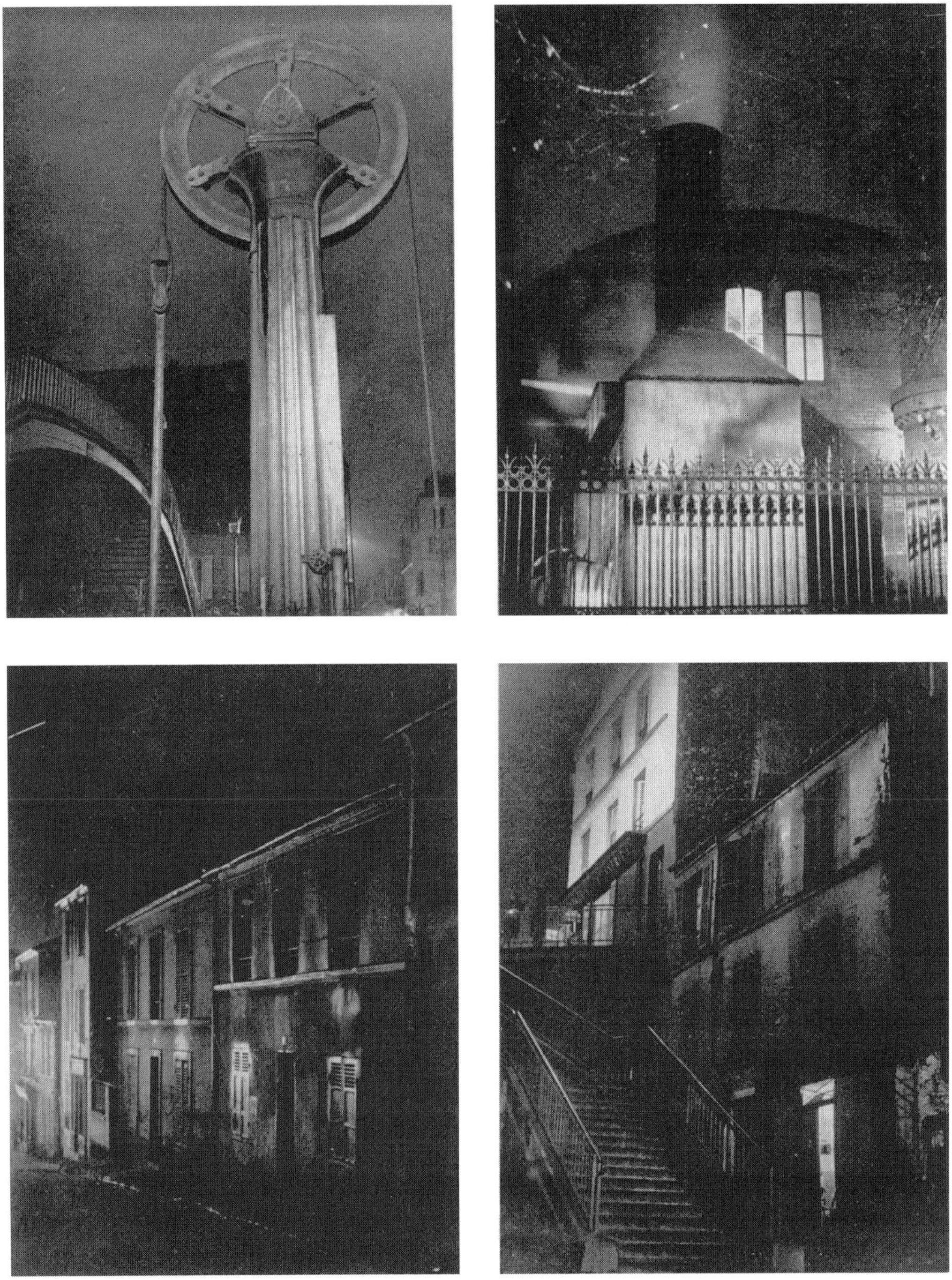

Fig 56 Brassaï, 'Nuits parisiennes', *Minotaure*, 7 (1935). © Estate Brassaï.

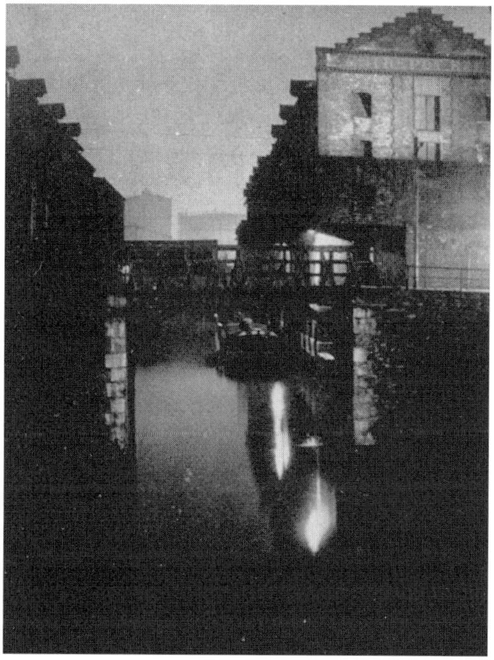

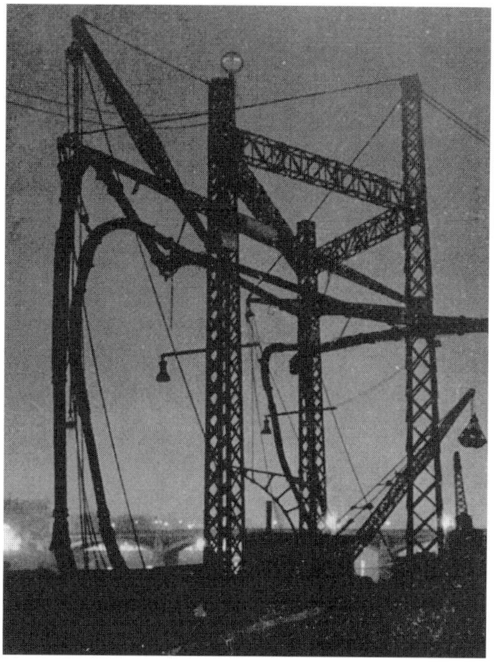

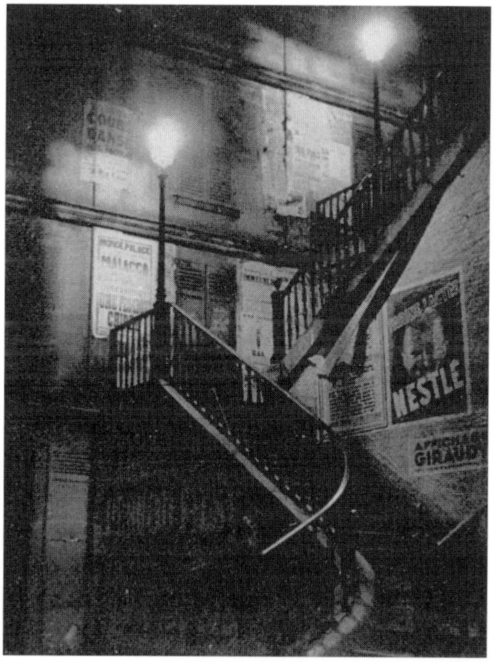
NESTLE
GIRAUDY

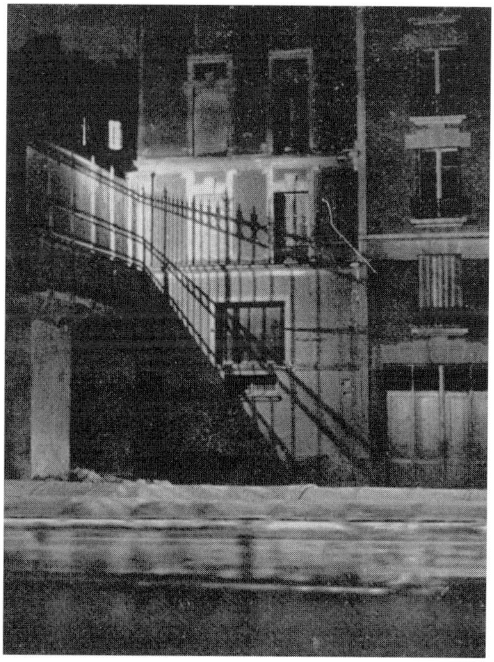

why the particular selection of pictures for *Minotaure* was made.

Eight of Brassaï's pictures in issue no. 7 were reproduced in one double spread – *Nuits parisiennes* – in two blocks of four, all in the same vertical format (figure 56).[15] I will return to the effect of this layout, but here I want to concentrate on the nature of the places depicted in the photographs. Of the scenes shown, only one is readily recognisable: the great wheel on the canal at the Pont de Crimée, an industrial monument as opposed to the tourist sites in *Paris de nuit*.[16] All the photographs depict a working Paris resting from its daily round; places that would be bustling by day are strangely silent at night. The effect of the images is heightened by our knowledge of the other, diurnal existence of these places, an existence which will reawaken shortly and go about its business again. The uncanny emptiness of the sleeping city may help to explain the placement of these particular *Nuits parisiennes* in *Minotaure*. As we know, the Surrealists loathed the drudgery of physical work.[17] Here then was workaday Paris, an industrial Paris that seemed to exist only for work, transformed into something other, essentially unknowable, the banal rendered other-worldly. If the four images across the top of the layout show the places of this work themselves, those at the bottom depict the working-class residential districts of the city, filled now with the dreams that filter from behind these anonymous facades. As if the night makes the logic and rationality that dominates the day simply untenable.

A later image in the same issue suggests that the city itself also dreams. A buttress on the corner of a solid wall casts a shadow that immediately reads as the profile of a face (figure 57); Brassaï himself wrote that it reminded him of 'one of those giant statues from Easter Island'.[18] This is in actuality the exterior of a metro station, but the dramatic title that Brassaï later gave the picture emphasises its metaphoric power: *From the great shadow will surge forth destiny*.[19] If not quite so profound as that hyperbole suggests, the photograph nonetheless is a potent found instance of Dalí's 'paranoiac-critical' re-readings of objects, a real life version of the Surrealist game *l'un dans l'autre*, where one thing is described as another. As with many of his night-time pictures, Brassaï here plays with the dialectic between the solidity of the architecture and the transient play of light and shade across it. Yet it is the shadow profile, so dark and sharp, which seems an immovable presence, despite one's knowledge that in the morning it will have vanished.

These two examples – the block of eight *Nuits parisiennes* and the single image of the shadow – suggest the range of possible Surrealist readings of Brassaï's night pictures in *Minotaure*, from implied critique to melodramatic effect. In both these instances, though, the photographs are granted their own space and we must make of them what we will; no text accompanies them. However, a few pages after the profile photograph in issue no. 7 of *Minotaure*, Brassaï's nocturnal photography comes into direct contact with Surrealism in the form of André Breton's essay 'La Nuit du tournesol'.[20] Two years later, this account of a night spent wandering Paris with his future wife, Jacqueline

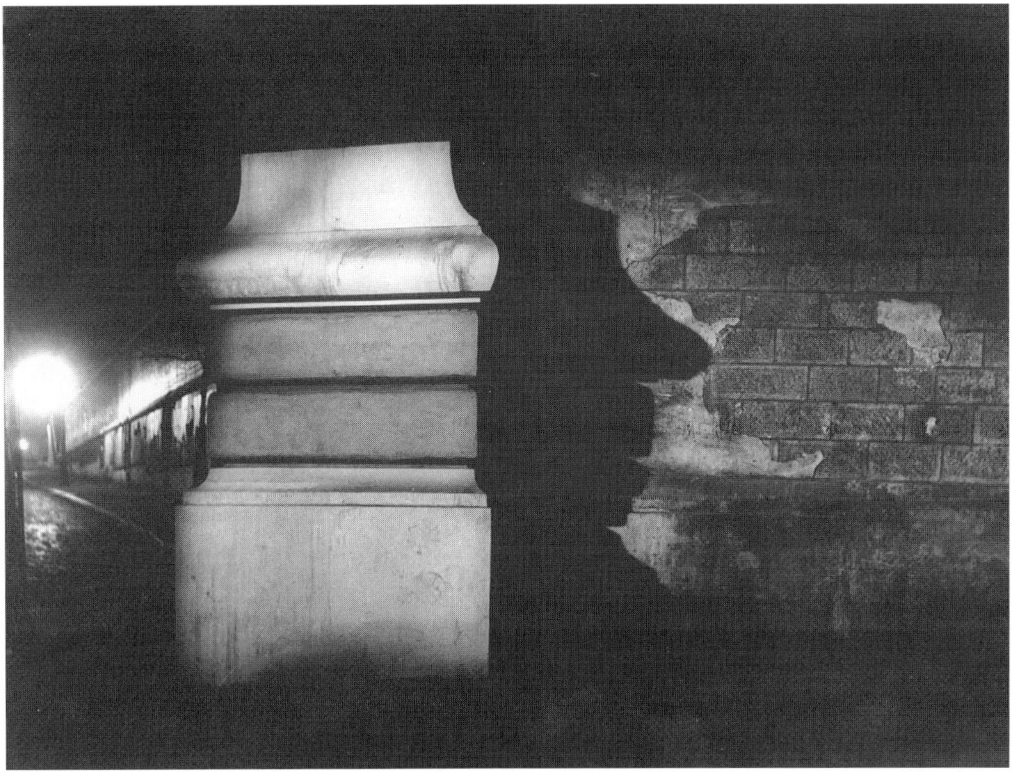

Fig 57 Brassaï, *Buttress of the Elevated (Pilier de Métro aérian Corvisart)*, 1933. The Museum of Modern Art, New York. © Estate Brassaï.

Lamba, would form the central part of Breton's *L'Amour fou*, and in both magazine and book, the text was accompanied by three of Brassaï's night photographs of sites the couple passed on their walk: Les Halles, the Tour Saint-Jacques and the flower market. Breton, it seems, had asked Brassaï to take the pictures of these sites, but as Brassaï later recounted, 'Contrary to what the author of *Nadja* thought at the time, however, these photographs had not been made specially for him. I had had them for some time – even one of the Tour Saint-Jacques as he had described it, "beneath its ghostly veil of scaffolding".'[21]

Brassaï's account suggests the tension between his own perception of his *oeuvre* as independent and self-sufficient and the illustrative uses Breton made of it. Moreover, his description of Breton as 'the author of *Nadja*' suggests that Brassaï was well aware that his images in *L'Amour fou* were in competition with those of Boiffard in *Nadja*. But in fact the two sets of pictures – and the picture-making tactics employed by Boiffard and himself – were very different. Brassaï's images were not taken on commission from Breton, they made their own aesthetic statement and, placed next to Breton's text, are independent but complementary. Boiffard's images do not have that same individual presence when removed from *Nadja*. However, the quality of the reproductions in *L'Amour fou* – small illustrations placed against the flow of the text – proved inadequate in conveying the subtle range of blacks and whites and the accumulation of detail through which Brassaï's photographs create their sense of presence and mystery. In this context, Brassaï's pictures become merely insufficient, whereas with Boiffard's images in *Nadja*, that 'insufficiency' is partly why those modest photographs are so puzzling and unsettling.[22]

In fact, Brassaï's images work far better in the original presentation of 'La Nuit du tournesol' in *Minotaure* than they do later on in *L'Amour fou*. The more innovative layout of the magazine operated to increase their effect, the three photographs centred in the middle of the large pages, with the text flowing around them (figure 58). The cumulative effect produced by the luxurious context of the magazine, the lushness both of Brassaï's photographs and of Breton's text is very far from the distanced asceticism of *Nadja*.[23] This, however, is in keeping with the mood of *L'Amour fou*, written for Jacqueline to read while *Nadja* would never be read by Nadja herself.[24] As George Melly has written, the depiction of the lovers' walk through night-time Paris is 'more romantic than surrealist', closer to the imagery of Chagall than to de Chirico.[25] And that difference is also evident in the gap between Boiffard's photographs and Brassaï's, which, as Melly says, are 'less matter of fact, more beautiful, and in consequence less convincing'.

Indeed, we need to look away from Surrealism itself to fully understand the cultural placement of Brassaï's night-time photographs, even those which were published in *Minotaure*. When they first appeared in the early 1930s, Brassaï's images must surely have been read as a response to the example of Atget, a contemporary Paris set against an antiquated image, the dark shadows of night opposed to the clarity of early morning daylight, a deliberate negative to Atget's positive. Pierre MacOrlan had already presaged this duality in his text on Atget: 'Photographic views of Paris offer two different worlds: that of the day and that of the night. It is easier to exploit the night if you want to stir the public's curiosity. The elements of night are the great stage directors of a social fantastic which is rather naïve and always easy to understand.'[26]

Convincing parallels have been suggested by Marja Warehime between Brassaï's photographs of Paris by night and MacOrlan's concept of the 'social fantastic'.[27] Though Brassaï was one of the few major photographers in Paris at the time that MacOrlan didn't write about,[28] one can understand something of this connection by looking at the essay that MacOrlan wrote for André Kertész's 1934 monograph. There, MacOrlan described an oneiric Paris he rather extravagantly perceived in Kertész's photographs: 'A bridge in Paris calls forth a strange, larval and nocturnal life; a deserted square is peopled with ghosts; an empty street allows us to foresee the corteges of murder and the end.' That might as well be a description of Brassaï's photographs. However, as MacOrlan himself argued, the mysteries of the night are more obvious and established than those of broad daylight. The uncanny atmosphere of Atget's images arises out of their very clarity; whatever ghosts are there emerge, in Baudelaire's phrase, 'en plein jour' and are all the more disquieting. One expects ghosts at night.

toute l'insécurité qui est en moi dès que, cette nuit-là, je me reprends à lire dans l'avenir ce qui pourrait, ce qui devrait être si le cœur *disposait*. La liberté à l'égard des autres êtres, la liberté à l'égard de celui qu'on a été semble ne se faire alors si tentante que pour mieux m'accabler de ses défis. Qui m'accompagne à cette heure dans Paris sans me conduire et que, d'ailleurs, moi non plus, je ne conduis pas? Je ne me rappelle pas avoir éprouvé de ma vie si grande défaillance. Je me perds presque de vue, il me semble que j'ai été emporté à mon tour comme les figurants de la première scène. La conversation qui, tant que ma trop belle interlocutrice est demeurée assise en face de moi, glissait sans obstacle d'un sujet à l'autre, n'effleure plus maintenant que le masque des choses. Je me sens avec effroi la conduire à sombrer malgré moi dans l'artificiel. J'en suis réduit à m'arrêter de temps à autre pour immobiliser devant moi le visage que je ne puis supporter plus longtemps de voir s'offrir de profil, mais cette démarche enfantine ne me rend, à vrai dire, qu'une très courte assurance. Il me deviendrait peut-être brusquement impossible de faire un pas, sans le secours d'un bras qui vient s'unir à mon bras et me rappeler à la vie réelle en m'éclairant délicieusement de sa pression le contour d'un sein.

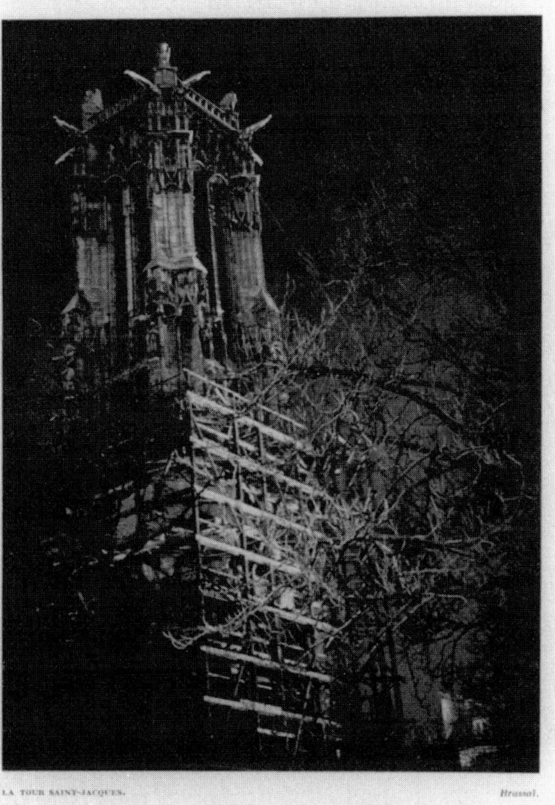

LA TOUR SAINT-JACQUES. *Brassaï.*

Tandis que nous nous attardons une heure plus tard dans les petites rues du quartier des Halles, j'éprouve d'autant plus durement l'éclipse de ce sein, commandée par les difficultés de la circulation à deux parmi les camions dans cette rumeur qui s'enfle sans cesse, qui monte comme la mer vers l'appétit immense du prochain jour. Mon regard, des magnifiques cubes blancs, rouges, verts des primeurs glisse malencontreusement sur le pavé luisant de déchets horribles. C'est aussi l'heure où des bandes de fêtards commencent à se répandre en ces lieux pour y finir la nuit dans quelque petit torchon renommé, jetant dans la cohue robuste et franche du travail, la note noire, mousseuse et équivoque des tenues de soirée, des fourrures et des soies. Allons ! c'est seulement dans les contes qu'il est impossible au doute de s'insinuer, qu'il n'est pas question de glisser sur une écorce de fruit. Je vois le mal et le bien dans leur état brut, le mal l'emportant de toute la facilité de la souffrance : l'idée qu'il est au loin, peut-être seul créateur de bien ne m'effleure même plus. La vie est lente et l'homme ne sait guère la jouer. Les possibilités d'atteindre l'être susceptible de l'aider à la jouer, de lui donner tout son sens, se perdent dans la carte des astres. Qui m'accompagne, qui me précède cette nuit encore une fois? Demain reste fait de déterminations bon gré mal gré acceptées sans tenir compte de ces boucles charmantes, de ces chevilles pareilles à des boucles. Il serait temps encore de reculer.

Quel avertisseur fonctionnera jamais pour faire entendre la voix de la déraison, si je parle le langage qu'on m'a appris, et soutenir que demain sera *autre*, qu'il s'est mystérieusement, complètement déchiré d'hier? J'étais de nouveau près de vous, ma belle vagabonde, et vous me montriez en passant la Tour Saint-Jacques sous son voile pâle d'échafaudages qui, depuis des années maintenant contribue à en faire, plus encore, le grand monument du monde à l'irrévélé. Vous aviez beau savoir que j'aimais cette tour, je revois encore à ce moment toute une existence violente s'organiser autour d'elle pour nous comprendre, pour contenir l'éperdu dans son galop nuageux autour de nous :

A Paris la Tour Saint-Jacques chancelante
Pareille à un tournesol (*)

ai-je dit assez obscurément pour moi dans un poème, et j'ai compris depuis que ce balancement de la tour était surtout le mien entre les deux sens en français du mot *tournesol*, qui désigne à la fois cette espèce d'hélianthe, connue aussi sous le nom de grand soleil et le réactif utilisé en chimie, le plus souvent sous la forme d'un papier bleu qui rougit au contact des acides. Toujours est-il

(*) Cf. *Le Revolver à cheveux blancs* (Les Cahiers libres, édit.).

Fig 58 Extract from André Breton, 'La Nuit du tournesol', with photograph by Brassaï, *La tour Saint-Jacques*, in *Minotaure*, 7 (1935). Photograph © Estate Brassaï.

Obviously, there is a relationship here between MacOrlan's 'social fantastic' and the Surrealist vision of Paris in *Nadja* and *Le paysan de Paris* (and the Paris that Desnos and Valentin had found in Atget's images). But it is not the same vision. Where the Surrealist dream-image is hard and lucid – one thinks also of the paintings of de Chirico, Magritte, Dalí or the films of Buñuel – Brassaï's photographs of the fog-bound city in *Paris de nuit* have the softness of reverie.

They are, to use a distinction employed by the Surrealists themselves, 'mysterious' rather than 'marvellous'.[29] And it was the marvellous they valued most, the transformative experience that Breton described as 'like the feeling of feathery wind brushing across my temples to produce a real shiver'.[30] Moreover, that experience can strike in the most banal of situations; indeed, as we have seen with *Nadja*, its power might in part be due to this banality. On such occasions, the city seems to crack open. In most of Brassaï's images, however, it remains swathed in its fogs and its mysteries, hiding rather than revealing its inner life.

This was a common image of Paris in the inter-war years, and alongside MacOrlan's *fantastique sociale*, there was also the concept of *réalisme poétique*. Though the term had been coined by Jean Paulhan, editor of the *Nouvelle revue française*, to describe a trend in the contemporary novel, we now more usually associate 'poetic realism' with the series of films made in the late 1930s by Marcel Carné from scripts by the former Surrealist Jacques Prévert, based on novels such as Pierre MacOrlan's *Quai des brumes* (figure 59). In discussing the work of Carné, Edward Baron Turk has made a useful distinction between the two terms *réalisme poétique* and *fantastique sociale*. The phrases, he says, may denote 'the same two concepts: reality and fantasy. The difference lies in their order. In French, a noun followed by an adjective tends to emphasise the qualifier. Thus *réalisme poétique* suggests that the prime aesthetic gesture involved is the poeticisation of reality ... *Le fantastique sociale*, on the contrary, emphasises the tempering of fantasy by attention to the "real" or social'.[31] This is not a clearcut distinction, and such emphases were often elided, but in general, it is also an appropriate way to read the photographs of Kertész and Brassaï. Their work sometimes shifted into formalism and sometimes into reportage; on occasion, it was more disorientating, closer to Surrealism itself. But it was always both 'poetic' and 'realist', and in this regard one must place the work next to Surrealism rather than within it.[32]

But this does not mean that the images made by these photographers hold no interest for Surrealism. In later years, Brassaï sought to emphasise the distance between him and the Surrealists. Speaking to Tony Ray-Jones in 1970, he said: 'For years I worked with them. I did not like Surrealism however as I was very objective. But they liked my photographs. They found a kind of surrealism in my pictures even though I was objective. They thought the night photos were unusual and amazing. André Breton wanted me in the Surrealist group. I was opposed to their ideas but I was friends with them all anyway.'[33] In a second interview published in 1980, he elaborated on this relationship: 'the "surrealism" of my images was only the real made fantastic by vision. I sought only to express reality, because nothing is more surreal ... My ambition was always to make visible an aspect of everyday life as if we were uncovering it for the first time. That is what separated me from the surrealists'.[34]

Next to these extended comments by Brassaï, one might place André Kertész's more succinct statement of refusal: 'I am not a Surrealist; I am

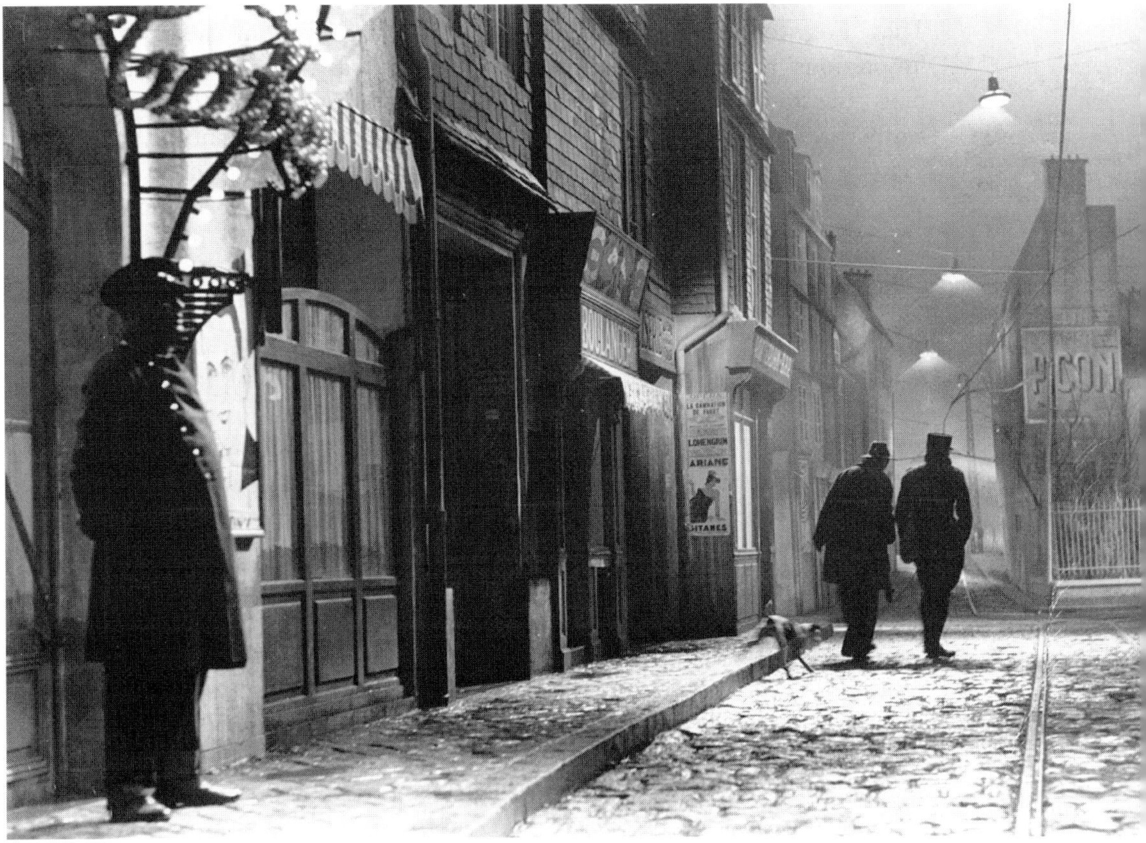

Fig 59 Production still for Marcel Carné, *Quai des brumes*, 1938.

absolutely a realist.'[35] The two photographers took parallel positions, opposing Surrealism to something supposedly quite different called 'realism'. It was an understandable attitude for a photographer of the urban scene to hold, especially in a context where sides were taken and groups joined, and they were surely reacting against the perceived 'literary' aspects of Surrealism. But their comments betrayed a more fundamental misunderstanding of the nature of Surrealism. The Surrealists, ultimately, did not seek an eradication of 'realism' but a more complex understanding of it. They would have agreed with Brassaï's assertion that nothing is more surreal than the real. And there one can see why Surrealism would be interested in such 'realistic' images – and also why, despite themselves, these photographers sometimes made surrealist images from that realism. But only sometimes, and at this distance, we need to be careful about slurring the 'surrealist', the 'fantastic' and the 'poetic' into one overall, rather indistinct effect.

One avoids this only by closely observing individual images or sets of images. Looking back at the three examples I have cited from *Minotaure* – the *Nuits parisiennes* in the working-class areas of the city, the profile caught on the edge of the Métro station, the pictures chosen to illustrate 'La Nuit du tournesol' – one can see that each is differently poised between these categories of the 'fantastic', the 'poetic' and the 'surrealist'. Ironically, it is the example which seems most securely sited within a Surrealist context – the images accompanying Breton's text – which now seem most 'poetic', indeed romantic. The profile is more obviously 'surrealist', yet that obviousness robs it of a subtler resonance; the picture seems merely 'fantastic'.

Oddly, then, it is the spread of eight anonymous *Nuits parisiennes* which are finally most unsettling. For we are not invited into these pictures as we usually are with Brassaï's images. We are kept at a distance, estranged, even alienated by the emphatically severe, depopulated spaces. This effect resembles more the power of Atget's or de Chirico's images, or of Boiffard's pictures in *Nadja*, than the more insinuating pleasures offered by most of Brassaï's nocturnal photographs. Ironically, it was Brassaï himself who later defined this distinction: 'The surreal exists ... in the things which have become so banal that we no longer notice them, and in the normality of the normal.'[36] Yet he apparently could not see that this was indeed an integral aspect of Surrealism itself, which he persisted in defining as interested only in the bizarre and the imagined.

It is not only the nature of the individual photographs in the *Nuits parisiennes* spread which makes them resonate in this way. The impact of this double-page spread lies also in the selection of pictures – all taken at a similar distance, full of angular architectural forms, and free of foggy diffusion – as well as their placement within an insistently regular layout, each picture a small element in the overall pattern. This configuration may not be the creation of Brassaï himself; indeed one must wonder if he would have recognised the difference between these images and the rest of his work. Rather the effect has been created through the decisions of the anonymous picture editor, working within an aesthetic already established within Surrealism and deriving from Atget and de Chirico via Boiffard and Lotar.[37]

But if the effect of this spread can be related to that Surrealist aesthetic, the pictures themselves have emerged from Brassaï's overall *oeuvre*, and carry with them echoes of his other work. Between the pictures and their presentation, then, we must see these pages as the result of a multiple authorship. When Brassaï said that 'the "surrealism" of my images was only the real made fantastic by vision', his comments are ambiguous. What is this vision? Is it his own artistic vision, his authorship of the work? Is it the vision of the camera, that unblinking eye which both records and transforms the real? Brassaï could have meant either. But from a more distanced perspective, this question of transformative vision may also be seen to engage decisions of layout and placement. For Brassaï's constructions of night-time Paris are far from cohesive. They offer many different readings, which are constantly being shifted through successive contexts of publication. If Surrealism is not central to the making of Brassaï's photographs, it is nevertheless a productive frame through which to view them.

At the same time he was publishing his images of Paris by night, Brassaï embarked on another project – the extended photography of Parisian graffiti. Aside from a single publication, also in *Minotaure* in 1933, this work was not seen until after the Second World War and consequently it made less of a mark than his nocturnal photography. Yet in many ways, the Surrealist credentials of Brassaï's graffiti photographs are more convincing. In these pictures, Brassaï recorded the marks left by the true 'Paris peasants' and in the process called into question the values of civilised urbanity. In this, Brassaï's work interlocked with the Surrealist concern for the primal and the peripheral considered in the previous chapter. Yet where depictions of the Zone, the ruin and the abattoir were fragmentary, Brassaï worked on his project for over thirty years to form a coherent and extensive body of images, the most fully worked through of all these explorations of the urban primitive.

The first siting of the graffiti photographs in *Minotaure* in 1933 carried a title which conveyed the sense of continuity that Brassaï felt between his images and the art of prehistoric time: 'From Cave Wall to Factory Wall'.[38] Brassaï himself stated that the title was suggested by Paul Eluard,[39] and although the graffiti photographs were to be recontextualised several times over, their initial placement was in relation to Surrealism. In his later statements about this work, Brassaï was usually direct and to the point. His text in *Minotaure*, however, is opaque and elusive, suggesting perhaps a desire to emulate the writing of the Surrealist poets elsewhere in the magazine. Nevertheless, his argument is clear. Brassaï romanticises both cave art and graffiti, seeing in each 'the same agony ... the frenzy of the unconscious'. Like cave art, graffiti returns to 'the origins of writing', an essential magic, indeed a mythology of monsters, demons, heroes and 'dieux phalliques'. It lies at the base of creativity 'as insistent and as irrational as breathing or sleeping'.

For Brassaï, the expressiveness of graffiti 'announces that the equilibrium, broken between man and nature, has once again been restored by art'. Indeed, in the city, graffiti 'replaces nature'.[40] Graffiti, he says, is natural in its ephemerality, in its flux 'where all is being formed, transformed, deformed'. This 'natural' subversion elides, in Brassaï's argument, into a more conscious subversion of the mores of culture; graffiti takes place 'around the word "Forbidden", the first one the child deciphers on the wall'. Brassaï however is at pains to distinguish graffiti from child art: 'From the supervised to the anonymous, the character of the expression changes.' 'The liveliness of fantasy' in child art 'gives way to the magical spell' of graffiti.

Brassaï was not, of course, the first artist to be interested in graffiti. When he described graffiti as 'the bastard art of the infamous streets', the phrase has a nineteenth-century ring to it, graffiti as an *art maudit*. Kirk Varnedoe sees here the 'legacy of Baudelaire's nostalgic love for the piss-stained corners of Paris'.[41] Presenting the work for the first time in 1933, Brassaï emphasised that the images 'were gathered in Paris itself by chance on several walks'.[42] This description placed them firmly in the context of an urban *flânerie*, the same

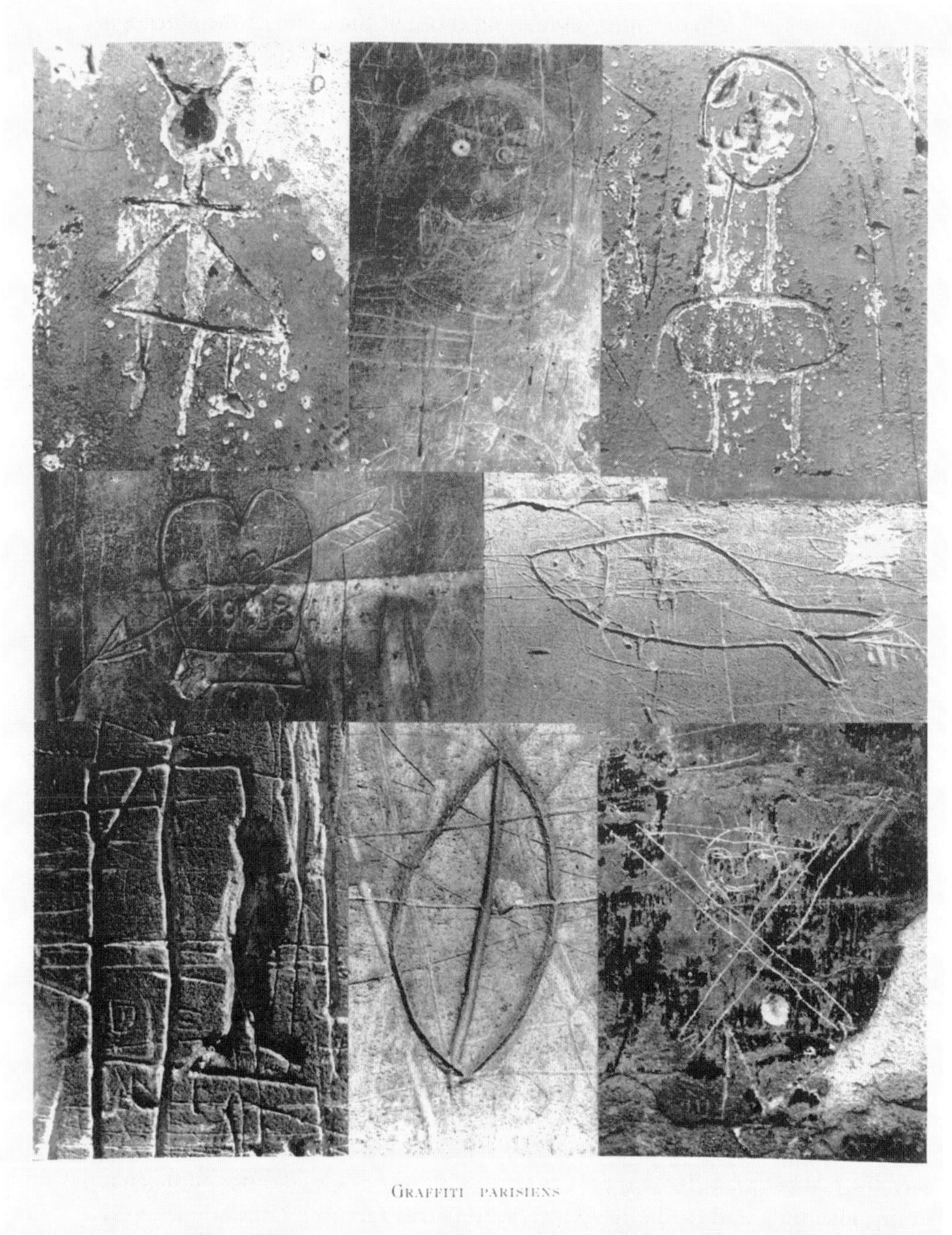

Fig 60 Brassaï, 'Graffitis parisiens', *Minotaure*, 3–4 (1933). © Estate Brassaï.

process that produced the images in *Paris de nuit*. But this is another city, though it intersects with that experienced by the tourist and the worker: 'In 1933, and two steps from the Opéra, signs resembling those in the caves of the Dordogne, the Nile and Euphrates valleys, surge into view on the walls'.[43] These scrawled and gouged forms, then, represent a different form of the urban unconscious to that evoked by the images of Paris by night, and they have been discovered through a different form of *flânerie* – exploring the underside of the city rather than the grand boulevards.

As Varnedoe recognises, what was new was Brassaï's emphasis on the violence of graffiti. His concentration on images that were scratched and gouged, to the exclusion of drawn, painted or written signs, was not a purely documentary response to what he found on the street. Rather, it came out of an attitude to the material that was allied with Surrealism's interest in the dark power of the *id* bursting through the veneer of civilisation. These graffitied signs acquired a different range of meanings in a post-Freudian context.

As might be expected in *Minotaure*, the layout of the photographs was inventive, with eight images montaged together, three verticals at the top, three at the bottom, with two horizontals in the middle (the original photographs being cropped as necessary) (figure 60). This creates a sensation that one is looking at one wall and gives the imagery the quality of ubiquity that Brassaï claimed for it. Moreover, the arrangement suggests the form of a single body, with a grinning head at the top and female genitalia at the bottom (Kim Sichel compares it with an 'exquisite corpse').[44] Again, this underlines Brassaï's argument that we are seeing here the base of our own humanness.

One could argue, however, that the visual patterning in this layout, while making the photographs more engaging, also decreases their power. For it is surely when the presentation is most simple that the imagery is most effective. For Brassaï, it is the graffiti that is the art, not the photograph. With this project, Brassaï seems to negate his own role as image-maker in a desire to promote the worth of the graffiti itself. He is not the creator, but the collector of these images, an ethnographer of the present.[45] Yet it is also the fact that we are seeing them through – and as – photographs that helps to make them so compelling. Brassaï's framing, though undemonstrative, is firmly centred, four-square and concentrated. All context and extraneous information is removed, and paradoxically the marks seem to speak for themselves directly to the viewer, as they might not *in situ*.

After their initial appearance in *Minotaure* in 1933, there was almost no significant publication or exhibition of Brassaï's graffiti photographs for two decades.[46] When they did reappear in the 1950s, they carried different meanings from those they had at the height of Surrealism. *Harper's Bazaar* published a portfolio of six images in 1953.[47] In 1956, Edward Steichen exhibited them at the Museum of Modern Art in New York. Their visibility reached its zenith in 1958, when the photographs were published in a number of divergent sites: photographic (*U.S. Camera*), artistic (*XXe Siècle*) and social (*The Saturday*

Book).[48] The same year, they were exhibited at the Institute of Contemporary Arts in London, with a catalogue introduction by Roland Penrose.[49] Finally, in 1960, the pictures were comprehensively collected in book form.[50]

Much of what Brassaï wrote about the graffiti photographs to accompany them in these new contexts was familiar. He again elided the 'natural' and the 'primitive', emphasising that the images represented 'this other "nature", artificial and town-made, perspiring with humanity' and 'a psychic ego, furtive, stifled, a reminder of a primitive existence'.[51] But some things had changed between the early 1930s and the late 1950s. The cultural contexts in which the photographs were now found would suggest that the savagery that the graffiti had previously represented had become widely palatable, for the images had come to resemble what by this time was 'Modern Art'. When Brassaï wrote about his pictures, he allied them with the work of his close friend Picasso, and quoted Picasso's own comments on the images.[52] And by 1960, Picasso was no longer the avant-garde ally of the Surrealists; he was a Modern Old Master.

For Brassaï, Picasso's comments on the graffiti photographs provided their ultimate validation. The more so in that Picasso echoed Brassaï's own comments, referring to the democracy of the wall: 'Graffiti belongs to everyone and to no one',[53] and to the aesthetic value of the images: 'That is as rich as the facade of a cathedral! ... Your book links art with the primitive arts.'[54] Picasso spied connections with other modern artists: 'This is a Rouault, That a Klee', but mostly, he talked of the relationship of graffiti to his own art: 'I have often done faces like this myself.'[55] Although Brassaï also briefly recorded the relationship of the graffiti images to the work of other artists,[56] it was Picasso to whom he constantly referred, indeed deferred. There were personal reasons for this – they had been close friends since the 1930s, and shared ideas born in the days of high modernism – but it must also be considered a desire on Brassaï's part to attach his work to Picasso's genius.

If in the short term, this increased the profile of the work, it also had the effect of deflating the genuine threat and disturbance that the graffiti images had held in 1933. There were, in fact, other connections with more contemporary art practice that would, in the 1950s, have maintained that edge, but Brassaï passed over them. He briefly conceded that there might be a new context for the images in 'the "realisation of the wall" by Klee, Miró, Dubuffet etc., the Informel School of artists, the School of Action, the *Tachistes*'.[57] But he went no further. In particular, it is curious that Brassaï did not fully acknowledge the close parallel with Jean Dubuffet's espousal of *Art Brut*. Dubuffet himself recognised the connection between *Art Brut* and Brassaï's graffiti and, in 1947, he wrote to Brassaï proposing a publication of the graffiti images as part of the *Art Brut* collection, but it seems that Brassaï did not respond.[58] Perhaps the parallel was too close, and Brassaï wished to assert his priority in the field.[59] Moreover, Dubuffet was one of the few post-war French artists to acknowledge his debt to Surrealism and actively seek the collaboration of André Breton in his project, a connection that Brassaï now seemed to disavow.

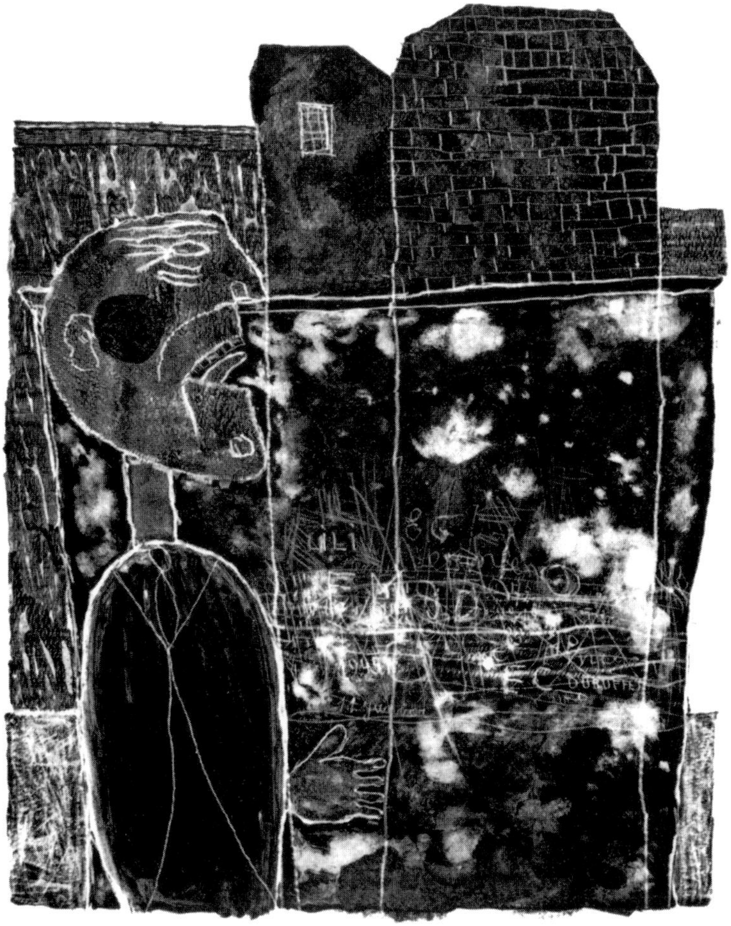

Fig 61 Jean Dubuffet, *Man Caught in the Walls* from *Les Murs*, 1950. © ADAGP, Paris and DACS, London, 2001.

Of course, *Art Brut* consisted of more than graffiti – the art of children and the insane – and Brassaï's graffitists were surely neither mad nor innocent. But the graffiti in the photographs does have the quality of 'surging into view completely spontaneous and ingenuous in its brute purity', as Dubuffet claimed for the work of the artists he championed.[60] When, in 1951, Dubuffet asserted, 'I believe very much in the values of savagery. I mean instinct, passion, mood, violence, madness' and attacked official culture as 'a dead language, without anything in common with the language spoken in the street',[61] he was closer to the Brassaï of the 1933 essay in *Minotaure* than the Brassaï who would later support the work with the comments of Picasso. Within Dubuffet's own work, it was the sequence of lithographs *Les Murs* (figure 61),[62] which were most directly related to Brassaï's work, and one early writer made the connection: the poet Francis Ponge in his text for Dubuffet's *Matière et memoire* (1945).[63]

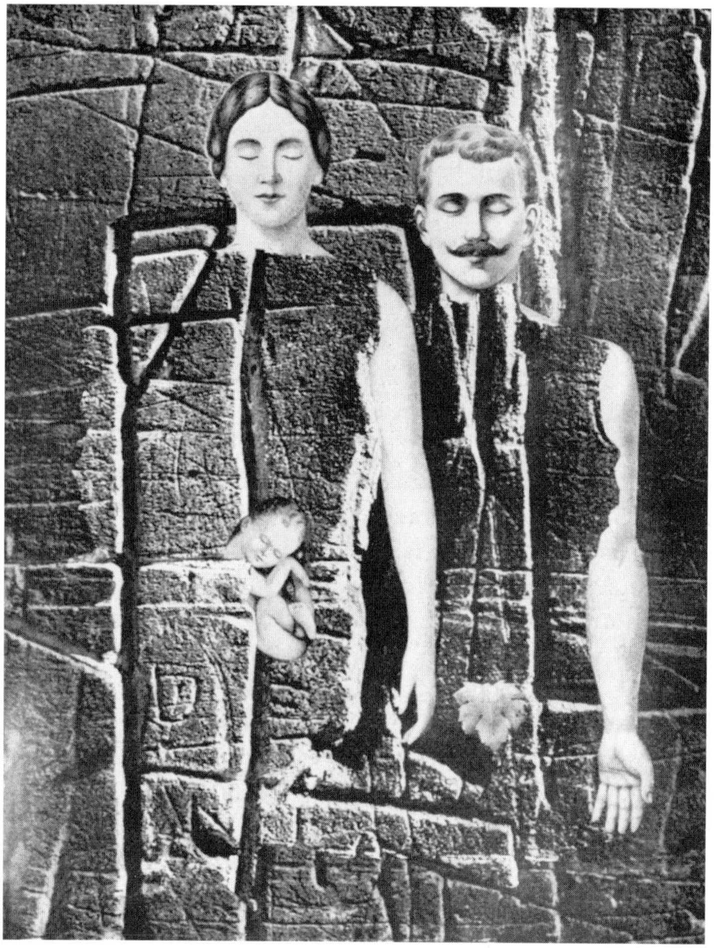

Fig 62 Jacques Prévert, *Homme, Femme, Enfant*, 1958. © ADAGP, Paris and DACS, London, 2001.

Dubuffet's direct inspiration for *Les Murs* came from the Zone, and the fact that this had been the frequent site of war-time executions now added a darker note to its atmosphere of estrangement.[64]

In the work of both Brassaï and Dubuffet, there is a tension between their aspirations towards the populist and the actual positioning of their work within the avant-garde. There was, however, one moment when Brassaï's graffiti was sited at the confluence of the popular and the avant-garde in post-war French culture: the placement of one of his photographs on the cover of the first edition of Jacques Prévert's book of poems *Paroles* in 1945. Indeed, it seems that the small edition of 334 copies used an actual photographic print of graffiti wrapped round the cover, so that the word ANE (ass) appeared on the front and a figure with horns or large ears (the ass itself?) on the back. Prévert's name and the title PAROLES was printed over the top as if daubed in red paint which had dripped a little, another layer of graffiti.[65] Both photographer and poet wished to place their work between the street as it is lived and the street transmuted into art. At this historical moment, as French culture emerged from the Occupation, such a siting was widely resonant, and the success of *Paroles* was enormous and immediate.[66] However, when this rare first edition was followed by a much larger second edition in 1947, the book had a plain cover.[67]

In 1993, several of Brassaï's graffiti photographs were exhibited in the Tate Gallery exhibition *Paris Post War: Art and Existentialism 1945–55*, alongside the paintings of Fautrier, Wols, Artaud and Dubuffet. The elements that the graffiti had in common with these paintings were apparent – passion inscribed directly into the surface, a dark irony and sense of anguished achievement. However, the roots of this philosophy of the *informel* in Surrealist automatism were ignored, and the exhibition espoused an Existentialist myth of originality where a 'beginning at the beginning ... was the only way to begin at nothing'.[68] As a result, the connections between Brassaï's graffiti and Surrealism – connections that indeed Brassaï himself had sought to deny – were further severed. What I want rather to emphasise is the journey that Brassaï's graffiti photographs make from Surrealism in the early 1930s through Existentialism in the late 1940s to find cultural acceptance in the late 1950s. The meanings that these photographs carried in 1933, in 1945 and in 1960 may have shifted, but this does not mean that the later contextualisations invalidated the first.

Jacques Prévert often used prints given to him by his photographer friends to form the basis of his own collages, and in 1958, he included one of Brassaï's graffiti photographs in the collage *Homme, Femme, Enfant* (figure 62).[69] It's hard to tell whether the three figures are emerging out of the gougings on the wall or sinking back into it; Prévert has skilfully placed them so that the incisions begin to suggest the shapes of their bodies. Their eyes are closed – in birth, death or dream. Though they seem to be naked, the figures are thoroughly bourgeois; the man has a carefully cultivated moustache and a fig leaf, the woman's hair is demurely parted in the centre. However, the graffiti that lies behind them – a gouged out figure hanging from a scaffold – undermines their poise.[70] Graffiti represents here (as it does in Brassaï's images themselves) the collective unconscious, that irruption of the repressed that Surrealism looked for in its exploration of popular culture. And that was a project which Brassaï and Breton, Dubuffet and Prévert would all, in their different ways, have endorsed.

Brassaï's photography of graffiti was the most extensive exploration of the subject, but elsewhere, within and without Surrealism, it was a theme that concerned many photographers in the 1930s and 1940s. Humphrey Jennings and Humphrey Spender in Bolton for Mass-Observation, Helen Levitt in New York, Izis and Robert Doisneau in Paris all photographed graffiti on the street.[71] But where Brassaï in 1933 had resisted the connection of graffiti with child art, these other photographers emphasised it, concentrating on ephemeral chalk drawings rather than the gouged and incised images typical of Brassaï's images.[72] Seldom did their work present graffiti as social challenge in the way that Brassaï had originally hoped; in the hands of many later photographers, graffiti lost its sense of threat and disruption, becoming merely a picturesque backdrop to the sympathetic evocation of working class life.

Perhaps only two major exceptions stand out. Within Surrealism, there is the work of Czech photographers such as Jindřich Štyrský, Jíří Sever, Vilém Reichmann, and above all Emila Medková, who also made the city walls her particular subject.[73] In Paris, meanwhile, the sense of graffiti as social critique was maintained by the Situationists, who, following the Surrealists, saw in graffiti an expression of the repressed in society – the 'real' which might yet unsettle the 'spectacle' of mass consumer culture. This could take many forms. Asger Jorn, for example, scrawled over kitsch paintings bought in the flea market as well as editing a book on the medieval graffiti of churches in Normandy.[74]

A different sort of graffiti, though still derived from Surrealism via the Situationists, was to cover the walls of Paris during the uprising of 1968. One now famous example quizzically announced: 'Sous les Pavés, Les Plages' (beneath the pavements, the beaches). The phrase sums up many of the concerns outlined in these chapters: the awareness of the primitive so close beneath the civilised, the natural beneath the cultural, flow and flux undermining order, pleasure undermining work. In 1968, the statement represented an upheaval in values that was both poetic and physical (the paving stones were there to be torn up and thrown at the cops). But, as Edouard Jaguer has commented, 'for these "Paris peasants" who were and are always the Surrealists, the pavement *is* the beach'.[75] To discover these other values, the Surrealists did not need to leave the city, only to see it differently.

Notes

1 Thomas Michael Gunther, 'Man Ray and Co.: la fabrication d'un buste', in Pierre Barbin (ed.), *Colloques Atget*, special number of *Photographies* (March 1986), p. 72. He further states that Man Ray planned to make this album of photographs of Paris with Jacques-André Boiffard, which would suggest an intriguing relation with the latter's photographs for *Nadja*.

2 See Chapter 3, n. 41.

3 For a fuller discussion of these books, see David Travis: 'Kertész and his Contemporaries in Paris', in Sandra S. Phillips *et al.*, *André Kertész of Paris and New York* (London: Thames and Hudson, 1985), pp. 75–81.

4 Germaine Krull, *100 x Paris* (Berlin: Justh, 1929). Kim Sichel, *Germaine Krull* (Cambridge, MA: MIT Press, 1999), p. 115, describes the layout of *100 x Paris* as 'retrograde', but this is in comparison with the dynamism of Krull's previous book *Métal*. Next to the other books cited here, it is innovative.

5 *Paris vu par André Kertész* (Paris: Librarie Plon, 1934).

6 Robert Doisneau, *La Banlieue de Paris* (Paris: Seghers/Lausanne: La Guide du Livre, 1949), Willy Ronis, *Belleville-Menilmontant* (Paris: Arthaud, 1954) and Izis, *Paris de rêves* (Lausanne: La guide de livres, 1950). For a sympathetic account of the continuum between

the work of Brassaï and Kertész in the 1930s and these post-war photographers, see Marie de Thézy, *La photographie humaniste 1930–60* (Paris: Contrejour, 1992). On Breton's contribution to *Paris de rêves*, see below, n. 71.

7 Brassaï, *Paris de nuit* (Paris: Arts et métiers graphiques, 1932).

8 Miller wrote his essay on Brassaï in 1932, the year of *Paris de nuit*, but it was not published until the late 1930s in *Max and the White Phagocytes* (Paris: Obelisk Press, 1938), pp. 240–52.

9 For details of their meeting, see Brassaï, 'My Memories of E. Atget, P. H. Emerson and Alfred Stieglitz', *Camera*, 48:1 (January 1969), 3–43.

10 For broader examinations of Brassaï's *oeuvre*, see Kim Sichel, *Brassaï: Paris le jour, Paris la nuit* (Paris: Musée Carnavalet, 1988); Manuel Borja-Villel (ed.), *Brassaï: Del Surrealismo al informalismo* (Barcelona: Fundació Antoni Tàpies, 1993); Marja Warehime, *Brassaï: Images of Culture and the Surrealist Observer* (Baton Rouge: Louisiana State University Press, 1996); Anne Wilkes Tucker, *Brassaï: The Eye of Paris* (Houston: Museum of Fine Arts, 1999), and Alain Sayag and Annick Lionel-Marie, *Brassaï* (Paris: Centre Pompidou/Editions Seuil, 2000).

11 Brassaï himself planned to publish these images in the early 1930s with a text by Pierre MacOrlan. But when the book eventually appeared in 1934 as *Voluptés de Paris*, it had been changed so much by the publishers that Brassaï disowned it.

12 In concentrating here on Brassaï's night photographs, I am passing over other important work that he published in *Minotaure*: his photographs of Picasso's studio, his nudes, the collaborative projects with Salvador Dalí (see Chapter 1, n. 57). In issue no. 6 (Winter 1934/35), he had already published some of his night photographs, including the well-known image of the statue of Marshal Ney in the fog. After issue no. 7, his contributions largely ceased, perhaps due to the fact that Tériade left in 1937 to found a new journal *Verve*. But at least one important image – 'Troglodyte', discussed in n. 46 – appears in *Minotaure* after this.

13 Brassaï, 'Interview avec France Bequette', *Culture et communication*, 27 (1978), 15.

14 Borja-Villel (ed.), *Brassaï*, p. 15.

15 *Minotaure*, 7 (June 1935), 24–5.

16 This wheel was evidently a landmark; it was also photographed by Kertész in *Paris vu par André Kertész* (unpaginated) and Krull (two of her images of the wheel are in *Germaine Krull: Photographie 1924–1936* (Arles: Musée Reàttu, 1988), pp. 75 and 77).

17 See Chapter 4, n. 43.

18 Brassaï, *Picasso and Company* (London: Thames and Hudson, 1967), p. 180. The photograph as reproduced in *Minotaure* (31) was a vertical crop from the larger horizontal frame. By concentrating on the profile itself, this version over-simplified the image, removing the profile from its urban context. In the full frame, the receding perspective on the left seems to push forward the sharply defined buttress from which the profile emerges, while the mottled textures on the wall to the right suggest that the profile is breathing, speaking or indeed dreaming.

19 This title is given in Sichel, *Brassaï*, cat. no. 80. Both this image and the photograph of the Pont de Crimée were later used in the decor for the ballet *Le Rendez-vous* (1945), written by Prévert with music by Kosma (see Tucker, *Brassaï*, pp. 106–7).

20 *Minotaure*, 7 (June 1935), 48–55.

21 Brassaï, *Picasso and Company*, p. 38.

22 For positive views on the role of Brassaï's pictures in *L'Amour fou*, see Dawn Ades, 'Photography and the Surrealist Text', in Rosalind Krauss and Jane Livingston (eds), *L'Amour fou* (Washington: Corcoran Gallery/New York: Abbeville Press, 1985), p. 183, and Warehime, *Brassaï*, p. 80. For an argument placing Brassaï's images for *L'Amour fou* at the heart of Surrealism, see Rosalind Krauss, 'Nightwalkers', *Art Journal* (Spring 1981), 33–8.

23 In retrospect, Brassaï was rather scathing about the Surrealists' involvement in *Minotaure*: 'this sumptuous review ... could only find an audience among the bourgeoisie it professed to scorn ... Faced with the eternal alternatives of surrealism – "go out in the streets with a revolver in your hand" or "to return home to art" – Breton and Eluard chose the later path. Their participation in *Minotaure* brought an end to the "radical break with the world" and marked the formal entrance of surrealist art and poetry into the world.' (Brassaï, *Picasso and Company*, pp. 11–2). This attack is somewhat unjust. There was intense Surrealist political activity in the 1930s, though it is true that it did not appear in *Minotaure*. The two sides of the Surrealist project – the artistic and the political – which in the 1920s had been locked together in an intense dialectic, had now become disengaged.

24 There is one version of *L'Amour fou* which emphasises its private nature as an extended love letter from Breton to his wife: the copy that he presented to her, now in the Musée d'art moderne, Paris. It is a luxurious object, bound in thick leather with a mirror of Venus embedded in the cover (designed by Georges Hugnet). Inside, the book was augmented with many additional objects – the wedding invitation, their horoscopes – and photographs: the couple in Tenerife and the star-shaped castle at Prague, sites represented in the published book by impersonal, probably bought, images, but here shown through the intimacy of personal snapshots, most likely Breton's own. (My thanks to the museum staff for allowing me to study this object.)

25 George Melly and Michael Woods, *Paris and the Surrealists* (London: Thames and Hudson, 1991), p. 139.

26 Pierre MacOrlan, 'Preface to *Atget Photographe de Paris*', in Christopher Phillips (ed.), *Photography in the Modern Era* (New York: Metropolitan Museum of Art/Aperture, 1989), p. 47.

27 Warehime, *Brassaï*, pp. 75–6.

28 Despite their plans to collaborate in the early 1930s, MacOrlan first wrote about Brassaï in 1953 ('La photographie et la poésie du monde', *Mercure de France* (1 February 1953), 305–8).

29 Breton himself employed this distinction in an essay on nineteenth-century French poetry: 'Le merveilleux contre le mystère' (*Minotaure*, 9 (1936), 25–31), translated as 'Marvellous versus Mystery', in *Free Rein* (Lincoln: University of Nebraska Press, 1995), pp. 1–6.

30 André Breton, *Mad Love* (Lincoln: University of Nebraska, 1987), p. 8.

31 Edward Baron Turk, *Child of Paradise: Marcel Carné and the Golden Age of Cinema* (Cambridge, MA: Harvard University Press, 1989), p. 109.

32 On the tangible links between Carné, Prévert and Brassaï, see Tucker, *Brassaï*, pp. 44–5.

33 Tony Ray-Jones, 'Brassaï talking about Photography', *Creative Camera* (April 1970), 121.

34 Brassaï, 'Interview avec France Bequette', 15.
35 Paul Hill and Thomas Cooper, *Dialogue with Photography* (New York: Farrar, Straus and Giroux, 1979), p. 48.
36 Quoted by Sayag and Lionel-Marie, *Brassaï*, p. 160, from a speech given by Brassaï in 1963.
37 It's impossible now to determine who might have been responsible for this layout. Formally, Albert Skira was the Administrative Director of *Minotaure* and E. Tériade the Artistic Director, but their roles were never so clear cut. Several of the Surrealists were involved with the magazine – in particular Breton and Eluard – but it's hard to tell what decisions they made beyond their own contributions. Likewise, one can't know if Brassaï himself played any part in the layout of his work.
38 Brassaï, 'Du mur des cavernes au mur d'usine', *Minotaure*, 3–4 (14 December 1933), 6–7. For a full translation, see the British edition of Sayag and Lionel-Marie, *Brassaï*, p. 292, which I have used in translating the extracts given here, but with several variations.
39 Brassaï, *Picasso and Company*, p. 38.
40 This phrase is from a later statement in *Brassaï* (Paris: Bibliothèque Nationale, 1963), p. 24.
41 Kirk Varnedoe and Adam Gopnik, *High and Low: Modern Art and Popular Culture* (New York: Museum of Modern Art, 1991), p. 79.
42 Brassaï, 'Du mur des cavernes au mur d'usine'.
43 It is not a coincidence that Brassaï refers to the Opéra here, since it represents high culture and an elaborate architectural style as well as being a central feature in Haussmann's attempt to order the city. Raoul Ubac would later make it the subject of one of his 'fossil' photographs (see Chapter 6, n. 34), while René Magritte had also undermined its pretensions in a collage published in *La Révolution surréaliste* (12 (15 December 1929), 46), where a herd of cows are shown grazing in front of the Opera House. (The collage is now in the collection of the Detroit Institute of Art; it's illustrated in Krauss and Livingston (eds), *L'Amour fou*, p. 106.)
44 Sichel, *Brassaï*, p. 20.
45 The anthropological analogy, implicit in the 1933 text, was later amplified by Brassaï himself (see Chapter 9).
46 In issue no. 9 of *Minotaure* (1936), Brassaï published a single image titled 'Troglodyte', which can serve as a coda to the graffiti photographs, the title recalling Brassaï's parallel with cave art. The photo was taken from inside a cave looking out through two holes, which are reminiscent of the gouged out eyes in some of the graffiti. Moreover, the play between inside and outside, positive and negative is reminiscent of the way that, in the graffiti photos, the negative shadows of the gouged out shapes can be read as positive forms.
47 'Walls of Paris', *Harper's Bazaar* (July 1953), 42–5.
48 See 'Language of the Wall', *U.S. Camera* (1958), 6–15, 290 and 294; 'Graffiti parisiens', *XXe Siècle* (March 1958), 21–4; and 'The Art of the Wall', in John Hadfield (ed.), *The Saturday Book* (New York: Macmillan, 1958), pp. 237–40.
49 *Language of the Wall* (London: Institute of Contemporary Arts, 1958).
50 *Graffiti* (Stuttgart: Belser, 1960).
51 *Language of the Wall*, unpaginated. Two other later texts by Brassaï on graffiti, from 1958 and 1976, are translated in Borja-Villel, *Brassaï*, pp. 169–70 and pp. 173–4.

52 In his text to the 1960 collection, Brassaï made much of the interest of Picasso in the images, ending the volume with discussions that were to be reprinted in the book *Conversations avec Picasso* four years later.

53 Brassaï, *Picasso and Company*, p. 184.

54 *Ibid.*, p. 242.

55 *Ibid.*, p. 241.

56 He records a comment by Matisse on the resemblance between the graffiti images of the female genitals and coffee beans (*Ibid.*, p. 221).

57 *Language of the Wall*, unpaginated.

58 The letter of 16 August 1947 from Dubuffet to Brassaï was included in Brassaï's 1963 exhibition at the Bibliothèque Nationale (listed on p. 23 of the catalogue).

59 In his previously unpublished text 'Le Procès des Graffiti', added to the 1993 edition of *Graffiti*, Brassaï quotes with great satisfaction a review from *The Times* (29 September 1958), stating that the work of contemporary painters 'can never attain the same degree of force and authenticity that many of these photographs do' (p. 144).

60 Jean Dubuffet, *L'Art Brut* (Paris: Musée des Arts decoratifs, 1967), p. 7.

61 From a lecture delivered on 20 December 1951, at the Arts Club of Chicago. Reproduced in facsimile in Jean Dubuffet, *Dubuffet and the Anticulture* (New York: Richard Feigen and Co., 1969).

62 Eugène Guillevic and Jean Dubuffet, *Les Murs* (Paris: Les Editions du Livre, 1950). For a recent commentary on *Les Murs*, see Harry Gilonis, 'Reinvented from Scratch: Dubuffet and Guillevic's *Les Murs*', in *Dubuffet's Walls* (London: Hayward Gallery, 1999), pp. 13–20.

63 Francis Ponge and Jean Dubuffet, *Matière et memoire* (Paris: Mourlet, 1945).

64 Noted by Sarah Wilson, 'Paris Post-War: In Search of the Absolute', in Frances Morris (ed.), *Paris Post War: Art and Existenialism 1945–55* (London: Tate Gallery, 1993), p. 33.

65 This description is based on an examination of a copy of the rare first edition in the Bibliothèque Nationale.

66 On this period in French cultural history, see Brian Rigby, *Popular Culture in France* (London: Routledge, 1991).

67 On *Paroles*, see also Chapter 2. Another of Brassaï's graffiti photographs was used on the cover of a later book by Prévert, *La pluie et le beau temps* (Paris: Livre de poche, 1962). Brassaï's pictures were also included in one other post-war French publication: Camille Bryen and Alain Gheerhardt (eds), *Anthologie de la poèsie naturelle* (Paris: Editions K., 1949).

68 Wilson, 'Paris Post-War', p. 26.

69 Published in Jacques Prévert, *Fatras* (Paris: Gallimard, 1966), p. 281, along with collages based on photographs by Izis, Halsmann and Doisneau. The image was also reproduced in Patrick Waldberg, *Surrealism* (London: Thames and Hudson, 1965), illus. 114, where it was returned to a Surrealist context.

70 This graffiti had been one of the first photographed by Brassaï and is at bottom left in his 1933 montage in *Minotaure*.

71 A photograph by Humphrey Jennings of a 'child's graffiti from Lancashire' was reproduced in the *London Bulletin*, 4–5 (July 1938), 22. Spender also photographed graffiti in Bolton;

for one example, see Humphrey Spender, *Worktown People* (Bristol: Falling Wall Press, 1982), p. 35. An image by Helen Levitt accompanied Roger Caillois' essay 'The Myth of Secret Treasures of Childhood', in *VVV*, 4 (1942), 4; her photographs of graffiti were collected in *In the Street* (Durham, North Carolina: Duke University Press, 1987). Robert Doisneau's photograph 'Le mur de graffiti: initiation des filles' (*La Banlieue de Paris*, illus. 8) unusually showed young female graffitists. In Izis' *Paris de rêves* (pp. 154–5), a photograph of a boy drawing a face on a fence was accompanied by a brief text from André Breton, who referred to the images on the fence as 'une page de grimoire', eliding the three meanings of 'grimoire': illegible scrawl, obscure language and book of spells. Evoking the work of Klee, Miró and Arp, Breton ended by suggesting that the boy was 'adding the last touches to the portrait of Prévert', a reference, perhaps, to the contemporary caricature portraits by Dubuffet.

72 On the back cover of the 1993 edition of *Graffiti*, there is a photograph by Brassaï of a boy scribbling in chalk on a wall; in Sichel, *Brassaï*, p. 19, the picture is dated to 1931–34 and titled 'A la sauvette'. But Brassaï himself never seems to have used the photograph, and its posthumous appearance serves to undercut his earlier presentation of the work as primitive and permanent.

73 However, where Brassaï photographed marks made deliberately through human agency, Medková generally recorded processes of time, weathering, change and damage. As Jan Kříž put it in his text for Medková's 1965 monograph, Brassaï's work 'possesses a much stronger element of expressive aggression', where Medková 'sets up a more magical symbolic expression' with a 'more complex content' (*Emila Medková* (Prague: SNKLU, 1965)).

74 Asger Jorn, *Signes gravés sur les églises de l'Eure et du Calvados* (Copenhagen: Edition Borger, 1964).

75 Edouard Jaguer, *Les mystères de la chambre noire* (Paris: Flammarion, 1982), p. 152.

8

Henri Cartier-Bresson: *Images à la sauvette*

In 1976, Henri Cartier-Bresson, then at the height of his reputation as one of the most important and influential of documentary photographers, decided to use a quotation from André Breton as the epigram for an anthology of his pictures:

> Actually it's quite true that he's not waiting for anyone since he's not made an appointment, but the very fact that he's adopting this ultra-receptive posture means that by this he wants to help chance along, how should I say, to put himself in a state of grace with chance, so that something might happen, so that some one might drop in.[1]

The source of the quote is given simply as *Entretiens* – the book that was compiled in 1952 from a series of radio interviews that Breton gave to André Parinaud. There is no explanation of who the 'he' is that Breton refers to, but in this context, it is Cartier-Bresson himself who becomes that 'he'. It is now the photographer who is 'in a state of grace with chance'.

Not only did Cartier-Bresson, through this quotation, emphasise the vital role that Surrealist notions of chance had in the formation of his working method in the early 1930s, but he also seemed to imply that this influence had underpinned his work ever since. Yet this emphasis on the accidental and the arbitrary was surely at odds with the dominant idea of Cartier-Bresson, developed during the post-war years, as a great humanist photographer operating out of the framework of traditional reportage, with its imperative to observe established forms of narrative.

In a number of interviews during the 1970s, Cartier-Bresson continued to affirm the place of Surrealism in his work, and explained why he had made the shift from 'surrealist' to 'photojournalist'. He described this apparent move through an anecdote, dating back to 1946:

> My friend Robert Capa told me 'Henri, be very careful. You must not have a label of a surrealist photographer. If you do, you won't have an assignment and you'll be like a hothouse plant. Do

> whatever you like, but the label should be "photojournalist"'. And Capa was extremely sound. So I never mentioned surrealism. That's my private affair. And what I want, what I'm looking for – that's my business.[2]

It seems, then, that there have been two Cartier-Bressons. The second, the post-war version, though never in fact purely a photojournalist, certainly made his reputation as a photographer with a notably warm and affirmative attitude towards the human condition. The reputation of this Cartier-Bresson, enormously high for many years, has perhaps waned in the last couple of decades as documentary photography acquired a harder edge, throwing into doubt the values of the 'Family of Man' tradition which Cartier-Bresson seemed to exemplify.[3] The post-war Cartier-Bresson is still respected as a past master, but not, it seems, as a continuing example for contemporary radical photography. In this regard, interest shifted in the 1980s to the Cartier-Bresson of the early 1930s. That Cartier-Bresson was an individualistic artist, self-consciously poetic in his approach, working on the edge of the medium, making images that were difficult, troubling, somewhat unnerving.

As Charles Hagen points out, 'a central purpose behind the vast majority of photography ... is to define a communal perception of reality ... it repeats and seems to certify unchanging verities of narrative, of the nature of the world, of the varieties of human character and incident'. That is what the humanist post-war Cartier-Bresson did, brilliantly. But, as Hagen goes on to suggest, Cartier-Bresson's early images work against these communal narratives, in an 'unrelenting, sometimes subtle and sometimes blunt contradiction of this web of expectation and purpose'.[4] In this, the Cartier-Bresson of the 1930s seems closer to those photographers of the 1960s who redefined the nature of documentary in reaction to the affirmative pieties of the 'Family of Man'; a Cartier-Bresson as acerbic and amoral as Gary Winogrand, as self-referential as Lee Friedlander. The work of these latter photographers was endorsed by exhibitions at the Museum of Modern Art as it swung away from the grand projects of the 1950s,[5] and the Museum was in turn to place its imprimatur of approval on the early Cartier-Bresson with an major exhibition in 1987.[6] This was, in a sense, the reversal of a process that had begun forty years earlier in 1947, when MOMA had mounted the exhibition which established the burgeoning reputation of 'Henri Cartier-Bresson: Photographic Humanist'.[7]

Whereas Brassaï and Kertész came into contact with Surrealism when they were already well established, Cartier-Bresson discovered it before he began to make photographs and the influence was much deeper. Moreover, unlike them, he was happy to acknowledge the importance of that influence. Indeed, his adherence to the fundamental principles of Surrealism were such that 'there is justification for the opinion that in the early 1930s Cartier-Bresson was the best and most mature of the Surrealist photographers, although his work does not appear in any of the Surrealist periodicals'.[8] Paradoxically, then, Cartier-Bresson's early work is crucial to an understanding of Surrealist photography, even as it was peripheral to the movement itself.

Cartier-Bresson was born in 1908 into a prosperous manufacturing family, but rather than enter the family business, he gradually moved towards a career as an artist. In 1927, at the age of nineteen, he began to study with the minor Cubist painter, André Lhote, but already his main interest was elsewhere. For Cartier-Bresson was also discovering Surrealism: 'Very young, around 1926–1927, I was marked, not by surrealist painting, but by the ideas of Breton. I went regularly to the reunions at the "Café de la Place Blanche", although I was not a member of the group. Breton's conception of surrealism delighted me, the role of spontaneity and of intuition, and, above all, the attitude of revolt.'[9] Though the young Cartier-Bresson hardly knew the magisterial Breton, he did become more friendly with other Surrealists such as Max Ernst and René Crevel.

His earliest photographic work dates from 1929 and was made with a view camera; his first influence was Atget.[10] By the end of the 1920s, it was probably impossible for an aspiring young photographer in Paris *not* to know of Atget, so quickly had his reputation spread. Cartier-Bresson's surviving images from 1929 certainly are full of Atgetian simulacra – a group of male mannequins outside a shop in Rouen, moulds of hands thrown in a pile – but already these pictures have an unbalanced quality which anticipates Cartier-Bresson's work of the 1930s and feels distinctly different from Atget's formal poise.

In 1930, Cartier-Bresson journeyed to the Ivory Coast, a personal response to the French fascination with Africa which had inspired his hero Rimbaud to quit France in the 1870s, which had fuelled Cubism in the first decade of the twentieth-century and which would later account for the popular appeal of the 1931–33 Mission Dakar–Djibouti. The search for an 'other' to set against European bourgeois society would be integral to Cartier-Bresson's work in the 1930s, whether he found it on the periphery of the urban environment, in the impoverishment of Mediterranean peasant life or, in 1934, in the radically different culture of Mexico.

The photographs Cartier-Bresson took on his African trip were destroyed by damp, and he himself fell dangerously ill. He returned to France, recovered, continued to travel in Europe. And in 1932 he acquired a Leica 35mm camera, the photographic instrument that was to become central to his photography. This new technology offered the possibility of making pictures rapidly and invisibly, with no delay between shots. It enabled Cartier-Bresson to create images expressive of a philosophical position fundamentally tempered by Surrealism. Later, in 1952, he described this encounter:

> I had just discovered the Leica. It became an extension of my eye, and I have never been separated from it since I found it. I prowled the streets all day, feeling very strung up and ready to pounce, determined to 'trap' life – to preserve life in the act of living.[11]

If this sounds an echo of Aragon wandering through the Passage de l'Opéra, it is no accident, for Cartier-Bresson had certainly read and absorbed *Le paysan de Paris*.[12] His close friend of these years, André Pieyre de Mandiargues, later elaborated upon the almost obsessive interest this aspect of Surrealism held for them:

> what we were seeking ... was violent emotion, rupture with the disciplines of everyday life as we knew and barely tolerated it, a certain dizziness and a certain convulsion ... I asked for reality to become a dream. On occasion reality fulfilled my desire. For example when, with Henri Cartier-Bresson, I went to follow the example of Aragon in the brothels of provincial France, at Rouen or Nancy.[13]

But Cartier-Bresson showed (and has continued to show) little interest in Surrealist art: 'I have been influenced by Surrealism as a concept, as an attitude to life, but I have great reservations about Surrealist painting, which seems too literary for me.'[14] He has expressed much the same reservation about Surrealist photography, describing the bulk of Man Ray's work also as too *littéraire*.[15] (He makes an exception for Man Ray's portraits, which he admires for their directness.) 'The only aspect of the phenomenon of photography that fascinates me, and will always interest me, is the intuitive capture through the camera of what is seen. That is exactly how Breton defined objective chance (*le hasard objectif*) in his *Entretiens*.'[16]

It was around this concept of 'objective chance' that Cartier-Bresson formed his version of a Surrealist realism. For the Surrealists themselves, this was a central idea, and it is worth returning to the original source of the quotation that opened this chapter. Breton is in fact describing not the actions of an actual person, but of a character, Monsieur Létoile, in *S'il vous plaît*, a play written by Breton and Philippe Soupault in 1920. Breton comments: 'We were stalking that "objective chance" (to use Hegel's term) whose manifestations I'd never stop watching out for, not only in *Nadja*, but later in *Les Vases communicants* and *L'Amour fou* as well.'[17] This theme ran through the movement like a rich vein of ore, as one of its most fundamental concerns. It was however not theorised by Breton until the early 1930s – the point at which Cartier-Bresson's own ideas were being formed by his contact with Surrealism.

Breton's first extensive explication of 'objective chance' comes in *Les Vases communicants* in 1932, where he cites Frederick Engels: 'Causality cannot be understood except as it is linked with the category of objective chance, a form of the manifestation of necessity.'[18] However, as Margaret Cohen has demonstrated, in *L'Amour fou*, published five years later in 1937, 'Breton uses the term not to suggest that obscured objective forces are at issue in chance but rather that chance makes manifest repressed desire'.[19] It was then a matter of emphasis whether objective cause or subjective response was foregrounded;

what was most important though was the intersection of the two. As the very concept of the 'communicating vessels' demonstrates, these two sites of interior and exterior were never to be seen as opposites, but rather as dialectically linked realities, neither of which could be meaningfully apprehended without the other. Breton himself commented in *L'Amour fou*, 'the spectacle playing itself out before me ... suddenly appears to be set up for me alone, conforming in every way to my *previous* image of it ... implying between events imagined and real a constant parallelism'.[20]

Cartier-Bresson tempered Breton's apparent shift towards subjectivity through an emphasis on the operation of 'objective chance' in actuality. But he does think of 'the intuitive capture through the camera of what is seen' as a process parallel to automatism.[21] Pieyre de Mandiargues later wrote: 'I thought he used [his Leica] rather as the Surrealists tried to use automatic writing: as a window that one leaves permanently open for the visitations of the unconscious and the unpredictable.'[22] Where the Surrealists sought to exploit automatism as a means of entry into the web of poetic relationships inside the human unconscious, so 'objective chance' seemed to offer access to the 'optical unconscious' of the exterior world.

The term 'optical unconscious' was coined by Walter Benjamin; in his essay 'A Small History of Photography' (1931), he wrote:

> Whereas it is a commonplace that, for example, we have some idea of what is involved in the act of walking ... we have no idea at all what happens during the fraction of a second when a person *steps out*. Photography, with its devices of slow motion and enlargement, reveals the secret. It is through photography that we first discover the existence of this optical unconscious, just as we discover the instinctual unconscious through psychoanalysis.[23]

In one sense, Benjamin is expanding here on his interest in chronophotography and the 'New Vision' of German photography; he had elsewhere praised Blossfeldt's flower photographs in similar terms.[24] Yet he goes further and glosses this effect by seeking a parallel with the psychoanalytic probing of the human mind. In his later 'Artwork' essay, Benjamin amplified the concept: 'It thereby becomes tangible that a different nature speaks to the camera than to the eye. For in place of a space interwoven with human consciousness, one interwoven with unconsciousness steps in.'[25]

It is a provocative analogy, but also perplexing. As Rosalind Krauss has asked: 'Can the optical field – the world of visual phenomena: clouds, sea, sky, forest – *have* an unconscious?'[26] The concept of the 'optical unconscious' becomes more intriguing when it is brought to bear upon the urban environment of buildings, streets, signs, things that have in fact themselves been formed through the impulses of human culture, the complex products of conscious intent and unconscious desire. The camera, it would seem, can be particularly effective in revealing these impulses. As Esther Leslie has written, 'Film and photography, through the optical unconscious, tap transformative potentials embedded in actuality'.[27]

However, this still makes it sound as if the camera undertakes this all by itself. In one sense, photographs are indeed made by the indifferent but incisive mechanism of the *appareil* – the machine – and its *objectif* – the lens. The camera may well see more than the human eye can, but what it cannot do is decide what to look at. What is caught and what escapes, what is valued and what is not, is due in part to the photographer's choice of where to point the camera and when to press the shutter. But those decisions may not be altogether consciously controlled, as Cartier-Bresson himself suggested by his phrase 'the intuitive capture through the camera of what is seen'. Seen, one might ask, by what? By the cold eye of the camera and the 'intuition' of the photographer, working in tandem together. And in the case of Cartier-Bresson, working not in the service of dominant modes of existence, but rather, guided by the subversive impetus of desire, seeking to catch the parapraxes of culture.[28]

The years of Cartier-Bresson's initial discovery of the Leica and the possibilities it opened for street photography, 1932–33, was a period of great intensity in his work. As Ben Maddow has written, the pictures made during this time have 'the feeling of being seized rather than merely taken'.[29] In retrospect, a key moment occurred in 1932, on the Pont de l'Europe behind the Gare St Lazare in Paris, when Cartier-Bresson indeed captured 'the fraction of a second when a person *steps out*' (figure 63). 'A wooden fence surrounded some roadworks', he later wrote.[30] Through the railings, he saw a man crossing the flooded ground. 'I put my lens through a gap just at the moment that the man jumped.' Indeed, one can just see the fence at the edge of the published print, which – perhaps uniquely in Cartier-Bresson's work – has been cropped in from the larger negative.

The resulting photograph is justly famous and brings together a number of photographic and thematic tropes. Most often, it is discussed as a supremely 'decisive moment' – that term which Cartier-Bresson was later to adopt to describe his photographic philosophy. And indeed the central *punctum* of the image – that space between the man's foot and its reflection – seems miraculous, as small as it could be without disappearing.[31] The water appears as a mirror-like surface and it is difficult to convince oneself that the man is not either going to land somehow *on* the surface or alternatively disappear beneath it completely. Leslie elaborates on Benjamin's 'optical unconscious' in terms that connect strongly with the effect of this picture: 'a fragment that now figures as a representation of the real is blasted out of the incessant movement of experience by its reproduction. As representation, it is held up, made still for an instant of conscious reflection on its significance'.[32]

As a 'decisive moment', the picture might be read primarily as an image of formal grace and harmony – the central figure supported by the curved forms in the foreground and echoed by the rhyming presence of the leaping dancer on the

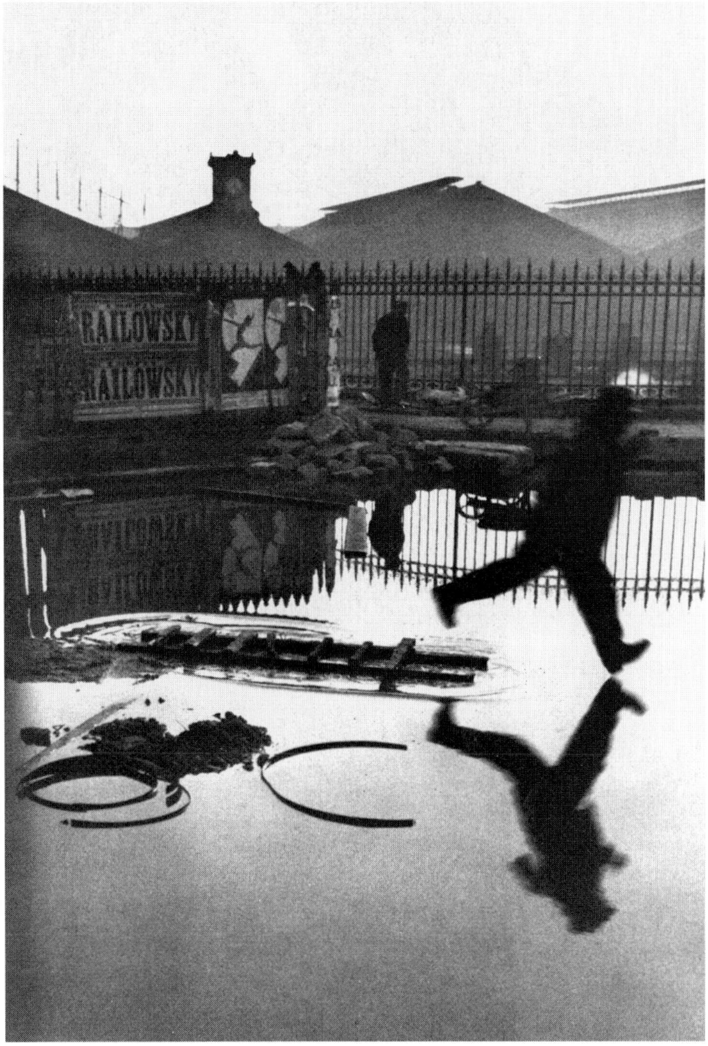

Fig 63 Henri Cartier-Bresson, *La Place de l'Europe, Paris, 1932.*
© Henri Cartier Bresson/Magnum Photos.

poster in the background. Thus the photograph would be pulled into line with Cartier-Bresson's post-war work. But 'objective chance' is a more problematic concept than the 'decisive moment', and this image has an unsettling quality which its fame has not quite erased. The image is unusually dark for Cartier-Bresson, the gloom of a northern city in winter. The rhyme between workman and dancer has the nagging pointlessness which Breton and Aragon had both found so haunting in the chance juxtapositions of street posters and reality.[33] There are also echoes in the image of de Chirico. The clocktower on the railway station is reminiscent of the one which de Chirico placed (or saw?) on the Gare Montparnasse, while the figures are relatives of the black silhouettes which stand silently in many of the deserted city spaces in his paintings. Finally, the

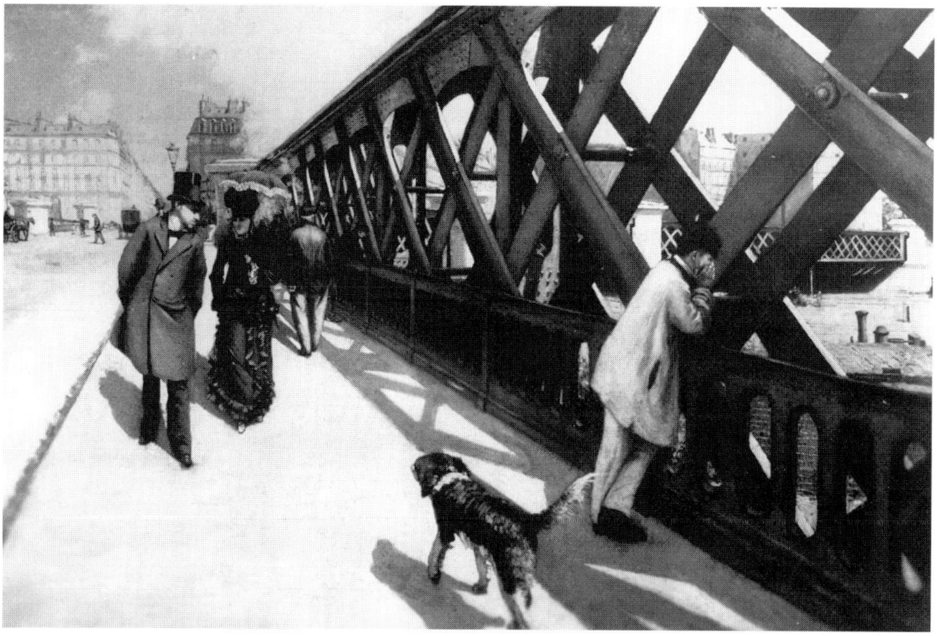

Fig 64 Gustave Caillebotte, *Le Pont de l'Europe*, 1876. Musée du Petit Palais, Geneva.

disquieting nature of the photograph lies also in its setting, a sort of *terrain vague* in miniature, a wasteland of indecisiveness. Even the site itself, behind a railway station, is a site of passage and flux – a place that is also a 'non-place'.[34]

The Pont de l'Europe had been built in 1868 to hold up several roads as they crossed above the railway leaving the Gare St Lazare, and in 1876, it had been the setting for two of Gustave Caillebotte's great paintings of Parisian modernity (figure 64).[35] Though Caillebotte's images were much busier and visually clearer than Cartier-Bresson's would be, there was already in Caillebotte's depiction of this site a strong sense of the flux and indeterminacy which this new urbanity had brought with it. Cartier-Bresson's photograph, however, serves no social purpose. Rather it indelibly records a sliver of time and space. Records *and* creates, for it is a supremely photographic image, an image that could only exist as a photograph. And it could only be meaningful as a photograph, for its surreality rests in the welding together of the indexical and the constructed. That man was once there, a corporeal being with a life to go to. Now he is a flat silhouette, dynamic yet forever frozen, his suspension in mid-air a function of the camera's ability to stop motion. But this doesn't explain the picture. Indeed, like many of Cartier-Bresson's early pictures, its power lies precisely in its refusal of explanation.

There were other occasions when this refusal was more deliberate. In Valencia in 1933, Cartier-Bresson photographed a small boy against a gouged and battered wall (figure 65). The boy gazes upward with an expression which suggested to Ben Maddow a 'universal experience of intense happiness'.[36] It

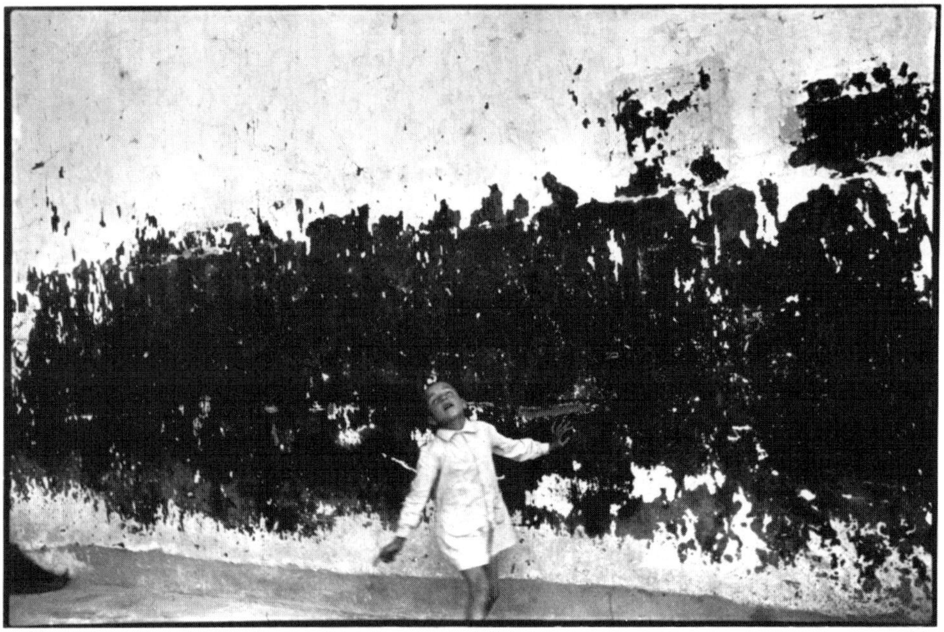

Fig 65 Henri Cartier-Bresson, *Valencia, 1933*. © Henri Cartier-Bresson/Magnum Photos.

might equally represent the disorientation of mental disturbance. In fact, Maddow reports, the boy has thrown a ball into the air and is waiting for it to come down. But the words 'in fact' are misleading. It may have been the fact of the original event, but that has long since gone; the fact of the photograph is that the boy is ambiguously, disturbingly poised in the caught moment of the photograph and the ball will never come down. The ball is a red herring; eliminated from the frame at the crucial instant the image was made, it no longer exists (just as the man jumping the water will never land). Photographically this may be a 'decisive moment', but it is hardly one that draws together the elements of the scene in order to explicate them, as Cartier-Bresson's later work seems to do. In narrative terms, the photograph is actually rather inconclusive – the nature of the photographic moment used to render the event altogether ambiguous.[37]

A comparison between the work of Cartier-Bresson and other photographers working in Paris round 1930 also helps to demonstrate the particularity of his work at that time. Earlier, I contrasted Cartier-Bresson's photograph made at the abattoir of La Villette with the pictures made there by Eli Lotar.[38] But the most direct contrast is with the work of the other Parisian photographer to have seized on the possibilities offered by the Leica: André Kertész. Kertész was older, having come from his native Hungary in 1925; in 1928, he bought one of the first Leicas to arrive in Paris, recognising in the new camera the ideal tool for his own peripatetic and improvisatory approach to photography.[39] One of his earliest 35mm pictures, taken that same year in the Paris suburb of Meudon, has

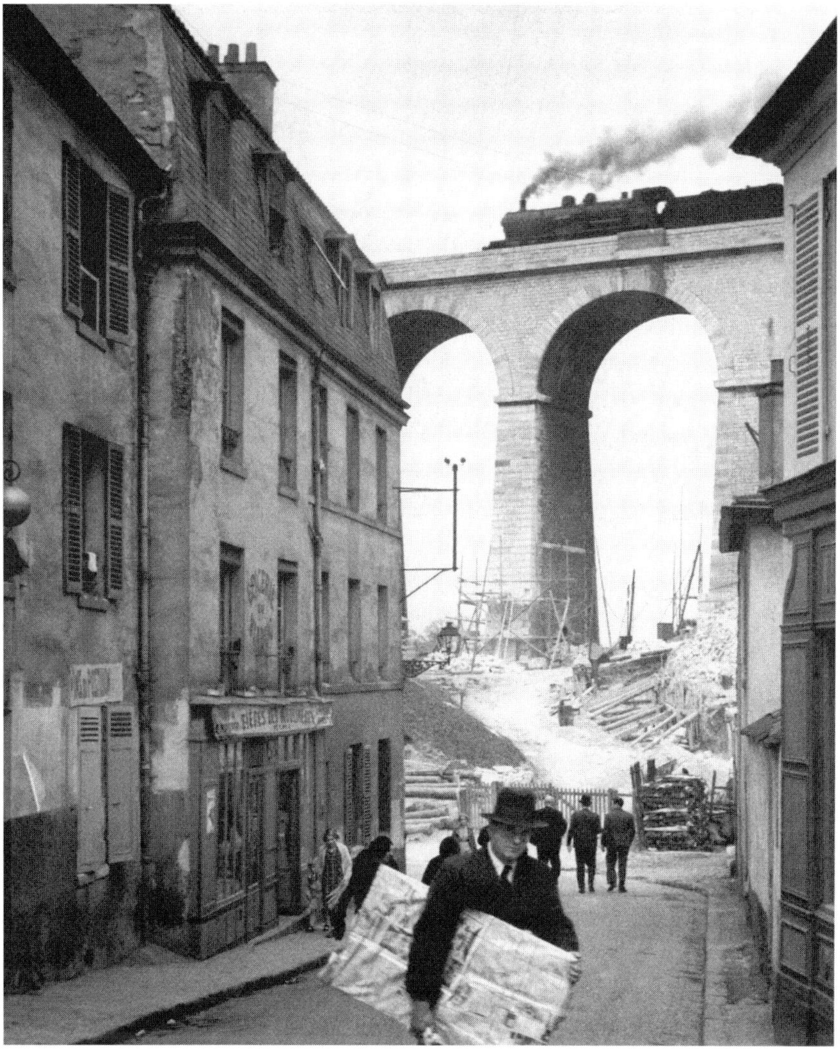

Fig 66 André Kertész, *Meudon, 1928.* © Ministère de la Culture-France.

become one of the key images in a Surrealist reading of his photography (figure 66).[40] It has some features in common with the photograph that Cartier-Bresson made four years later behind the Gare St Lazare. The setting is also an indeterminate *terrain vague*, dominated by the passing railway line. Moreover, these elements are again reminiscent of de Chirico; indeed, as Michel Frizot has remarked, there is a danger that Kertész's photograph is 'valorised by the associative recollection of a Chiricesque iconography (town, viaduct, train)'.[41]

Both photographs capture a fleeting moment when relationships are formed by the camera that a split second later will have gone. But beyond that, the pictures are quite different. Rather than the single, startling event on which Cartier-Bresson's photograph is centred, the effect of Kertész's image relies on 'the spacing of simple but disjunctive objects',[42] a series of oblique, fragile relationships – between the man and the train, the man and his parcel, the man and the photographer. It is important that eye contact, albeit mistrustful, is established, for through it we also are able to enter the scene. Where Cartier-Bresson's vision is fragmented, disassociative, Kertész's photography is more integral. The fabric of urban experience holds together for him in a way that it does not for Cartier-Bresson.

All in all, Cartier-Bresson shows the city as a scrappy sort of place, a picture grabbed here, a picture there – all quite decontextualised. He can shift suddenly from the alienation of the bourgeoisie to the raw edges of deprivation, can as easily photograph dogs copulating on the pavement as the funeral of a former Prime Minister.[43] It is difficult to know how much the sense of fragmentation is due to the fact that what one sees now is a radical stripping down of the work by both time and the will of the author. (Cartier-Bresson destroyed most of the negatives he considered unsuccessful.) Unlike Atget, Brassaï or Kertész in their different ways, in the 1930s Cartier-Bresson evidently harboured no desire to build up a body of consistent work. Moreover, Cartier-Bresson was not a photographer of Paris as were the other three.[44] Travel was at the core of his work, to an almost obsessive extent. In 1931, he was in Eastern Europe; from 1932–33, there are surviving photographs taken in Brussels, Marseilles, Italy, Spain and Morocco. In 1934, he left Europe for an extended stay in Mexico and later New York.

Nevertheless, it is possible to place Cartier-Bresson, for all his globetrotting, essentially in the tradition of *flânerie*, indeed to see him as one of its foremost exponents. Quoting Baudelaire's eulogy of 'the painter of modern life', Mark Haworth-Booth has commented: 'This is the aptest account of the young Henri Cartier-Bresson, who wandered the streets of France, Mexico and Spain in the early 1930s, a Leica in hand and Baudelaire's poems in his pocket.'[45] It is of course a romanticised version of Cartier-Bresson's project in the 1930s, but then there was a self-romanticisation on the part of Cartier-Bresson at the time.

After his return to Paris from New York in late 1935 or early 1936, Cartier-Bresson seemed to shift tack, making fewer photographs with diminished intensity. He worked briefly in the cinema, both as assistant to Jean Renoir and attempting his own documentary film in Spain in 1937. His photography also changed direction; for the first time, he worked in reportage, for the Communist journals *Ce Soir* and *Regard*. With the war, he enlisted, was captured by the Germans, escaped and joined the Resistance. He made little work until 1944, when he photographed the liberation of Dessau prison camp. In 1946 his work was exhibited at the Museum of Modern Art in New York; in 1947 he co-founded the photographic agency Magnum, together with Robert Capa, 'Chim' (David Seymour) and George Rodger.

As this narrative suggests, the post-war Cartier-Bresson did not suddenly appear, changing his title from surrealist to photojournalist after the war, as the Capa anecdote would suggest. Rather than a break between his pre-war and post-war work, there was a gradual evolution. As early as the mid-1930s, when he took up reportage, more comprehensible narratives appeared in his pictures. The experience of working with Jean Renoir, that most humanist of film directors, also influenced the direction of his work.[46] The political experiences of the Spanish Civil War and the German Occupation of France would also leave their mark.

His post-war work would not only be different in style; the format in which it was presented also suggests a different attitude on Cartier-Bresson's part. In *The Decisive Moment*, he inserted a brief note: 'the images in this book do not pretend to give a general idea of the look of this or that country'.[47] But in his later books, this is what he does seem to want to show. There is hardly a continent or major country in the world which does not have a volume devoted to it: *Bali* (1954), *The Europeans* (1955), *China in Transition* (1956), *People of Moscow* (1958), *China* (1964), *Tokyo* (1966), *Cartier-Bresson's France* (1970), *The Face of Asia* (1972), *About Russia* (1973), *Henri Cartier-Bresson in India* (1987), *America in Passing* (1991), *Mexican Notebooks* (1994), *Europeans* (1998).[48]

This is in marked contrast with the earlier work made on his travels, the very decontextualisation and fragmentation of which enables it to escape accusations of touristic voyeurism. He did not attempt to tell stories but rather to show ambiguously framed situations, where the lack of comprehension on the part of the viewer (and perhaps Cartier-Bresson himself) was often part of the picture's effect. When he went to Mexico in 1934, he was not moved, as was André Breton four years later, to claim the country for Surrealism and thus fall into a problematic romanticisation of that country's otherness.[49] Several of his Mexican images are very reminiscent of those made by his friend Manuel Alvarez Bravo. But where, for Bravo, such images would have been part of a long and continuing process of mirroring his own culture, for Cartier-Bresson, they were moments he saw, something to make photographs with. He did not pretend to speak for their 'Mexicanness'.[50]

Yet in the later Cartier-Bresson there did remain elements of the earlier one, and there are many individual pictures that still have something inexplicable about them. Peter Galassi has pointed to one of the photographs made in Mexico on Cartier-Bresson's return visit in 1963: 'like many of the best later pictures – far more than commonly acknowledged – this one shares with the early work a lively independence from the conventions of narrative logic and the pat explanations of the caption writer'.[51] But there is rarely in the later work the 'certain convulsion' to which Pieyre de Mandiargues (echoing Breton's demand for a 'convulsive beauty') had referred and which was the main attribute that made the work of the young Cartier-Bresson relevant for Surrealism.

If, however, this element never entirely disappeared, our sense of it has been diminished by familiarity and perhaps by the cultural context in which the work has latterly been sited. Cartier-Bresson's first major book of 1952 was titled in English *The Decisive Moment*; in French, it was *Images à la sauvette*.[52] *A la sauvette* is a slang term usually applied to traders operating on a street corner,

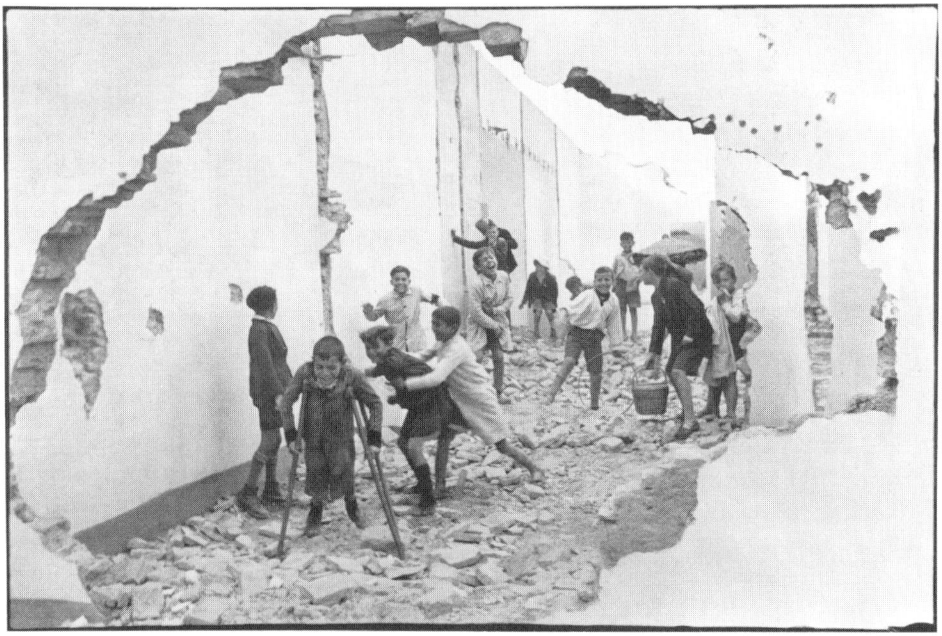

Fig 67 Henri Cartier-Bresson, *Seville, 1933*. © Henri Cartier-Bresson/Magnum Photos.

looking out for the police and ready for a quick getaway. This gives the French title a more edgy, furtive connotation than its English equivalent. Furthermore, the anthology of photographs which in 1968 updated *The Decisive Moment* was in English blandly (if revealingly) entitled *The World of Henri Cartier-Bresson*; its French title however was *Flagrants délits* ('caught in the act'), another term with guilty, even dangerous resonances.[53] Whereas in the introduction to *The Decisive Moment* Cartier-Bresson had written that he had been 'determined to "trap" life – to preserve life in the act of living', in *Images à la sauvette* he described himself as 'cherchant dans les rues à prendre sur le vif des photos comme des flagrants délits'.[54] It is not only his subjects who have been 'caught in the act'; even while his reputation as the great photographic humanist developed, it seems that Cartier-Bresson himself continued to court – and value – the voyeurism implicit in his way of working, slipping in and out of the life that flowed past, a life that others lived as he spied.

The placement of Cartier-Bresson's early work as emblematic of a particular sort of Surrealist documentary photography is largely retrospective. In the 1930s, there seems to have been only two actual sitings of his work within a Surrealist context. One of them though was at the heart of the movement – the use by André Breton of a Cartier-Bresson photograph as the last image in his 1937 book *L'Amour fou*. It appears at the point where Breton is addressing his baby daughter Aube; he tells her that, despite his feelings about the Civil War in Spain, it is for her sake that he will not go to fight there: 'I loved in you all the

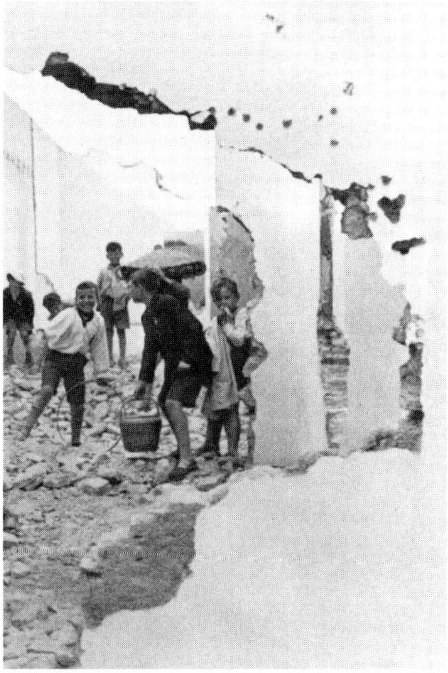

Fig 68 Henri Cartier-Bresson, *Seville, 1933*, as reproduced in André Breton, *L'Amour fou*, 1937. © Henri Cartier-Bresson/Magnum Photos.

little children of the Spanish militia, like those I saw running naked in the outer district of Santa Cruz, on Tenerife. May the sacrifice of so many human lives make of them one day happy beings.'[55] (Cartier-Bresson's photograph of a group of boys playing in a ruined building had been made in Seville in 1933 (figure 67), but Breton has not been the only one to connect the picture with the Civil War.[56])

As George Melly has written, the last part of *L'Amour fou* 'becomes almost sentimental; no, it *is* sentimental'.[57] Breton is surely striving too hard to be optimistic, placing all his hopes in the children who will grow to be the next generation, and falling into an uncharacteristic Panglossism. In turn, one may wonder if this was a factor in the most striking and curious aspect to the reproduction of this photograph in *L'Amour fou*. Cartier-Bresson had given the print to Breton 'out of admiration for surrealism';[58] however, when it later appeared in the book, the picture has been sliced in half with only the right side of the original image left (figure 68). Cartier-Bresson himself never knew why this had been done. It cannot have been because of space or layout; horizontal images by Brassaï and Cézanne are both used. Rather it must have been because of the content.

Cartier-Bresson made many images of children during the early 1930s and they are notably unsentimental, filled with incipient, hardly-understood lusts and cruelties. The central feature of the original Seville image is a crippled child on crutches who is seemingly being chased by the other boys; it's hard to tell if he shares their hilarity. The cropping by Breton removes that incident entirely, and leaves only a group of laughing children seen inside a ruined building. It seems that this ambiguous intimation of childhood cruelty could not be admitted by Breton's panegyric to childish innocence.

There are several ironies in this use of Cartier-Bresson's image. First, that the maker of such unsettling images of children should be bowdlerised by a writer who in earlier circumstances had been as tough-minded as he was. Second, that the artist who exploited with such uncomfortable energy the framing of his images should in turn have his image reframed. (It is doubly ironic in view of Cartier-Bresson's later insistence on the use of the full frame in reproductions.) But above all, it is the waste of this image in this context that is so striking. Julien Levy wrote that 'Breton in *L'Amour fou* used one of the photos (by Cartier-Bresson) to illustrate his theory of *hasard objectif* – convulsive, indifferent, eternal'.[59] Unfortunately, that is just what Breton did not do. *L'Amour fou* (in its earlier sections) is indeed one of the key texts of 'objective chance'; likewise, many of Cartier-Bresson's images of the 1930s exemplify the truly convulsive quality of the phenomenon. But this one siting of Cartier-Bresson's work in relationship to Breton's text is fudged and its power altogether dissipated.

There was another placement of Cartier-Bresson's work in a Surrealist context in the mid-1930s: in Julien Levy's own 1936 book *Surrealism*. In a brief sequence on photography, Levy reproduced the work of Man Ray and Bellmer to exemplify staged Surrealist photography, while Atget was represented by the photograph of the corset shop from *La Révolution surréaliste*. All this involved the selection of work already published in a Surrealist context. However, Levy, who had a very good knowledge of advanced photography in both Europe and the USA, then went further, with the reproduction of two previously unpublished images by Cartier-Bresson: the boy with his hand on the battered wall in Valencia and an image from Brussels of two men looking through a canvas screen.

Opposite these was a letter to Julien Levy from one 'Peter Lloyd'; in fact, it had been written by Levy himself for the catalogue of the first exhibition of Cartier-Bresson's work at his gallery in New York in 1933.[60] Part of this text was an attack on 'the photo gods, my gods too, the purists, the three great S's – Stieglitz, Strand, Sheeler – and their school'. In contrast to the fine print aesthetic which then dominated art photography in the USA, Levy/Lloyd called Cartier-Bresson's work 'rude and crude ... septic as opposed to the mounting popularity of the anti-septic photograph. Call the exhibition amoral photography ... equivocal, ambivalent, anti-plastic, accidental photography. Call it anti-graphic photography'.[61] These qualities may not precisely coincide with Surrealist notions of the photographic, though there are obvious intersections. But what Levy's text does convey is just how unnerving and extreme Cartier-Bresson's photographic tactics must have seemed in the 1930s.

Such a response cannot now be recovered. Our view of those early pictures is inevitably affected by the development of Cartier-Bresson's long career, by his enormous reputation, by the tendency to anthologise his work in ways that make it seem homogeneous. Only by cutting the images of 1929–34 out of these later contexts can something of their effect be regained. Then one recognises a consistency of attitude in that work despite its fragmentariness. Even while concentrating on the broken and grubby, photographing *à la sauvette*, he nevertheless manages to suggest further qualities – strange, unnerving rhythms and patterns – that make these images valuable both for Surrealism and for documentary. Locking together the particular indexicality and constructedness of street photography, the young Cartier-Bresson simultaneously recorded *and* created his images. If, on the one hand, he exploited the 'photographicness' of photography, blatantly imposing a frame on reality and stopping action dead, he also proposed that through this process, we are able to glimpse something of reality asserting itself.

In 1995, Henri Cartier-Bresson paid his most extensive tribute to André Breton with the publication of a selection of his portraits of the elderly writer, at home in his Paris apartment or in the country, gathering stones on the banks of the River Lot. The title of the book expressed some of the awe with which Cartier-Bresson still regarded Breton – *André Breton: Roi Soleil* – and the accompanying text concluded with a reaffirmation of his debt: 'It is to surrealism that I owe allegiance, for it has taught me to allow the camera lens to rummage in the debris of the unconscious and of chance.'[62]

Notes

1 Henri Cartier-Bresson, *Henri Cartier-Bresson* (New York: Aperture/London: Gordon Fraser, 1976), unpaginated. For a different translation, see André Breton, *Conversations: The Autobiography of Surrealism* (New York: Paragon House, 1993), p. 106.

2 Sheila Turner-Seed, 'An Interview with Henri Cartier-Bresson', *Popular Photography* (May 1974), 108.

3 *The Family of Man* exhibition was mounted by Edward Steichen at the Museum of Modern Art, New York, in 1955 and remains one of the most ambitious and controversial of photographic exhibitions. For an attempt to balance the arguments, see Eric J. Sandeen, *Picturing an Exhibition* (Albuquerque: University of New Mexico Press, 1995). Eleven Cartier-Bresson images were included in the exhibition, from Indonesia, India, China and Iran as well as France and the United States.

4 Charles Hagen, 'Mystery in a Hat', *Artforum* (October 1987), 119.

5 This shift was marked by the change of curatorship from Edward Steichen to John Szarkowski in 1962. See the Introduction, n. 10, for further references to the exhibition policy of MOMA.

6 *Henri Cartier-Bresson: The Early Work* (New York: Museum of Modern Art, 1987). This catalogue is an invaluable collection of Cartier-Bresson's early images (several previously unpublished) and Peter Galassi's introductory essay remains the central text on the subject.

7 This is the title of the essay by Lincoln Kirstein in *The Photographs of Henri Cartier-Bresson* (New York: Museum of Modern Art, 1947).

8 Van Deren Coke and Diana C. Dupont, *Photography: A Facet of Modernism* (San Francisco: Museum of Art/New York: Hudson Hills Press, 1986), p. 76.

9 Henri Cartier-Bresson and Gilles Mora, 'Conversation', *Les Cahiers de la photographie*, 18 (1985), 117.

10 See Henri Cartier-Bresson, *The Decisive Moment* (New York: Simon and Schuster, 1952), unpaginated.

11 *Ibid.* As discussed below, the original French has markedly different resonances.

12 Interview with the author (Paris: 1979).

13 Translated in *Henri Cartier-Bresson: The Early Work*, p. 15, from André Pieyre de Mandiargues, *Le Désordre de la mémoire* (Paris: Gallimard, 1975), pp. 67–70.

14 Paul Hill and Thomas Cooper, *Dialogue with Photography* (New York: Farrar, Straus and Giroux, 1979), p. 75.

15 Interview with the author (Paris: 1979).

16 Hill and Cooper, *Dialogue with Photography*, p. 75.

17 Breton, *Conversations*, p. 106. Translation amended to give original titles of Breton's books.

18 André Breton, *The Communicating Vessels* (Lincoln: University of Nebraska Press, 1990), pp. 91–2.

19 Margaret Cohen, *Profane Illumination* (Berkeley and Los Angeles: University of California Press, 1993), p. 142.

20 André Breton, *Mad Love* (Lincoln: University of Nebraska, 1987), p. 39.

21 Interview with the author (Paris: 1979).

22 In Henri Cartier-Bresson, *A Propos de Paris* (London: Thames and Hudson, 1994), p. 160.

23 Walter Benjamin, 'A Small History of Photography', in *One-Way Street* (London: New Left

Books, 1979), p. 243.

24 Benjamin's 1928 review of Blossfeldt's *Urformen der Kunst* is translated as 'New Things about Plants', in David Mellor (ed.), *Germany: The New Photography 1927–33* (London: Arts Council of Great Britain, 1978), pp. 20–1. Blossfeldt's photographs were also of interest to the Surrealists; Bataille published a selection of his images in *Documents*, accompanied by his own essay 'Le langage des fleurs', 3 (June 1929), 160–8.

25 I have used here the translation by Detlef Mertins, 'Walter Benjamin and the Tectonic Unconscious: Using Architecture as an Optical Instrument', in Alex Coles (ed.), *The Optic of Walter Benjamin* (London: Black Dog Publishing, 1999), p. 207. Mertins continues: 'Such a space interwoven with unconsciousness was palpable for Benjamin, who consistently located the unconscious in the material world itself, not outside, behind, above or below it, but within.'

26 Rosalind E. Krauss, *The Optical Unconscious* (Cambridge, MA: MIT Press, 1994), p. 179.

27 Esther Leslie, 'Telescoping the Microscopic Object: Benjamin the Collector', in Coles (ed.), *The Optic of Walter Benjamin*, p. 63.

28 When published in French, the 1987 MOMA catalogue of Cartier-Bresson's early work was wittily retitled *De l'Objectif hasardeux au Hasard objectif*.

29 Ben Maddow, *Faces* (Boston: New York Graphic Society, 1977), p. 494.

30 Cartier-Bresson, *The Decisive Moment*, unpaginated.

31 My use of *punctum* here deviates from Roland Barthes' own usage (see *Camera Lucida* (New York: Farrar, Straus and Giroux, 1991), p. 27). This particular event is too generally remarkable to truly fit Barthes' definition, which, as discussed in Chapter 1, emphasises the subjective response of the individual viewer.

32 Leslie, 'Telescoping the Microscopic Object', p. 62.

33 Aragon in *Le paysan de Paris* muses on many of the signs in the Passage de l'Opéra (see, for example, *Paris Peasant* (London: Jonathan Cape, 1971), pp. 104 and 111) while Breton is disturbed by a poster for Mazda lightbulbs which reminds him of Nadja (*Nadja* (New York: Grove Press, 1960), p. 129).

34 This term has recently been used by Marc Augé to refer to sites of passage in contemporary 'super-modern' society (see *Non-Places: Introduction to an Anthropology of Supermodernity* (London: Verso, 1995)), but it is an experience which has its roots in earlier versions of modernity.

35 The larger of the two paintings, illustrated here, is in the Musée du Petit Palais, Geneva, and the smaller in the Kimbell Art Museum, Fort Worth, Texas. On Caillebotte and his probable use of photography, see Kirk Varnedoe, *Gustave Caillebotte* (New Haven: Yale University Press, 1987).

36 Maddow, *Faces*, p. 494.

37 For a related reading of another early Cartier-Bresson, see Max Kozloff, *The Privileged Eye* (Albuquerque: University of New Mexico Press, 1987), pp. 3–17.

38 See Chapter 6.

39 Kertész's personal photography is different in this respect from the often more formal work he was simultaneously making for illustrated magazines. For many examples of the latter, see André Kertész, *Ma France* (Paris: Ministére de la Culture, 1990).

40 However, this placement is entirely retrospective, for *Meudon, 1928* was not published until

1946 in Kertész's monograph *Day of Paris* (New York: J. J. Augustin, 1946). For sitings of the image in a Surrealist context, see Nancy Hall-Duncan, *Photographic Surrealism* (Cleveland: New Gallery of Contemporary Art, 1979), p. 21, and Edouard Jaguer, *Les mystères de la chambre noire* (Paris: Flammarion, 1982), p. 39.

41 Kertész, *Ma France*, p. 160.

42 Hall-Duncan, *Photographic Surrealism*, p. 9.

43 See pp. 71 and 81 in *Henri Cartier-Bresson: The Early Work*. The funeral was that of Aristide Briand, who died in 1932.

44 Photographs of Paris made across Cartier-Bresson's career were collected in *A Propos de Paris*.

45 Mark Haworth-Booth, *Old and Modern Masters of Photography* (London: Arts Council of Great Britain, 1980), p. 45.

46 Cartier-Bresson worked on three films for Renoir: *La vie est à nous* (1936), *La partie de campagne* (1937) and *Les régles du jeu* (1939). He also had small acting parts in the latter two films, as a priest and an English butler respectively.

47 Cartier-Bresson, *The Decisive Moment*, unpaginated.

48 For full details on these books, see the bibliography in Jean-Pierre Montier, *Henri Cartier-Bresson and the Artless Art* (London: Thames and Hudson 1996).

49 Breton's essay 'Souvenir de Mexique' was published in the final issue of *Minotaure* with a lavish selection of illustrations, including ten photographs by Manuel Alvarez Bravo. For a translation, see André Breton, *Free Rein* (Lincoln: University of Nebraska Press, 1995), pp. 23–8.

50 Cartier-Bresson's Mexican photographs have been collected in *Mexican Notebooks* (London: Thames and Hudson, 1995). For a reading of Cartier-Bresson's early work which places it in the context of the Surrealist interest in travel, see Peter Osborne, *Travelling Light: Photography, Travel and Visual Culture* (Manchester: Manchester University Press, 2000), pp. 166–8.

51 *Henri Cartier-Bresson: The Early Work*, p. 46.

52 In Turner-Seed, 'An Interview with Henri Cartier-Bresson', 142, Cartier-Bresson gives an account of how 'the decisive moment' came to be selected as the title for the English edition of *Images à la sauvette*.

53 Henri Cartier-Bresson, *Flagrants Délits* (Paris: Delpire, 1968).

54 Cartier-Bresson, *Images à la Sauvette*, unpaginated. Cartier-Bresson's English is exceptionally good and he would certainly have appreciated fully the different inflections in the two languages. Possibly, he wished to present a more benign image of his work to the English-speaking world.

55 André Breton, *Mad Love*, p. 117.

56 See John Szarkowski's account of his own misreading in Eugenia Parry Janis and Wendy McNeil, *Photography within the Humanities* (Danbury, New Hampshire: Addison House, 1977), p. 93.

57 George Melly and Michael Woods, *Paris and the Surrealists* (London: Thames and Hudson, 1991), p. 130.

58 Communication to the author from Cartier-Bresson, February 2001. His full statement reads: 'Regarding my photograph that André Breton used in *L'Amour fou*, I have no idea

why he used only half that photograph. I had given him it as a present – my youth was formed by Surrealism sitting at the meetings at the Café Blanche – though I knew quite well he had no feelings for painting or photography! I had given him that print out of admiration for Surrealism as a literary concept and way of life.'

59 Julien Levy, 'Henri Cartier-Bresson', *Les Cahiers de la photographie*, 18 (1985), 70.

60 The letter is dated 3 June 1933 and the exhibition took place in October.

61 Julien Levy, *Surrealism* (New York: Black Sun Press, 1936), p. 61.

62 Henri Cartier-Bresson, *André Breton: Roi soleil* (Paris: Fata morgana, 1995), unpaginated.

9

Phantom Africa: a Surrealist ethnography?

In Paris, in the Musée de l'Homme, in the gallery devoted to artifacts from tropical Africa, in a rather dusty glass case, is a small photograph. It depicts a native of the Dogon tribe wearing an extraordinary mask, the face and false breasts of which are decorated with rows of white shells (figure 69). According to the label, this is a *Masque 'jeune fille'*, and the image is displayed next to an actual mask of the same type. In this context, then, the photograph has a seemingly simple documentary role: to show how the museumised, decontextualised mask hanging next to it might have originally been worn in a Dogon ceremony.

But just as there has been in the last two decades an intense questioning of the supposed objectivity of photography, so a parallel acknowledgement of the inevitable presence of cultural attitudes and subjective impulses has filtered into anthropology's understanding of its own scientific practice. Photographs as ethnographic documents are, we now realise, far from simple objects.[1] The photograph of the *Masque 'jeune fille'* has travelled a long way to this site in the museum (not only in space but also now in time) and it has passed through a great many culturally mediated screens on the way.

We may think of our sensitivity to these issues as comparatively recent – post-colonialist, post-modernist. But when one looks back to the point in time – Paris in the early 1930s – when this image first came to Europe, it is perhaps already possible to discern an anticipation of these repositionings within the complex and ambiguous relationship between Surrealism and ethnography. In the wake of James Clifford's 1981 essay, 'On Ethnographic Surrealism',[2] the debate about this relationship has comprised a crucial aspect of both the rethinking of the relevance of Surrealism and the development of a more critically self-reflexive ethnographic practice.

Clifford's argument that in the 1930s Surrealism and ethnography were closely bound together has been both very influential and much criticised and I do not have the space here to fully rehearse those arguments.[3] Rather, I want to extend a consideration of this relationship in two directions. First, I will take as examples two particular photographs of Dogon masks made at that point in time and examine their placement in a number of different contexts (of which

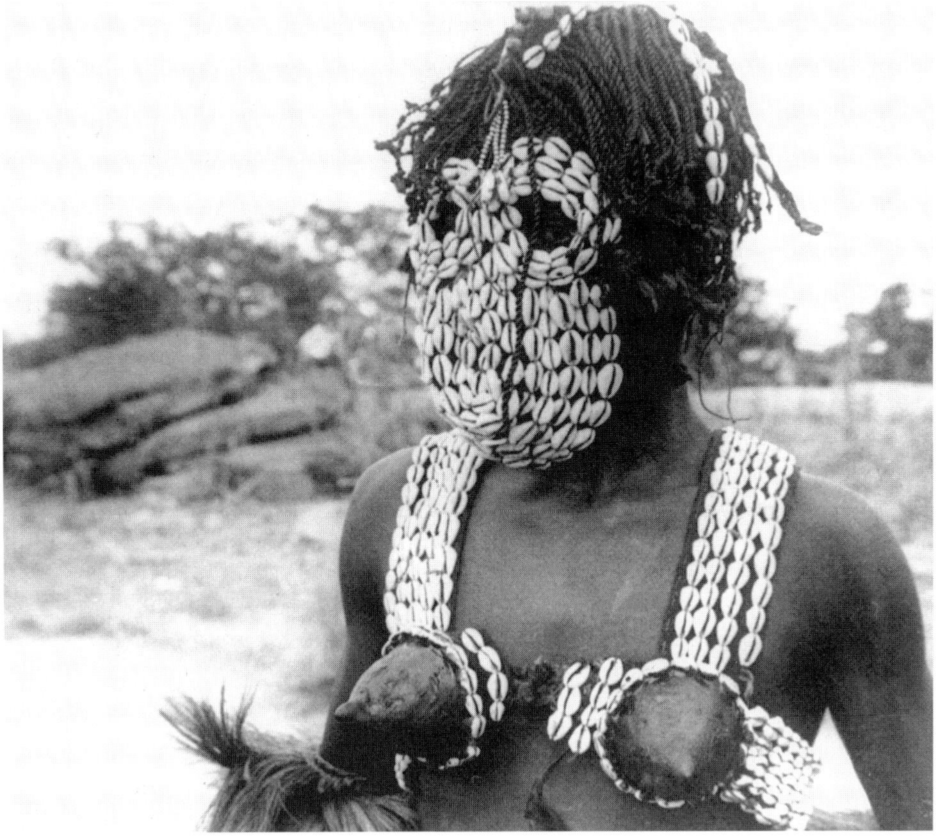

Fig 69 Marcel Griaule, *Masque 'jeune fille'*, 1932. Musée de l'Homme, Paris.

the Museum is the first). Second, I want to relate this 'ethnographic surrealism' to the 'documentary surrealism' which has been the main focus of this book, illuminating from another direction the status of these images as ethnographic 'documents' and demonstrating how their apparently obvious directness can also be revealed as complex and ambiguous.

The photograph of the *Masque 'jeune fille'* is but one image brought back from what was perhaps the most extraordinary of French ethnographic expeditions: the Mission Dakar–Djibouti which traversed central Africa between 1931 and 1933. The Mission was, of course, primarily a scientific expedition, gathering material and data for the new Musée de l'Ethnographie in Paris (the institution that was to become the Musée de l'Homme). It collected a great deal, including 3500 objects, 200 sound recordings and several zoological specimens.[4]

6000 photographs were also collected, of which this was one. These were primarily taken by the leader of the expedition, Marcel Griaule, an avowed believer in the use of photography to provide a context for the artifacts collected by the Mission. Griaule's understanding of the cultural implications of his ethnographic practice was in many ways highly sophisticated, and in a text such as 'Un coup de fusil', published in *Documents* in 1930, he had written about it with considerable scepticism.[5] Nevertheless, he did believe that the primary role of the ethnographer was documentation and interpretation came later. When the findings of the mission were placed on display in the Musée in 1933, a special issue of the new magazine *Minotaure* was produced to accompany the exhibition. In his 'Introduction méthodologique', Griaule listed the many forms that ethnographic investigation could take, but ended by saying 'The direct observation of facts ... seems to be the most certain procedure, the most natural, the most simple there is'.[6] For Griaule, photography appears to have been a part of that process of 'simple', 'natural', 'direct' observation.

Certainly, this is the role photographic images are intended to play in Griaule's own massively detailed study *Masques Dogon*, first published by the Musée de l'Homme in 1938. The same photograph of the *Masque 'jeune fille'* appears as one aspect of the recording of the mask and its function. These documentations include Griaule's description of the mask, a transcription of the chants that accompany the ceremony in which it was featured (both in Dogon and translated into French) and drawings of variations on the mask type.[7] There is no sense that we are witnessing here different representational systems each coded to signal the authenticity and neutrality of this ethnographic observation. Griaule's dry, precise description is notably lacking in evaluative adjectives, the drawings have a naive crudity, the photograph is undemonstrative and frontal. None of these images or texts is meant to have any visual or literary value in itself. They are 'records' and together they elaborate and reinforce an overall sense of documentation.

The siting of this photograph in the museum and the siting of it in Griaule's book are of course different in several respects, each context offering what it offers best (given that we ourselves cannot travel to west Africa) – an apparently direct confrontation with the object on the one hand and, on the other, an elaboration of its cultural placement. But they are parallel in that they each use the photograph as unproblematic primary material, first hand evidence. And beyond these sites lies a third, less accessible siting which subtly underlines this status. For the original glass plates and a set of first generation prints from the Dakar–Djibouti expedition are carefully filed in the archives of the Musée de l'Homme, and it is partly their very inaccessibility which lends them that aura of the primary which the archival so often effects. When a picture such as the *Masque 'jeune fille'* emerges into the light of the public gallery or the book, it brings with it something of this aura, precisely because the image carries no artistic overtones. It appears to be, and we are asked to take it as, the purest, simplest form of evidence, document, fact.

However, the status of the Dakar–Djibouti expedition was a far more complex and multiple phenomenon in the Paris of the early 1930s than this suggests. Certainly it was a serious scientific expedition. But, as Jean Jamin has described, the Mission also became enmeshed with the contemporary fashion for all things 'Negro'.[8] At the same time, it intersected crucially with the artistic avant-garde. The Mission's departure was signalled in George Bataille's magazine *Documents* with an essay by Michel Leiris,[9] and, as already mentioned, its findings were displayed in 1933 in a special number of the new magazine *Minotaure* (issue no. 2). The materials collected by the Mission had been put on display in the Trocadéro, and this publication acted both as publicity and as catalogue.

Scanning this issue of *Minotaure* today, its version of the Mission Dakar–Djibouti remains a sober and detailed account of the expedition's findings. Yet in the context of the early 1930s, the account of the expedition – and the photographs that represented it – must have had additional dimensions, both social and artistic. Although *Minotaure* was independently produced by Albert Skira, its tone was heavily influenced by Surrealism. But, as we have seen with the way that Brassaï's photographs were reproduced in the magazine, *Minotaure* was also a most luxurious production, with large format pages, an elegant layout and lavish use of colour reproduction, very different from the asceticism of *La Révolution surréaliste*. It signalled in other words the shift of Surrealism from 'the street to the salon' which Susan Rubin Suleiman has described.[10] However, these two aspects of the presentation of both the Mission and of *Minotaure* – the fashionable and the avant-garde – cannot quite be conflated and still need, for the moment, to be considered separately.

On a second level, then, beyond the specifically ethnographic, the materials presented in *Minotaure* must have acquired a 'Surrealist' meaning, within the context of an advanced taste which could admire them both for their aesthetic *frisson* and for the anti-colonial stance their presence represented. It's true, though, that one would probably not be able to grasp such a meaning from viewing this issue of *Minotaure* alone. But it must certainly come into play when one views issue no. 2 next to issue no. 1, published in fact on the same date: 1 June 1933. There one would have found Picasso's 'Une Anatomie', Dalí's 'paranoiac-critical' interpretation of Millet's *Angélus*, Maurice Heine on Sade, Eluard on Baudelaire, Masson's drawings of 'Massacres', Dr Lacan's study of paranoia.

Seen in that context, the ethnographic materials presented in issue no. 2 of *Minotaure* become entangled in a web of meanings which fascinated the Surrealists – the desire to espouse the 'primitive' in opposition to 'high' or 'fine' art, the desire to emphasise the unconscious, disquieting urges which erupt from behind the facade of bourgeois rectitude. Although its luxuriousness meant that its audience had, in part, to be members of the bourgeoisie, *Minotaure* was nevertheless a prime site for such a continuing Surrealist quest, and however distinctive the Dakar–Djibouti issue was, its reception must at the same time have been affected by the magazine's wider context.

James Clifford largely centred his 1981 essay on the role of Georges Bataille and *Documents* in bringing together ethnography and dissident Surrealism. His text was thus part of the more general burgeoning of interest in Bataille's work

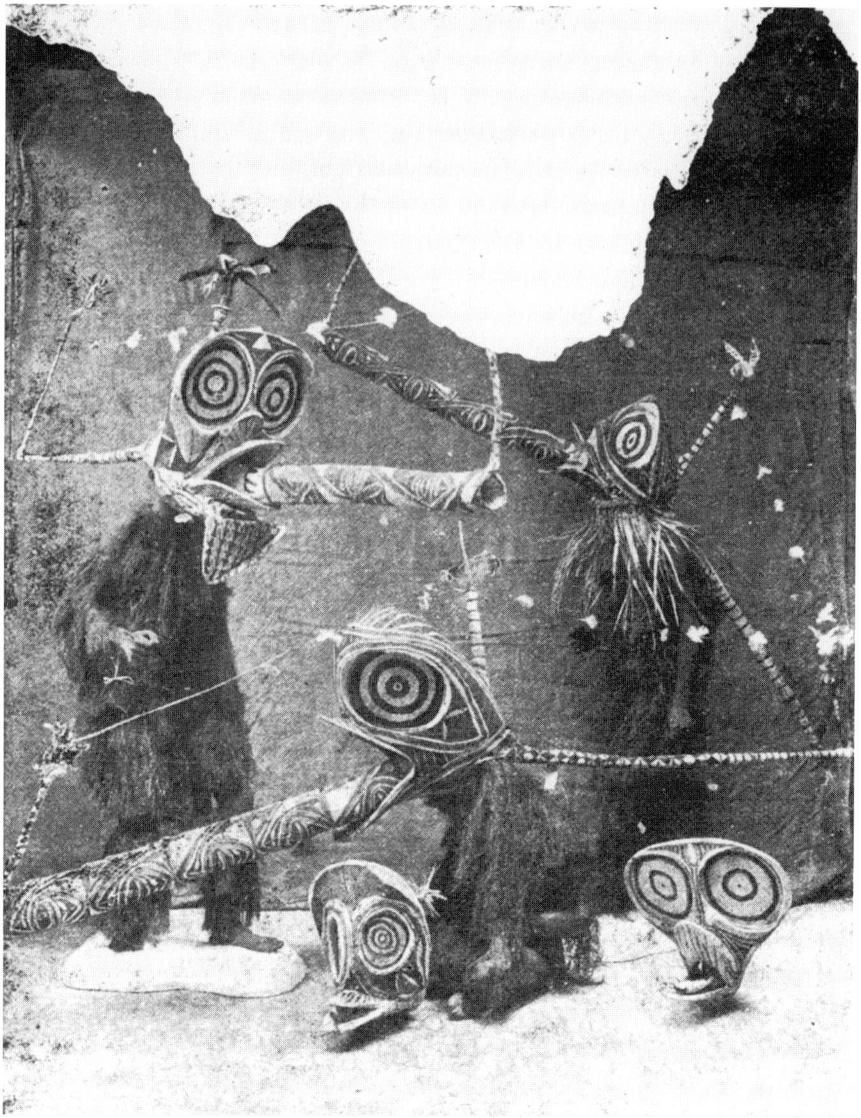

Fig 70 'Scene rituelle (Nouvelle-Bretagne)', *La Révolution surréaliste*, 7 (1926).

at that time.[11] Certainly it is in Bataille's denigration of the values of modern Western culture in favour of the base and the primal where one finds the most extreme espousal of the 'Primitive'. But this desire to embrace the otherness of other cultures ran through all of Surrealism. In 1926, *La Révolution surréaliste* had placed a photograph of a 'Scène Rituelle: Nouvelle-Bretagne' in the middle of a poem by Philippe Soupault (figure 70).[12] As Dawn Ades comments, 'It is there, not to illustrate a text, but as a 'text' in its own right ... Nor is there any attempt to mediate the strangeness of the ritual scene.'[13]

There would have been no mistaking the challenge posed by the image of the ritual dropped into *La Révolution surréaliste* or by the uncomfortable juxtapositions of tribal and modern in *Documents* and that other fascinating site of Surrealist magazine montage, *Variétés*.[14] But the Surrealist dimension of the Dakar–Djibouti pictures in *Minotaure* is far less evident, only perceptible if one is aware of the broader context in which they take their place. That status remains ambiguous. It can be read as evidence of a new respect for the self-sufficient scientific nature of the Mission, indeed as an example of the fascination that such rigour held for Surrealism. Or it can be seen as a symptom of the taming of Surrealism by the luxuriousness of *Minotaure*. Or simply as a sign of Skira's insistence on the pluralism of his new magazine.[15]

Jean Jamin has commented that 'the Dakar–Djibouti Mission was principally interested in the spectacular dimension (let us say) of African societies' (though, he adds, it did not ignore 'what animated those spectacles').[16] The term 'spectacular' might also be used to describe the presentation of *Minotaure*. And it might also be used negatively to describe at least the visual aspect of *Minotaure*'s version of the Mission – a collection of images that are rich and tantalising but which intrigue without fundamentally challenging the preconceptions of the reader, a (re)presentation running dangerously close to the touristic.

But perhaps there was more to *Minotaure*'s version just as there was to the Mission itself. In the magazine, the photographs were generally attributed to the 'Mission Dakar–Djibouti' and the magazine's preface made a point of this anonymous collectivity.[17] Jamin notes however that the issue was organised and coordinated by Michel Leiris, who refused Skira's offer of an editorial credit out of loyalty to that collective spirit.[18] The main essay by Leiris himself was on 'Masques Dogon',[19] and above the title was a photograph of several dancers wearing masks – an image which in 1986 was included as an example of collage in an exhibition of Surrealist art.[20] Which indeed it can be made to represent, but in the original context there was not a whiff of anything obviously 'Surrealist' to either the presentation or Leiris' text. His approach seems to have been as resolutely detached and descriptive, as was the rest of this issue of the magazine. The photographs that accompanied his text amplified but did not clash with it.

Only now and then, by reading between the lines with a degree of hindsight that derives from what one knows Leiris will later make of the images, can one presume to look beyond the straightforward use of the photographs as documentation. One of the most striking images that illustrated Leiris' article was the *Masque 'jeune fille'* photograph (figure 71). This was placed next to a text which described the taboos surrounding the use of such a mask (for example if women came into contact with it, they would become obsessed). Then below the image of the *jeune fille* was placed another photograph of a pile of 'Masques usés, abandonnés sous une roche'. (The captions are, of course, important here in focusing our reading of the images; would we otherwise know that those masks have been 'abandoned'? As, in a different way, the very title *Masque 'jeune fille'* gives us the frame in which we now must see that object.)

puis broyé et repris par l'eau ; on peut y mélanger les excréments d'un serpent tacheté.

Au repos, ces masques sont conservés partie dans les cavernes spéciales, partie dans les maisons de jeunes hommes.

Lors de la danse, ceux qui portent le masque sont l'objet d'un grand nombre de tabous. On ne doit pas, par exemple, prononcer leur nom, car il importe que le danseur masqué ne soit pas reconnu. Pour la même raison, celui dont le masque se détache est immédiatement entouré par les sociétaires, qui dansent autour de lui pour empêcher que les assistants le voient. Celui dont le masque se détache et qui est reconnu doit, pour éviter de mourir, retourner immédiatement à la caverne avec son masque, briser celui-ci en le foulant aux pieds et en disperser les morceaux. Par ailleurs, le danseur masqué n'a pas le droit de parler autrement qu'en langue secrète.

La nuit qui précède et la nuit qui suit une sortie de masques, celui qui porte le masque ne doit coucher avec aucune femme ; ce serait mauvais pour celle-ci, qui risquerait d'avorter ou de devenir stérile. Femmes et enfants peuvent regarder la danse mais seulement de loin, montés sur les terrasses.

La femme qui se trouverait en contact avec un masque ou rencontrerait un danseur revêtu du déguisement deviendrait possédée. On dirait que le masque « lui a pris la tête » ou « est monté sur sa tête ». Elle ne pourrait guérir qu'après une longue et coûteuse série d'offrandes, suivie d'une cérémonie d'intronisation à la suite de laquelle elle serait dite *ya siguinè* ou « sœur des masques », aurait le droit, contrairement aux autres femmes, d'approcher ces derniers et vivrait très respectée, comme une illuminée.

Les masques reproduits ici étaient en activité lorsque la mission se les est procurés. Toutefois le masque *dégué* a été trouvé dans une caverne et le masque *kâ* (antilope-cheval) — fabriqué par un homme qui fut tué lors de l'occupation de Sanga par les Français — dans un de ces trous de rochers où les Dogon ont coutume de laisser pourrir ou disparaître, rongés par les termites, les masques usagés. Quant à ceux de Songo, ils ont été découverts dans un massif rocheux où les habitants du village avaient relégué les masques et leurs accessoires après s'être convertis à l'islamisme.

M. L.

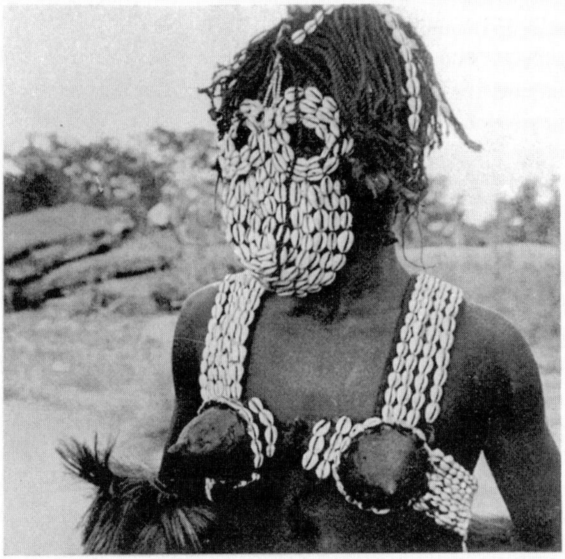

En haut : MASQUE « JEUNE FILLE ». *En bas :* MASQUES USÉS, ABANDONNÉS SOUS UNE ROCHE.

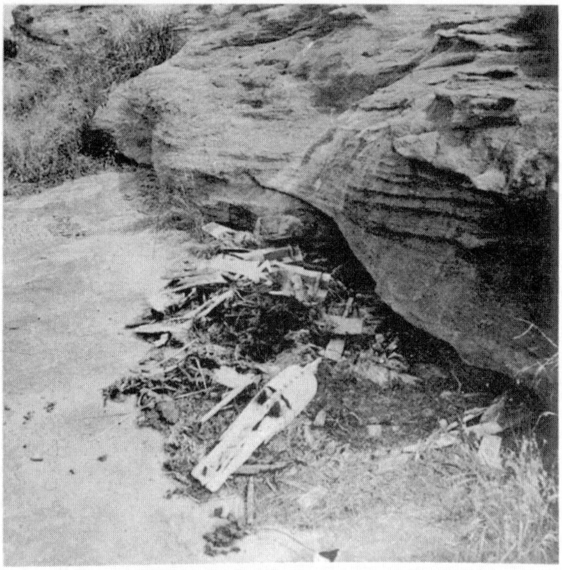

Fig 71 Extract from Michel Leiris, 'Masques dogon', with photographs by Marcel Griaule, in *Minotaure*, 2 (1933).

In this layout then, the Dogon mask is shown above as spectacle and below as debris, while the text speaks of it as ritual and belief. Caught thus between various significations, one begins to realise the limitations of demanding any single fixed meaning for these objects – either for us as European viewers, or perhaps for the Dogon themselves. It may be that one only reads so much into this juxtaposition of images and text because such intertextual meanings are common within the Surrealist magazines of the period. Nevertheless, one can start to see these juxtapositions as creating connotations that might operate around this apparently objective documentation. However, even if that is so, it is a minimal gesture – perhaps all that Leiris could manage in this context controlled by the demands of both the Mission and *Minotaure*.

But some of those suppressed implications had been gathering over the previous two years within Leiris' private expedition diary and were to pour out in public in the book that he made from that journal, *L'Afrique fantôme*, published the following year.[21] That first edition of *L'Afrique fantôme* carried the dedication 'A mon ami Marcel Griaule'. This is missing from later editions and Leiris referred to the publication of his book as 'le premier coup' to their friendship.[22] Evidently, Leiris' project was very different from what Griaule thought of as 'documentation'.

Michel Leiris, former Surrealist turned dissident, now trained as an ethnographer but continuing to practice as a *littérateur*, stood in a unique position astride the differing sites of scientific fieldwork and avant-gardist reflexivity. It was not necessarily a very comfortable position, but it was this complexity that made *L'Afrique fantôme* such an extraordinary and perhaps unique document. By its very nature, Leiris' book defies definition, but James Clifford, at one point in his essay 'On Ethnographic Surrealism', briefly reverses his terms and seeks examples of a 'surrealist ethnography'.[23] One is *L'Afrique fantôme*. (The other he cites – in a footnote – is Mass-Observation, the project formed in Britain in the late 1930s; it is a parallel which suggests intriguing possibilities that cannot be explored here.[24])

L'Afrique fantôme is the final siting of the Dakar–Djibouti photographs that I want to discuss, containing as it does a small selection of the images.[25] In the first instance, Leiris had a very direct relationship with the photographs, for one of his jobs as 'Secrétaire-Archiviste' of the Mission was to record in a *carnet photographique* the details of each image as Griaule took it.[26] In this context, the factual descriptiveness of the photograph on the one hand and the text on the other would operate in mutual confirmation, and this seems initially to be the way that the photographs in *L'Afrique fantôme* relate to the text. But the more subjective elements in Leiris's text break down this naturalising convention and reveal the photographs themselves as potentially disruptive and disturbing. To the extent that, in his 'Préambule' to the 1981 edition of the book, Leiris could describe the photographs as 'au gré presque de ma fantaisie' ('almost as my fantasy would have it').[27] Not, it should be noted, in accordance with the 'factual' account he made at the time, nor even with his memory of those events, but rather with his *fantasy*.

On the cover of the first edition of *L'Afrique fantôme* was reproduced a photograph of a very similar mask to the *Masque 'jeune fille'*, again worn in a ceremony by a Dogon male (figure 72). It was presumably considered provocative, exotic – indeed 'spectacular' – enough to act as advertisement. But within the book itself, the image played a far more problematic role. It was captioned 'The mask "wife of the shoemaker" with breasts made from baobab fruit (Sangra, 1 November)'.[28] Moving to that date in the text, one reads, 'The wife of the shoemaker has marvellous pointed and erect breasts, made from half-baobab fruits, much more exciting than the real thing. The cloak of fibre entirely covered with cowrie shells, surmounted by a headdress with a three pointed crest, gives the dancer a lunar face which is extraordinarily seductive.'[29]

Whatever the complex impulses that lay behind Leiris's reaction here, it is hard not to situate them now in terms of fetishism, indeed to read them as a fusing together of the anthropological sense of that term with the psychoanalytic. (For, as Dawn Ades points out more generally, 'Surrealism was constituted in an awareness of what Foucault later called the "confrontation, in a fundamental correlation" of ethnography and psychoanalysis'.[30]) Evidently, one part of Leiris' excitement did lie in the unknowability of the mask, a crucial example of this 'surrealist ethnography' that did not seek to explicate but rather to celebrate otherness. But the more overtly sexual aspect of Leiris' pleasure, with its emphasis on the 'marvellous pointed and erect breasts', is a classically Freudian example of fetishism, seeking signs of the missing phallus elsewhere on the female body. Though that is complicated by the irony that this 'phallic female', behind – below – 'her' disguise, actually does possess a penis.

However one wishes to analyse the implications of Leiris's description, one can certainly see how he suffused his text with personal and emotive elements in a manner that must have earned the disapproval of Griaule. Leiris was unafraid, indeed unashamed, of merging his observations and his fantasies – to the point of being unnervingly frank in the inclusivity of his remarks. The next entry – 2 November – began with a note about a 'nocturnal pollution, after a slightly erotic dream'. He didn't say whether this 'wet dream' was related to the 'extraordinarily seductive' face he'd seen the day before, but the proximity of these two entries does demonstrate the extent to which he was interested not only in documenting Dogon culture, but also in documenting himself.

This is an admittedly extreme example, but it nevertheless represents something of Leiris' tactics with *L'Afrique fantôme*. The tone of his text was coolly descriptive, yet all the time, he showed himself to be highly sceptical of any pretence of a scientific neutrality supposedly removed from its object of study. He deliberately wove into his factual narrative another account – that of his own implication. Sometimes, this implication was personal (as here); at other points, it involved his own strong sense of colonial guilt, when, for example, he found himself in the uncomfortable position of 'honorary' colonial administrator.[31]

Looking back in 1981, Leiris described *L'Afrique fantôme* as 'essentially a succession of relative flashes of subjective facts as well as exterior things (lived, seen or acquired) … seen from an angle semi-documentary, semi-poetic'.[32] This last comment sounds a striking echo of Kathleen Raine's equally hybrid description of Mass-Observation as 'half-poetic, half-sociological',[33] for what

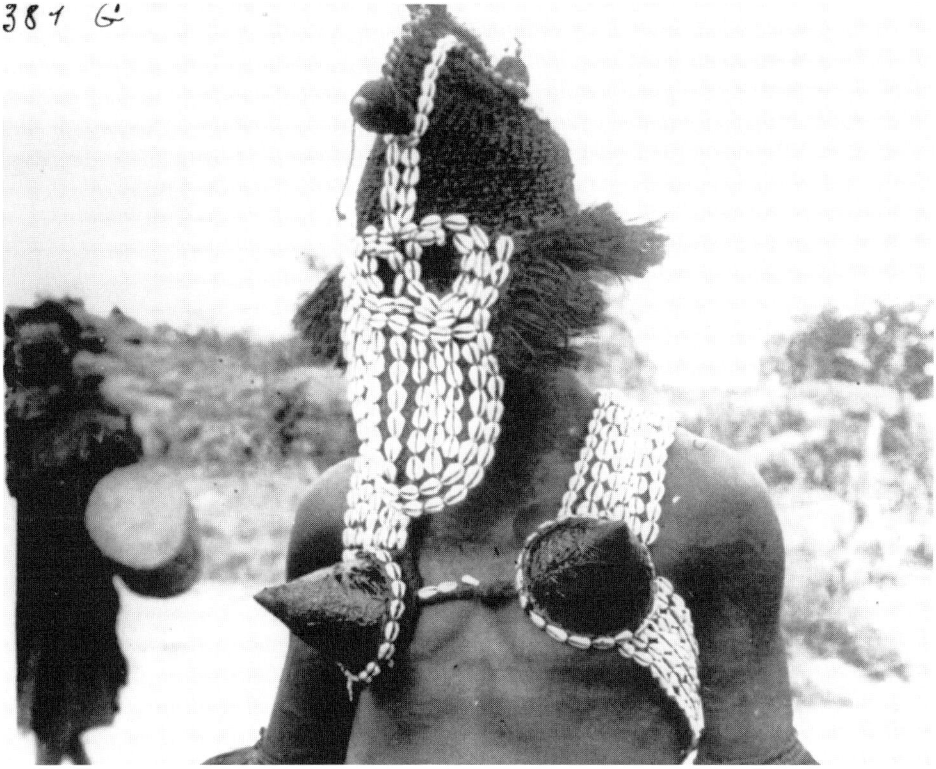

Fig 72 Marcel Griaule, *Masque 'femme du cordonnier'*, 1932. Musée de l'Homme, Paris.

the two projects shared was an understanding, unusual for their time, that the collection of evidence can never stand alone, can never attain a self-sufficient scientific 'objectivity'. It must inevitably be intermeshed with the subjectivity – indeed, the desires – of the person collecting the evidence. More than he or she might know, and in ways often not acknowledged, the 'participant–observer' must participate, if not in the observed event itself, then certainly in the construction of its meaning. There is no observation that is free of interpretation.

James Clifford has written of Leiris's presentation of his unadorned notes in *L'Afrique fantôme* as 'stubbornly naive, holding off acceptable forms of narrative', exploiting 'the merely chronological collection of citations and snapshots'.[34] The photographic term 'snapshot' is particularly appropriate, with its dual connotations of spontaneous directness and personal witness. Such a combination of effects has often been exploited in ethnography (and documentary photography) to lend authenticity to the observer's records and comments. This in turn can give an authority to those observations, the authority of first hand experience. Leiris however refuses any such authority; his text does not attempt to tell us how Dogon culture is, rather how it seems through a screen of eurocentric subjectivity. Leiris cannot help but be simultaneously implicated in what he is studying and distanced from it, as he observes the Dogon and observes himself observing them.

For Leiris, the experience recorded in *L'Afrique fantôme* was unique and unrepeatable. Leiris' later writings are divided between his professional work as an anthropologist based at the Musée de l'Homme and a sequence of autobiographical volumes, the first of which was *L'Age d'homme*, published in 1939.[35] Yet these latter books were also written as a form of anthropological exploration; as Michael Richardson says, 'Starting with the objective data of his everyday life, collected in a systematic way, Leiris moves inward to engage in a sort of ethnography of the self'.[36]

In his introduction to *L'Age d'homme*, entitled 'The Autobiographer as Torero', Leiris himself invoked a photographic metaphor for his procedure in this book, describing it as 'a kind of surrealist collage or rather photomontage, since no element is utilised which is not of strict veracity or of documentary value'.[37] And a little later, he amplified his metaphor: 'Looking on my enterprise as a sort of photomontage and choosing for my expression a tone as objective as possible, trying to gather my life into a single solid block (an object I can touch, as though to insure myself against death, even when, paradoxically, I am claiming to risk everything), even if I opened my door to dreams (a psychologically justified element but tinged with romanticism ...), I was imposing on myself a rule quite as severe as if I had intended to compose a classical work.'[38]

Again, what is most important to note here is the deliberate conjunction of the objective, the cool and 'classical' with the subjective and 'romantic'. As we have seen, it is a common dialectic within Surrealism, and in his introduction to *L'Age d'homme*, Leiris is explicit about the continuing influence of Surrealist method on his autobiographical enterprise: 'Receptivity to what appears to be given without our having sought it (automatic writing, *objet trouvé*) ... repugnance for everything that is a transposition or arrangement, in other words a fallacious compromise between real facts and the pure products of the imagination.'[39]

Within the same passage, Leiris cited André Breton's *Nadja* as a primary example of these fundamental Surrealist attitudes and tactics, and indeed there were several parallels with his own project. Michel Beaujour, writing in 1967, compared *Nadja* and *L'Afrique fantôme*, commenting that '*Nadja* is the account of an ethnological expedition into the interior of a city'.[40] In both books, the use of the diary form serves to place the subjective responses of the author at the centre of the text, but both Breton and Leiris adopt an air of removed factuality, however extraordinary the events described. And, of course, both used photographs to add to the effect of veracity. Griaule's images in *L'Afrique fantôme* were unattributed – as were the street photographs in the first edition of *Nadja* – which worked to affirm their status as direct, almost unmediated, records.

As I suggested earlier, there are a number of parallels between the 'ethnographic surrealism' explored here and the 'documentary surrealism' which developed after *Nadja* in the late 1920s and early 1930s. But photographers such as Brassaï and Lotar did not need to go to Africa to find their material; in this, they prefigured what Lydia Davis has claimed for Leiris in his autobiographical books: 'with a sort of ethnographic objectivity ... he examines what is familiar, to him and often to us, so closely and from such an odd angle that in the end it becomes strange'.[41] In some cases, an ethnographic model was explicitly acknowledged. As we have seen, Brassaï drew a parallel between his exploration of Parisian graffiti and the work of the ethnographer, writing in 1960: 'Attracted as we are by the strangeness of primitive customs, we know more about the habits of the pygmy or African bushman than we do about a Parisian from the rue des Solitaires.'[42] His own work, he claimed, was ethnography brought home, what Marc Augé has recently called 'an anthropology of the near'.[43]

Brassaï, however, like the Surrealists themselves, was not interested in the mainstream of culture, but rather in the hidden, marginal and unacknowledged elements which undermined the structures of that culture. Much the same attitude pervaded the pages of *Documents*, which offered 'a sort of ethnography of the everyday in which there was a two way movement between the exotic and the commonplace ... No methodological distinction was made between social facts taken from 'exotic' societies and those drawn from Western society'.[44] Lotar's abattoir photographs, for example, were not explicitly offered as ethnographic evidence, but in the context of *Documents*, surrounded by texts from writers such as Leiris and Griaule, they took on that role, their restraint and formality giving them an apparent authority.[45]

In his autobiography *My Last Breath*, Luis Buñuel claimed that he himself was asked to go on the Mission Dakar–Djibouti, to make a documentary film about the journey. But he refused – 'I just wasn't that interested in Africa' – and his place was taken by Michel Leiris.[46] Instead Buñuel went to one of the poorest areas of Spain and (with Eli Lotar as his cameraman) made his own documentary film *Las Hurdes* (*Land without Bread*). The apparent factuality of the film masks an intense critique, which works through a familiar double-coding: a rigorous visual objectivity placed against a caustic and often reflexive narrative.[47] Buñuel's own later comment emphasised that this was both a realist and a surrealist film: 'I made *Las Hurdes* because I had a Surrealist vision and because I was interested in the problem of man. I saw reality in a different manner from the way I'd seen it before Surrealism.'[48]

As much might have been said by Leiris or Breton, by Brassaï, Lotar or any of the Surrealist or Surrealist influenced writers, artists, photographers and film-makers of the period. For Surrealism – contrary to how it has often been characterised – was never only about the development of individual subjectivity; it always emphasised the necessity to seek out a heightened interaction between that subjectivity and the reality around it. The usual opposition between the inner and the outer, the individual and the world, the subjective and the objective should thus become meaningless as these elements are merged together in a heightened state of existence – *sur*reality. Just as the facts that Griaule discovered about the Dogon masks should not be separated from the emotions that the object aroused in Leiris.

The moment of 'surrealist ethnography' was brief and quickly passed. *L'Afrique fantôme* and Mass-Observation were two different products of a particular moment in time and a particular confluence of effects. Yet they do in some ways seem to prefigure later developments. When Fred Inglis in 1990 defined ethnography as a 'highly specific narrative about the form of life in front of us, but a narrative always suspicious of its own common sense',[49] it was a very contemporary definition, which at the same time sounded an echo of Marcel Griaule's 1930 comment that ethnography is 'self-doubting (because it is a white science, and therefore tainted with prejudice)'.[50] What Leiris did in *L'Afrique fantôme*, however, was to double up on that suspiciousness, to apply it not only to his cultural positioning but also to his own subjectivity. Thus he deliberately questioned the objectifying distance that Griaule sought to maintain, at one point in *L'Afrique fantôme* expressing his 'resentment against ethnography which makes you take so inhuman a position, that of an observer, in situations where it would be best to let go'.[51]

But, as with Breton's use of photography in *Nadja*, one might here ask to what extent Leiris was also suspicious of the documentary veracity of the photographs he used. Did both he and Breton take that veracity for granted, a solid – indeed stolid – *donnée* against which to throw the uncertainties of their texts? Or did they recognise that the juxtaposition of images and text cast a shadow of doubt not only across their written accounts, but also across the photographs they used? In 1981, Leiris was aware that the photographs in *L'Afrique fantôme* were 'au gré presque de ma fantaisie', but had he been aware of it in 1934? To what extent can more contemporary understandings (both Leiris's and ours) of the complexity of representation be retrospectively applied? Can one extrapolate back to the 1930s and find there an understanding of these issues?

It has been a central tenet of some recent theory that 'reading' (and indeed 're-reading') is more important than the original act of 'writing'. In such an argument, perhaps, it doesn't matter that we don't know if what *Nadja* and *L'Afrique Fantôme* now seem to mean is what they meant to Breton, Leiris and their contemporary audience. But this stance is surely only one element in how we should approach these texts. The place of intentionality and historical positioning must necessarily be reconsidered within this different context, and we must attempt an 'archaeology' of this recent past that now seems so far away, even if in the process we run the danger of over-estimating the radical intentions behind these images and texts. For in the end, we cannot know how much of what has been proposed here was intended, or indeed how much of it was noticed, since such issues were not at the time discussed, let alone theorised.

Nevertheless, and with all that in mind, it is possible to trace in the 'Surrealist ethnography' of *L'Afrique fantôme* a significant problematisation, however untheorised, of its own production, a complex celebration of otherness that at the same time suggests its own self-critique. In his response to the 'wife of the shoemaker' mask, Leiris throws into question the neutrality of any relationship one might have with that object. His immediate reaction, in the heart of Africa, was in the context of a direct confrontation with the mask itself. But in *L'Afrique fantôme*, the mask was now only to be seen *through* the photograph, seen as a 'phantom', as part of the phantomatic structure that Leiris constructed from his African experience. In the process, the apparent straightforwardness of the photograph itself was also implicitly thrown into question, and one can already see there an intuitive apprehension that no document is ever just a document. Or rather that what we call a document can be – indeed must be – threaded through with enculturation, with subjectivity, with desire: 'au gré presque de [la] fantaisie'.

Notes

1 For recent commentaries on the historical use of photography within anthropology, see Elizabeth Edwards (ed.), *Anthropology and Photography 1860–1920* (New Haven and London: Yale University Press, 1992), and Christopher Pinney *et al.*, *The Impossible Science of Being* (London: Photographers' Gallery, 1995).

2 Originally published as 'On Ethnographic Surrealism', *Comparitive Studies in Society and History*, 23–4 (October 1981), 539–64; reprinted in a revised form in *The Predicament of Culture* (Cambridge, MA: Harvard University Press, 1988), pp. 117–51.

3 A summary of this debate and references to further discussion around it can be found in Michael Richardson, 'An Encounter of Wise Men and Cyclops Women', *Critique of Anthropology*, 13:1 (1993), 57–75.

4 The acquisition of the actual mask in the Musée de l'Homme is credited to the Mission H. Labouret, but many of the other objects in these glass cases are either from the Mission Dakar–Djibouti or from Marcel Griaule's later expeditions, and Griaule's photographs are used in several parts of the display.

5 Originally published in *Documents*, 2:1 (1930), 46, translated in Georges Bataille *et al.*, *Encyclopaedia Acephalica* (London: Atlas Press, 1995), pp. 96–9. See the quotation from this essay towards the end of this chapter. Griaule was to spend the rest of his life studying Dogon culture, and his enterprise was to develop enormously in complexity from these early stages. For a sympathetic account of his work, see Genevieve Calame-Griaule and Jean Guiart, 'Dakar–Djibouti, *Minotaure* and Marcel Griaule', in Charles Georg (ed.), *Focus on Minotaure* (Geneva: Musée d'Art et d'Histoire, 1987), pp. 89–94, while a more critical view is that of Clifford, *The Predicament of Culture*, pp. 55–91: 'Power and Dialogue in Ethnography: Marcel Griaule's Initiation'.

6 Marcel Griaule, 'Introduction méthodologique', *Minotaure*, 2 (1 June 1933), 10.

7 Marcel Griaule, *Masques Dogon* (Paris: Institut d'Ethnologie, Musée de l'Homme, 1938), pp. 536–41. The *Masque 'jeune fille'* is fig. 139 on p. 539.

8 Jean Jamin, 'On the Human Condition of *Minotaure*', in Georg (ed.), *Focus on Minotaure*,

pp. 79–87. On the fashionable 'negrophilia' of the period, see Petrine Archer-Straw, *Negrophilia: Avant-Garde Paris and Black Culture in the 1920s* (London: Thames and Hudson, 2000).

9 Michel Leiris, 'L'oeil de l'ethonographie: A Propos de la Mission Dakar–Djibouti', *Documents*, 2:7 (1930), 404–14.

10 Susan Rubin Suleiman, 'Between the Street and the Salon: the Dilemma of Surrealist Politics in the 1930s', *Visual Anthropology Review*, 7:1 (1991), 39–50.

11 For a development of his initial essay in these terms, see James Clifford, 'Documents: Decomposition', in Sandra Stich (ed.), *Anxious Visions* (Berkeley: University Art Museum/New York: Abbeville Press, 1990), pp. 177–99.

12 *La Révolution surréaliste*, 7 15 June 1926), 16. The taste of André Breton and the 'official' Surrealist group was for tribal art other than African – in particular Oceanic and American Indian sculpture – perhaps because the African connection had already been so well worked by the Cubists. Thus the concern in *Documents* for African culture was not only an extension of the popular and ethnographic interest of the time, but may also have been a position taken up in opposition to Breton.

13 Dawn Ades, 'Paolozzi, Surrealism, Ethnography', in Eduardo Paolozzi, *Lost Magic Kingdoms and Six Paper Moons from Nahuatl* (London: Museum of Mankind, 1985), p. 63.

14 For examples from *Variétés* involving ethnographic materials, see the pages reproduced in Hal Foster, *Compulsive Beauty* (Cambridge, MA: MIT Press, 1993), pp. 138–9.

15 Skira initially wanted to bring Breton and Bataille together in *Minotaure* and one can perhaps see a deliberate balance between the first issue, which is dominated by Breton with his long essay on Picasso, and the second issue, devoted to the ethnographic concerns that had been established in *Documents*.

16 Jamin, 'On the Human Condition of *Minotaure*', p. 86.

17 This collective credit continued to be used through the various editions of Leiris's *L'Afrique fantôme* (see n. 21) and in the Musée de l'Homme itself.

18 Jamin, 'On the Human Condition of *Minotaure*', p. 87 n. 9, indicates that this information came directly from Leiris himself.

19 Michel Leiris, 'Masques Dogon', *Minotaure*, 2 (1933), 45–51.

20 Alexander Robertson (ed.), *Surrealism in Britain in the Thirties* (Leeds: City Art Galleries, 1986), p. 111.

21 Michel Leiris, *L'Afrique fantôme* (Paris: Gallimard, 1st edn: 1934; 2nd edn: 1951; 3rd edn: 1981). The second and third editions both had updated 'Préambules' added by Leiris; on the various versions of *L'Afrique fantôme*, see Jean Jamin, 'Les Metamorphoses de *L'Afrique fantôme*', *Critique*, 418 (1982), 200–12. Subsequent page references here are to the 1981 edition. It is a great omission that *L'Afrique fantôme* has not been translated into English. For some extracts, see the special issue of *Sulfur* dedicated to Leiris (15 (1986), 30–4 and 42–5), introduced by another essay by James Clifford, 'The Tropological Realism of Michel Leiris' (4–18).

22 'Préambule' to the 1951 edition (Leiris, *L'Afrique fantôme*, p. 12). Leiris himself gave more detailed information on the context of *L'Afrique fantôme*, including Griaule's disapproval, in Sally Price and Jean Jamin, 'A Conversation with Michel Leiris', *Current Anthropology*

(October 1987), 157–74.

23 Clifford, *The Predicament of Culture*, pp. 142–3.

24 Mass-Observation was formed in 1937 by Tom Harrisson, an anthropologist recently returned from Borneo, Charles Madge, a journalist and poet, and Humphrey Jennings, film-maker, photographer, painter, poet and member of the English Surrealist group. Their proposition was to make an ethnographic study of British culture itself – including its 'collective unconscious'. Mass-Observation was thus an extraordinary hybrid of anthropology, journalism and surrealism. Much of the most interesting material is in the detail of the participants' diaries; see Angus Calder and Dorothy Sheridan (eds), *Speak for Yourself: A Mass-Observation Anthology 1937–1949* (Oxford: Oxford University Press, 1985).

25 Thirty-two in the first edition, thirty-six in the 1981 edition.

26 Leiris, *L'Afrique fantôme*, p. 67.

27 Leiris, *L'Afrique fantôme*, p. 8. One might be reminded here of the comment by André Breton in *L'Amour fou* previously quoted in Chapter 8: 'the spectacle playing itself out before me ... suddenly appears to be set up for me alone, conforming in every way to my *previous* image of it'.

28 Opposite p. 80 in the 1934 volume; plate 6 (between pp. 234–5) in the 1981 edition. The reproduction is slightly different, with the 1934 version showing more of the head-dress and more of the background, including part of a drum on the left. In the full frame, the drummer can also be seen, watching the photograph being taken. He was presumably cut out of published versions so as not to distract from the mask itself (and in order not to draw attention to the act of photography).

29 Leiris, *L'Afrique fantôme*, p. 148. There is incidently no indication why the mask is called the 'wife of the shoemaker' (*femme du cordonnier*), but again the different name affects the reading of the image in small but significant ways.

30 Dawn Ades, 'Surrealism: Fetishism's Job', in Anthony Shelton (ed.), *Fetishism* (London: South Bank Centre/Brighton: The Royal Pavilion, Art Galleries and Museums, 1995), p. 68. The quotation is from Michel Foucault, *The Order of Things* (London: Tavistock, 1970), p. 379.

31 See Clifford, *The Predicament of Culture*, chapter 6: 'Tell about your Trip: Michel Leiris', p. 169.

32 Leiris, *L'Afrique fantôme*, p. 9.

33 Kathleen Raine, *The Land Unknown* (London: Hamish Hamilton, 1975), p. 81.

34 Clifford, *The Predicament of Culture*, p. 172.

35 Following *L'Age d'homme* (translated as *Manhood* (London: Jonathan Cape, 1968)), Leiris wrote the four part *La Règle du jeu: I: Biffures* (1948); *II: Fourbis* (1955); *III: Fibrilles* (1966) and *IV: Frêle bruit* (1976). The first two have been translated by Lydia Davis as *Scratches* and *Scraps* (both Baltimore: Johns Hopkins University Press, 1997). Leiris also wrote extensively about art, particularly the painting of Francis Bacon and it has emerged that Bacon used the photographs in a copy of *L'Afrique fantôme* given to him in 1966 by Leiris as the basis for a series of ink drawings (see David Alan Mellor, *The Barry Joule Archive: Works on Paper Attributed to Francis Bacon* (Dublin: Irish Museum of Modern Art, 2000), pp. 14–15).

36 Michael Richardson, *Georges Bataille* (London: Routledge, 1994), pp. 44–5.
37 Leiris, *Manhood*, p. 16.
38 *Ibid.*, p. 19.
39 *Ibid.*, p. 15.
40 Michel Beaujour, 'Qu'est-ce que *Nadja*?', *Nouvelle Revue Française*, 15:172 (April 1967), 797.
41 Lydia Davies, 'An Excerpt from *Fourbis*', *Yale French Studies*, 81 (1992), 3.
42 Brassaï, *Graffiti* (Stuttgart: Belser, 1960), p. 10. This translation is from Marja Warehime, *Brassaï: Images of Culture and the Surrealist Observer* (Baton Rouge: Louisiana State University Press, 1996), p. 88.
43 Marc Augé, *Non-Places: Introduction to an Anthropology of Super-modernity* (London: Verso, 1995), p. 7.
44 Richardson, *Georges Bataille*, p. 52.
45 There are intriguing parallels here with the work of contemporary artists who utilise an anthropological model in their work. However as Hal Foster comments in his essay 'The Artist as Ethnographer', in *The Return of the Real* (Cambridge, MA: MIT Press, 1996), pp. 171–203, the institutional context in which this later work is placed makes any resemblance somewhat superficial.
46 Luis Buñuel, *My Last Breath* (London: Flamingo, 1985), p. 138.
47 The dialectic of inflammatory subject-matter and flattened, almost disengaged technique can be found throughout Buñuel's work, from *Un Chien andalou* (1928) to *That Obscure Object of Desire* (1977).
48 Francisco Aranda, *Luis Buñuel: A Critical Biography* (London: Secker and Warburg, 1975), pp. 90–1. In Chapter 6, I have related *Land without Bread* to the work of Lotar and Painlevé. Both Jeffrey Rouff ('An Ethnographic Surrealist Film: Luis Buñuel's *Land Without Bread*', *Visual Anthropology Review*, 14:1 (Spring–Summer, 1998), 45–57), and Nicholas Thomas ('Colonial Surrealism: Luis Buñuel's *Land without Bread*', *Third Text*, 26 (1994), 25–32) site the film in relation to the 'Surrealist ethnography' of the early 1930s. But Thomas's highly critical view of the film as colonialist is surely reductive and misses its profoundly dark and anti-humanist irony. It should be added however that contemporary Hurdeans apparently view the film with distaste (see Geoffrey McNab, 'Buñuel and the Land That Never Was', *The Guardian* (9 September 2000), 6).
49 Fred Inglis, *Media Theory: An Introduction* (Oxford: Blackwell, 1990), p. 82.
50 Bataille *et al.*, *Encyclopaedia Acephalica*, p. 98.
51 Leiris, *L'Afrique fantôme*, p. 433.

Select bibliography

Abbott, Berenice, *The World of Atget* (New York: Horizon Press, 1964).

Ades, Dawn, *Dada and Surrealism Reviewed* (London: Arts Council of Great Britain, 1978).

Ades, Dawn, *Dalí* (London: Thames and Hudson, 1982).

Ades, Dawn, 'Paolozzi, Surrealism, Ethnography', in Eduardo Paolozzi, *Lost Magic Kingdoms and Six Paper Moons from Nahuatl* (London: Museum of Mankind, 1985), pp. 61–6.

Ades, Dawn, 'Photography and the Surrealist Text', in Krauss and Livingston (eds), *L'Amour fou*, pp. 153–87.

Ades, Dawn, *An Introduction to Photography and Surrealism* (London: Arts Council of Great Britain, 1986).

Ades, Dawn, 'Reviewing Art History', in A. L. Rees and Frances Borzello (eds), *The New Art History* (London: Camden Press, 1986), pp. 11–18.

Ades, Dawn, 'Surrealism: Fetishism's Job', in Anthony Shelton (ed.), *Fetishism: Visualizing Power and Desire* (London: South Bank Centre/Brighton: The Royal Pavilion, Art Galleries and Museums, 1995), pp. 67–85.

Ades, Dawn, *Dalí's Optical Illusions* (Hartford, CT: Wadsworth Atheneum/London: Yale University Press, 2000).

Apollinaire, Guillaume, *Alcools*, trans. Anne Hyde Greet, foreword by Warren Ramsey (Berkeley: University of California, 1965).

Aragon, Louis, 'Introduction à 1930', *La Révolution surréaliste*, 12 (15 December 1929), 57–64.

Aragon, Louis, *La peinture au défi* (Paris: Goemans, 1930), reprinted in *Les Collages* (Paris: Herman, 1965).

Aragon, Louis, *Paris Peasant* (London: Jonathan Cape, 1971), trans. Simon Watson Taylor from *Le paysan de Paris* (Paris: Gallimard, 1926).

Aranda, Francisco, *Luis Buñuel: A Critical Biography* (London: Secker and Warburg, 1975).

Archer-Straw, Petrine, *Negrophilia: Avant-Garde Paris and Black Culture in the 1920s* (London: Thames and Hudson, 2000).

Armstrong, Carol, *Scenes in a Library* (Cambridge, MA: MIT Press, 1998).

Arrouye, Jean, 'La photographie dans *Nadja*', *Melusine*, 4 (1981), 123–51.

Ashbery, John, 'Introduction to Fantômas', in Marcel Allain and Pierre Souvestre, *Fantômas* (London: Picador, 1987), pp. 1–9.

Atget, Eugène, *Atget: Photographe de Paris*, text by Pierre MacOrlan (Paris: Henri Jonquières/New York: E. Weyhe Gallery, 1930). German edition: *Eugène Atget: Lichtbilder*, text by Camille Recht (Leipzig: Jonquières, 1930).

Augé, Marc, *Non-Places: Introduction to an Anthropology of Super-modernity* (London: Verso, 1995).

Badger, Gerry, 'Garden of Critical Delights: The Meaning of Atget', in Peter Turner and Gerry Badger, *Photo-Texts* (London: Travelling Light, 1988), pp. 108–18.

Bakhtin, Mikhail, *Rabelais and his World* (Cambridge, MA: MIT Press, 1968).

Balakian, Anna, *André Breton: Magus of Surrealism* (New York: Oxford University Press, 1971).

Bancquart, Marie-Claire, *Paris des surréalistes* (Paris, Seghers, 1972).

Barbin, Pierre (ed.), *Colloques Atget*, special number of *Photographies* (March 1986).

Barrows, Susanna, *Distorting Mirrors: Visions of the Crowd in Late Nineteenth Century France* (New Haven: Yale University Press, 1981).

Barthes, Roland, *Elements of Semiology* (London: Jonathan Cape, 1967), trans. Colin Smith from *Eléments de sémiologie* (Paris: Editions du Seuil, 1964).

Barthes, Roland, *Camera Lucida* (New York: Farrar, Straus and Giroux, 1991), trans. Richard Howard from *La Chambre claire* (Paris: Editions du Seuil, 1980).

Barthes, Roland, *The Responsibility of Forms* (Berkeley and Los Angeles: University of California Press, 1991), trans. Richard Howard from *L'obvie et l'obtus* (Paris: Editions du Seuil, 1982).

Bataille, Georges, 'Abattoir', *Documents*, 6 (November 1929), 328–30.

Bataille, Georges, *Oeuvres complètes, Vol. II: Ecrits posthumes, 1922–1940* (Paris: Gallimard, 1970).

Bataille, Georges, *The Absence of Myth*, ed. Michael Richardson (London: Verso, 1994).

Bataille, Georges *et al.*, *Encyclopaedia Acephalica* (London: Atlas Press, 1995).

Batchen, Geoffrey, *Burning with Desire* (Cambridge, MA: MIT Press, 1999).

Bate, David, *Photography and Surrealism: Sexuality, Colonialism and Social Dissent* (London: I. B. Tauris, 2002).

Baudelaire, Charles, *The Painter of Modern Life and Other Essays*, trans. Jonathan Mayne (London: Phaidon, 1965).

Baudelaire, Charles, *The Flowers of Evil*, trans. Richard Howard (Brighton: Harvester Press, 1982).

Bazin, André, 'The Ontology of the Photographic Image', in *What is Cinema?: Vol. I* (Berkeley: University of California, 1967), pp. 9–16, trans. Hugh Gray from *Problemes de la Peinture* (1945).

Beaujour, Michel, 'Qu'est-ce que *Nadja?*', *Nouvelle Revue Française*, 15:172 (April 1967), 780–99.

Beaumelle, Agnès Angliviel de la, Isabelle Monod-Fontaine and Claude Schweisguth, *André Breton: la beauté convulsive* (Paris: Musée nationale d'art moderne, 1991).

Beaumont-Maillet, Laure, *Atget's Paris* (London: Thames and Hudson, 1993; originally published Paris: Hazan, 1992).

Beauvoir, Simone de, *The Second Sex* (Harmondsworth: Penguin, 1983), trans. H. M. Pashley from *Le deuxième sexe* (Paris: Gallimard, 1949).

Bellows, Andy Masaki and Marina McDougall, *Science is Fiction: The Films of Jean Painlevé* (Cambridge, MA: MIT Press, 2000).

Benayoun, Robert, *The Look of Buster Keaton* (New York: St. Martin's Press, 1983), trans. Randall Conrad from *Le regard de Buster Keaton* (Paris: Editions Herscher, 1982).

Benjamin, Walter, 'The Work of Art in the Age of Mechanical Reproduction', in *Illuminations* (London: Fontana, 1973), pp. 219–53, trans. Harry Zorn from 'Das Kunstwerk im Zeitalter seiner technischen Reproduzierbarkeit' (1936).

Benjamin, Walter, *Charles Baudelaire: A Lyric Poet in the Era of High Capitalism*, trans. Harry Zorn (London: New Left Books, 1976).

Benjamin, Walter, 'A Small History of Photography', in *One-Way Street* (London: New Left Books, 1979), pp. 240–57, trans. Kingsley Shorter from 'Kleine Geschichte der Photographie' (1931). Also trans. Stanley Mitchell as 'A Short History of Photography', *Screen* (Spring 1972), 5–26, and Phil Patton as 'Walter Benjamin's Short History of Photography', *Artforum* (February 1977), 46–51.

Benjamin, Walter, 'Surrealism, the Last Snapshot of the European Intelligentsia', in *One-Way Street* (London: New Left Books, 1979), pp. 225–39, trans. Edmund Jepcott from 'Der Sürrealismus: Die letze Momentaufnahme der europäischen Intelligenz' (1929).

Benjamin, Walter, *The Arcades Project* (Cambridge, MA: Harvard University Press, 1999), trans. Howard Eiland and Kevin McLaughlin from *Gesammelte Schriften: Vol. V: Das Passagen-Werk* (Frankfurt: Suhrkamp Verlag, 1982).

Berg, Brigitte (ed.), *Jean Painlevé* (Paris: Les Cahiers cinématographiques, 1991).

Berman, Marshall, *All That is Solid Melts into Air* (London: Verso, 1983).

Bois, Yves-Alain and Rosalind Krauss, *Formless: A User's Guide* (New York: Zone, 1997); originally published as *L'Informe: mode d'emploi* (Paris: Centre Pompidou, 1996).

Bolton, Richard (ed.), *The Contest of Meaning* (Cambridge, MA: MIT Press, 1989).

Bonnet, Marguerite, *André Breton et la naissance de l'aventure surréaliste* (Paris: José Corti, 1975).

Borja-Villel, Manuel (ed.), *Brassaï: Del Surrealismo al informalismo* (Barcelona: Fundació Antoni Tàpies, 1993); English edition: *Brassaï: From Surrealism to Art Informel.*

Brassaï, *Paris de nuit* (Paris: Arts et métiers graphiques, 1932); English edition: *Paris After Dark* (London: Batsford, 1933). (Republished Paris: Flammarion/London: Thames and Hudson, 1987.)

Brassaï, 'Du mur des cavernes au mur d'usine', *Minotaure*, 3–4 (14 December 1933), 6–7.

Brassaï, 'Walls of Paris', *Harper's Bazaar* (July 1953), 42–5.

Brassaï, *Language of the Wall: Parisian Graffiti Photographed by Brassaï*, introduction by Roland Penrose (London: Institute of Contemporary Arts, 1958).

Brassaï, 'Graffiti parisiens', *XXe Siècle* (March 1958), 21–4.

Brassaï, 'Language of the Wall', *U.S. Camera* (1958), 6–15, 290 and 294.

Brassaï, 'The Art of the Wall', in John Hadfield (ed.), *The Saturday Book* (New York: Macmillan, 1958), pp. 237–40.

Brassaï, *Graffiti* (Stuttgart: Belser, 1960). (French edition, Paris: Les Editions du Temps, 1961; republished Paris: Flammarion, 1993.)

Brassaï, *Brassaï* (Paris: Bibliothèque Nationale, 1963).

Brassaï, *Picasso and Company* (London: Thames and Hudson, 1967), trans. Francis Price from *Conversations avec Picasso* (Paris: Gallimard, 1964). Also trans. Jane May Todd as *Conversations with Picasso* (Chicago: University of Chicago Press, 1999).

Brassaï, 'My Memories of E. Atget, P. H. Emerson and Alfred Stieglitz', *Camera*, 48:1 (January 1969), 3–43.

Brassaï, *The Secret Paris of the 30s* (London: Thames and Hudson, 1976), trans. Richard Miller from *Le Paris secret des Années 30* (Paris: Gallimard, 1976).

Brassaï, 'Interview avec France Bequette', *Culture et communication*, 27 (1978), 8–15.

Breton, André, *Nadja* (New York: Grove Press, 1960), trans. Richard Howard from *Nadja* (Paris: Gallimard, 1928). Reprinted Harmondsworth: Penguin, 2000, introduction by Mark Polizzotti. (Revised French edition, Paris: Gallimard, 1963).

Breton, André, *Manifestoes of Surrealism* (Ann Arbor: University of Michigan, 1969), trans. Richard Seavor and Helen R. Lane from *Manifestes du surréalisme* (Paris: J. J. Pauvert, 1962).

Breton, André, *Surrealism and Painting* (New York: Icon, 1972), trans. Simon Watson Taylor from *Le Surréalisme et la peinture* (Paris: Gallimard, 1928; enlarged edition: 1965).

Breton, André, *Mad Love* (Lincoln: University of Nebraska, 1987), trans. Mary Ann Caws from *L'Amour fou* (Paris: Gallimard, 1937).

Breton, André, *Oeuvres Complètes, Vol. I*, ed. Marguerite Bonnet (Paris: Gallimard, 1988).

Breton, André, *The Communicating Vessels* (Lincoln: University of Nebraska Press, 1990), trans. Mary Ann Caws and Geoffrey T. Harris from *Les Vases communicants* (Paris: Gallimard, 1932).

Breton, André, *Conversations: The Autobiography of Surrealism* (New York: Paragon House, 1993), trans. Mark Polizzotti from *Entretiens* (Paris: Gallimard, 1952).

Breton, André, *Earthlight* (Los Angeles: Sun and Moon Press/Toronto: Coach House Press, 1993), trans. Bill Zavatsky and Zack Rogow from *Clair de terre* (Paris: Gallimard, 1923).

Breton, André, *Free Rein* (Lincoln: University of Nebraska Press, 1995), trans. Michel Parmentier and Jacqueline d'Amboise from *La clé de champs* (Paris: Editions de Sagittaire, 1953).

Breton, André, *The Lost Steps* (Lincoln: University of Nebraska Press, 1996), trans. Mark Polizzotti from *Les Pas perdus* (Paris: Gallimard, 1924).

Breton, André and Paul Eluard (eds), *Dictionnaire abrégé de surréalisme* (Paris: Galerie des Beaux-Arts, 1938; reprinted Paris: José Corti, 1991).

Briers, David, 'Some Notes on the Relation of Photography/Performance', *Creative Camera*, 238 (December 1984), 1627–9.

Brunius, Jacques, *E. L. T. Mesens* (Knokke Le Zoute Albert Plage: Salle 'La Reserve', 1963).

Bryen, Camille and Alain Gheerhardt (eds), *Anthologie de la poèsie naturelle* (Paris: Editions K., 1949).

Buñuel, Luis, *My Last Breath* (London: Flamingo, 1985), trans. Abigail Lane from *Mon dernier soupir* (Paris: Robert Lafont, 1982).

Burck-Morss, Susan, 'The Flâneur, the Sandwichman and the Whore: the Politics of Loitering', *New German Critique*, 39 (Autumn 1986), 99–140.

Burgin, Victor, *In/Different Spaces* (Berkeley and Los Angeles: University of California Press, 1996).

Burgin, Victor (ed.), *Thinking Photography* (London: Macmillan, 1982).

Calder, Angus and Dorothy Sheridan (eds), *Speak for Yourself: A Mass-Observation Anthology, 1937–1949* (Oxford: Oxford University Press, 1985).

Campbell, Kathleen, 'Ideology versus History: Deconstructing Surrealist Photography', *Exposure*, 26:1 (Spring 1988), 38–49.

Cardinal, Roger, 'Soluble City: the Surrealist perception of Paris', *Architectural Review*, 2–3 (1978), 143–9.

Cardinal, Roger and Robert Stuart Short, *Surrealism: Permanent Revelation* (London: Studio Vista, 1970).

Carroll, Paul, *The Luke Poems* (Chicago: Big Table Publishing Company, 1971).

Cartier-Bresson, Henri, *The Photographs of Henri Cartier-Bresson*, essays by Lincoln Kirstein and Beaumont Newhall (New York: Museum of Modern Art, 1947).

Cartier-Bresson, Henri, *Images à la sauvette* (Paris: Editions Verve, 1952). American edition: *The Decisive Moment* (New York: Simon and Schuster, 1952).

Cartier-Bresson, Henri, *Flagrants délits* (Paris: Delpire, 1968). English edition: *The World of Henri Cartier-Bresson* (London: Thames and Hudson, 1968).

Cartier-Bresson, Henri, *Henri Cartier-Bresson* (New York, Aperture/London: Gordon Fraser, 1976).

Cartier-Bresson, Henri, *Henri Cartier-Bresson: The Early Work*, essay by Peter Galassi (New York: Museum of Modern Art, 1987). French edition: *De l'Objectif hasardeux au Hasard objectif* (Paris: Arthaud, 1991).

Cartier-Bresson, Henri, *A Propos de Paris*, essays by Vera Feyder and André Pieyre de Mandiargues (London: Thames and Hudson, 1994). French edition: *Paris à vue d'oeil* (Paris: Musée Carnavelet, 1984).

Cartier-Bresson, Henri, *André Breton: Roi soleil* (Paris: Fata morgana, 1995).

Cartier-Bresson, Henri, *Mexican Notebooks*, essay by Carlos Fuentes (London: Thames and Hudson, 1995). French edition: *Carnets mexicains* (Paris: Hazan, 1995).

Cartier-Bresson, Henri and Gilles Mora, 'Conversation', *Les Cahiers de la photographie*, 18 (1985), 117–25.

Cassou, Jean, 'L'Art sous-marin', *Art et Décoration*, 59 (January–June 1931), 143–50.

Castellin, Philippe, *René Char* (Paris: Editeur les Evidents, 1989).

Caws, Mary Ann, *The Poetry of Dada and Surrealism* (Princeton: Princeton University Press, 1970).

Cendrars, Blaise, *Du monde entier: poésies complètes 1912–1924* (Paris: Gallimard, 1975).

Certeau, Michel de, *The Practice of Everyday Life* (Berkeley and Los Angeles: University of

California Press, 1984).
Char, René, *Le tombeau des secrets* (Nîmes: privately published, 1930).
Char, René, *Le Marteau sans maître* (Paris: José Corti, 1st edn: 1934; 2nd edn: 1945).
Clark, T. J., *The Painting of Modern Life: Paris in the Art of Manet and his Followers* (Princeton: Princeton University Press, 1984).
Clifford, James, 'The Tropological Realism of Michel Leiris', *Sulfur*, 15 (1986), 4–18.
Clifford, James, *The Predicament of Culture* (Cambridge, MA: Harvard University Press, 1988).
Clifford, James, 'Documents: Decomposition', in Sandra Stich (ed.), *Anxious Visions* (Berkeley: University Art Museum/New York: Abbeville Press, 1990), pp. 177–99.
Cohen, Margaret, *Profane Illumination: Walter Benjamin and the Paris of Surrealist Revolution* (Berkeley and Los Angeles: University of California Press, 1993).
Coke, Van Deren and Diana C. Dupont, *Photography: A Facet of Modernism* (San Francisco: Museum of Art/New York: Hudson Hills Press, 1986).
Coles, Alex (ed.), *The Optic of Walter Benjamin* (London: Black Dog Publishing, 1999).
Collins, Phillip, 'Dickens and the City', in William Sharpe and Leonard Wallock (eds), *Visions of the Modern City* (Baltimore: Johns Hopkins University Press, 1987), pp. 101–21.
Conan Doyle, Arthur, *Sherlock Holmes: The Complete Short Stories* (London: John Murray, 1963).
Crary, Jonathan, 'Spectacle, Attention, Counter-Memory', *October*, 50 (Autumn 1989), 97–107.
Crastre, Victor, *André Breton: trilogie surréaliste* (Paris: Sedes, 1971).
Crevel, René, 'La Grande Mannequin cherche et trouve sa peau', *Minotaure*, 5 (May 1934), 18–19.
Daeninckx, Didier, *Murder in Memoriam* (London: Serpent's Tail, 1991), trans. Liz Heron from *Meurtres pour mémoire* (Paris: Gallimard, 1984).
Davies, Lydia, 'An Excerpt from *Fourbis*', *Yale French Studies*, 81 (1992), 3–20.
Debord, Guy, *Society of the Spectacle* (London: Rebel Press, 1987), trans. from *La societé du spectacle* (Paris: Editions Buchet-Chastel, 1967).
Debord, Guy, *Comments on the Society of the Spectacle* (London: Verso, 1990), trans. Malcolm Imrie from *Commentaires sur la societé du spectacle* (Paris: Gérard Lebovici, 1988).
Delpire, Robert (ed.), *Identités* (Paris: Centre Nationale de la Photographie/Editions du Chêne, 1985).
Desnos, Robert, 'Pamphlet contre Jerusalem', *La Révolution surréaliste*, 3 (15 April 1925), 8–9.
Desnos, Robert, 'Imagerie Moderne', *Documents*, 1:7 (1929), 337.
Desnos, Robert, 'Pygmalion et le Sphinx', *Documents*, 2:1 (1930), 33–8.
Desnos, Robert, *Cinéma* (Paris: Gallimard, 1966).
Desnos, Robert, *Nouvelles-Hebrides et autre textes 1922–1930* (Paris: Gallimard, 1978).
Desnos, Robert, *Liberty or Love!* (London: Atlas, 1993), trans. Terry Hale from *La Liberté ou l'amour* (Paris: Gallimard, 1927).
Doisneau, Robert, *La banlieue de Paris*, text by Blaise Cendrars (Paris: Seghers/Lausanne: La Guide du Livre, 1949; republished Paris: Denoël, 1983).
Donald, James, 'Metropolis; the City as Text', in Robert Bocock and Kenneth Thompson (eds), *Social and Cultural Forms of Modernity* (Cambridge: Polity Press, 1992), pp. 417–70.
Dubuffet, Jean, *L'Art Brut* (Paris: Musée des Arts decoratifs, 1967).
Dubuffet, Jean, *Dubuffet and the Anticulture* (New York: Richard Feigen and Co., 1969).
Dufek, Antonín, *Vilém Reichmann* (Ceské Budéjovice: Foto Mida, 1994).
Duhamel, Marcel, *Raconte pas ta vie* (Paris: Mercure de France, 1972).
Dumas, Marie-Claire, *Robert Desnos ou l'exploration des limites* (Paris: Librarie Klincksieck, 1980).
Eagleton, Terry, *Walter Benjamin: Towards a Revolutionary Criticism* (London: Verso, 1981).
Edwards, Elizabeth (ed.), *Anthropology and Photography 1860–1920* (New Haven and London: Yale University Press, 1992).
Edwards, Steve, 'Gizmo Surrealism', *Art History*, 10:4 (December 1987), 509–17.

Eliot, T. S., *Selected Poems* (London: Faber and Faber, 1954).
Eluard, Paul, *La vie immédiate* (Paris: Gallimard, 1932).
Eribon, Didier, *Conversations with Claude Lévi-Strauss* (Chicago: University of Chicago Press, 1991), trans. Paula Wissing from *De près et de loin* (Paris: Editions Odile Jacob, 1988).
Evans, Walker, 'The Reappearance of Photography', *Hound and Horn* (October–December 1931), 125–8. Reprinted in Jeff L. Rosenblum and Douglas Eklund, *Unclassified: A Walker Evans Anthology* (New York: Metropolitan Museum of Art/Zurich: Scalo, 2000), pp. 80–4.
Faber, Monika, *Das Innere der Sicht* (Vienna: Osterreichisches Fotoarchiv im Museum moderner Kunst, 1989).
Fernández, Horacio, *Fotografía Pública (Photography in Print 1919–1939)* (Madrid: Museo Nacional Centro de Arte Sofia, 1999).
Finkelstein, Haim (ed.), *The collected writings of Salvador Dalí* (Cambridge: Cambridge University Press, 1998).
Foresta, Merry (ed.), *Perpetual Motif: The Art of Man Ray* (Washington: National Museum of American Art/New York: Abbeville Press, 1989).
Foster, Hal, 'L'Amour Faux', *Art in America* (January 1986), 117–28.
Foster, Hal, *Compulsive Beauty* (Cambridge, MA: MIT Press, 1993).
Foster, Hal, *The Return of the Real* (Cambridge, MA: MIT Press, 1996).
Foucault, Michel, *The Order of Things* (London: Tavistock, 1970).
Francis, Mark and Randolph T. Hester (eds), *The Meaning of Gardens* (Cambridge, MA: MIT Press, 1990).
Franju, Georges and Jean Painlevé, 'Le sang des bêtes', *L'Avant-scène du cinéma*, 41 (1 October 1964), 48–50.
Freud, Sigmund, 'Beyond the Pleasure Principle', in *The Pelican Freud Library, Vol. XI: On Metapsychology* (Harmondsworth: Penguin, 1984), pp. 271–338, trans. Angela Richards from 'Jenseits des Lustprinzips' (1920).
Freud, Sigmund, 'The Uncanny', in *The Pelican Freud Library, Vol. XIV: Art and Literature* (Harmondsworth: Penguin, 1985), pp. 335–76, trans. Alix Strachey from 'Das Umheimliche' (1919).
Fuller, John, 'Atget and Man Ray in the Context of Surrealism', *Art Journal*, 36:2 (1976/77), 130–8.
Gablik, Suzi, *Magritte* (London: Thames and Hudson, 1970).
Georg, Charles (ed.), *Focus on Minotaure* (Geneva: Musée d'Art et d'Histoire, 1987).
George, Waldemar, 'Le Salon de la photographie au Salon de l'Escalier', *Presse et Patrie* (11 June 1928).
George, Waldemar, 'Photographie: Vision du monde', in *Photographies*, special issue of *Arts et métiers graphiques*, 16 (1 March 1930), 134–8. (Republished in fascimile, Neuchatel: Paul Attinger, 1980.)
Gilonis, Harry, 'Reinvented from Scratch: Dubuffet and Guillevic's *Les Murs*', in *Dubuffet's Walls* (London: Hayward Gallery, 1999), pp. 13–20.
Graham, Dan, 'Legacies of Critical Practices in the 1980s', in Hal Foster (ed.), *Discussions in Contemporary Culture, no. 1* (New York: Dia Art Foundation/Seattle: Bay Press, 1987), pp. 88–91.
Graham, Dan, *Rock My Religion* (Cambridge, MA: MIT Press, 1993).
Griaule, Marcel, 'Introduction méthodologique', *Minotaure*, 2 (1 June 1933), 7–12.
Griaule, Marcel, *Masques Dogon* (Paris: Institut d'Ethnologie, Musée de l'Homme, 1938; republished in fascimile, 1994).
Grundberg, Andy, 'Art and Photography, Photography and Art: Across the Modernist Membrane', in Elizabeth Janus (ed.), *Veronica's Revenge* (Zurich: Scalo, 1998), pp. 43–52.
Guillevic, Eugène and Jean Dubuffet, *Les Murs* (Paris: Les Editions du Livre, 1950).
Hagen, Charles, 'Mystery in a Hat', *Artforum* (October 1987), 119–24.
Hall-Duncan, Nancy, *Photographic Surrealism* (Cleveland: New Gallery of Contemporary Art,

1979).

Hall-Duncan, Nancy, 'Out of Context', *Afterimage* (April 1986), 18–19.

Hambourg, Maria Morris, 'Atget, Precursor of Modern Documentary Photography', in David Featherstone (ed.), *Observations: Essays on Documentary Photography* (Carmel: Friends of Photography, 1984), pp. 24–39.

Hammond, Paul (ed.), *The Shadow and its Shadow* (London: British Film Institute, 1978).

Hammond, Paul, *L'Age d'or* (London: British Film Institute, 1997).

Haworth-Booth, Mark, *Old and Modern Masters of Photography* (London: Arts Council of Great Britain, 1980).

Hill, Paul and Thomas Cooper, *Dialogue with Photography* (New York: Farrar, Straus and Giroux, 1979).

Hollier, Denis, *Against Architecture: The Writings of Georges Bataille* (Cambridge, MA: MIT Press, 1989), trans. Betsy Wing from *La Prise de la Concorde* (Paris: Gallimard, 1974).

Hollier, Denis, 'Surrealist Precipitates (Shadows Don't Cast Shadows)', *October*, 69 (Summer 1994), 111–32.

Holmes, Richard, *Sidetracks* (London: Harper Collins, 2000).

Horning, Ron, 'Atget's Street Theater', *Aperture*, 101 (Winter 1985), 60–5.

Horning, Ron, 'An Argument with History', *Aperture*, 103 (Summer 1986), 2–6.

Hughes, Robert, *Shock of the New* (London: BBC Books, 1980).

Inglis, Fred, *Media Theory: An Introduction* (Oxford: Blackwell, 1990).

Izis, *Paris de rêves* (Lausanne: La guide de livres, 1950). English edition: *Paris Enchanted* (London: Harvill, 1951).

Jaguer, Edouard, *Les mystères de la chambre noire* (Paris: Flammarion, 1982).

Jamin, Jean, 'Les Metamorphoses de *L'Afrique fantôme*', *Critique*, 418 (1982), 200–12.

Janis, Eugenia Parry and Wendy McNeil, *Photography within the Humanities* (Danbury, New Hampshire: Addison House, 1977).

Jorn, Asger, *Signes gravés sur les églises de l'Eure et du Calvados* (Copenhagen: Edition Borger, 1964).

Kertész, André, *Paris vu par André Kertész*, text by Pierre MacOrlan (Paris: Librarie Plon, 1934).

Kertész, André, *Day of Paris* (New York: J. J. Augustin, 1946).

Kertész, André, *Ma France*, texts by Michel Frizot and Jean-Claude Lemagny (Paris: Ministére de la Culture, 1990).

Kozloff, Max, *The Privileged Eye* (Albuquerque: University of New Mexico Press, 1987).

Král, Petr, *Fotografie v surrealismu* (Prague: Torst, 1994).

Krauss, Rosalind, 'Nightwalkers', *Art Journal* (Spring 1981), 33–8.

Krauss, Rosalind E., *The Originality of the Avant-Garde and Other Modernist Myths* (Cambridge, MA: MIT Press, 1985).

Krauss, Rosalind E., *The Optical Unconscious* (Cambridge, MA: MIT Press, 1994).

Krauss, Rosalind and Jane Livingston (eds), *L'Amour fou* (Washington: Corcoran Gallery/New York: Abbeville Press, 1985).

Krauss, Rosalind and Margit Rowell, *Joan Miró: Magnetic Fields* (New York: Guggenheim Museum, 1972).

Krull, Germaine, *100 x Paris* (Berlin: Justh, 1929).

Krull, Germaine, *Germaine Krull: Photographie 1924–1936* (Arles: Musée Reàttu, 1988).

Lacassin, Francis, *Louis Feuillade* (Paris: Seghers, 1964).

La Charité, Virginia A., *The Poetics and the Poetry of René Char* (Chapel Hill: The University of North Carolina Press, 1968).

Leblanc, Gérard, *Georges Franju: une esthétique de la déstabilisation* (Paris: Maison de la Villette, 1991).

Lecoq, Dominique, 'Jacques-André Boiffard ou l'histoire d'un oeil', in *Georges Bataille et Raymond Queneau 1930–1940* (Clermont-Ferrand: L'association Billom-Bataille, 1982), pp. 38–51.

Leenhardt, Jacques, 'Le Passage comme forme d'expérience: Benjamin face à Aragon', in Heinz Wismann (ed.), *Walter Benjamin et Paris* (Paris: Cerf, 1986), pp. 163–71.

Léger, Fernand, 'The Spectacle: Light, Color, Moving Image, Object-Spectacle', in Edward Fry (ed.), *Functions of Painting* (London: Thames and Hudson, 1965), pp. 35–47, trans. from 'Le Spectacle: Lumière, Couleur, Image Mobile, Objet-Spectacle', *Bulletin de l'effort moderne* (1924).

Leiris, Michel, 'L'oeil de l'ethonographie: A Propos de la Mission Dakar–Djibouti', *Documents*, 2:7 (1930), 404–14.

Leiris, Michel, 'Masques Dogon', *Minotaure*, 2 (1933), 45–51.

Leiris, Michel, *L'Afrique fantôme* (Paris: Gallimard, 1st edn: 1934; 2nd edn: 1951; 3rd edn: 1981).

Leiris, Michel, *Manhood* (London: Jonathan Cape, 1968; reprinted Chicago: University of Chicago Press, 1992), trans. Richard Howard from *L'Age de homme* (Paris: Gallimard, 1939).

Leiris, Michel, *Scraps* (Baltimore: Johns Hopkins University Press, 1997), trans. Lydia Davis from *Fourbis* (Paris: Gallimard, 1955).

Leiris, Michel, *Scratches* (Baltimore: Johns Hopkins University Press, 1997), trans. Lydia Davis from *Biffures* (Paris: Gallimard, 1948).

Leja, Michael, 'Peirce, Visuality and Art', *Representations*, 72 (Autumn 2000), 97–122.

Leroy, Jean, 'Who was Eugène Atget?', *Camera* (March 1978), 40–1.

Leroy, Jean, 'The Truth about Atget', *Camera* (November 1979), 41–2.

Levitt, Helen, *In the Street*, essay by Robert Coles (Durham, NC: Duke University Press, 1987).

Levy, Julien, *Surrealism* (New York: Black Sun Press, 1936; republished in fascimile, New York: Arno/Worldwide, 1968).

Levy, Julien, *Memoirs of an Art Gallery* (New York: Putnam, 1977).

Levy, Julien, 'Henri Cartier-Bresson', *Les Cahiers de la photographie*, 18 (1985), 70.

Lionel-Marie, Annick, *Eli Lotar* (Paris: Musée national d'art moderne, 1993).

MacOrlan, Pierre, 'La photographie et la poésie du monde', *Mercure de France* (1 February 1953), 305–8.

Maddow, Ben, *Faces* (Boston: New York Graphic Society, 1977).

Magritte, René, *La fidelité des images*, text by Louis Scutenaire (Brussels: Service de la Propagande Artistique du Ministère de la Culture française, 1978).

Magritte, René, *Ecrits complets*, ed. André Blavier (Paris: Flammarion, 1979).

Malet, Léo, *120, rue de la Gare* (London: Pan, 1991), trans. Peter Hudson (originally published Paris: SEPE, 1943).

Marcus, Greil, *Lipstick Traces* (London: Secker and Warburg, 1989).

Martin, Jean-Hubert, *Man Ray Photographs* (London: Thames and Hudson, 1982; French edition: Paris: Centre Pompidou, 1981).

Mathieu, Jean Claude, *La Poèsie de René Char: Vol. I: Traversée du surréalisme* (Paris: José Corti, 1984).

Matthews, J. H., *An Introduction to Surrealism* (University Park: Pennsylvania State University Press, 1965).

McDonough, Thomas F., 'Situationist Space', *October*, 67 (Winter 1994), 59–77.

McNab, Geoffrey, 'Buñuel and the Land That Never Was', *The Guardian* (9 September 2000), 6.

Medková, Emila, *Emila Medková*, text by Jan Kříž (Prague: SNKLU, 1965).

Mellen, Joan (ed.), *The World of Luis Buñuel* (Oxford: Oxford University Press, 1978).

Mellor, David (ed.), *Germany: The New Photography 1927–33* (London: Arts Council of Great Britain, 1978).

Mellor, David Alan, *The Barry Joule Archive: Works on Paper Attributed to Francis Bacon* (Dublin: Irish Museum of Modern Art, 2000).

Melly, George and Michael Woods, *Paris and the Surrealists* (London: Thames and Hudson, 1991).

Michalski, Sergiusz, *Public Monuments: Art in Political Bondage 1870–1997* (London: Reaktion, 1998).

Michelson, Annette, 'Dr. Crause and Mr. Clair', *October*, 11 (Winter 1979), 31–53.

Miller, Henry, *Max and the White Phagocytes* (Paris: Obelisk Press, 1938), 240–52.

Mitchell, W. J. T., *Picture Theory* (Chicago: University of Chicago Press, 1994).

Moerkerken, Emiel van, *Reportages in licht en schadeuw* (Amsterdam: Geert van Oorschot, 1947).

Moerkerken, Emiel van, *Foto's* (Amsterdam: De Bezige Bij, 1989).

Montier, Jean-Pierre, *Henri Cartier-Bresson and the Artless Art* (London: Thames and Hudson 1996), trans. Ruth Taylor from *L'Art sans art d'Henri Cartier-Bresson* (Paris: Flammarion, 1995).

Morise, Max, 'Les yeux enchantés', *La Révolution surréaliste*, 1 (1 December 1924), 26–7.

Morris, Francis (ed.), *Paris Post War: Art and Existenialism 1945–55* (London: Tate Gallery, 1993).

Naeyer, Christine de, *Paul Nougé et la photographie* (Brussels: Didier Devillez, 1995).

Naville, Pierre, 'Beaux Arts', *La Révolution surréaliste*, 3 (15 May 1925), 27.

Naville, Pierre, *L'Espérance mathématique: Vol. I: Le temps du surréal* (Paris: Galilée, 1977).

Nečas, Vincenc, Jindřich Štyrský and Toyen, *Pruvodce Paříží a Okolím* (Prague: Odeon, 1927).

Nesbit, Molly, *Atget's Seven Albums* (New Haven and London: Yale University Press, 1992).

Nezval, Vítězslav, *Rue Gît-le-Coeur* (Paris: Editions de l'Aube, 1988), trans. Katia Krivanek from *Ulice Gît-le-Coeur* (Prague: Odeon, 1936).

Nickel, Doug, 'Roland Barthes and the Snapshot', *History of Photography*, 24:3 (Autumn 2000), 232–5.

Nougé, Paul, *L'Experience continue* (Brussels: Les Lèvres nues, 1966).

Nougé, Paul, *Subversion des images* (Brussels: Les Lèvres nues, 1968).

Nougé, Paul, *René Magritte (in extenso)* (Brussels; Didier Devillez, 1997).

Osborne, Peter, *Travelling Light: Photography, Travel and Visual Culture* (Manchester: Manchester University Press, 2000).

Oxford Companion to French Literature (Oxford: Oxford University Press, 1959).

Pacteau, Francette, *The Symptom of Beauty* (London: Reaktion, 1994).

Paquet, Marcel, *Photographies de Magritte* (Paris: Contrejour, 1982).

Peirce, Charles Sanders, *Collected Papers: Vol. II: Elements of Logic* (Cambridge, MA: Harvard University Press, 1960).

Péret, Benjamin, *Oeuvres complètes: Vol. III* (Paris: Eric Losfeld, 1979).

Péret, Benjamin, 'Ruines: ruine des ruines', *Minotaure*, 12–13 (1939), 57–61.

Phillips, Christopher (ed.), *Photography in the Modern Era* (New York: Metropolitan Museum of Art/Aperture, 1989).

Phillips, Sandra S., David Travis and Weston J. Naef, *André Kertész of Paris and New York* (London: Thames and Hudson, 1985).

Pierre, José (ed.), *Investigating Sex* (London: Verso, 1992), trans. Malcolm Imrie from *Recherches sur la sexualité, janvier 1928–aôut 1932* (Paris: Gallimard, 1990).

Pieyre de Mandiargues, André, *Le Désordre de la mémoire* (Paris: Gallimard, 1975).

Pinkney, David H., *Napoleon III and the Rebuilding of Paris* (Princeton: Princeton University Press, 1972).

Pinney, Christopher, Rosalind Poignant and Chris Wright, *The Impossible Science of Being* (London: Photographers' Gallery, 1995).

Polizzotti, Mark, *Revolution of the Mind: The Life of André Breton* (London: Bloomsbury, 1995).

Ponge, Francis and Jean Dubuffet, *Matière et memoire* (Paris: Mourlet, 1945).

Prévert, Jacques, *La pluie et le beau temps* (Paris: Livre de poche, 1962).

Prévert, Jacques, *Selections from Paroles* (Harmondsworth: Penguin, 1965), trans. Lawrence Ferlinghetti from *Paroles* (Paris: Editions du point du jour, 1945).

Prévert, Jacques, *Fatras* (Paris: Gallimard, 1966).

Price, Mary, *The Photograph: A Strange, Confined Space* (Stanford: Stanford University Press, 1994).
Price, Sally and Jean Jamin, 'A Conversation with Michel Leiris', *Current Anthropology* (October 1987), 157–74.
Rabaté, Jean-Michel (ed.), *Writing the Image after Roland Barthes* (Philadelphia: University of Pennsylvania Press, 1997).
Raeburn, Michael (ed.), *Salvador Dalí: The Early Years* (London: Thames and Hudson, 1994).
Raine, Kathleen, *The Land Unknown* (London: Hamish Hamilton, 1975).
Ray, Man, *Photographs 1920–34* (Paris/Hartford, Connecticut: James Thrall Soby, 1934; reprinted New York: Dover Press, 1979).
Ray-Jones, Tony, 'Brassaï talking about Photography', *Creative Camera* (April 1970), 121.
Reichmann, Vilém, *Fotografien*, texts by Antonín Dufek and Zdenek Primus (Berlin: Ex pose, 1989).
Renders, Hans, *Verijdelde Dromen* (Haarlem: Joh. Enschede en Zonen, 1989).
Rewald, Sabine, *Balthus* (New York: The Metropolitan Museum of Art/Harry Abrams, 1984).
Richardson, Michael, 'An Encounter of Wise Men and Cyclops Women', *Critique of Anthropology*, 13:1 (1993), 57–75.
Richardson, Michael, *Georges Bataille* (London: Routledge, 1994).
Rifkin, Adrian, *Street Noises: Parisian pleasure, 1900–40* (Manchester: Manchester University Press, 1993).
Rigby, Brian, *Popular Culture in France* (London: Routledge, 1991).
Roberts, John, *The Art of Interruption: Realism, Photography and the Everyday* (Manchester: Manchester University Press, 1998).
Robertson, Alexander (ed.), *Surrealism in Britain in the Thirties* (Leeds: City Art Galleries, 1986).
Robinson, Fred Miller, *The Man in the Bowler Hat: His History and Iconography* (Chapel Hill: University of North Carolina Press, 1993).
Roh, Franz, *photo-eye* (Stuttgart: Akademischer Verlag, 1929; reprinted in fascimile, New York: Arno Press, 1973).
Ronis, Willy, *Belleville-Menilmontant*, text by Pierre MacOrlan (Paris: Arthaud, 1954; republished 1984 and 1989).
Rose, Barbara, *Miró in America* (Houston: Museum of Fine Arts, 1982).
Rosemont, Franklin, *André Breton and the First Principles of Surrealism* (London: Pluto Press, 1978).
Rouff, Jeffrey, 'An Ethnographic Surrealist Film: Luis Buñuel's *Land Without Bread*', *Visual Anthropology Review*, 14:1 (Spring–Summer 1998), 45–57.
Rousseau, Jean-Jacques, *Reveries of the Solitary Walker* (Harmondsworth: Penguin, 1979), trans. Peter France from *Rêveries du promeneur solitaire* (1778).
Sadler, Simon, *The Situationist City* (Cambridge, MA: MIT Press, 1998).
Salles Gomes, P. E., *Jean Vigo* (London: Secker and Warburg, 1972; originally published Paris: Editions Seuil, 1957).
Sandeen, Eric J., *Picturing an Exhibition* (Albuquerque: University of New Mexico Press, 1995).
Sayag, Alain and Annick Lionel-Marie, *Brassaï* (Paris: Centre Pompidou/Editions Seuil, 2000). English edition: *Brassaï: 'No Ordinary Eyes'* (London: Thames and Hudson, 2000).
Seawright, Paul, *Paul Seawright*, text by Ian Walker (Salamanca: Ediciones Universidad de Salamanca, 2000).
Sers, Philippe (ed.), *Atelier Man Ray* (Paris: Centre Georges Pompidou, 1982).
Sever, Jiří, *Jiří Sever*, text by Ludvika Soucka (Prague: Odeon, 1968).
Shattuck, Roger, 'The Nadja File', *Cahiers Dada Surréalisme*, 1 (1966), 49–56.
Sheringham, Michael (ed.), *Parisian Fields* (London: Reaktion, 1996).
Sichel, Kim, *Brassaï: Paris le jour, Paris la nuit* (Paris: Musée Carnavalet, 1988).
Sichel, Kim, *Germaine Krull: Photographer of Modernity* (Cambridge, MA: MIT Press, 1999).
Slater, Don, 'Consuming Kodak', in Jo Spence and Patricia Holland (eds), *Family Snaps* (London:

Virago, 1991), pp. 49–59.

Smith, John M., *Jean Vigo* (London: November Books, 1972).

Solomon-Godeau, Abigail, 'Canon Fodder: Authoring Eugène Atget', in *Photography at the Dock* (Minneapolis: University of Minnesota Press, 1991), pp. 28–51.

Sontag, Susan, *On Photography* (New York: Farrar, Straus and Giroux, 1977).

Soupault, Philippe, *Last Nights of Paris* (Cambridge, MA: Exact Change, 1992), trans. William Carlos Williams from *Les dernières nuits de Paris* (Paris: Seghers, 1928).

Spender, Humphrey, *Worktown People* (Bristol: Falling Wall Press, 1982).

Spies, Werner, *Max Ernst – Collagen, Inventar und Widerspruch* (Munich: DuMont Verlag, 1988).

Stallybrass, Peter and Allon White, *The Politics and Poetics of Transgression* (London: Methuen, 1986).

Stanley, Nick, *The Extra Dimension: A Study and Assessment of the Methods Employed by Mass-Observation in its First Period, 1937–1940* (Birmingham Polytechnic: unpublished Ph.D. dissertation, 1981).

Stott, William, *Documentary Expression and Thirties America* (Oxford: Oxford University Press, 1973).

Suleiman, Susan Rubin, *Subversive Intent: Gender, Politics and the Avant-Garde* (New Haven: Harvard University Press, 1990).

Suleiman, Susan Rubin, 'Between the Street and the Salon: The Dilemma of Surrealist Politics in the 1930s', *Visual Anthropology Review*, 7:1 (1991), 39–50. Reprinted in Lucien Taylor (ed.), *Visualizing Theory* (New York and London: Routledge, 1994), pp. 143–58.

Švankmajer, Jan, *Tales from Prague* (BBC Television, 1990).

Sylvester, David, *Magritte* (London: Thames and Hudson, 1992).

Sylvester, David, Dawn Ades and Michel Leiris, *André Masson: Line Unleashed* (London: South Bank Centre, 1987).

Szarkowski, John and Maria Morris Hambourg, *The Work of Atget: Vol. II: The Art of Old Paris* (New York: Museum of Modern Art, 1982).

Szarkowski, John and Maria Morris Hambourg, *The Work of Atget: Vol. IV: Modern Times* (New York: Museum of Modern Art, 1985).

Tagg, John, *The Burden of Representation* (London: Macmillan, 1988).

Tester, Keith (ed.), *The Flâneur* (London and New York: Routledge, 1994).

Thézy, Marie de, *La photographie humaniste 1930–60* (Paris: Contrejour, 1992).

Thirion, André, *Revolutionaries without Revolution* (London: Cassell, 1975), trans. Joachim Neugroschel from *Révolutionnaires sans révolution* (Paris: Robert Laffont, 1972).

Thomas, Nicholas, 'Colonial Surrealism: Luis Buñuel's *Land without Bread*', *Third Text*, 26 (1994), 25–32.

Timms, Edward and David Kelley (eds), *Unreal City: Urban Experience in Modern European Literature and Art* (Manchester: Manchester University Press, 1985).

Tucker, Anne Wilkes, *Brassaï: The Eye of Paris* (Houston: Museum of Fine Arts, 1999).

Turk, Edward Baron, *Child of Paradise: Marcel Carné and the Golden Age of Cinema*, Cambridge, MA: Harvard University Press, 1989.

Turner-Seed, Sheila, 'An Interview with Henri Cartier-Bresson', *Popular Photography* (May 1974), 108–98.

Varnedoe, Kirk, *Gustave Caillebotte* (New Haven: Yale University Press, 1987).

Varnedoe, Kirk and Adam Gopnik, *High and Low: Modern Art and Popular Culture* (New York: Museum of Modern Art, 1991).

Vialle, Georges, *Georges Franju* (Paris: Seghers, 1968).

Waldberg, Patrick, *Surrealism* (London: Thames and Hudson, 1965).

Walker, David H., 'Cultivating the *Faits Divers*: *Détective*', *Nottingham French Studies*, 32:2 (Autumn 1992), 71–83.

Walker, Ian, *Contrariwise: Surrealism and Britain*, text by J. H. Matthews (Swansea: Glynn Vivian Gallery, 1986).

Walker, Ian, *Paris as the Site of Surrealist Photography 1924–1939* (University of Sussex: unpublished D.Phil. dissertation, 1994).
Walker, Ian, 'Desert Stories, or Faith in Facts', in Martin Lister (ed.), *The Photographic Image in Digital Culture* (London and New York: Routledge, 1995), pp. 236–52.
Walker, Ian, 'Documentary Fictions?', *Art and Design*, 10:9/10 (September 1995), 29–33.
Walker, Ian, 'Phantom Africa: Photography between Surrealism and Ethnography', *Cahiers d'études africaines*, 147 (1997), 635–55.
Walz, Robin, *Pulp Surrealism: Insolent Popular Culture in Early Twentieth Century Paris* (Berkeley and Los Angeles: University of California Press, 2000).
Warehime, Marja, *Brassaï: Images of Culture and the Surrealist Observer* (Baton Rouge: Louisiana State University Press, 1996).
Warner, Marina, *L'Atalante* (London: British Film Institute, 1993).
Westerbeck, Colin and Joel Meyerowitz, *Bystander: A History of Street Photography* (London: Thames and Hudson, 1994).
Wilson, Elizabeth, *The Sphinx in the City* (London: Virago, 1991).
Winston, Brian, *Claiming the Real: The Documentary Film Revisited* (London: British Film Institute, 1995).
Wollen, Peter, *Signs and Meaning in the Cinema* (London: Secker and Warburg, 1969).
Woolf, Janet, 'The Invisible *Flâneuse*: Women and the Literature of Modernity', *Theory, Culture and Society*, 2–3 (1985), 37–46.

Index

Note: numbers in *italic* refer to illustrations.